History of the
Fifth West Virginia Cavalry

FORMERLY
SECOND VIRGINIA INFANTRY,

AND OF
BATTERY G, FIRST WEST VA. LIGHT ARTILLERY

BY
Frank S. Reader
Author of the Life of Moody and Sankey

New Brighton, PA
Daily News, Frank S. Reader, Editor and Prop'r
1890

History of the
Fifth West Virginia Cavalry

Formerly the Second Virginia Infantry

And of Battery G, First West Va. Light Artillery

Frank S. Reader

© Copyright 2015 by 35th Star Publishing
All Rights Reserved.
Printed in the United States of America

35th Star Publishing
Charleston, West Virginia
www.35thstar.com

No part of this book may be reproduced in any form or in any means, electronic or mechanical, including photocopying, recording, or by any information storage and retrieval system, without permission in writing from the publisher.

ISBN-10: 0966453492
ISBN-13: 9780966453492
Library of Congress Control Number: 2015952632

On the cover: Private Charles F. Demoss
Courtesy of Rick Wolfe, Bridgeport, West Virginia

Photo Credits:
Gen. Robert H. Milroy: National Archives
George Latham: Ronnie Tront
Alexander Scott (back cover): Ronnie Tront
Alexander Scott (seated): Rutherford B. Hayes Presidential Center
Frank H. Singer and wife: U.S. Army Military History Institute
William W. Averell: National Archives
John Horle: Denise Staresina
Thornsbury Bailey Brown: West Virginia State Archives
William Schmolze: U.S. Army Military History Institute

Design by: Studio 6 Sense • studio6sense.com

Special thanks to the following individuals who assisted in this project: Terry Lowry, Bill Clements, and Rick Wolfe.

Steve Cunningham, 35th Star Publishing

TABLE OF CONTENTS

Chapter I: Loyal Western Virginia. 1

Chapter II: Organization of the Regiment. 17

Chapter III: Company Histories. 35
    Company A. 36
    Company B. 48
    Company C. 62
    Company D. 70
    Company E. 79
    Company F. 92
    Company G. 97
    Company H. 110
    Company I. 115
    Company K. 124

Chapter IV: The Quartermaster's Department. 135

Chapter V: The Chaplain and His Work. 157

Chapter VI: In Camp At Beverly, 1861. 167

Chapter VII: Relief Of Cheat Mountain. 173

Chapter VIII: In Camp At Elkwater. 179

Chapter IX: Camp At Cheat Mountain Summit. 189

Chapter X: Mountain Department. 199

Chapter XI: The Army Of Virginia. 213

Chapter XII: Return To Western Virginia. 231

Chapter XIII: Fourth Separate Brigade. 241

Chapter XIV: Rocky Gap Expedition 249

Chapter XV: Droop Mountain. 263

Chapter XVI: The Salem Raid 273

Chapter XVII: Campaigns Of 1864. 291

Chapter XVIII: Scouting Service. 301

Chapter XIX: Prison Life. 323

Chapter XX: Escape From Prison. 337

Index 359

Major General Robert H. Milroy

PREFACE

This work has been written at the request of the Author's comrades of his old regiment, and he has endeavored to give in a plain way, without exaggeration, the facts, and some of the incidents, that made up the life of the regiment in its service of over three years. The basis of the work is the diary kept by the Author during most of his service, on which he has built from all the sources of information that could be reached. Dates, places, and facts, it is believed, can be relied upon, though there may be a few unimportant errors, which will in no wise affect the correctness or value of the history. No pains or expense have been spared, and no labor avoided, that would secure the facts needed; and whatever omissions may be found, are not the result of the want of care or labor, on the part of the Author.

He is indebted to many of the comrades, officers and men, for valuable information supplied, and help given, but the names are so many, that they cannot be given here. Much credit is due them for the completeness of the work, and for the valuable assistance given in doing justice to the brave men of our regiment.

It is well to state, perhaps, that these pages are not intended as a history in full of any of the battles or campaigns mentioned, or of the armies that took part in them, but rather of the part our own regiment took in them. Other commands, no doubt, did as good service as our own, and they are not given the prominence they would have in a more general history, because this is intended solely as a regimental history, in which other regiments and commands are incidentally mentioned.

The writing of the history was a labor of love, for which the Author has received no compensation, and would under no circumstances accept any, being glad of the opportunity to set forth the services of his noble, brave comrades, who were as brothers to him in their long association together. The work is theirs, the cheerful gift of one who has a just appreciation of their patriotic services, and it is hoped that they will find in it a faithful portraiture of the work they did for their country.

THE AUTHOR.

ABOUT THE AUTHOR

Francis Smith Reader
(1842 – 1928)

On January 10, 1842, Frank and Ellen B. Smith were united in marriage. A little over ten months later their first child, Francis Smith Reader, was born in Greenfield (later Coal Centre), Washington County, Pennsylvania. Francis, known to his friends as Frank, attended public schools in the winter in the Pollock school house, Union Township, and in Greenfield. When the American Civil War erupted, Francis S. Reader was the assistant postmaster at Greenfield and a clerk residing at Pike Run, Pennsylvania. On April 27, 1861, Reader enlisted at Greenfield as a private in Company I, 2nd Loyal West Virginia Infantry, later designated 5th West Virginia Cavalry. During his military service he was externally poisoned by some vines at Woodville, Virginia, in August of 1862, which resulted in severe diarrhea until October. He served as a clerk on the staffs of Gen. William W. Averell in July of 1863, Gen. Franz Sigel in May of 1864, and afterwards with Gen. David Hunter. He served in the capacity of orderly throughout the campaigns. On June 24, 1864, he was captured at Greenbrier Bridge, West Virginia, by Confederate guerillas but later escaped and reported for duty on August 8, 1864, although he was officially discharged from the service on July 28, 1864, at Wheeling, West Virginia, too broken in health to return to active duty.

After the war, Francis Reader took up residence at New Castle, Pennsylvania, from July of 1865 to September 1866. He taught school in the winter, and finished a course in bookkeeping at Iron City College, Pittsburgh, Pennsylvania. He accepted a position in the office of Hon. David Sankey, collector of internal revenue, New Castle, Pennsylvania, in which capacity he served for ten years, as chief deputy collector of the district for eight years, and as acting collector for several months. While at New Castle he became friends with Ira D. Sankey, the singing evangelist. On December 15, 1865, he joined the Methodist Episcopal Church of New Castle. He then removed to New Brighton, Beaver County, Pennsylvania, from September of 1866 to March of 1868, at which time he was appointed preacher in charge of a circuit of nine appointments but was forced to resign after one year due to voice failure. Francis attended Mount Union College, Ohio, in 1867 and on December 24, 1867, married Merrian Darling at New Brighton. From March of 1868 to January of 1869, he lived in Greencastle and then returned to New Brighton and Beaver Falls, Pennsylvania, for the remainder of his life. His postwar occupations were primarily in the ministry and as a newspaper editor and journalist. On May 22, 1874, along with Major David Critchlow of the 100th Pennsylvania Volunteers, he established The Beaver Valley News, a weekly newspaper in Beaver County in 1883. His wartime experience as a clerk to both generals Averell and Sigel, as well as his newspaper background, would serve him well when he published History of the Fifth West Virginia Cavalry, formerly the 2nd West Virginia Infantry, and of Battery G, 1st West Virginia Light Artillery at New Brighton in 1890, considered by many as one of the finest regimental histories.

Francis Reader authored a number of other books, including Moody and Sankey: An Authentic Account of Their Lives and Service (1876), a book on the life of the great evangelist, Dwight L. Moody, and the singing evangelist, Ira D. Sankey; Some Pioneers, Washington County, Pa., A Family History (1902); History of the Newspapers of Beaver County, Pennsylvania (1905); History of Primary Laws in Pennsylvania (1906); and Old Brighton (1908).

Francis Reader was a Republican and served several years as a member and secretary of the Republican Committee of Beaver. In 1878, while so engaged, he prepared and presented to the state the first law enacted in Pennsylvania for the governing of primary elections, and was also an alternate to the Chicago Convention. He also served for several years as secretary of building and loan associations, and was a director in the American Porcelain Company of New Brighton.

Along with his son, Willard, Frank Reader served as editor and proprietor of The Beaver Valley News, but on September 15, 1925, he fell and injured his right knee and hip. At this time his physician also said he suffered from "neutral regurgitation and pronounced sclerated condition of his arteries" and added, "his mental faculties are perfectly normal." Francis S. Reader died at Beaver Falls, Pennsylvania, on December 31, 1928.

Those wishing to learn more about Francis Smith Reader can refer to the Francis S. Reader Papers in the manuscripts collection at the United States Army Military History Institute at Carlisle Barracks, Pennsylvania, and to the Frank Smith Reader Diary (Collection 019) at Washington and Lee University

ABOUT THE AUTHOR

Library, Lexington, Virginia. This personal diary covers the period from March 10 to June 25, 1864, and details the battle of New Market and his wartime capture and escape. There is also a biography of him in this history of the 5th West Virginia Cavalry (see chapter on Company I), and in his Washington County, Pennsylvania, history book, which also features a detailed account of his escape from capture during the Civil War.

FRANK S. READER, CO. I.

CHAPTER I.

LOYAL WESTERN VIRGINIA.

The determination of the loyal people of Western Virginia not to yield to the demands of the Secessionists of the State, created a great deal of enthusiasm in the bordering states of Pennsylvania and Ohio, and did much to attract volunteers from those states, to the support of the brave loyalists of this section. The treason of Richmond furnished the occasion to the West to assert its dignity and independence. The triumph of secession on the James, led to the triumph of loyalty in the mountains but it was a struggle such as few people have ever gone through, and fixed for all time the undaunted courage, the sublime devotion to principle, and the patient endurance, of the noble people of this western section. While Gov. Letcher was training the State militia for use against the government, the people of the western counties were holding Union meetings for the support of the government. The militia in the western part of the State were called into action, but largely refused, many of the officers and men becoming gallant officers in the regiments that were soon formed for the defense of the Nation. The sketches of many officers, and of companies, in the succeeding chapters, will show the work of some of them, and give a tolerably fair idea of the intense loyalty of these men. For a number of years, there had been a heated contest between the contending principles that were fully developed by the war, and there was no neutral ground upon which any persons could stand. This so completely defined the positions of the two, that when the war actually broke its dark and hideous cloud upon the rugged mountains and fair valleys of Western Virginia, the people were in line where they belonged, and the battle was on. The dominant party of the State being naturally for the principle of states rights, the Unionists suffered much at their hands, and it was no easy matter after all to be for the Union. Speakers were mobbed, meetings were broken up, rough and tumble fights were frequent, and neighbors were arrayed against neighbors, yet there was no yielding of the loyalty of the people.

During all this stormy period, there were a number of avowed abolitionists along the border of the state, some also in the interior of the state, but their influence was abridged. They could not get access to the masses. The preachers of the M. E. Church North, had a large membership in the state, and were closely watched. They were pressed by the M. E. Church South, and other denominations, on account of their anti-slavery tendency. Hon. F. H. Pierpont, one of the leading men of the state, though not a member of that church, wrote one of his most effective letters and published it in a local paper, vindicating the preachers of the M. E. Church, maintaining that they were simply living under the rule promulgated by Wesley. This letter had wide circulation, and served the end designed.

In the fall of 1860, the Virginia legislature was called in extra session; then came the state convention; then on the 17th of April 1861, the ordinance of secession was passed, and on the 25th of the same month the state, by secession commissioners, acting under authority of the convention in session at Richmond, was annexed to the Southern Confederacy at Montgomery, Ala. Of this the people knew nothing. They were called upon to go through the farce of an election on the fourth Thursday in May following, to vote on the adoption or rejection of the ordinance of secession, the time for electing members of the senate, house of delegates and members of congress. The news of the passage of the ordinance spread like wild fire. The Union members of the convention escaped from Richmond, some at the hazard of their lives. Hon. John S. Carlisle was among the first to escape. As soon as he arrived at Clarksburg, his home, he called a public meeting, and that meeting called a convention, to consist of ten men from each county, which would send delegates to a convention to be held in Wheeling on the 11th of May following. In the meantime, public meetings were called in every county, the shortest notice calling out large concourses and they were addressed by Union men and secessionists.

All the leading offices, civil and military, were held by rebels. Orders were issued from Richmond to assemble the militia by companies, battalions and regiments, and to push forward the militia officers' training. Rebel military companies were being raised in every county, their rendezvous being Grafton. What were called the "terror men" were active: A few of the most determined men in each county called on militia officers, and notified them that they must go with the state or resign; also on Union men, to admonish them that if they did not go with the state, they might expect serious consequences. Mr. Pierpont was among the most active of the speakers, and was approached, to learn what he meant by stirring up sedition in the state, and opposing the organized commonwealth of Virginia; and assured that if he persisted, he would be arrested and sent to Richmond, and tried and hung for treason

CHAPTER I.

against the great state. He had been in four or five principal counties, and the old men asked him what the Union people could do. He expected advice from them, and in his own language, "the very heavens appeared as brass without a single rift." His neighbors in the midst of this terror, asked him what they should do. He simply said, "hold on to the Union."

In this depressed state of mind, he went to his office and took down the Constitution of the United States. Audibly he said, "Old constitution, I will give you one more reading." He does not know why he had not done it before, but he commenced at the preamble, carefully reading article by article and section by section, until he came to the section which provides- "The Government of the United States shall guarantee a republican form of government to each state in the Union, repel invasion, and suppress insurrection and rebellion when called on by the legislature, or by the Governor, if the legislature cannot be convened in time." When he got through the section, he sprang to his feet, threw the book with force on the table and exclaimed, "I have got you." The cold chills ran from his head to his feet and his hair stood on end. He walked the floor for a few minutes in brisk step, and in less than a minute the whole proceedings of the convention, its representation, the declaring of all offices held by secessionists vacant, representation in Congress and division of the State, passed before him like a panorama. He went into his house and told his wife that it was clear. He met one of his neighbors on the street and remarked to him, "It will all come out right." He knew at that stage that success could only be had by secrecy.

The meeting at Wheeling, on the 11th of May, came off in a few days, and was presided over by Dr. John W. Moss, of Parkersburg. It was a great mass convention. The wealth and talent of the Union men in the State were there, earnest and determined, without reference to numbers from counties. Thirty odd counties were represented. They assembled in the afternoon in a large hall. A large number of resolutions were presented, all breathing a strong Union spirit. Daniel Lamb, Geo. McPorter and F. H. Pierpont were appointed a committee to whom all the resolutions were referred, with request to report next morning. Pierpont met with the committee and told them that they could report that he had three resolutions, which he desired adopted before the convention adjourned. They were about as follows:

1st. That this convention call a delegate convention, to be composed of all the Delegates and Senators elected at the ensuing election, and a number of delegates from each county, equal to twice the number of its representatives in the house of delegates; these delegates to be elected under the direction of a committee of safety to be appointed by this convention.

2nd. That this convention so elected, should meet in Wheeling the 13th day of June next following.

3rd. That this convention appoint - members as a committee of safety, whose duty it should be to direct the manner of electing members to the convention, who were not members of the Legislature, and to attend to such other affairs as they deemed necessary for the Union cause.

Pierpont put these resolutions in his pocket, and said he would wait for a proper opportunity to offer them. Speech-making began in earnest at an early hour in the evening. Mr. Carlisle led off, advocating the division of the state at once, the new state to be composed of two congressional districts, and he had a strong following. He was followed by Gen. Jackson, of Parkersburg, Hon. W. T. Willey, Hon. C. D. Hubbard, Campbell Tarr, J. S. Burdett, Daniel H. Polsley, and others, nearly all of whom had been members of the Richmond convention. Various propositions were suggested. About half an hour before dinner next day, Pierpont was called for; he took the stand and spoke until adjournment for dinner, and promised to finish after dinner. In the meantime he saw Wm. G. Brown, member of congress-elect of Kingwood. He told Brown that he did not care about speaking, but he wanted to wear out the convention so as to get in some practical resolutions; that after dinner he would resume his remarks, but he knew be would get hoarse in a short time, and would call upon him to finish, he being fully in possession of his, Pierpont's, views. This line was followed. After Brown had been speaking some time, Pierpont left the platform and went down one aisle of the hall, and met Carlisle. He took the resolutions out of his pocket, and said to Carlisle, "here is what you want." Carlisle read them carefully and said "that suits me exactly. Why did you not show them to me before?" Pierpont said it was not time. Carlisle addressed the President with a motion to refer all resolutions back to the General Committee with instructions to report as soon as possible. The committee retired, Pierpont's resolutions were presented, and the sub-committee was instructed to report them.

The convention reassembled just before sun-down. News had gone out that all disagreements were settled. A number of ladies and gentlemen were on the large platform. The convention was called to order, the resolutions were read, and unanimously adopted with great enthusiasm. The chairman then announced the committee of safety. Immediately a clerical gentleman stepped forward and struck up the star spangled banner, in which the band and all on the platform joined, the ladies acquitting themselves with great honor. Then another and another patriotic song, then the doxology, "Praise God, &c.," and the convention adjourned amid ringing cheers. This meeting was of national importance. The great daily papers of Boston, New York, Philadelphia, Pittsburg, Cleveland, Columbus, Cincinnati and Chicago had their reporters there. An intense Union feeling was developed and it greatly encouraged the sentiment in the North.

CHAPTER I.

The next day the committee of safety organized. The committee appointed a sub-committee to remain at Wheeling and take charge of affairs. Then the next day when the sub-committee met, some one who had heard that Pierpont had a plan of action asked him to explain it. He admitted that he had; and that it was this: "On principle the loyal people of the state are entitled to the protection of the laws of the state and United States. When our convention assembles I have no doubt we will know that the Governor of the state has joined the Southern Confederacy. The convention will pass resolutions declaring, in the language of the declaration of independence, that he has abdicated his office by joining a foreign state, and that it is the right of this convention to appoint a Governor and Lieutenant-governor, and pass such other ordinances as are necessary to turn out of office all disloyal men and to fill them by loyal men, and do anything else that may be necessary. Our actions must go to the whole state. We will call the legislature together immediately if necessary. You observe the convention is composed of double the number of delegates of the lower house. It may be we will need a legislature and convention both at once. We will elect Senators to fill the places made vacant by resignation of Hunter and Mason. We will commission our members elected and send them to Congress. The Governor will call upon the President for military aid to suppress the rebellion. In the meantime, we will get the United States Army to occupy the Monongahela and Kanawha valleys, drive the rebels beyond the mountains, and we will organize below. Now if we carry out this program, we will represent the State of Virginia, and divide the State by the consent of Congress and the consent of the Legislature of Virginia." The committee unanimously assented, and worked diligently, attending to all the details necessary to strengthen the Union cause.

On Saturday before the fourth Thursday in May, election day, Pierpont's friends at Fairmont thought it safe for him to come home and stay until the election. There was great commotion, on the day before the election, and a regiment from Georgia and the Valley of Virginia arrived at Philippi and Grafton. A large rebel meeting was held in Fairmont the same evening. Threats were freely made. About 2 o'clock at night, a lady living near called to Pierpont and told him that she had been watching all night, that she heard of threats, and feared that he would be killed or his house burned that night. He told her not to be alarmed, they would not hurt him, but he watched from that to daylight, got an early breakfast, and went to his office. A friend came in excitedly and declared there was present danger, and insisted on his leaving at once on the train for Wheeling. He went and got to the office of the committee at Wheeling at half past 3 p. m. The committee was there. They gibed him about not being at home voting. He replied, "The time of voting is past. I move that Mr. Carlisle be sent, at once, to Washington, to demand troops to drive the Rebels out of Western Virginia." Carlisle readily consented to go on the next train, at 8 o'clock that night. He had to go by Harrisburg and Baltimore. He got to Washington at 3 p.m. next day. He told the hackman to drive him to the White House as quick as his horses could go, got there and inquired for the President; was informed he could not see the President, as all the Cabinet were there in cabinet meeting. Carlisle said he wanted to see all the Cabinet and President together, and demanded that his card be taken in. The President called him in. "Well," said the President, "Mr. Carlisle, what is the best news in Western Virginia." Carlisle, without answering that question, said, "Sir, we want to fight. We have one regiment ready, and if the Federal Government is going to assist us we want it at once." "You shall have assistance," said the President. This was on Friday afternoon. On Sunday morning, United States troops, from Ohio and Indiana, crossed the river at Wheeling and Parkersburg, and on the third of June the first fight in the State came off at Philippi.

Before the assembling of the convention, a number of Union gentlemen in Wheeling, held a kind of informal caucus, and discussed the men who would likely be prominent for governor. They finally agreed on Pierpont and appointed a gentleman to see him and ascertain if he would accept; if so they would work to that end. Pierpont was seen, the matter submitted, he declared "that he had never thought of occupying the place. He had been looking to older men." After hearing all his friend had to say, he replied: "I am in for the war to lead or drive, and if the convention so orders I will do the best I can." Two days before the meeting of the convention, the members began to arrive in Wheeling. The first question to leading Union men was, "What are we going to do?" They were told to see Pierpont, he had worked up a plan of action. So they went to him singly and by numbers. He explained the proposed action in detail. All inquired, "Have you consulted the President or any of his cabinet?" He answered, "No. We don't want to consult them. This action by our enemies will be called revolutionary. The government of the United States is watched in this country and Europe, and we don't want to compromise it in any way. But we will submit our work and I will guarantee its acceptance."

The convention assembled on the 13th of June 1861. It was agreed that all the members before taking their seats, should take an oath to support the constitution of the United States, as the supreme law of the land, notwithstanding anything to the contrary in the ordinance of secession passed at Richmond on the 17th of April 1861. About thirty-five counties were represented, and every delegate elected but one, took his seat. Hon. A. I. Boreman was elected President of the convention. Appropriate committees were appointed on fundamental principles and plan for reorganizing the state. The committees went to work in earnest, and in a few days they reported in substance that the loyal people of the state were entitled to the benefit of state and national government; that the offices of Governor and Lieutenant-governor were vacant by reason of the officers who were elected to their places having joined

CHAPTER I.

a foreign government; and that it was the duty of the convention to elect a Governor and Lieutenant-governor for six months until the offices could be filled by an election of the people. They made it the duty of the Governor to require all the officers in the state to take the oath to support the constitution of the United States, as the supreme law of the land; and the restored government of Virginia as vindicated by the convention assembled at Wheeling on the 13th of June 1861, notwithstanding anything to the contrary in the ordinance passed at Richmond on the 17th of April 1861. It was made the duty of the Governor on the refusal of any office-holder of a state or county office to take this oath; to declare the office vacant, and order an election to fill the vacancy with a loyal man. By the 21st, all the preliminaries were completed, speeches of explanation made and election of Governor ordered for that day. Pierpont was asked privately to leave the hall.

Daniel Lamb, Esq., nominated him, in a short speech, for Governor of the Restored Government of Virginia. No other nomination was made, and the vote was unanimous. Pierpont was sent for, and informed of the action of the convention by the President, who asked him if he was ready to take the oath of office. He said he was. The oath was then administered on the President's platform, in the presence of the convention. Pierpont turned to the convention and said he thanked them for this expression of their confidence, and would serve them to the best of his ability.

Francis Harrison Pierpont was born in Monongalia County, Va., about five miles east of Morgantown, January 25, 1814. The same year his father, Francis Pierpont, and mother, Catharine, removed into Harrison County, three miles southwest of what is now Fairmont. They settled in a log cabin in an unbroken forest. In 1827 his father removed to what is now Fairmont, West Va. What work Francis did until thirteen years old, was on the farm. After he was of school age, he went about two and one-half miles to a log school house, four terms of three months each, in the winter time. From thirteen years old to twenty-one and one half he worked in his father's tan yard, then he started on foot to seek an education at Allegheny College, at Meadville, Pa., about one hundred and eighty miles distant. He remained at Allegheny College four and one-half college years, and was graduated in the class of 1839, visited home three times, in vacation, travelling as he first started most

HON. FRANCIS H. PIERPONT.

of the distance. After he left college he taught school for three years in Virginia and Mississippi. In political opinion he was a Whig. His father taught him that slavery was a moral, social and political evil. During his college life this sentiment was increased. While residing in Mississippi, his personal observations of the institution intensified this sentiment. After leaving college and while teaching, he studied law. In consequence of the failing health of his father, he returned home in 1842, and was admitted to the bar in that year. He was an amateur politician, though never a candidate for office, and frequently addressed the people on political subjects. He was placed by his party on the State electoral ticket for President, in 1848. His district contained ten counties, six mountain counties of which were overwhelmingly Democratic. It was proposed and agreed upon that the two electors should hold joint discussions of the points of difference between the parties, in all the counties in the district, at the county seats, and at such other points as they could attend. The meetings were largely attended and the canvas lasted over three months. Much of the capital of Democratic politicians then was to abuse abolitionists. Abolitionism was the sum of all villainies in politics. Socialism, free love, negro equality, slave insurrection and general spoliation of women and property, were attributed to designing abolitionists. But Pierpont did not suffer himself to be put on the defensive, but assumed the aggressive at the start. Whatever accusations were brought against the abolitionists, he knew that the people of Western Virginia knew the slavocracy of the State only by its oppression of the white laboring people; that the Democratic party had always held the political power in the State, and that the part east of the Blue Ridge, though largely in the minority in population, held controlling power in the legislature. The west had had but one United States Senator and never a judge of the Court of Appeals or a Governor. By the laws of the State, they to a great extent exonerated their slaves from taxation, and taxed all the laboring man had, from a pig to an engine. By law, a poor man with three sons over sixteen years, with himself, might be called to work the roads ten or twenty days in the year, while the gentleman owning two male slaves over sixteen years, was exempt from road working, and his land was seldom taxed for road purposes. The children were without free schools, and almost without schools of any kind. He pointed them to Pennsylvania and Ohio, with their free institutions; on the one side of an imaginary line you could see thrift, intelligence of the children and prosperity of the people; not so where slavocracy reigned. He declared that Western Virginia wanted free schools, a sound currency and a tariff for protection. He continued this line of attack on the oppression of slave holders, through the local press and before the people, in 1852, 1856, and in the Governor's election in 1859. When the Democratic party divided in 1860, and nominated Breckenridge and Douglas for President, Pierpont at once announced that the Breckenridge party meant secession, rebellion, division of

CHAPTER I.

the Union and war. He maintained this country could not be divided without war. Breckenridge Democrats vehemently denied this charge. Pierpont pressed it the harder, so that when the rebellion came, a large number of Democrats were on the Union side. He was not an Abolitionist in their sense of the term, but he hated the institution of slavery, the intolerant spirit of pro-slavery men, and their oppression. At the age of seventeen Gov. Pierpont joined the M. P. Church, was an active superintendent of the Sunday school for eighteen years before the war, has had a class ever since, and says that the most valuable knowledge is that received in this grand work. The Governor is now an honored resident of Fairmont, West Va., and though beyond three score years and ten, is active in good works. The Second Virginia regiment has many reasons to be grateful to him, and he is held in the highest esteem by every member of the old organization.

After his election, Governor Pierpont at once entered upon the duties of his office. The collector of the port offered him an office, with a bare table, half quire of paper and pen and ink, in the custom house. Some friends came in to congratulate him, and some of them remarked that he was the first man they had ever known to thank men for putting a rope around his neck. The Governor replied that success was never convicted of treason. He immediately addressed a letter to the President of the United States, in substance informing him that there was an insurrection and rebellion in the state; that certain evil minded men in the state had banded themselves together and had joined with like minded men from other states; that they had formed strong military organizations and were pressing Union men into their army, and taking their substance to support their organizations; that their object was to overthrow the government of the state and United States, and that he had not sufficient military force at his command to suppress the rebellion. He called upon the President for military aid, and signed his letter, "F. H. Pierpont, Governor of Virginia."

About the fourth day after, the Governor received a letter from Secretary of War (Cameron) acknowledging receipt of his letter, saying that he was directed by the President to congratulate the people of Virginia on their so soon resuming their relations with the United States Government, and authorizing Gov. Pierpont to raise volunteer regiments for the United States Army and to appoint company and field officers. This letter was read to the convention and greatly strengthened their faith in the movement.

The second week of the convention was nearing its close. Serious trouble was ahead. Landlords were informing members that they would expect their pay at the end of the second week. Money was exceedingly scarce. The Governor was informed of the situation. "Yes," said he, "I have been actively thinking about that. Tell them to hold on until next week." This was on Saturday. On Monday morning Gov. Pierpont said to Mr. P. G. Vanwinkle, "We must have money. I want you, after breakfast, to go with me to the N. W. and M. M. banks, and endorse my notes for $5,000, one on each bank. I intend to have $10,000 from these banks." Vanwinkle said he would do it. They got the cashiers together. The Governor told them what he wanted. They raised the objection that they could not make the loan to the State without a vote of the stockholders. The Governor replied, "I want it on my own individual note and Mr. Vanwinkle will endorse it. I want it to pay the mileage and per diem of the members of the convention. If my government succeeds you are sure of your money. If it does not succeed, your money is not worth a bubble." One of the cashiers replied, "You shall have five thousand from this bank, what shall we do with it?" The Governor replied, "Place it to my credit officially and I will so draw my checks." The other cashier said he would like to do the same, but nearly all his directors were of the secession party, and they would not meet until Thursday. Governor Pierpont said, "Please give them my compliments, and tell them to place that money to my credit, and I don't want any higgling about it." On Wednesday the cashier informed him that $5,000 was placed to his credit in the other bank. The Governor went immediately to the convention, asked the President to inform all the members that if they would get a certificate from the Sergeant at Arms of the mileage and per diem due them, and bring it to the Governor, he would give them a check for the money. This gave great strength to the convention. Thus the Governor became Auditor and Treasurer also.

The convention soon brought its work for the present, to a close, and convened the legislature, which elected United States Senators to fill the vacancies made by the resignation of Mason and Hunter. The Governor procured proper seals, and issued commissions to Senators and Representatives in Congress, who were admitted to seats in the extra session called by the President to meet on the 4th of July 1861.

The restored government being recognized by the legislative and executive branches of the Federal Government, they were ready to divide the state. Accomac, Northampton, Fairfax and Alexandria were now represented in the legislature. The legislature gave its consent and called on the people in the bounds of the proposed new state, to elect delegates to a convention to frame a constitution. That convention met and submitted its work for adoption or rejection in the spring of 1862. The people adopted the constitution so submitted with great unanimity. It was then submitted to Congress. The senate passed a bill admitting the new state of West Virginia. The lower house took objections to the constitution on the ground of the provisions on slavery, and required alterations in that particular. The state convention was reassembled and alterations were made to conform to the views of Congress. In December 1862, at the reassembling of Congress, all alterations had been made, the lower house passed the act, and it was approved by the President; and the new state

CHAPTER I.

was to be admitted on the proclamation of the President to be thereafter issued on proper certificates of ratification by the people of the alterations Congress proposed. Elections were held in the spring of 1863, in the old and new state, at the usual time of holding elections, and the constitution was adopted, and the government of West Virginia was organized June 17, 1863.

Governor Pierpont went into the loyal part of the old state, not embraced in West Virginia. The people were anxious for him to follow the restored government, which he decided to do. "I feared" said he, "if it failed the young state might fail." The people elected him to take the office of Governor of Virginia, for the full term from the 1st of Jan. 1864. Then he removed the seat of government of Virginia from Wheeling to Alexandria, and in 1865, after the rebellion collapsed, he went to Richmond and completely restored the government of the state. He was governor for seven years, and was superceded by the "Force Acts" of Congress passed in 1867.

Gov. Pierpont says the formation of West Va. was not the act of any one man, nor was it the act of the politicians of the State, as they were in the rebellion. It was simply the carrying out of an enthusiastic determination of a large body of serious, determined men, who felt that they had been oppressed by the slave power of the State, which power was then, forcing them to antagonize the Union they so dearly loved, to enlarge the slave power they so cordially hated. This intense power was behind him, and he also had the counsel of true, intelligent men. The *Wheeling Intelligencer*, the only daily paper in the State, edited with great ability and discretion by A. W. Campbell, Esq., was a tower of strength in support of the movement.

The movement forming the restored government and the new state, was of vast importance in determining the fate of the Union. It checked rebellion in Maryland, Kentucky and Missouri; it strengthened Union sentiment in the north; it added backbone to the administration at Washington, and it dampened the ardor of the rebels at Richmond. The Western Virginia politicians promised the Confederacy 50,000 Western Virginia troops. Rebels in the cotton states in the spring of 1861, said to the people, "Plant your broad acres of corn and cotton. The war is transferred to the Potomac and the Ohio." The intention was to make these rivers the picket line, but the first movement in Western Virginia removed the picket line from the Ohio far back into the Allegheny mountains. Gov. Pierpont mustered into the United States service about 19,500 men, as brave as ever shouldered a musket or drew a saber. Some of them were brave Pennsylvanians and Ohioans, who wanted to help Western Virginia. The rebels were paralyzed in that section, and it is believed that less than 5,000 of them were in the Confederate regular service.

The threatening advance of the Confederate forces in the latter part of May, 1861, necessitated the advance of Union troops to repel them and on the 27th of May, Col. B. F. Kelley with his noble First Virginia Infantry, left Wheeling, followed by other troops, and by May 31st 7,000 or 8,000 men were collected at Grafton under Gen. Morris. The enemy retreated to Philippi, where they made a stand under command of Colonel Porterfield. An advance was made, on June 2nd, by the forces under Gen. Morris, to capture Philippi by surprise. They moved in two separate columns; one, under Col. Dumont, proceeded on the N. W. Va. railroad to Webster, twelve miles from Philippi, and thence marched against the enemy's front, while Colonel Kelley, accompanied by Col. Lander, moved another column eastward to Thornton, from which point they marched twenty-two miles, and got in the rear of Porterfield's forces. The troops advanced through the peltings of a fierce storm. The darkness was so intense, and the mud so deep, that travel was exceedingly difficult, and it was daylight before they reached Philippi. The plan of the attack was for Col. Dumont to attack in front, and Col. Kelley in the rear, simultaneously. The attack was to be made at 4 o'clock, but Col. Kelley, having the longer distance to travel, could not possibly reach the point desired at the time, so that Col. Dumont waited till daylight to reveal his presence to the enemy. Seeing the enemy's camp in confusion, the colonel then ordered an attack, and about the same time Col. Kelley came in sight across the river below the camp and charged forward with great cheering. Col. Kelley's forces charged into the town but found it deserted. Passing along, Col. Kelley was shot through the body by some concealed person, but recovered and became one of the honored and brave generals of the State.

A large force of the enemy was firmly entrenched on Laurel Hill under Gen. Robert S. Garnett, and a smaller force under Col. John Pegram at Rich Mountain. On July 11th General McClellan ordered an attack on the forces on Rich Mountain. General Rosecrans was sent with some Indiana and Ohio regiments to get in the rear of the Confederate forces. This was accomplished, but the plan of attack was disclosed to the enemy, by the capture of a courier from McClellan to Rosecrans. This put the enemy on their guard and they hastily marched 2,500 men, with three pieces of artillery to the summit of the mountain, where they intrenched themselves. Rosecrans had no artillery, as he had to march his weary columns through almost impenetrable woods, by mountain bridle paths, under a cold, intermittent rain. About noon he reached the Confederate position, when the enemy opened on him with their artillery. The bushes were so thick that the location of the enemy could not be made out, and their whereabouts was known only by the explosions of their guns. Colonel Lander with twenty sharp shooters found position among the rocks close to the enemy's artillery, where they picked off their gunners as fast as they took their places. In the meantime an Indiana regiment came up, and the order to fix bayonets was given. The next moment an Ohio regiment posted on a high piece of ground, poured in a terrible volley, and the Indianians charged with a cheer that carried terror to the hearts of the enemy, who at once retreated,

CHAPTER I.

leaving their artillery, wagons, tents, provisions and stores, with 135 dead. The enemy were driven about 300 yards, when a recall was sounded and the column formed in line of battle, to meet the forces of Pegram at the foot of the mountain. But Pegram fully understanding the position of Rosecrans' forces, became alarmed for his own safety, and ordered an immediate retreat, but was compelled to surrender the next day. General McClellan then marched to Beverly.

General Garnett on Laurel Hill, hearing of Pegram's defeat, retreated through the mountains. General Morris took possession of the camp, and next day five regiments of Ohio and Indiana troops started in full pursuit, forcing the enemy directly over the mountains, toward the Cheat river. The rain fell without intermission, making the marching miserable in the narrow valley of the Cheat river. No guide was needed to point out their track, the trampled mud, haversacks, blankets, tents, etc., that strewed the valley, showing plainly enough the route taken. It was a wild chase and when open ground was reached, skirmishes were frequent. Four companies of a Georgia regiment were cut off and captured, and at Corrick's Ford Gen. Garnett made a stand, his artillery being posted on a bluff, while the infantry were concealed behind the bushes. A desperate fight followed, the enemy's forces far exceeding the Union troops, but they were compelled to retreat in great disorder. Gen. Garnett bravely exerted himself to stop the demoralized command, but his efforts were fruitless, and while so doing, he was shot through the body and died without a groan. The pursuit was continued only two miles beyond the ford, when the Union troops camped for the night. The remainder of the enemy under Col. Ramsey, made their way across the mountains, joining Gen. Jackson at Monterey. Our loss in these fights was not more than sixty, while the killed of the enemy was nearly two hundred, and about one thousand captured.

Both armies now settled down to the organization needed for the conflicts that were certain to follow. Enlistments came in rapidly from this time forward, and side by side with the other loyal sections of the Union, Western Virginia did her full share for the maintenance of the National Government. As showing the readiness of the people to support the flag, it is proper to state here, that there were placed in the field of Western Virginia soldiers as brave a body of men as anywhere fought for the Union cause. As showing the patriotic spirit existing, it is well to note that out of a population of 393,234 in Western Virginia, in 1860, afterward the state of West Virginia, including the slaves, there were furnished 32,068 soldiers, or 8.1 per cent of the population; and the character of the troops may be shown, by the following statement of the losses of the several organizations:

HISTORY OF THE FIFTH WEST VIRGINIA CAVALRY

REGIMENTS	KILLED	DIED	TOTAL
1st Cavalry	81	126	207
2nd Cavalry	81	115	196
3rd Cavalry	46	136	182
4th Cavalry	-	30	30
5th Cavalry	71	118	189
6th Cavalry	61	174	235
7th Cavalry	33	203	236
Loudoun Rangers	-	14	14
Light Artillery	33	131	164
1st Infantry	54	138	192
4th Infantry	83	158	241
5th Infantry	61	90	151
6th Infantry	8	169	177
7th Infantry	142	158	300
9th Infantry	99	108	207
10th Infantry	95	146	241
11th Infantry	67	148	215
12th Infantry	59	131	190
13th Infantry	61	108	169
14th Infantry	88	157	245
15th Infantry	53	99	152
16th Infantry	-	7	7
17th Infantry	1	24	25
1st Veteran	9	31	40
2nd Veteran	1	16	17
Total	1287	2735	4022

This showing hardly does justice to the West Virginians, since the regiments were, as a rule, under the average size, and owing to the difficulties of recruiting, they had, from first to last, fewer men on their rolls, so that the apportionment of mortality to the total number was greater than would appear from a similar showing in regiments from more Northern States. As an instance, take our own regiment. The muster out rolls show a total enrollment of 1,069 men from first to last, of whom about sixty-five were discharged before the arduous campaigns of 1862 began, and Company G was detached for artillery service, making the real strength of the regiment before leaving Cheat Mountain, about 900 men. The losses given were really from this

CHAPTER I.

number of men. As a rule, when a West Virginia regiment was once formed and mustered into the service, it had to depend on its original members for its future strength. But few recruits were received, and as comrades fell in battle or by disease, their places were forever left unfilled, sad reminders of the horrible realities of war. In our own regiment, but 19 recruits were received in the whole of the three years service.

In justice to some Western Virginia regiments that were brigaded with our regiment during the service, we here recall them, in order that the readers of this book, may have a better idea of what the organizations were, as they read their noble records in the battles herewith given. The State and country had no abler defenders, and a truer, nobler set of men could not be found anywhere in the land. They were a tower of strength in the shock of battle, and brothers and comrades in the camp and on the march. Our sufferings together made us brothers in fact, and the memory of all of them is one of the most precious recollections of the war.

The Third Regiment Virginia Infantry was organized at Clarksburg, Va., in July 1861, by Col. David T. Hewes, and at once began operations in Western Virginia, having companies stationed in different places in the State, engaged in scouting and fighting bushwhackers, until it joined the brigade under Gen. Robt. H. Milroy in the spring of 1862, and proceeded to McDowell, where the Mountain Department was formed under Gen. Fremont. From this time on, until after the battle of Cloyd Mountain, in May 1864, this regiment and ours were in the same brigade. When the regiments were mounted in June 1863, and the Second became the Fifth Western Virginia Cavalry, the Third became the Sixth Western Virginia Cavalry, the two regiments bearing the same relative rank as when infantry. The two regiments were thus constantly together for over two years, and when their time of enlistment expired, the veterans and recruits of the two regiments were consolidated, taking the name of the Sixth West Virginia Cavalry.

The Fifth Regiment Virginia Infantry was organized at Ceredo, Va., during the summer of 1861, and was mustered into the United States service October 18, 1861. It was engaged in protecting the loyal citizens of the Kanawha Valley, and ridding it of the Confederates, until ordered to Parkersburg on Dec. 10. A principal part of the regiment was sent to New Creek and in February 1862, accompanied Colonel Dunning of the Fifth Ohio, commanding brigade, on his expedition to Moorefield, against Col. Harness of the Confederate army. On the 2d of April the regiment left New Creek, and went to McDowell, joining the command of Gen. Milroy, and taking part in the battle at that place, and after that battle became a part of General Milroy's brigade. They remained with the brigade all through Pope's campaign, participating in all the battles in which the brigade took a part, from Cedar Mountain to the second battle of Bull Run. The regiment returned to the Kanawha Valley in October 1862, and was detached from Milroy's brigade, and in May 1864, it became a part of Gen. Crook's command, participating in his expeditions. It took a part in Gen. Hunter's advance on Lynchburg, and the battle at that place June 18. Returning, it proceeded with Gen. Hunter's army to the Shenandoah Valley, forming a part of the Army of West Va. under General Crook in the brigade commanded by Col. I. H. Duvall, 9th W. Va. Infantry. On the 9th of November 1864, the Fifth and Ninth Western Virginia Infantry were consolidated by order of the War Department, and designated the First Regiment, West Virginia Veteran Infantry, and were mustered out of service, July 21, 1865.

The Eighth Regiment Virginia Infantry was organized in the Kanawha Valley, during the fall of 1861, headquarters being at Charleston. The regiment was ordered to New Creek in April 1862, becoming a part of Gen. Fremont's Mountain Department, and with the Sixtieth Ohio Infantry, was organized as an advance brigade, and placed under the command of Col. Cluseret A. D. C. to Gen. Fremont. In the pursuit of Jackson up the Valley, this brigade had the advance, and were engaged in several skirmishes with Ashby's cavalry, followed him closely to Harrisonburg, where they engaged him, resulting in the death of Ashby. This brigade occupied the centre at the battle of Cross Keys and was complimented by Gen. Fremont for its gallantry. The regiment became a part of Gen. Bohlen's brigade, Sigel's corps, in Pope's campaign, and served with great gallantry in all the engagements of that campaign. On arriving at Washington City, the regiment was transferred to Gen. Milroy's brigade, and returned with him to Western Virginia, and was again assigned to duty in the Kanawha Valley. In November 1862, it was transferred to Col. Moor's brigade at Buckhannon. On the assignment of Gen. Averell to the Fourth separate brigade, this regiment was mounted, and became a part of his brigade, as the Seventh West Virginia Cavalry, with which it served as long as the organization existed. It was mustered out of the service August 1, 1865.

CHAPTER II.

ORGANIZATION OF THE REGIMENT.

The three months men who had so gallantly and successfully carried the flag over Laurel Hill and Rich Mountain, were now sent to the rear to be mustered out, their term of service having expired, and the field was being occupied by three years troops. Ohio and Indiana were sending their brave men to the front, some of whom were encamped at Beverly, and Col. Bosley, Sixth Ohio Infantry, had command of the post at that place. Loyal Western Virginia was busy raising troops for its own defense and the support of the national authority, and men from all over the section were inquiring for the best place to give their services. The Second Regiment Virginia Volunteer Infantry, now being enlisted in various sections, was ordered to rendezvous at Beverly for organization, the first regiment in the state enlisted for the three years service. Company after company reported at Camp Carlisle, and were mustered into the United States service. This camp was located in the Fair grounds on Wheeling Island, at Wheeling, and was named after Hon. John S. Carlisle, one of the most prominent loyalists of the state, distinguished for his services to his country, and one of the ablest Representatives of the state in Congress.

Companies A, D, F and G came from Pittsburg, Pa.; Company I from Greenfield and California, Washington county, Pa.; Company H from Ironton, O.; Company B from Grafton, Va.; Company C from Wheeling, Va.; Company E from Monroe and Belmont counties, O., and Wetzel, Taylor and Ritchie counties, Va.; and Company K from Parkersburg, Va., and Bridgeport, O. The companies met together at Beverly, Va., in the latter part of July, and were organized as the Second Regiment Virginia Infantry. Dr. John W. Moss, of

Parkersburg, Va., was commissioned Colonel, Robert Moran Lieutenant Colonel, J. D. Owens Major, Rev. J.W.W. Bolton Chaplain, Dr. R. W. Hazlett Surgeon, Dr. Sample Ford Assistant Surgeon, Lieut. H. G. Jackson Adjutant, and Lieut. Webster A. Stevens Regimental Quartermaster. The following are the field officers, and non-commissioned staff, with the date of entering service, and the record of each.

NAME AND RANK	DATE OF COMMISSION	RECORD
John W. Moss, Colonel	July 3, 1861	Resigned May 20, 1862
George R. Latham, Colonel	May 25, 1862	Mustered out with regiment. Wounded at Second Bull Run.
Robt. Moran, Lieutenant Colonel	July 3, 1861	Resigned May 20, 1862
Alex. Scott, Lieutenant Colonel	May 20, 1862	Mustered out.
John D. Owens, Major	July 3, 1861	Resigned July 7, 1862
Thomas Gibson, Major	July 7, 1862	Transferred to 14 Pa. Cavalry
H. C. Flesher, Major	Nov. 9, 1862	Resigned Feb. 23, 1863
F. P. McNally, Major	Mar. 24, 1863	Killed Rocky Gap, Aug. 26, 1863
D. D. Barclay, Major	May 11, 1864	Mustered out.
H. G. Jackson, Adjutant	Aug. 23, 1861	Resigned Oct. 8, 1861
Chas. McC. Hays, Adjutant	Nov. 26, 1861	Resigned Jan. 11, 1862
D. F. Williamson, Adjutant	Feb. 7, 1862	Resigned Mar. 25, 1863
John Combs, Adjutant	June 12, 1862	Promoted to Cap. April 27, 1864
Jno. C. French, Adjutant	Apr. 27, 1864	Declined promotion. Not mustered.
Webster A. Stevens, First Lt. & R.Q.M.	July 27, 1861	Resigned July, 1862

CHAPTER II.

A. J. Pentecost, First Lt. and R.Q.M.	July 7, 1862	Mustered out.
R. W. Hazlett, Surgeon	July 25, 1861	Resigned Mar. 2, 1863
Eli N. Love, Surgeon	Mar. 13, 1863	Mustered out.
Sample Ford, Assistant Surgeon	Aug. 6, 1861	Resigned Sept. 18, 1862
Eli N. Love, Assistant Surgeon	Dec. 29, 1862	Promoted Surgeon, Mar. 23, 1863
Theo. Millspaugh, Assistant Surgeon	Sep. 20, 1862	Mustered out.
J. W. W. Bolton, Chaplain	Aug. 20, 1861	Mustered out. Wounded at Cloyd Mountain, May 1864.
John J. Ebert, Sergt. Major	June 1, 1861	Discharged for disability, Jan. 13, 1863
Geo. W. Miller, Sergt. Major	May 25, 1861	Promoted 1st Lt, Co. H
Wm. H. Silver, Sergt. Major	June 24, 1861	Mustered out.
E. F. Seaman, Q.M. Sergt.	Sept. 1, 1863	Mustered out with Co
Geo. Kirkpatrick, Com. Sergt.	July 29, 1861	Mustered out with Co
Jno. R. Thomas, Prin. Mus.	June 13, 1861	Mustered out with Co Wounded in ankle at Rocky Gap.
Danl. McK. Martin, Hospital Steward	Mar. 22, 1862	Mustered out.

An earnest effort has been made to secure a good sketch of the life and services of each of the field officers and non-commissioned staff, which has been accomplished except in a few cases. In a few instances, it was not possible to get the desired information, and no sketch is made, but the name is simply placed in the roll of honorable record and service, of itself glory enough for anyone. The individual sketches will be found very interesting and valuable, and as much as any other part of the work, show the struggles and heroic deeds, that led to the formation of the grand army that saved the nation. The writer very much regrets that he could not have a complete notice of everyone, but he found it impossible. The sketches of the chaplain, quartermaster, and others connected with the quartermaster department, will be found in the special articles in later chapters of this work.

COLONEL JOHN W. MOSS.

Dr. John W. Moss was born in Fairfax county, Va., October 4, 1816. He received a collegiate education in a Virginia school, and was graduated in medicine at the University of Pennsylvania, and located at Parkersburg, Va., in 1840, to practice his profession. Politically he was devoted to the principles of the Whig party, and was regarded as one of its leaders in that section of the state. He was opposed to the theory of state's rights, and strong in the belief that a citizen's just allegiance was due to the general government. After the passage of the ordinance of secession by the Virginia convention at Richmond, he aided in inaugurating the movement to save his part of the state to the Union, and was president of the convention held for that purpose in the city of Wheeling, May 13, 1861. He was also a member of the convention of June 11, 1861 at Wheeling, called to form the "Reorganized Government of Virginia," which was recognized by the Federal authorities. He was elected to the House of Delegates of the general assembly, which met in Wheeling July 1, 1861, and while serving in that body, he was commissioned colonel of the Second Virginia Infantry. Colonel Moss commanded his regiment with ability, and had the respect of his command, resigning his commission May 20, 1862. On August 22, 1862, he was commissioned surgeon of the Fourteenth West Virginia Infantry, and served as such until his death at Petersburg, W. Va., January 2, 1864.

COLONEL JOHN W. MOSS

COLONEL GEORGE R. LATHAM.

George Robert Latham was born in Prince William County, Virginia, in sight of the Bull Run battle ground, March 9, 1832. His father's name was John; mother's, Juliet A. - maiden name, Newman. He is the third of ten children, eight of whom grew to man or womanhood. Of five brothers living at the breaking out of the rebellion, four entered the army. James W., then living in Iowa, entered Col. Fitz Henry Warren's First Iowa Cavalry, and was with

CHAPTER II.

Wilson's cavalry which captured Jeff. Davis. John T. was a lieutenant in Bat. E., First W. Va. Lt. Art., and Benj. F. was lieutenant, and adjutant, Seventeenth W. Va. Infantry. Abner O. was not physically able for military service, and is now chief of the Diplomatic and Consular Bureau in the Fifth Auditor's office, Washington, D. C. James W. and Benj. F. have died since the war.

GEORGE R. LATHAM, COLONEL AND BREVET BRIGADIER GENERAL

His father was a farmer, and he was reared on the farm. In November, 1849, his father moved with his family into Western Virginia, and settled in Taylor County. George R., as a youth, was of very studious habits and good memory, but enjoyed limited means of acquiring an education, having access to such schools only as the state of Virginia then afforded, and that during the winter months only. In January 1850, he was taken with a severe attack of pleurisy, followed by general prostration, from which he was totally disabled for farm work for three years, and which broke up the plan of home study he had marked out and just entered upon. In 1852, having partially regained health, he took a country school and followed teaching in Taylor, and Barbour counties, Va., until the winter of 1859. From 1855 to 1861 he was a citizen of Grafton, where he married December 24, 1858, Miss Caroline A. Thayer, a daughter of Franklin and Mary Thayer, then of Monongalia county, Va. While teaching school he turned his attention to the study of the law and in the last week of 1859, passed the necessary examination and was admitted to the bar, opening the first law office in Grafton.

At this time, Rev. Simeon Siegfried was publishing the Grafton Sentinel, Grafton's first newspaper, to which Mr. Latham became an occasional contributor, participating to some extent, without an interest, in its management. About the time of the Presidential nominations for 1860 the Sentinel suspended, and he took the office and published a campaign paper called the *Western Virginian*, in the interest of Bell and Everett. After the election it became evident to those who watched the sentiment, and knew the reckless determination of those who controlled it, in the south, that there would be "unpleasantness." In this border section business was now practically suspended, and all was excitement and preparation.

Upon the passage of the ordinance of secession, the Union delegates from Western Virginia returned home, many of them leaving Richmond in disguise at night in order to escape with their lives. No one who had voted against the ordinance was safe to remain after it had passed, who did not immediately "flop over," as some did. Mr. L., in view of these facts, published an editorial about this time in which he said: "Considering the treatment of the Western Virginia delegates to the convention, we do sincerely hope that no Western Virginia constituency will ever again be represented in the present capital of the state." Viewed in the light of subsequent history, this wish partakes of the nature of prophecy. He also wrote for publication about this time, a call for a convention in Western Virginia - the first that was written.

Col. Porterfield, with a battalion of troops from Augusta and adjoining counties, was now at Philippi, sixteen miles south of Grafton, where he was joined by Barbour county volunteers. W. P. Thompson had organized a company at Fairmont, Marion county, and moved to Fetterman, one and one-half miles west of Grafton, where he was joined by a company of Taylor county rebels under Hansbrough. The Union leaders, though at a disadvantage, the rebels having the start by way of organization, were by no means inactive, and Mr. Latham was in constant correspondence with all the leading Union men of the State.

About two weeks before the election, Mr. Latham hoisted a large United States flag over his law office and turned it into a recruiting office. Maj. James Oakes, as mustering officer, and Capt. Wm. Craig, as quartermaster, of the regular army, had, in the meantime, been stationed at Wheeling, to muster into the United States service, such volunteers from Virginia as might present themselves. Mr. Latham at once placed himself in communication with them, often visiting them at Wheeling, and they gave him all the information and advice he needed. By the 20th of May he had a full company enrolled, which afterwards became Company B, and was the first Union company recruited in the interior of the State. He and the company determined to remain in Grafton and vote before leaving for Wheeling. About this time a little incident occurred which is probably worthy of note. The flag, before mentioned, was suspended over Main street on a rope, one end of which was tied to the chimney of Mr. Latham's house, and the other to that of Mr. Lewis, opposite. One day when Mr. Latham was in Wheeling, a committee of citizens called upon his wife and advised her to have the flag taken down, stating that from threats they had heard, the house would be in danger if it remained up over night. She replied that Mr. Latham had left it flying when he went away, and, so far as she was concerned, it should fly until he came back. The alarmists, however, frightened Mr. Lewis and he took the rope off his chimney, and the flag into an upper window of Mr. Latham's house, leaving the rope still tied to his chimney. On the afternoon of the day before the election, Capt., afterwards Col., Thompson, commanding at Fetterman, for the purpose of intimidating the citizens of Grafton, marched his force, about one hundred and sixty strong,

CHAPTER II.

through Grafton and back, passing up Main street and down the railroad. When it became known to the citizens of Grafton that they were coming, the excitement was intense, and it was with the utmost difficulty that a bloody street fight was prevented. A single shot fired would have proved most disastrous, but the calmer counsels prevailed and bloodshed was deferred to await legal organization. As the rebel column marched up Main street Mr. Latham was standing in front of his office. A half dozen of fiery young men rushed past him into his house, threw the flag out of the window, and, rushing down again, dragged it through the rebel column and tied the other end of the rope to a tall post across the street, and it remained there all the evening, hanging so low as to obstruct passage, the horsemen following at the rear of the rebel column being compelled to turn back. There was in the town a company, probably fifteen to twenty-five, of little girls, who had been accustomed to meet and sing patriotic songs. As if by magic, these appeared on the platform at the Grafton House, in white dresses, carrying small Union flags, and gave the rebels a strain of Union music as they passed back to Fetterman. Mr. Latham had sent his family, consisting of wife and two small children, to her father's. The election passed off as quietly as a funeral, the largest vote ever polled at Grafton to that time being cast, and only one for the ordinance.

Porterfield had moved on that day from Philippi to Webster, four miles south of Grafton, and he and Thompson were to unite their forces at Grafton on the next day. Latham therefore collected his company after night, and while the rebels at Fetterman were really fearing an attack, marched around them, striking the railroad at Valley Falls, six miles below, in time to intercept a 3 a.m. train for Wheeling. The latter part of June, Capt. Latham was ordered with his company to Grafton, where he met Gen. McClellan and, knowing the locations, distances, &c., assisted him in preparing his Western Virginia campaign. The company was then assigned to Gen. Morris' command at Philippi, and took part in the campaign to Corrick's Ford. Capt. Latham had charge of Garnett's body, dressed and boxed it, and it was sent in charge of a staff officer to Manassas and delivered to Gen. Beauregard several days before the first battle of Bull Run. This company also buried the body of a mere youth who fell by the side of his general, and placed at his head a board with the inscription, written by First Lieutenant F. A. Cather, "Here lies the body of a youth (name unknown) who fell defending his general while his comrades ran away." The most interesting trophies captured by Company B in this race were the patent leather wallet of George W. Hansbrough, with his name on it, and a cartridge box with the following inscription: "D. S. K. Knight who killed the first yankee in Virginia."

Capt. Latham and his company were left at Belington to protect the line of transportation. From this time on until his muster out in March 1865, his history is incorporated with that of the regiment. Toward the close of his service, Secretary of War Stanton nominated Col. Latham as brevet brigadier general, after a thorough investigation of his record, thus placing upon this gallant officer, one of the proudest honors of his life. Col. Latham had the confidence and love of the entire regiment. The men believed in him, admired his courage, trusted his honesty and relied on his ability and intense devotion to country, and he never disappointed them. With a knowledge of his conduct during the service of the regiment, the writer cheerfully bears testimony to the worth and ability of this noble and brave officer. He never failed in any emergency, and his men would follow him wherever he called to duty.

In the fall of '64, Col. Latham was elected a member of the Thirty-ninth Congress for the Second District of West Virginia, from March 4th, '65, to March 4th, '67, and was mustered out of the service March 10th. During his term in Congress he served on the committees of printing and of public buildings and grounds. This was probably the most exciting Congress the country has ever experienced. It was during the Reconstruction period and the quarrel with President Johnson. Col. Latham, though an ardent Republican, did not approve of some of the measures and doctrines advocated by a majority of his party. While favoring the amendments which were offered to the constitution, in order to harmonize it with the altered condition of things, he would not agree that the *reconstruction of the government* was necessary in order to restore the states to their proper places in the Union, or to "guarantee" future loyalty; and was in favor of local self-government in and for the states, and the seating of *loyal* members of Congress, legally elected, whenever and from whatever state presented; but he was opposed to *ever* admitting to a seat in Congress, or to other important *Federal* offices, *any who had not been continuously loyal*. His position on these momentous questions is fully presented in his own language, in speeches delivered in the house on January 8th and May 28th, 1866.

On account of the failure of his health, Col. Latham declined to be a candidate for renomination, and about two weeks before the adjournment, at the request of the Secretary of State, he agreed to accept an appointment as United States Consul at Melbourne, Australia. For this position he was nominated by President Johnson and promptly confirmed by the Senate, and left for his post of duty on the 10th and sailed from Boston on the 20th of April, 1867. This service continued three years, he returning in 1870. While in Melbourne he detected a whisky fraud upon the revenue of the United States, which was compromised by the payment of $75,000 into the treasury. He also collected from the Fiji Islands an indemnity claim of long standing, amounting to $45,000. The white residents, of all nationalities, united with the native authorities of Fiji, and presented, through him, an application or petition to the Government of the United States to extend its jurisdiction over the group. President Grant and his cabinet, however, rejected the petition. They then applied to Great Britain, which promptly accepted the offer. Col. Latham

CHAPTER II.

delivered one lecture in Melbourne on the "American War," for the benefit of the building fund of the church which he and his family attended. The largest hall in the city was filled and the committee realized between $400 and $500. He was urgently requested to repeat the lecture in other places and for similar objects, but declined because the State Department, in a general way, disapproves of its foreign representatives lecturing on matters relating to our public institutions and governmental pollcy. When about to leave Melbourne, he was feted, banqueted and presented with addresses as no other consul of any nation, to Melbourne, had ever been. It is regretted that we have not a full copy of his reply to an address presented to him by the Consular Corps. In this he congratulated them especially upon the fact that during his connection with them, all the nations represented had been at peace; and predicted in the near future the settlement of international disputes by an international congress, and consequently practical disarmament.

Since 1870 Col. Latham has retired mostly from public life, though still taking a lively interest in all the social and political questions of the day. He was elected and served one term of two years, about 1875, as Superintendent of public schools for Upshur county, West Va., and was appointed by President Hayes, in 1880, Supervisor of Census for the first census district of West Virginia. This is his last public office, to date. He received a grape shot wound in his left foot at Lee's Springs on the Rappahannock River, in August, 1862, which was thought to be but trifling at the time and for some years after, but which is now giving him much trouble and pain at times. Col. Latham has a wife and eight children living - four sons and four daughters, and he is now fifty-eight years of age.

LIEUTENANT COLONEL ROBERT MORAN.

Robert Moran, was born on the banks of White Day creek, Monongalia Co., Va., near the village of Smithtown, December 27, 1822. Shortly after this his father moved into what is now Marion County, West Va., where he remained until his death. During the boyhood of the subject of this sketch, there was but little opportunity in that section of securing an education especially by the common people, who had to work both summer and winter, clearing out their farms. His father being a poor man with a large family, he received but a few months schooling. In his boyhood he had strong military inclinations, and when he attended the drills of the State Militia with his father, he determined to be an officer if he reached manhood. At twenty-one years of age he was elected Captain of a militia company for five years, and after that was elected lieutenant colonel of the One Hundred Forty-seventh Regiment of Virginia Militia, and six years later was elected colonel of the same regiment, which commission he held until the war began. Upon reaching his majority, Col.

Moran married, and began clearing a farm for himself. In 1852 he rented his farm and moved to the village of Winfield, about four miles from Fairmont, where he kept a general store and tavern, until April 1, 1861. Seeing that war was inevitable, he sold his goods at auction, at a sacrifice of nearly $3,000, and on the first call for troops for the support of the government, he cast his fortunes with the Union, and began to enlist troops for the Second Virginia Infantry, of which he was appointed lieutenant colonel, upon its organization in July, 1861. At the convention held in Wheeling, May 13, 1861, Col. Moran was a delegate, and took a prominent, and positive part in its proceedings. Col. Moran participated in all the campaigns of his regiment, until May 20, 1862, when he resigned his office. His health had become so bad that he had to retire, and was so worn down at the time, that he had to be hauled in an ambulance to New Creek, and it was weeks before he was able to reach his home. After his return home, Gen. Jones, of the Confederate army, made a raid through Fairmont and that part of the state, and Col. Moran did good service in the defense made against the raider.

After the war he was assessor of Internal Revenue for two years, and in 1875 was land commissioner for one-half of Marion county, to place a valuation on all real estate for taxation. In the spring of 1876, he moved to Platte County, Nebraska, of which he was elected county commissioner one term, and since then his health has been so bad, that he has declined to serve in any office, though often solicited by the people to do so. He is now living on his farm of 640 acres, greatly enfeebled by disease.

LIEUTENANT-COLONEL ALEXANDER SCOTT.

Alexander Scott was a native of Franklin County, Pa., and of Scotch-Irish origin. His parents' relatives, as well as those of his wife, fled to this country during the Irish Rebellion, and are of a sturdy, courageous stock. Col. Scott's grandfather, Alexander Scott, was a soldier in the Revolutionary war, and the colonel comes honestly of his soldierly qualities. His father, Samuel Scott, was, a farmer, and moved to Wooster, Ohio, in 1836, when the son went to Pittsburgh to study music. He gave up his studies to enter the service in the Mexican war, and went out from Pittsburgh with the "Rough and Ready Guards," commanded by Capt. Rowley. This company was mustered in as Company F, Maryland and District of Columbia volunteers, October 8, 1847, and was on duty until July 24, 1848, when it was mustered out. At the close of the Mexican war, Col. Scott married Eleanor G. Smith, daughter of Prof. James M. Smith, of Pittsburgh, formerly of Londonderry, Ireland, and went to reside in Nashville, Tenn., and from there to Mississippi, and engaged in the furniture business. They remained there until the breaking out of the rebellion. He was at that time a member of the Aberdeen Masonic Lodge, and commanded the Monroe

CHAPTER II.

Rifle Volunteers. This company was ordered to report for duty at Macon, Ga., to go into a Confederate regiment, and the colonel was given command, but he declined the offer, and left the South, returning to Pittsburgh. Here he aided in recruiting Company F of the regiment of which he became lieutenant-colonel, entering the service as captain of the company. He was in all the battles in which the regiment took part, and his history is intimately connected with all the operations of the army recorded in the following chapters. At the battle of Second Bull Run, August 30, 1862, he had his horse shot under him. At the battle of Droop Mountain, November 6, 1863, he commanded the remnant of the regiment, and was complimented on the field by General Averell, for his gallant conduct. He had the entire confidence of his men,

ALEXANDER SCOTT, LIEUTENANT-COLONEL ALEXANDER SCOTT

and they cheerfully followed his leadership, though they knew that it meant danger, and perhaps death. He rendered good service on the famous Salem Raid, where he contracted a severe cold, from which he never recovered, and which caused his death May 29, 1870, in his 49th year. He was mustered out with the regiment, and returned to private life at Pittsburgh. He left a widow, who resides in their home city, and three children, Mary Ray Scott, and Wm. Graham and Henry Brown Scott. The two sons are employed in the offices of the Pennsylvania railroad. The daughter is one of the talented singers of that city, having a very fine contralto voice, and sings in the choir of the Third Presbyterian church. The name is also perpetuated in two grandsons, Josiah R. B. and Armor G. Scott. Colonel Scott was an able, brave officer, a good leader, and was a worthy representative of the volunteer soldiery of the country.

MAJOR J. D. OWENS.

J. D. Owens was one of the organizers of the Plummer Guards, going to Wheeling as the captain of that company. He was commissioned the first major of the regiment, and served in that capacity until he resigned his commission, July 7, 1862. He commanded the detachment of the regiment that went to the battle of Allegheny Mountain, and was in command of the regiment at the battle of Cross Keys, June 1862, where he performed his duty, and handled his regiment, to the satisfaction of his superiors. It was a task of more than ordinary severity, but he met it bravely. The first colonel and lieutenant-colonel had resigned, and Major Owens followed them after the active campaign was over, the regiment thus losing its first officers, of the first three ranks, as also that of adjutant and quartermaster.

MAJOR H. C. FLESHER.

Henry C. Flesher, a native of Weston, Lewis County, Va., was born October 27, 1838, and lived at that place until he was 17 years of age. He studied law and was admitted to practice in 1858, opening an office in Wheeling January 1, 1859, and there remained until he was mustered into the service, as first lieutenant of the company, and was promoted captain May 1862. In October 1862, he was promoted to major of the regiment, which position he held until he resigned. He served as A. A. G. for Gen. Milroy before and after the Pope campaign in 1862. While in the valley with Gen. Fremont, Capt. Flesher was directed to carry a dispatch from Fremont at Harrisonburg, to Gen. James Shields at Luray, just before the battle of Cross Keys, and was mentioned by Fremont and Milroy for his bravery and efficiency. He was with the regiment in its hard work, and did his full share of it. He settled in Jackson C. H., W. Va., in March 1869, and was married in September of that year to Mrs. Miriam F. Hopkins, where he has since been engaged in the practice of his profession. He has three children, Paul 19, Pearl 17 ,and Pauline 11 years of age. The major is a member of the G. A. R., and has held the position of Judge Advocate for the Department of West Va. G. A. R.

MAJOR H.C. FLESHER

MAJOR F. P. M'NALLY.

Francis Patrick McNally was born in County Goet, Ireland, and came to America when about seventeen years of age. When about the age of eighteen, he went with the expedition of Commodore Perry to Japan. The expedition sailed on the 24th of November, 1852, and returned from Japan upon the

MAJOR F.P. MCNALLY

CHAPTER II.

completion of the Treaty, February 22d, 1855, receiving an honorable discharge at Norfolk, Va. He was married to Miss Mary McNamara, on February 14th, 1860, at Ironton, Lawrence County, O., by Rev. Philip Donahue. Both were adherents of the Catholic church. Upon the outbreak of the rebellion, Mr. McNally raised the first company that left Ironton for the three years service. He was wounded, at the battle of Rocky Gap, August 26th, 1863, was taken prisoner, and died at White Sulphur Springs, September 22d, 1863.

MAJOR D. D. BARCLAY.

D. D. Barclay was born in Conemaugh township, Indiana County, Pa., April 13th, 1838. His parents, J. M. L. Barclay and Jane Ferguson Barclay, were natives of the same county, and born within one-half mile of each other. The subject of this sketch served his minority with his parents on the farm, and at the age of twenty-one went to McKeesport, Allegheny County, Pa., where he served his apprenticeship at boat building. As soon as he had completed his trade, he went to boating on the Ohio and Mississippi rivers, and continued in the same until the breaking out of the war, when he went to Pittsburgh, and enlisted in Company D. When mustered in to the United States service at Wheeling, he was elected second lieutenant of the company. On the 22d of March, 1862, he was promoted to first lieutenant, and on July 7th to captain of the company. By his bravery and good fellowship, he soon became a great favorite in the company. He took an active part in all the battles and skirmishes in which the company was engaged, and could always be found where the danger was the greatest, and where duty called. On several occasions he acted as major of the regiment. This was notably the case on General Averell's famous Droop Mountain raid, and in the battle that closed the campaign, November 6th, 1863, and on the Salem raid in December of the same year. On April 24th, 1864, he received the well merited promotion of major of the regiment. He took part in all the work of the regiment, until mustered out August 25th, 1864. During his term of service he served under Generals McClellan, Rosecrans, Milroy, Fremont, Pope, Averell, Crook and Hunter. The regiment had not a more popular man in it, and he had but to give the command, when his brave boys would follow him anywhere. They had the utmost confidence in his solid sense, good

MAJOR D.D. BARCLAY

judgment, fidelity and bravery, and never in all his service did he do any act to lose the high regard of his men. His bravery is attested by the gallant work under Milroy, his faithful service at Rocky Gap, Droop Mountain, and Salem Raid, and by his grand work on the final expedition under Gen. Crook.

Major Barclay was married on March 4, 1862, to Mrs E. P. Reinbeau, to whom have been born two sons and two daughters. After returning home from the army, he again followed his trade of boat building, and went to work for W. H. Brown, one of Pittsburgh's greatest coal merchants, and continued with him until Mr. Brown's death, when the firm was changed to W. H. Brown's Sons, and the major is now superintendent of their entire works at Brown's station, Twenty-third ward, Pittsburgh, on the B&O R.R. The major is a deacon in the Christian church at Hazelwood, and ever since leaving the army has been an active and enthusiastic worker in the Sunday school. His wife often accompanied him in the army, and is most highly esteemed by the men in the command. Major Barclay is a true American, a typical citizen soldier, a patriotic citizen, and a Christian gentleman, in whom his old comrades find a good friend.

ADJUTANT HAYS.

Charles McClure Hays, a native of Pittsburgh, enlisted in the Plummer Guards as a private. He was a lawyer by profession, and a nephew of Judge McClure, who was famous as a lawyer and jurist before the war. Mr. Hays was a man of magnificent presence, remarkably handsome, with a large and brainy head, and polished in speech and manner. November 6, 1861, he was promoted to be adjutant of the regiment, which office he resigned January 11, 1862. Returning to Pittsburgh, he enlisted in Captain Young's company of Heavy Artillery, stationed at Fort Delaware. He died at Harrisburg, Pa., about the close of the war.

ADJUTANT WILLIAMSON.

D. F. Williamson was by birth an Englishman, and about 40 years of age when he entered the service, as a member of Company K. He had served 12 years in the English army, and was one of the best drilled men in the regiment, especially with the sword. While the regiment lay at Elkwater, the officers specially had the opportunity to learn his skill in this respect. Many, if not all, of the line officers at that time, were drilled in the use of the saber by him. He was a well built man, and made a splendid appearance in uniform; and in addition was well educated and of the most genial disposition. He was appointed first lieutenant of Company I in the fall of 1861, and on February 7, 1862, was appointed adjutant of the regiment, resigning this office March 25, 1862. It may be said of

CHAPTER II.

Lieut. Williamson, that he was generally liked, and he had few enemies among the officers and men of the regiment.

SURGEON R. W. HAZLETT.

R. W. Hazlett, M. D., was born at Washington, Pa., in 1828. He was educated at Washington College, Washington, Pa., but was prevented by illness from graduating; but subsequently the degree of A. B. was conferred on him by the college. Adopting the profession of medicine, he was graduated at Jefferson Medical College, Philadelphia, Pa., in 1851, and practiced medicine at Wheeling, Va., until the breaking out of the war of the rebellion. Dr. Hazlett was commissioned surgeon of the Second Regiment Virginia Volunteer Infantry, June 15th, 1861, serving in that capacity until the fall of 1862, when he was appointed surgeon of Gen. Milroy's "Independent Brigade." He resigned his commission as surgeon of the regiment March 2d, 1863, and was appointed one of the surgeons in the United States General Hospital at Grafton, West Va., in the summer of 1863. While at this place, the doctor was commissioned by the Secretary of War, Surgeon of the Board of Enrollment, of the First District of West Virginia, which embraced about one-half of the State, and was mustered out of service June 15, 1865.

R.W. HAZLETT, M.D.

The doctor was present at the surrender of Gen. Pegram, after the battle of Rich Mountain, July, 1861, and participated in the battles of Monterey, McDowell, Cross Keys, Cedar Mountain, Waterloo Bridge, White Sulphur Springs, Freeman's and Kelly's Fords, Warrenton, Second Bull Run, Centreville and Chantilly, in the summer of 1862.

Since his retirement from the army, he has practiced medicine at Wheeling, and has held a number of civil and medical appointments. Among the latter, the doctor was for twenty years a Pension Examining Surgeon, which position he resigned upon the election of Grover Cleveland as President. The doctor located for a company in 1858, the first productive oil well in the state of West Virginia.

SURGEON E. N. LOVE.

Eli Nathan Love was born in Loudoun County, Va., Sept. 28, 1820. At the age of 17, he commenced teaching school, and continued in this occupation until he became of age. Having inherited some money he entered the mercantile business, but he soon tired of it, and began reading medicine. In 1847, he entered the University of Maryland, from which he was graduated in 1849.

He then went to Virginia, where he was married to Miss Caroline Moore, Sept. 3, 1850, and practiced his profession until the breaking out of the rebellion. After the secession of Virginia he was forced to leave his home on account of his loyalty, became a refugee, and in company with several others, left Virginia July 13, 1861, and waded the Potomac River to the Maryland side, where he found some Federal soldiers, and went with them to the Point of Rocks, thence to Washington. He next went to Ohio, but soon found his way to Wheeling, where he was commissioned assistant surgeon of the Second Virginia Infantry. Upon the resignation of the surgeon, Dr. R. W. Hazlett, he was appointed surgeon of the regiment, serving until it was mustered out.

After the expiration of his term of service, he resumed the practice of his profession at Waterford, Loudoun County, Va. During the war his wife died, and after the war he married Miss Armida Athey, of Maryland, who survives him, the doctor having died August 14, 1882.

ELI N. LOVE, M.D.

ASSISTANT SURGEON S. FORD.

Dr. Sample Ford was born in Wheeling in 1827. He attended the West Alexandria Academy, Washington County, Pa., and read medicine with Dr. R. H. Cummins of Wheeling. He attended one course of lectures at the Pennsylvania University at Philadelphia, and practiced medicine near McKeesport, Pa. Dr. Ford was commissioned assistant surgeon of the Second Virginia Infantry in July 1861, and participated in the battles of Cross Keys, Freeman's and Kelly's Fords and Second Bull Run. He resigned his commission in the winter of 1862; and was near Cumberland, Md., in 1863, where he remained until the close of the war. He subsequently practiced medicine in Bridgeport, Ohio, and Wheeling, W. Va. He died at Wheeling in 1868 of hepatic disease.

CHAPTER II.

ASSISTANT SURGEON T. MILLSPAUGH.

Dr. Theodore Millspaugh was born in Ulster County, N. Y., May 24, 1838. He was educated at Montgomery Academy, N. Y., and Rutgers College Grammar school. He is a graduate of the College of Physicians and Surgeons of New York City, class of 1861. He was studying medicine at the outbreak of the rebellion, and was two months in the U.S. General Hospital at Alexandria, Va., immediately after the first battle of Bull Run, in the employ of the Sanitary Commission. After graduating, he entered the service as Acting Assistant Surgeon U. S. A., and joined General Fremont's command in the Shenandoah Valley, in June 1862. He was commissioned assistant surgeon of the Second Virginia Infantry August 1, 1862, and served with the regiment until mustered out. He has practiced medicine in Wallkill, N. Y., since the close of the war. He is a Republican in politics, and has represented his district in the state legislature, and has held several local offices.

THEODORE MILLSPAUGH, M.D.

SERGEANT MAJOR G. W. MILLER.

George W. Miller was residing in Grafton, West Va., at the breaking out of the rebellion and had been for several years previous to that time, but the place of his birth is unknown. His father's name was George. He enlisted with Company B and was mustered in with the company. He was twenty-eight years of age. August 1st, 1862, he was promoted from a sergeant to sergeant major, in which capacity he served to the end of the war. He was a soldier of much merit, intelligent, brave and trusty, and possessed a constitution to stand the hardships of a soldier's life. After the war he married and moved to Kansas.

PRINCIPAL MUSICIAN J. R. THOMAS.

John R. Thomas joined the party that left California for Pittsburgh, and became members of Company G. His parents were from Wales, sturdy people, from whom John inherited a strong constitution. He worked about town, like most boys of the day, at such work as he could get, securing by reading and at the public school the average information of the day in a village. His chief joy, however, was music, and he could readily learn to play on any instrument that was given him, but his special ability lay in leading in martial music. He naturally called about him many kindred spirits, and for a year or two before the war he led a band of fifers and drummers, that was unexcelled in skill in western Pennsylvania. During a great Republican parade in Pittsburgh, in 1860, the band was engaged, and was spoken of as the best in the large column. This band was the one that aroused the people of Greenfield and California, the first Sunday after Fort Sumter was fired upon, and rallied the loyal hearts in those towns, leading to the enlistment of Company I. This enlistment of Thomas in Company G soon caused the breaking up of the band, and all that were old enough, enlisted in the Second Virginia Infantry. Soon after the organization of the regiment, Mr. Thomas organized a regimental band, and afterward was appointed principal musician of the regiment. He remained in this position until the muster out, and was transferred to Company I after Company G was transferred to the artillery arm of the service. Mr. Thomas was a brave soldier, and while engaged at Rocky Gap was shot in the ankle and severely hurt. After the war he engaged in farming, and is now happily located in Iowa, one of the stalwart, noble citizens of that grand commonwealth.

CHAPTER III.

COMPANY HISTORIES.

In the following pages of this chapter, will be found the history of each company from its enlistment, until the organization of the regiment, including incidents of interest, in some cases conflict with the enemy, sketches of officers, and a roster of the Company, containing the rank of each officer and man, and his individual record. It is not claimed that these company histories are complete and full or absolutely correct in all the details, as it is feared that such is not the case in some, at least, of the companies. Nearly two years were devoted by the Historian to searching for the facts, but he was not always successful in securing them. The muster out rolls, as published in the Adjutant General's report of the state of West Virginia, were used as a basis, but were found to be imperfect, and officers and men were then asked to correct the rolls so far as it was possible. Scores of corrections were made of men who were killed, had died or were wounded, and the proper credit given after the names on the rolls; but after all the effort, the record is incomplete, and must so remain. Those who could give the information desired, are dead or beyond the reach of the writer, and the facts cannot now be ascertained. This is greatly regretted, as doubtless many comrades in reading the book will find omissions in their own cases, and will wonder why the proper credit has not been given them. Weeks of anxious effort were cheerfully and freely given by the writer to make the record of each of his comrades perfect, and he could do no more.

The company histories will be found one of the most interesting parts of the entire work. They clearly show the patriotism that animated the men, and their readiness to hurry to the defense of their country. All were volunteers, who entered the service without promise of reward, and had no mercenary motives whatever in the course they took. Their one anxiety was to defend the flag of their country, and aid in quelling the causeless rebellion that threatened the very life of the nation. It was a regiment of comparatively young men, the average age being about twenty-four years, a large number of them being but boys of eighteen, while a few reached the age of forty. They were young, active, strong and intelligent, the making of a splendid regiment, and their work for three years fully confirmed all that was expected of them.

An endeavor was made to secure individual sketches of the officers, and it was mainly successful. In a few cases it will be noticed that the sketch is absent, but it is because of the absolute impossibility of securing it. Hundreds of letters were written to find the whereabouts of certain officers, but they were not found, nor could any intelligent record be had of their lives. In most cases where an officer was promoted to the field, the sketch will be found in the regimental organization. These sketches will be found very valuable and interesting. They are often a history of themselves. After reading some of them, especially of men from West Va., it will not be difficult to understand whence came their intense love of their country and its institutions. Our officers, as a rule, were brave and efficient, and measured up well to the standard of patriots and heroes. It would be a source of great gratification were the histories of these men more complete and full, and if the lives of the brave men of the regiment could also be printed in these pages, but it was not possible. The large majority of the brave old comrades have answered to the last roll call, and many of them have left no record of their lives or life work. It is hoped that the following pages of this chapter will be found measurably free from errors, and as complete as the lapse of 26 years will permit.

COMPANY A.

The first company from Allegheny county, Pa., that entered the service of other states, was the organization that bore this name in the Second Virginia regiment. The company was organized in Pittsburgh and Allegheny by Major Abijah Ferguson, an old Mexican veteran, who being rather feeble for active service, the command devolved upon Captain A.C. Hayes, who was chosen to that office, with D.L. Smith, first lieutenant, and Oliver R. West, second lieutenant. It was among the first companies organized after the attack upon Fort Sumter, and immediately tendered its services to Gov. Andrew G. Curtin of Pennsylvania. So anxious were the men to serve their native state, that they sent Lieut. Smith to Harrisburg, personally to urge the acceptance of their services, presuming from the fact of his having recently been a member of the legislature, that he could prevail upon the Governor to accept them. The quota of the state having been filled, however, Lieut. Smith was informed that his company would have to wait another call for troops. The men now

CHAPTER III.

became impatient, and in the midst of the excitement of the occasion, news came that the enemy had captured Harper's Ferry, and taken possession of the Baltimore & Ohio railroad, were moving on the Pennsylvania line, and were menacing Wheeling, Va. The loyal people of Wheeling called for aid, and this company, then known as the "Washington Rifle Guards," chartered the steamer McCombs and took passage for Wheeling, arriving there on the 10th of May 1861. On the 21st of May 1861, Major James Oakes of the U.S. army, mustered them into the service of the United States for three years. This was the first company of Pennsylvanians that was mustered for three years service, all the troops that were mustered prior to that time, being known as three months men.

On the morning of the 25th of May 1861, the company, together with the First Virginia Infantry, three months troops under command of Col. B.F. Kelley, left Wheeling and advanced along the line of the Baltimore & Ohio railroad toward Grafton, which place was then held by the enemy.

At Glover's Gap, company A was detached to guard that important position, and more particularly to break up a rebel military organization, known to be in that section, under command of Captain Christian Roberts. On the morning of May 27th, a detachment of the company under command of Lieut. West, encountered Captain Roberts and a portion of his command, and in the fight that followed, Captain Roberts was killed, being the first armed rebel soldier that fell in the war. Thus the honor fell to this company of killing the first armed soldier of the Confederacy. Jackson, the slayer of the gallant Colonel Ellsworth, killed a few days previously, was a civilian, while Captain Roberts was a regularly mustered officer of the Confederacy. After this the company went to Grafton, where it lay while the battle of Philippi, the first battle of the war, was being fought some sixteen miles away.

Upon General George B. McClellan assuming command of the army in Western Virginia, Company A was detailed as his body guard, along with one company of infantry of the U. S. Regular Army, and remained at his headquarters as such, during the time he remained in command of that department, participating in his successful Western Virginia campaign which terminated in Beverly, from which point General McClellan was called to Washington, after the first battle of Bull Run, to take command of the armies of the United States. Company A always retained the most pleasant recollections of their campaign under General McClellan, as his body guard. His engaging manners, and sense of justice to his men, greatly endeared him to his soldiers.

The following is the muster out roll, showing list of members and their record. The company was mustered into the U. S. service at Wheeling May 21, 1861, and mustered out June 14, 1864. All the members not otherwise marked, were mustered out with the company. The recruits, and veterans were transferred to the 6th West Virginia cavalry when the company was mustered out.

HISTORY OF THE FIFTH WEST VIRGINIA CAVALRY

NAMES	RANK	RECORD OF SERVICE
Albert C. Hayes	Capt.	Resigned July 22, 1861
William Otto	Capt.	Promoted from 1st Sergt. Aug. 24, 1861. Resigned Mar. 13, 1862
John A. Hunter	Capt.	Promoted from 1st Lt. Co. F, Mar. 20, 1862. Relieved Aug. 1, 1863.
Oliver R. West	Capt.	Promoted 2d Lt to 1st Lt, Mar. 1, 1862, to captured Aug. 18, 1863. Wounded Allegheny Mountain.
David L. Smith	1st Lt.	Promoted to Capt & C.S. Feb. 17, 1862; to Lt Col & Chief C.S. 5th Army Corps
Alex. J. Pentecost	1st Lt.	Promoted to 1st Lt & R.Q.M. July 7, 1862
A. J. Chambers	2d Lt.	Promoted to 2d Lt Co D, July 7, 1862
James Black	2d Lt.	Promoted to 2d Lt Mar. 1, 1862. Relieved May 30, 1863.
Jas. R. Hutchinson	2d Lt.	Promoted to 2d Lt Aug. 18, 1863, Captured Cheat River, Sept. 25, 1863. Prisoner to close of war.
Geo. H. Kirkpatrick	Sergt.	Promoted to C.S. July 29, 1861.
George W. Given	Sergt.	
Harrison Smith	Sergt.	Captured Cheat River, Sept. 25, 1863. Prisoner till end of war.
Franklin H. Singer	Sergt.	Wounded Allegheny Mountain, Dec. 13, 1861. Captured Cheat River, Sept. 25, 1863. Exchanged.
Michael Campbell	Sergt.	Captured Cheat River, Sept. 25, 1863. Exchanged.
Samuel Scott	Sergt.	
Hannam Gray	Sergt.	Discharged for disability, March 12, 1863.
John Breen	Corporal	Captured Cheat River, Sept. 25, 1863. Exchanged.
Wm. H. Graham	Corporal	Wounded at Rocky Gap, Aug. 26, 1863.
Chas. Britch	Corporal	Wounded at 2d Bull Run. Captured Cheat River, Sep. 25, 1863. Exchanged.
Samuel K. Croco	Corporal	Captured Cheat River, Sept. 25, 1863. Exchanged.

CHAPTER III.

William Ray	Teamster	
Charles R. Curtis	Teamster	Deserted, May 20, 1863.
James Kincaid	Blacksmith	Wounded Second Bull Run.
Benj. F. Ackelson	Private	Wounded Cheat River, Sept. 25, 1863. Re-enlisted Jan. 5, 1864.
Marvin Annis	Private	Died consumption, Nov. 10, 1863.
Fred. Baxmeyer	Private	
William Bowser	Private	Wounded Beverly, Apr. 24, 1863.
Fred. H. Braun	Private	Captured 2nd Bull Run. Exchanged.
John Bailey	Private	Discharged June 20, 1861.
Frederick Baird	Private	Discharged June 20, 1861.
Amos M. Barbin	Private	Discharged May 25, 1863.
Joseph D. Croco	Private	Re-enlisted Jan. 5, 1864.
Matthew Coates	Private	Re-enlisted Jan. 5, 1864.
James Conway	Private	Wounded Beverly; wounded 2nd Bull Run. Died from wounds.
James Carrigan	Private	Died in Andersonville prison.
John Campbell	Private	Wounded Allegheny Mt., Dec. 13, 1861.
Alexander Campbell	Private	Wounded Huntersville. Died from wounds.
William Dever	Private	
John C. Dalzell	Private	
Casper Diehl	Private	
Fred'k Dickroger	Private	Captured Cheat River, Sept. 25, 1863. Exchanged.
George Dixon	Private	Captured Cheat River, Sept. 25, 1863. Exchanged.
Harmon Deinhart	Private	Re-enlisted Jan. 5, 1864.
Patrick Daly	Private	Died of typhoid fever, June 24, 1861.
Michael Donohue	Private	Died of pneumonia, May 12, 1863.
Thos. S. Eichbaum	Private	
Conrad Eicholtz	Private	
Adam Glistner	Private	Wounded Allegheny Mt., Dec. 13, 1861. Re-enlisted Jan. 5, 1864.
Daniel Green	Private	Re-enlisted Jan. 5, 1864.
William Heine	Private	Wounded at Cross Keys. Died in Andersonville.

Louis Heinrich	Private	Captured Cheat River, Sept. 25, 1863. Exchanged.
William Happoldt	Private	
John Johnston	Private	
William H. Jones	Private	Re-enlisted Jan. 5, 1864.
John Koehnlein	Private	
Patrick Kelly	Private	
Benj. F. Kurtz	Private	Wounded 2nd Bull Run. Captured Cheat River, Sept. 25, 1863. Exchanged.
Philip Kirsch	Private	Captured Cheat River, Sept. 25, 1863. Exchanged.
Jacob Kuenzler	Private	Discharged Nov. 4, 1861, disability.
Henry Kotlers	Private	Discharged Nov. 4, 1861, disability.
John B. Kelly	Private	Killed in action, Battle of Cross Keys.
Alex. Lane	Private	Discharged June 23, 1861, disability.
Jesse Lloyd	Private	Discharged.
William Ludaking	Private	Died in Andersonville prison.
Samuel Mitchell	Private	Discharged Nov. 11, 1861, disability.
Enoch C. Miller	Private	Discharged Apr. 17, 1863, disability.
Walter S. Marshall	Private	Re-enlisted Jan. 5, 1864.
John S. Miller	Private	Died Dec. 14, 1861, typhoid fever.
Adam Moninger	Private	Transferred to Co. D, Aug. 1, 1863.
Robert R. Morris	Private	Discharged by order of Secretary of War.
Jacob Miller	Private	
Louis Metz	Private	Captured Cheat River, Sept. 25, 1863. Exchanged.
John McClarren	Private	Captured Cheat River, Sept. 25, 1863. Exchanged.
F.H. McCleane	Private	Captured Cheat River, Sept. 25, 1863. Exchanged.
Hugh McMannis	Private	Wounded at Droop Mt., Nov. 6, 1863.
David C. McCuen	Private	Discharged Mar. 7, 1863, disability.
John A. McCrea	Private	Re-enlisted Jan. 5, 1864.
Richard Pyburn	Private	Re-enlisted Jan. 5, 1864.
Nicholas Rumple	Private	Re-enlisted Jan. 5, 1864.
Peter Romiser	Private	Killed Cheat River, Sept. 25, 1863.

CHAPTER III.

Michael Robel	Private	Died in Andersonville prison.
John Ramsey	Private	
Samuel L. Reynolds	Private	Captured Cheat River, Sept. 25, 1863. Exchanged.
John Stone	Private	Captured Cheat River, Sept. 25, 1863. Exchanged.
Thomas H. Swain	Private	Deserted Sept. 25, 1862.
Henry Stubbs	Private	
Henry C. Stevens	Private	
James Sloan	Private	
Charles Schmitz	Private	Wounded at Elkwater.
Joseph Swartz	Private	Discharged Mar. 7, 1863, disability.
Gustave Steider	Private	Killed in action Allegheny Mt., Dec. 13, 1861.
Edward Saladin	Private	Died in Andersonville prison.
Jacob Slayer	Private	Killed by bushwhackers.
William S. Taylor	Private	Captured Cheat River, Sept. 25, 1863. Exchanged.
George Wilson	Private	Captured Cheat River, Sept. 25, 1863. Exchanged.
Charles Werner	Private	Captured Cheat River, Sept. 25, 1863. Exchanged.
John Washington	Private	Wounded 2nd Bull Run. Captured Cheat River, Sept. 25, 1863. Prisoner till end of war.
Louis Wagner	Private	Re-enlisted Jan. 5, 1864.
S. Weisenberger	Private	Wounded at Bull Run. Died of wounds.
Henry Wagner	Private	Died in prison at Richmond.
L.H. Webster	Private	Died, returning from prison.
W.W. Youngson	Private	Re-enlisted Jan. 5, 1864.

CAPTAIN ALBERT C. HAYES

Albert C. Hayes, the first captain of Company A, was born in Pittsburgh, in the year 1837, being only twenty-four years of age when he assumed command in April, 1861. He had been but lately married to an exceedingly bright and handsome young lady, and on the evening before departing for the seat of war, he marched the company up to his residence, where his wife, on behalf of herself and other ladies, presented the company with a handsome bunting flag, which their own fair hands had made. This flag was carried by the company through its three years term, and is now in the custody of comrade Wm. H. Graham, of that company, to whom it was given by Cap. Oliver R. West, who brought the company home in June, 1864. Cap. Hayes served as commander of the company during Gen. McClellan's successful Western Virginia campaign, and resigned July 22, 1861. After returning home, he engaged in the planing mill business in Pittsburgh. He represented that city in the Legislature of Pennsylvania in 1874. He removed to the West about 1886, and his present whereabouts are unknown.

CAPTAIN WILLIAM OTTO.

William Otto, Company A's second captain, was born in Germany in 1828, and came over to this country when a young man. He enlisted in the regular army and served ten years on the western plains. Shortly before the war he left the army and accepted a position as first mate on an Ohio river steamer. While his boat was lying at the Pittsburgh wharf, Fort Sumter was fired upon, which aroused the old martial spirit in him and he enlisted in Cap. Hayes' company. On account of his army experience and knowledge of tactics, he was elected orderly sergeant. He was an excellent drill master and a brave officer, and upon the resignation of Cap. Hayes, he was commissioned captain and served as such until March 13, 1862, when, owing to a misunderstanding with a superior officer, he tendered his resignation. He afterwards served as an officer in Hancock's Veteran Corps, until the conclusion of the war, when he went back to his old employment on the Ohio river, and if now living his whereabouts are unknown.

CAPTAIN JOHN A. HUNTER.

John A. Hunter, Company A's third commander, was born in County Down, Ireland, in 1831, and came to this country when fourteen years of age. He located in Pittsburgh and learned the trade of cabinet making. He had an extensive furniture establishment there when the war broke out. He and Cap. Alexander Scott, afterwards lieutenant colonel of the regiment, recruited Company F, and as second lieutenant accompanied it to Wheeling, Va. He was promoted to first lieutenant and finally, March 20th, 1862, was promoted to captain and assigned to the command of Company A. He served with great gallantry during the Fremont and Pope campaigns. After the West Virginia campaign, August 1st, 1863, he was relieved from command and returned to Pittsburgh. After the war he engaged in business in the Pennsylvania oil regions, Venango and Crawford counties, for a number of years, but afterwards returned to Pittsburgh and engaged in the grocery business. He was

CHAPTER III.

elected school director and served as such several terms. He married Miss Mary Fowler and has seven children, all living. He has now retired from active business, though still residing in Pittsburgh.

CAPTAIN OLIVER R. WEST.

Oliver R. West, the fourth and last commander of Company A, was born in Allegheny county, Pa., October 17th, 1829. He learned the trade of machinist, and was employed as such when the war broke out. He was elected second lieutenant of the company and participated in all the marches, campaigns, skirmishes and battles of the company during its three years hard service. He was promoted to first lieutenant March 1st, 1862, and finally captain August 18th, 1863. He had a constitution like iron, that enabled him to be always ready for duty, and on hand in every fight. At the battle of Allegheny Mountain he was wounded in the knee, and narrowly escaped death. Lieut. Sickman, of Company G, who was temporarily acting as first lieutenant of Company A, was mortally wounded and died in his arms. His bravery and many sterling qualities endeared him to the men of his company and he was familiarly termed by them "Old Standby." He brought the company home to Pittsburgh, and then settled down to his trade of machinist, and as such is still employed in Allegheny. He never married, but faithfully supported and resided with his aged mother until her death in 1890.

LIEUT. DAVID L. SMITH.

David L. Smith was born in Cumberland county, Pennsylvania, Feb. 4, 1826, and moved with his parents to Pittsburgh in May 1836. He was married to Elizabeth Gordon in September 1852, who died in 1877; was married to Helen M. Armstrong in 1879, and moved to Chester county in December 1881, where he now resides and is engaged in farming. He was elected a member of the Common council of Allegheny City in 1854, and served one year; was elected to the legislature of Pennsylvania in 1854 and served in the session of 1855. He was a clerk by profession, and in 1861 when the war of the rebellion commenced, was chief clerk in the commissioner's office of Allegheny county. After the war, in 1861, he was again elected a member of common councils of Allegheny City, and a member of the school board, in which he served eleven years. At the election in 1867, he was again elected to the Legislature and represented Allegheny county in the session of 1868.

He took an active part in forming and organizing a company of volunteers, then known as the Washington Rifles, of which he became first lieutenant.

At Grafton on the 25th of May, he was detailed as acting assistant quartermaster and commissary of subsistence, in charge of posts all over Western

Virginia. In August 1861, on the resignation of Capt. A.C. Hayes, he was promoted to the captaincy of Company A and went to Beverly to take command of the company, but General McClellan would not relieve him from his detail as assistant quartermaster, remarking that "good quartermasters were harder to find than good captains."

On the 19th of February 1862, he was appointed by the Secretary of War a commissary of subsistence, with the rank of captain. In June 1862 he was ordered on duty on the staff of General Sigel at Martinsburg, Va. In September 1862, he was assigned as acting chief commissary of subsistence of the Twelfth Army Corps, General Mansfield commanding. In March 1863 he was assigned to 5th Corps Headquarters, General George G. Meade commanding, as acting chief commissary of the Corps, and on the 25th of September 1864, was made chief commissary of the Fifth Corps, with the rank of lieutenant-colonel. He served on the Fifth Corps staff until the corps was disbanded in September 1865, and was honorably discharged on the 16th of March 1866, having remained on duty as post commissary of subsistence at Baltimore, Md., until that date, when he was relieved from duty by one of the officers of the regular army, thus serving continuously from May 19th 1861 to March 16th 1866 or 4 years, 9 months and 27 days.

LIEUTENANT JAMES BLACK.

James Black was born in Canada, in 1826, and followed lumbering most of the time. He was sojourning in Pittsburgh when the war broke out, and enlisted as a private in Company A; was elected fifth sergeant and gradually worked his way up until March 1st, 1862, he was commissioned second lieutenant. He was a brave officer and served with credit through the campaigns under Gens. Fremont and Pope. After the battle of Antietam the regiment was transferred to Western Virginia, and while lying at Beverly, May, 30th, 1863, he returned to civil life. After the war he removed to Big Swamico, Brown county, Wis., where he engaged in the lumbering business and is still residing there. He led the squad while at Beverly, 1862-63, that captured Hornet, a bushwhacker in the mountains, and was with the picket at Beverly bridge, when the Confederate force attacked our camp in April, 1863.

JAMES BLACK

CHAPTER III.

LIEUTENANT JAMES R. HUTCHINSON.

James R. Hutchinson is a native of Pittsburgh, Pa., born in the year 1838. After receiving a common school education he worked in a printing office for a number of years. He then served an apprenticeship of four years at the engine works of Robinson, Minis & Miller. After thus learning his trade, he was employed on locomotive work in the Connellsville Railroad Shops. While serving his apprenticeship in 1857, he joined a volunteer rifle company and drilled faithfully in the manual of arms, marching and skirmish drills, thus obtaining that knowledge that was of such great service afterward in the dark days of the sixties. The opening of the war found him employed at the engine works of Nuttall & Kirkpatrick, in Allegheny. He promptly enlisted and was mustered into the service for three years in Company A as first duty sergeant. By strict attention to duty and bravery in action, he

JAMES R. HUTCHINSON

was promoted to orderly sergeant, and August 18th, 1863, to second lieutenant. He richly merited and deserved promotion to first lieutenant, and would undoubtedly have received it, but unfortunately was sent out, September 25th, 1863, to an exposed and defenseless picket post on Cheat river, thirteen miles from nearest support, with a small force of thirty men, where he was surrounded and surprised at night by a rebel battalion commanded by Major Lang, and after brief resistance, during which one of his command was killed and several wounded, he and the rest of the squad were captured. He was kept a prisoner until close of the war, being transferred from Richmond, Va., to the following rebel prisons: Danville, Va.; Macon, Ga.; Charleston and Columbia, S. C.; Goldsboro, Raleigh, and Charlotte, N. C. Lieut. Hutchinson was a universal favorite, not only in the company, but also in the regiment, on account of his good humor and jollity. He always had a smile or joke ready to enliven the gloomiest march. He was married April 26th, 1866, to Miss Mary E. Corken, whose father was a soldier and was killed in the battle of Cedar Mountain, Va. After Lieut. Hutchinson returned to civil life, he started in the steam engine and machine business, in Allegheny, and still continues at it. He has been commander of Post 88, G.A.R., and also commander of Encampment No. I, Union Veteran Legion.

CORPORAL GRAHAM.

Wm. H. Graham, corporal Company A, was born in Allegheny, Pa., August 3d, 1844. He attended the public schools until fourteen years of age, when, owing to the death of his father, he as the oldest son, was compelled to leave school and seek employment, to help support his widowed mother and family. He was in the employ of Maffit & Old, brass manufacturers, when Fort Sumter was fired upon, and although not seventeen years old, he managed to get enrolled in the Washington Rifle Guards, afterwards Company A, and was mustered into the United States service for three years. He participated in most all of the engagements, scouts, and campaigns with his regiment. Was wounded in the right arm in the battle of Rocky Gap, and after a few months sojourn in the West Penn Hospital, at Pittsburgh, rejoined his regiment in time to start with the expedition under Gen. Averell, culminating in the brilliant victory of Droop Mountain. Upon the expiration of his three years term, he accepted service in the quartermaster's department, and was attached to Gen. Sheridan's headquarters during that dashing general's brilliant campaign in the Shenandoah Valley, resulting in the great victories of Winchester, Fisher's Hill and Cedar Creek, where Sheridan made his famous ride. He also accompanied Sheridan in his march across Virginia and ride around Richmond, joining Gen. Grant at Petersburg; thence Gen. Sheridan, with his cavalry and the Fifth Corps of Infantry, swung around Lee's flank and fought the decisive battle of Five Forks, breaking Lee's line and capturing Petersburg, and compelling the evacuation of Richmond. During these operations and the vigorous pursuit of Gen. Lee's army, he served as a volunteer aid, and it was while carrying a message to Sheridan, the eventful 9th day of April, 1865, that he rode out between the two lines of battle to the little

WILLIAM H. GRAHAM

village of Appomattox, and there, in the house of Mr. McLean, had the rare good fortune to be one of the few spectators that witnessed the memorable interview between the two great generals, that terminated in the surrender of Gen. Lee. After taking part in the grand review at Washington he returned to civil life. He was engaged in the wholesale leather business in the firm of Graham & Spangler, then became chairman of Mansfield & Co., Limited, brass manufacturers. He also took an active part in Republican politics, being elected a member of common councils, Allegheny, in 1873, member of select

CHAPTER III.

councils 1874, and member of the House of Representatives, Pennsylvania, 1875, 1876, 1877 and 1878. He was elected recorder of deeds of Allegheny county in 1881, and is now serving his ninth year in that office. He was married September 30th, 1869, to Miss Sadie K. Shields, and they have had six children.

FRANK H. SINGER.

The subject of this sketch is a native of Armstrong county, Pa., born at Freeport, October 11, 1838. He received a common school education, and removed to Johnstown in 1859, where he engaged in the manufacture of fire brick until the spring of 1860, and then went to Miltenberger, Fayette county, Pa., and was employed as foreman in the Miltenberger fire brick works until he enlisted in Pittsburgh, becoming a member of Company A. He served his full enlistment, and was a brave soldier, almost to rashness, and as true as steel. He was a universal favorite, on account of his unfailing good humor, and good qualities as a man. When mustered out, he re-enlisted in an Independent Battalion of Pennsylvania troops, and served until November 14, 1864, when he was honorably discharged. He was so crippled with rheumatism that he had to give up the manufacture of fire brick, and accepted a position as salesman in the Cambria Iron Company's store, Johnstown, Pa., where he has been for nearly 21 years.

FRANK H. SINGER AND WIFE

BENJAMIN F. KURTZ

FRED H. BRAUN

COMPANY B.

The "Grafton Guards" were organized shortly after the firing on Fort Sumter, the leading spirits in forming the company being George R. Latham, Daniel Wilson, Bailey Brown, F. A. Cather, and others, the company being fully enrolled on May 20, 1861. At the time of forming the company, the Confederates were camped on the bridge across the Tygart's Valley river, on the Northwestern Virginia turnpike, nearly two miles below at Fetterman. When eighty men had been enrolled the company organized by the election of George R. Latham captain, F. A. Cather first lieutenant, and Daniel Wilson second lieutenant.

Previous to this time, George A. Porterfield, of Jefferson county, Va., who had seen service in the Mexican war, was appointed a colonel by Governor Letcher, and sent into northwestern Virginia to organize the companies being formed under the call of the State for troops. A company from Marion county under the command of William P. Thompson, which became Company A, Thirty-first Virginia, two companies from Taylor county, one under command of John A. Robinson, that became Company A Twenty-fifth Virginia, and one under G. W. Hansbrough, that was afterwards disbanded, rendezvoused at Fetterman May 20, and on the 22d were joined by the Harrison Guards of Clarksburg under command of William P. Cooper, which became Company C of the Thirty-first Virginia. The whole force marched that evening to Grafton and then back to Fetterman. On the night of the 22d, Daniel Wilson and Bailey Brown walked down towards Fetterman, and encountered the rebel picket on the railroad in the east end of town, where Daniel W. S. Knight and George Glenn, of Captain Robinson's company, were on guard. Knight ordered them to halt. Instead of doing so, they continued to advance, Knight repeating his order, until they got close to the pickets, when Brown fired his revolver shooting Knight through the ear. Knight, who was armed with an old-fashioned smooth-bore flint-lock musket, loaded with slugs, returned the shot, killing Brown almost instantly. There were three holes in Brown's body close together, in triangular shape, resembling wounds made by buck-and-ball cartridge, one slug passing through his heart. This occurred about 9 o'clock. When the firing took place Wilson retreated, receiving the load out of Glenn's gun in the heel of his boot. Brown's body was taken to the town hall by the rebels, which was occupied as quarters by the Harrison Guards, and properly cared for.

Major W. P. Cooper, Thirty-first Virginia, Confederate, from whom some of the facts of this shooting were obtained, relates that the next morning, in explaining to Colonel Porterfield how the affair happened, Knight said, he "halted Brown two or three times, but he didn't stop and came up and shot me through the ear, and it made me so mad I shot him. I hope I didn't do anything

CHAPTER III.

wrong, Colonel." The colonel told him that if he had done anything wrong it was in not shooting sooner, which seemed to relieve him very much.

A committee was sent to the Confederate commander asking for Brown's body, which was refused. When the committee reported back the refusal to give up the body, Captain Latham's company started for more active measures, when they were met by the enemy nearly half way to Fetterman, with the body on a hand car.

Bailey Brown, thus early a victim to the act of secession, was the first enlisted man in the U. S. volunteer service, killed in the war. He was enrolled as a member of his company May 20, 1861, though the company was not mustered in until the 25th. His death occurred on May 22, while that of the gallant Colonel Ellsworth did not occur until the 24th, two days later.

The Guards now started for camp at Wheeling, making a detour of twelve or fifteen miles around the enemy, who were closely watching them and stopping and searching all trains, and reached the Valley River Falls, about eight miles by rail west of Grafton, whence they took the train for Wheeling, where they were mustered into the U. S. service on May 25. On Monday, June 3, the company received their guns and accoutrements and began drilling, being now in sole charge of Camp Carlisle, which was relieved of all other troops then garrisoned there, which were pushed forward to the front.

In the latter part of June the company was ordered to the front, going to Mannington, where they were in camp for two days. About the first day of July they went to Grafton, and on the 4th were ordered to Philippi and were accorded the special honor of body guards to General Morris, commanding. On the night of the 6th the command advanced on the Confederates who were fortified at the foot of Laurel Hill, General Garnett in command, arriving there early on the morning of the 7th, remaining in front of the enemy until the 11th, when their forces being routed at Rich Mountain with a severe loss, our forces gained General Garnett's rear, when he attempted to make his escape through the mountains. Our command followed them, skirmishing with their rear several miles down Cheat river, overtaking them at Corrick's Ford, where a sharp encounter occurred on the 13th between the two armies, resulting, among other casualties on both sides, in the death of General Garnett, the first Confederate general officer killed in the war.

The company then went to Beverly, where it joined other companies forming the Second Virginia Infantry, of which it became Company B upon the organization of the regiment.

Company B was then ordered to Belington, where it went into camp and remained until January 25th, 1862, engaged in guarding the supply trains between Webster and Beverly and in sending scouting parties through the adjoining counties. One of the distinguishing features of the members of Company B was that they were crack rifle shots previous to enlistment, and were thus soon able to get all the effect out of an army gun, and they were more than ordinarily well equipped for the active and dangerous service that was required of them. Their efficiency as scouts was recognized and they were almost in constant service, in ferreting out the bushwhackers in the mountains.

On the 10th of October, C. E. Ringler, with four others of the company, went eight or ten miles out from camp at Belington, on the lookout for a noted guerrilla in that neighborhood. Near midnight the party was fired upon by a band of bushwhackers and Joe Wright of the party was mortally wounded. Ringler and another comrade dragged and carried Wright, a very heavy man, in a speechless and insensible condition, through four or five feet of water in the creek and up hill about a quarter of a mile, where Joe had to be abandoned and died. Ringler "borrowed" a horse at the muzzle of a gun, rode to camp, returned early next morning with twenty-five more men of his company, secured Wright's body, killed the man who had harbored the guerrillas, burned the house and barn where they had slept, and cleaned the place out generally. Concerning Wright, Ringler says, "I have often found men loth to follow where I was willing to lead, but Joe did deeds of cool bravery and daring that made me tremble." While at Belington a detachment of six of the company was detailed under Sergeant O.P. Bower to capture Paton G. Boothe, a Confederate scout. Arriving at the house where he was stopping, at the foot of Laurel Hill, Boothe came out the back way and was mistaken for one of Company B by T. W. Carpenter, who asked him if he was not, to which he replied affirmatively and then jumped the fence to escape, when Carpenter saw it was Boothe and fired at him, striking him just above the knee, inflicting a slight wound. The courtesy was returned, Boothe's bullet barely missing Carpenter's head. William Bibey, of Booth's party was captured.

January 5th, '62, Cap. Latham, with eighteen of his men, was ordered to Dry Fork, of Cheat river, to search for Bill Harper's gang of bushwhackers, who were stealing and driving stock away for the use of the southern army. They were joined by Lieutenant A.J. Weaver and a detachment from Company K. The party reached the river on the 7th, when Lieut. Weaver's men stopped at Snyder's farm house, and Cap. Latham's men proceeded up the valley about two miles, and lodged with an old bachelor by the name of Armentrout. Next day they proceeded up the river about a mile to the guerrilla captain's home, but found no one there, and then started on the return. Upon reaching an open bottom, about a fourth of a mile below where they lodged for the night, they were suddenly fired on by about forty guerrillas, who were in ambush in heavy timber about twenty paces from them. Being without regular formation, on hearing the click of the enemy's guns, our men instinctively dropped to the ground as a volley was poured into them from the timber. Our party then dropped back, under cover of the river bank, where, standing and crouching in the water through a thin ice, they engaged the guerrillas for about

CHAPTER III.

two hours, when the latter withdrew with a loss of one killed and three wounded, our party having six men wounded, one, Fred Doph, the oldest man in the company, supposed mortally, a ball having passed through his body immediately above his heart. Company K's squad had started on the morning of the 8th to camp and were not in the fight, except two of their men who joined us. After the firing had ceased Captain Latham gathered his men together, carrying Doph to the Snyder residence, and left him in charge of the family. He was taken prisoner to Richmond and recovered, was exchanged, rejoined his company, got married, and was discharged from the service for disability February 9, 1863. The men then pressed horses of the citizens into service and started with their wounded down the river. It began to snow and rain and they were compelled to wade streams filled with ice and plod on through rain and mud until Friday night of the 11th, when they reached Rowlesburg on the B. & O. railroad, thence by cars to Grafton, where the wounded were left in the hospital. After a few days rest here, Capt. Latham rejoined his company on Cheat Mountain, where it had joined the regiment.

Wm. E. Stafford relates how he and six other comrades of Preston county, A. C. Baker, J.G. Matlick, N.L. Lock, J.H. Dennison, R.M. Woodward and T.C. Nuzum, became members of Company B. Stafford was a captain in the militia, and went to Kingwood in May to drill, when Col. Hugh was to drill the men that assembled. They fell in line, but the colonel failing to appear, Col. John F. Martin took his place. At once Stafford stepped from the ranks, declaring he would not drill under a rebel officer, and started for home. At Fellowsville he met a crowd of Union men with their rifles, banded to stop the advance of rebels into their town, whom he joined, but the alarm over he went home, and was informed that a force of the enemy was coming to compel him to muster his company into the rebel service. The party named then attempted to make their way to Pennsylvania to join a Union regiment, and while at Grafton were met by Cap. Latham, and invited to join his company, which they did.

The following is the muster out roll, showing list of members and their record. The company was mustered into the U. S. service May 25, 1861, and mustered out June 4, 1864. All the members not otherwise marked, were mustered out with the company. The recruits and veterans were transferred to the Sixth West Virginia Cavalry, when the company was mustered out.

THORNSBURY BAILEY BROWN

NAMES	RANK	RECORD OF SERVICE
George R. Latham	Capt.	Promoted to Colonel, May 25, 1862. Wounded at Dry Fork, Jan. 8, 1862.
Fabricius A. Cather	1st Lt.	Resigned May 20, 1862.
Daniel Wilson	2d Lt.	Promoted to Captain, May 20, 1862. Resigned April 22, 1863.
Amos B. Hammer	2d Lt.	Promoted to Captain, Jan. 27, 1864.
Asbury C. Baker	Sergeant	Promoted to 2d Lt., May 20, 1862. Resigned Dec. 19, 1862.
Felix H. Hughes	Sergeant	Promoted to 2d Lt., Sept. 4, 1863.
Oliver P. Bower	Sergeant	
H. F. Brohard	1st Sgt.	
Daniel K. Shields	Sergeant	Promoted to 2d Lt., Co. K, Nov. 15, 1863.
William Jenkins	Sergeant	Wounded at Dry Fork Cheat River, Jan. 8, 1862; and Droop Mtn., Nov. 6, 1863.
Joseph W. Shahan	Sergeant	
Milton J. Thrayer	Sergeant	
Bailey Powell	Corporal	
Thomas Kenney	Corporal	
T. C. Nuzum	Corporal	
Martin T. Bailey	Corporal	
E. T. Nuzum	Corporal	
John S. Newlon	Corporal	
Robert S. Gabbert	Corporal	
Dennis Nuzum	Wagoner	
Jos. M. Ashby	Private	
Jos. M. Allen	Private	
John S. Behen	Private	Wounded
Launslot Behen	Private	
Thomas G. Bartlett	Private	Wounded Jan. 8, 1862, at Dry Fork Cheat River.
Samuel J. Boyles	Private	
Marshall Bayley	Corporal	
Samuel C. Bartlett	Private	Shot in knee, Cheat Mt., 1862. Discharged for disability.
John H. Bailey	Private	Died at Flemington, Aug. 19, 1861.

CHAPTER III.

James Callahan	Private	Wounded. Captured at Rocky Gap, Aug. 27, 1863.
Edward B. Creel	Private	Captured on Salem Raid, Dec. 19, 1863.
Reuben J. Corbin	Private	Discharged for disability, Nov. 16, 1862.
Jackson Cooper	Private	Discharged for disability, Sept. 6, 1862.
John E. Clarke	Private	Discharged for disability, Aug. 1, 1861.
David O. Carpenter	Private	Transferred to Company I, July 1, 1863.
Dennis Connell	Private	Deserted Sept. 1, 1862.
Jehu Champ	Private	Recruit July 5, 1863. Transferred to 6th W.Va. Cavalry. Shot in face at Belington, 1863.
David B. Curtis	Private	Recruit July 5, 1863. Transferred to 6th W.Va. Cavalry.
Thomas W. Carpenter	Private	Recruit July 5, 1863. Transferred to 6th W.Va. Cavalry.
Ephraim Conn	Private	Re-enlisted as veteran, Jan. 5, 1864.
C.G. Creel	Private	
John H. Dennison	Private	
David E. Duncan	Private	
Daniel Dillon	Private	Re-enlisted as veteran, Jan. 5, 1864.
John F. Drabell	Private	Re-enlisted as veteran, Jan. 5, 1864.
Charles F. Demoss	Private	Re-enlisted as veteran, Jan. 5, 1864.
Reuben H. Dillon	Private	Recruit March 7, 1864.
Fred Doph	Private	Shot through chest, Jan. 8, 1862, at Dry Fork. Discharged Feb. 9, 1863.
Alpheus Downey	Private	Died at Franklin, May 22, 1862.
Joab A. Demoss	Private	Deserted Feb. 28, 1863.
Nathaniel K. Grimm	Private	
G.M. Glendening	Private	
Amos F. Gandy	Private	
Elias J. Glenn	Private	Re-enlisted as veteran, Jan. 5, 1864.
John R. George	Private	Re-enlisted as veteran, Jan. 5, 1864.
David Hester	Private	
James T. Hebb	Private	Re-enlisted as veteran, Jan. 5, 1864.
John M. Harr	Private	Recruit July 5, 1863.

John P. Hardin	Private	Recruit July 5, 1863.
Joshua Hemins	Private	Discharged for disability, Sept. 6, 1862.
Edward Henderson	Private	Died October 10, 1862.
Eli Ice	Private	
G.H. Kirkpatrick	Private	
John Kerns	Private	Wounded, Bull Run, Aug. 30, 1862, and Droop Mt., Nov. 6, 1863.
Benjamin F. Kerns	Private	Discharged for disability, Jan. 29, 1862.
John B. Lafrance	Private	Deserted Nov. 27, 1862.
Nelinza L. Lock	Corporal	Died of wounds.
John W. Leese	Private	
John W. Moore	Private	
David P. Morgan	Private	
B.W. Maxwell	Private	
Ignatius G. Martin	Private	Re-enlisted as veteran, Jan. 5, 1864.
Thomson D. Means	Private	Re-enlisted as veteran, Jan. 5, 1864.
Martin Murray	Private	Re-enlisted as veteran, Jan. 5, 1864.
Jacob G. Matlick	Private	Captured on Salem Raid, Dec. 19, 1863.
E.W. Mulrine	Private	Discharged for disability, March 28, 1862.
George W. Miller	Private	Promoted to Sergeant Major.
Archibald McDonald	Private	Re-enlisted Jan. 5, 1864.
Joseph McVicker	Private	
Charles E. McGee	Private	Discharged Sept. 6, 1862.
John H. McCullough	Private	Killed at Monterey, Va., April 25, 1862.
James B. McMillan	Private	Killed at Bull Run, Aug. 30, 1862.
Stephen McMitt	Private	Deserted Feb. 28, 1863.
Salathiel J. Newlon	Private	
Otis J. Nye	Private	
Job Nuzum	Private	Re-enlisted as veteran, Jan. 5, 1864.
George W. Ordner	Private	Wounded Cross Keys. Wounded Bull Run, Aug. 30, 1862.
John M. Pfrom	Private	Wounded Jan. 8, 1862, at Dry Fork Cheat River.
John H. Powell	Private	

CHAPTER III.

William F. Pell	Private	Discharged Oct. 22, 1862.
Charles W. Pickett	Private	Wounded by shell at White Sulphur Springs, Aug. 1862. Drowned at Grafton, June 6, 1863.
Samuel P. Peterson	Private	Deserted Sept. 1, 1862.
Richard Ryan	Private	Transferred to Company D, June 1, 1861.
Cyrus E. Ringler	Private	Wounded Cross Keys. Wounded in hand at Bull Run.
Patrick Ryan	Private	
Isaac Roberts	Private	Discharged Nov. 8, 1862.
C.W.D. Smitley	Private	Wounded. Re-enlisted as veteran, Jan. 5, 1864. See Scout Chapter.
G. Shingleton	Private	Re-enlisted as veteran, Jan. 5, 1864.
William E. Stafford	Private	Captured on Salem Raid, Dec. 19, 1863.
John W. Shepler	Private	Died of wounds at Philippi, July 17, 1861.
Kidd S. Simpson	Private	Wounded and captured at Rocky Gap, Aug. 27, 1863.
Isaac L. Vincent	Private	
William D. Vanhorn	Private	Deserted Feb. 28, 1863.
Joseph M. West	Private	Re-enlisted as veteran, Jan. 5, 1864.
Alex. Watts	Corporal	Wounded at Cheat River, Dry Fork, Jan. 8, 1862.
James Whitehair	Private	Discharged Jan. 8, 1862, on account of wounds rec'd at Dry Fork, Jan. 8, 1862.
Joseph Wright	Private	Killed by guerillas, Oct. 10, 1861, Barbour County.
William Wyckoff	Private	Wounded Kelly's Ford.
John Wright	Private	
Samuel G. Wotring	Blacksmith	
R.M. Woodward	Private	Wounded at Cedar Mt., Aug. 1862.
Thomas Waldron	Private	
S.J. Willhide	Private	
John W. Willhide	Private	Wounded at Cheat River, right hip. See Scout Article.

CAPTAIN DANIEL WILSON.

Daniel Wilson was born in Guernsey county, Ohio, August 24th, 1824. His father's name was William F.; mother's, Jane - maiden name, Booth. His parents moved to Barbour county, Va., in 1825. He married Miss Naomi Reger, of Barbour county, in 1845, by whom he had seven children. She died before the close of the war, and he afterwards married a second wife, who bore him four children. He was engaged in farming till 1854, when he went to merchandizing, which he followed in Barbour and Taylor counties till 1860. He was a devoted friend of the Union, never flinching from any duty, no matter how arduous or hazardous. He ably assisted Col. Latham in the enlisting of Company B, in May, 1861, went to Wheeling with the company, and was mustered in as second lieutenant. He was promoted from second lieutenant to captain on the 20th day of May, 1862. He was never very robust in health, but was in all the engagements with his company and regiment, until compelled to resign on account of failing health, April 22d, 1863. In 1864 he was appointed post master at Grafton, which position he held until 1876, when he resigned and moved to Michigan, in 1877, on account of his health, and died there in 1878. He has one son, James L., who graduated with honors at West Point, and is now first lieutenant in the Fourth Artillery; and one son, Lloyd L., who is a practicing physician at Grafton, West Va.

DANIEL WILSON

CAPTAIN A. B. HAMMER.

Amos B. Hammer was born September 23d, 1835, in what was then Monongalia county, Va. He received a common school education in the schools of Virginia and Ohio, by choice he became a machinist and at the breaking out of the rebellion was engaged on the B. & O. R. R., with residence at Grafton. He was one of the first to join in the organization of a company and became identified with the interests of Company B, of which he was made a sergeant at the organization; and having a little knowledge of tactics, took an active part in drilling the men and bringing the company to an efficient standing. He was with his company during the Western Virginia campaign of '61, and while the company lay detached at Belington, took an active part in the suppression of the bushwhackers of that region. On one occasion, alone and in citizen's clothes, he penetrated the haunts of the noted Harper gang, and gained such information as led to the capture or driving out of most of these outlaws. In

CHAPTER III.

the spring of '62, at the solicitation of Gen. Schenck, the sergeant conducted the negotiations with a number of guerrilla chieftains, which were largely successful. On the 8th of May, 1862, at McDowell, Cap. Latham having been detached for staff duty, Sergt. Hammer was left in command of the company for a time, during which the company demonstrated its ability to meet an emergency, by taking a section of Johnson's battery into action, taking the guns up an almost perpendicular cliff to a plateau commanding the enemy's position. These were the only guns brought into action and determined the fate of our forces by enabling us to hold our position until after dark. On June the 8th, 1862, at the battle of Cross Keys, the company was in command of Lieut. Wilson. When Jackson succeeded in turning the left of Fremont's line, Milroy's brigade was compelled to change front under fire, and Companies B and D were ordered to the front as skirmishers and Sergt. Hammer placed in command. The conflict was desperate for a time, but the skirmishers were held to their work by the Sergeant, until the evolution was completed. Gen. Milroy, in view of these services, asked that a commission be given to Sergt. Hammer, and a commission as first lieutenant was issued in June to date May 15th. Lieut. Hammer did staff duty with Generals Sigel and Milroy until in June, 1863, returning to the regiment, on the resignation of Cap. Wilson, and remained in command until the company was mustered out at Wheeling in '64. During the three years service of Cap. Hammer, he participated in every campaign and engagement of his regiment except the battle of Droop Mountain, and during the entire period, though slightly wounded three times, and exposed to the most trying labors, was never in hospital and never absent but once, for two weeks on sick leave. In January of 1864 Lieut. Hammer was promoted to captain of Company B. After being mustered out in '64, Cap. Hammer located in Christian county, Ill. Finding his health impaired and being incapacitated for his former calling, he studied law, and in 1867 was admitted to the supreme court of his adopted state. Since that time he has continued, with occasional rests, to practice that profession, removing to Kansas in 1872, and to Texas in 1880, thence to Oklahoma City in the wild rush of 1889, where he now resides.

CAPT. AMOS B. HAMMER

LIEUTENANT FABRICIUS A. CATHER.

F. A. Cather was a native of Harrison county, Va., born May 12, 1840. His occupation before and after the war was farming. He was received into the membership of the Baptist church at Flemington, Va., and was baptized in 1856. He was a man of upright character, and of strong convictions in his devotion to his country. He cast his first vote in May 1861, against the ordinance of secession, and was firm and true in the trying scenes that preceded the war. He enlisted in Company B, and was commissioned First Lieutenant. He was with his company in all its service to January 1862. In consequence of exposure his health was much impaired, and he was assigned to recruiting service at Clarksburg, Va., Jan. 10, 1862. His health continued to grow worse, and May 20, 1862 he was pronounced unable to stand military duty, and he offered his resignation, which was accepted. He tried to regain his health by travel and seemed to improve, and desired to re-enlist, but his physician advised him not to do so. He was dissatisfied to remain at home while his comrades were serving their country so bravely. In March 1864, he enlisted in the First West Virginia Veteran Cavalry, and was commissioned First Lieutenant. He was promoted to Captain of Company K February 7, 1865, and Major June 8, 1865, and was honorably discharged in July 1865. He was in the campaign with Hunter and Sheridan in the valley of Virginia, and took part in the closing battles of the war, when General Grant's forces compelled General Lee to surrender. He was in several severe battles, having his horse shot under him on two separate occasions, and proved himself to be a brave and true soldier, a worthy member of his old regiment. Major Cather was married in Grafton, W.Va., August 17, 1865, to Miss Helen V. Mallonee. His health became very poor, and in 1871 he moved to Sedgewick county, Kansas, in the hope of finding relief and health, but he died at his home in that state October 7, 1876. He was steadfast in his faith in Christ, and the evening before his death he talked calmly about it, and said hoped soon to be with those who were rejoicing.

LIEUTENANT ASBURY C. BAKER.

Asbury C. Baker was born in Preston county, Va., August 3, 1839, and died August 16, 1885. At the beginning of hostilities in 1861, he was attending school at West Liberty, Va. Feeling it to be his duty to serve his country, he quit school and entered the Union army, as a private in Company B, serving with distinction, and was promoted to Second Lieutenant of the company. A few months later he was forced to resign on account of his failing health, a result of his arduous service. Soon after resigning, he was appointed adjutant of a regiment of militia of Preston county, and was appointed to an honorary position on the Colonel's staff, with the rank of Colonel. He was twice elected superintendent of public schools in Preston county, served one term in the state legislature as delegate from his county, and was twice elected prosecuting attorney of the same county, and held the office of county surveyor at

CHAPTER III.

the time of his death. He was a good lawyer, a fine scholar, and was deservedly popular with the people generally. His remains are interred in Bluemont cemetery, Grafton, W. Va.

SERGEANT O. P. BOWER.

Oliver P. Bower was born in Fairmont, Marion county, Va., September 3, 1836, where he worked on a farm during his early boyhood. After reaching manhood, he was engaged on the B. & O. railroad most of his time, until he enlisted in Company B, in which organization he served until the company was mustered out, bearing the rank of sergeant. He was orderly for General Benham, when that officer pursued and defeated General Garnett at Corrick's Ford, and was in the front when the Confederates were defeated. He served well and faithfully. After muster out, he returned to farming, and was married August 5, 1864. He now lives at Big Bend, W. Va., his wife being an invalid, and to whom he gives his time and faithful attention.

SERGEANT H. F. BROHARD.

Humphrey F. Brohard, a native Virginian, was born January 20, 1833, near Flemington, Taylor county, Va., now West Va. He remained on the farm with his father until 1855, when he followed teaching and carpentering until 1861. He enlisted in Company B, serving with fidelity and bravery until mustered out June 14, 1864. The history of the company is his history, and is therefore a noble and honorable one. He began merchandising in 1864, and has continued at that and farming ever since. He was married to Miss Mary F. Bailey December 6, 1866. Mr. Brohard was one of that noble class of Virginians to whom too much honor cannot be paid. Loyal, brave and true, they did their full duty to their country.

CORPORAL CYRUS E. RINGLER.

Cyrus E. Ringler was born in Johnstown, Pa., September 20, 1835. His father, Jonathan Ringler, a descendant of the Philadelphia Quakers, was killed on the railroad between Johnstown and Hollidaysburgh, Pa., in 1837. His mother was a native of Stoystown, Pa., and soon after the death of her husband migrated with her two little boys to the southeastern part of Maryland, where she married a Virginia carpenter, with whom she followed up the construction of the Chesapeake and Ohio

CYRUS E. RINGLER

canal, and then the extension of the B. & O. railroad, west of Cumberland. Mr. Ringler learned the printing trade before reaching his majority and applied himself to the improvement of his education. He grew up a strong pro-slavery Democrat, and held a military commission under Governor Henry A. Wise, of Virginia, but with the first acts of secession, he took a decided stand for the Union and was probably the first man in Harrison county, Va., to procure names for the Union service. He sought the first opportunity of becoming a soldier, a desire that had haunted him from boyhood, and became a member of Captain Latham's company in May, 1861. He was offered command of a company of volunteers as well as other positions, but preferred to remain in the ranks of his own company. He was the first member of the company inside of the Confederate lines at Laurel Hill, as a spy, near to General Garnett's headquarters, and only escaped capture by riding down the middle of the creek at night, and after scrambling in the brush and obstructions about the enemy's position, in the dense darkness and rain, and narrowly escaping being shot, he reached his camp at Philippi the next morning.

October 10, 1861, he took four others of his company at Belington and scouted on the lookout for a noted guerrilla, resulting in a combat with bushwhackers and the death of Joe Wright, an account of which is given in the history of the company. At Monterey he was detailed to the brigade department, yet at McDowell he was in the skirmish line with his company, and was stunned by a musket ball that shot the cord off his hat. At Cross Keys he was stunned by a rebel shell and later in open ground, he became the target for fully a hundred hostile muskets, escaping with a scratch on the face and a sting on the back of the neck. At Cedar Mountain he was chased back to the Union lines by five Confederate cavalry, and was arrested on suspicion by the Union pickets. The next day he was accosted beyond the lines by a Confederate general, who was reconnoitering, as to his regiment. "Second Virginia," he replied. "You're a little too far from your command, you'd better get back," was the general's response. There were, two Second Virginia regiments there. In hunting for his regiment in line of battle on the Rappahannock, he rode down to the river in front of a rebel cannon, and seemed as little disturbed as if a fly had buzzed between him and his horse's ears, instead of a cannon ball. Within ten minutes after Colonel Latham had asked him to help hunt up his scattered regiment, after the terrible repulse at the railroad cut, Bull Run, he was shot in the stomach and in the right hand. When asked to occupy an ambulance he replied "wait till I fall down," and the next day he was in a storm of grape and canister. He asked the surgeon for a pass that he might go where he pleased without being molested. "My God!" said the surgeon, "If you want any better pass than you have, I can't give it to you." Two days afterwards he succumbed to his wounds, helplessly prostrated in a hospital at Alexandria.

CHAPTER III.

Back in West Virginia, when Confederate General Jones raided part of that state he obtained leave to go to Grafton, where he and a comrade of his regiment went on a scout, and among other services captured two of General Jones' cavalrymen, whom he turned over with their horses to General Mulligan at Grafton, and on returning to his command at Beverly soon after, he was confronted with charges of desertion. Subsequently he was acting on the provost staff and employed in ferreting out and breaking up guerrilla dens in the mountains, and participated in the succeeding battles of Huntersville, Droop Mountain and the Salem Raid.

From January till April, 1864, he acted on courts martial and enquiry at Martinsburg, being no longer fit for active duty and was mustered out in June, 1864, and in about two months accepted a lieutenancy in the Seventeenth West Virginia Infantry, from Governor Boreman. Mr. Ringler often declared that he would rather be a private soldier in front of battle, than anything else, and his conduct fully verified his statement. He is a studious Bible reader, is identified with the Methodist Protestant church and believes in a full, free, personal salvation, in the loftiest and most liberal sense.

S. J. BOYLES.

S. J. Boyles was born in Marion county, Virginia, Jan. 21, 1835. He was one of the early members of the company, and served with honor as private soldier, until the company was mustered out in 1864.

SAMUEL J. BOYLES

PRIVATE CHARLES F. DEMOSS

JACOB G. MATLICK

COMPANY C.

This company was organized May 10th, 1861, with Capt. E. Plankey in command, and was mustered into the United States service June 1st, 1861, at Camp Carlisle. The company saw some service before being formally sworn into the service, and was active in whatever demands were made upon it before muster in, resulting in some splendid work. It was sworn for a special trip to Sistersville, where it was understood there were a few pieces of artillery. The steamer Woodside was chartered for the trip, and going down the river landed at midnight, when the company at once proceeded to secure the guns, which were hidden in an old stable. The trip was entirely successful, and the boat returned the next day. Among others who were on the trip, were D. Ritz, Vierheller, Klein, Getze and Graebe. A part of the company was stationed at Moundsville, for a short time, guarding public and private property.

Upon leaving Wheeling to join the regiment, the company went by the way of the B. & O. R. R. to Clarksburg, where they had a dress parade on July 4th. They then went with two other companies of the regiment to Beverly, by way of Rich mountain, joining the regiment, and were assigned as Company C. This company did its full share of the hard work of the regiment, and established a good reputation for faithful, brave service. They were always ready for duty, and were esteemed highly by all their comrades.

The following is the muster out roll, showing list of members and their record. The company was mustered into the United States service June 1, 1861, and mustered out June 14th, 1864. All the members not otherwise marked, were mustered out with the company. The recruits and veterans were transferred to the Sixth West Virginia Cavalry, when the company was mustered out.

NAMES	RANK	RECORD OF SERVICE
Edward Plankey	Capt.	Resigned March 5, 1863.
Jas. K. Billingsley	Capt.	Transferred from Co. I, and promoted Captain March 5, 1863.
August Rolf	1st Lt.	Resigned Sept. 10, 1862.
Henry Schultz	1st Lt.	Promoted from 1st Sgt. Sept. 10, 1862. Relieved Dec. 9, 1863.
Lewis P. Salterback	1st Lt.	Transferred from Co. H May 1, 1864.
Christian Petry	2d Lt.	Resigned July 25, 1862.
Chrisitan Vierheller	2d Lt.	Promoted from Sgt. July 25, 1862. Resigned April 11, 1863.

CHAPTER III.

Levi B. Keller	1st Sgt.	
William F. Graebe	1st Sgt.	Name on muster out roll incorrectly William Grave.
William Speaker	1st Sgt.	
Fred'k Schellhaas	1st Sgt.	
Charles Bearly	1st Sgt.	Drowned in Greenbrier River, W.Va., May 18, 1864.
Christian Schwedus	1st Sgt.	Discharged on account of wounds received, Feb. 26, 1862.
Christian Gaefke	1st Sgt.	Discharged for disability, Oct. 2, 1862.
William Adams	Corp.	
Christian Galleck	Corp.	
Herman Dietrick	Corp.	
Frank Walther	Corp.	Discharged for disability, Dec. 6, 1861.
Sigmund Gnam	Corp.	Discharged Sept. 24, 1863, to received promotion in Battery H, 1st W.Va. Art.
Jos. Wanzel	Corp.	Deserted May 27, 1862.
August Davis	Corp.	Killed in action at Bull Run, Aug. 29, 1862.
John B. Wiley	Corp.	Killed in action at Bull Run, Aug. 29, 1862.
William Young	Wag.	
Rudolph Armstrong	Private	Killed in action at Rocky Gap, W.Va., Aug. 27, 1863.
Daniel Brost	Private	
Theodore Batsch	Private	
Melchior Barley	Private	
Jos. Bermetlen	Private	
John Bavoridge	Private	
Hiram Burkett	Private	
Richard Bowman	Private	Re-enlisted as veteran, Jan. 5, 1864.
Joseph Blake	Private	Re-enlisted as veteran, Jan. 5, 1864.
Daniel Biehl	Private	Accidentally shot at Elkwater, W.Va., Oct. 8, 1861.
Jacob Bertsch	Private	Died at Wheeling, Oct. 8, 1862.
William Carr	Private	Wounded at Bull Run.
Antony Christy	Private	Re-enlisted as veteran, Jan. 5, 1864.

Anton Conrad	Private	Wounded at Bull Run. Discharged for disability, Oct. 29, 1862.
Benedict Coleman	Private	Died of typhoid fever at Elkwater, Nov. 19, 1861.
George Callahan	Private	Died July 21, 1863, at Ft. Delaware.
George Deitz	Private	
Anton Dentz	Private	
Philip Diek	Private	
Benj. Dingfeller	Private	Died of wounds rec'd in action at Bull Run, Sept. 20, 1862.
John Damury	Private	Died at Cheat Mountain, W.Va., March 21, 1862.
Jacob Dowler	Private	Died at Beverly, Jan. 7, 1863.
Christian Esslinger	Private	Discharged for disability, Aug. 15, 1862.
John J. Ebert	Private	Discharged for disability, Jan. 13, 1863.
Henry Emmerig	Private	Died Nov. 20, 1863, from wounds rec'd at Droop Mountain.
Thomas Faust	Private	
John Fox	Private	
William Finzel	Private	
August Fishman	Private	Discharged July 17, 1861. Served in another command.
Isaac Friess	Private	Discharged July 17, 1861. Served in another command.
Anton Glay	Private	
John Goedecke	Private	
Frank J. Guth	Private	
Frank Glatz	Private	Discharged for disability, Nov. 7, 1863.
August Gottschalk	Private	Deserted Nov. 23, 1863, at New Creek.
Henry Getze	Private	Transferred to V.R.C., Nov. 26, 1863.
Lewis Heitzman	Private	
Wm. Huey	Private	
Wm. Heidinger	Private	
Wm. Hinkleman	Private	
Thos. Hamm	Private	
Wm. Hamm	Private	

CHAPTER III.

Jos. Horwedel	Private	Discharged for disability, Jan. 26, 1863. Wounded at Bull Run.
Wm. Heim	Private	Deserted Nov. 17, 1862.
Henry Herbst	Private	Deserted May 8, 1863.
James Johnson	Private	
Jacob Klein	Private	Captured at Union, May 16, 1864. In Andersonville, exchanged.
Christian Kregor	Private	
John Koehline	Private	
Isador Keller	Private	Discharged for desertion, March 27, 1863.
Wm. Lauterbach	Private	
Henry Landbrohn	Private	
Louis M. Lang	Private	
Sebastian Lantner	Private	Re-enlisted as veteran, Jan. 5, 1864.
Conrad Miller	Private	Captured on Salem Raid, Dec. 1863. Died in Andersonville.
Henry Myers	Private	
Wm. Mereir	Private	Discharged for disability, Aug. 26, 1862.
John Neidhart	Private	
Anton Nolte	Private	Captured on Salem Raid, Dec. 1863. Died at Belle Island, Richmond.
Jenkins Neikles	Private	
Ernst Poggmeur	Private	Died at Florence, S.C.
Frank Plankey	Private	Discharged for disability, May 18, 1862.
Alex Primatty	Private	Discharged July 17, 1861. Served in another command.
Blassius Riester	Private	
Daniel Ritz	Private	
Christian Rohrer	Private	Discharged July 17, 1861. Served in another command.
Charles Ritz	Private	Killed in action at Droop Mt., Nov. 6, 1863.
F. Schwindig	Private	
Conrad Sturkel	Private	
Jacob Simon	Private	
Owen Sullivan	Private	Captured at Cloyd Mt., May 9, 1864. Exchanged.

Henry Schott	Private	Re-enlisted as veteran, Jan. 5, 1864.
John Sacksauer	Private	Discharged July 17, 1861. Served in another command.
John Sanner	Private	Discharged July 17, 1861. Served in another command.
John Schumacher	Private	Discharged July 17, 1861. Served in another command.
Matthias Schwartz	Private	Deserted May 28, 1862.
Jacob Schellenburg	Private	Deserted Sept. 28, 1862.
Lorenz Turk	Private	Killed in action at Rocky Gap, Aug. 28, 1863.
John Warnecke	Private	
Frederick Wenzel	Private	
John Will	Private	Discharged July 17, 1861. Served in another command.
F. Weisgarber	Private	Discharged for disability, April 24, 1863. Wounded at Bull Run.
Fiddius Zahn	Private	Discharged July 17, 1861. Served in another command.

CAPTAIN E. PLANKEY.

Edward Plankey was born in Germany, and came to the United States when but sixteen years old, settling at Wheeling, Va., where he learned the trade of carpenter. He afterwards went to Louisiana, where he enlisted as a private in an infantry company under Capt. C. Walker, which was known as the "Mexican Rangers," and served with great credit in the Mexican war. After the war with Mexico, he returned to Wheeling, and worked at his trade until he enlisted for service in 1861. Before the war he was captain of a rifle company at Wheeling, which enlisted for three years on Lincoln's first call. This company had been ordered by the Governor of Virginia to go to Richmond, but dissolved at once, and then pledged themselves to the national government. Among others in this company, was Wm. F. Graebe. Captain Plankey went with his company into the service, and did his duty faithfully, until failing health compelled him to resign. Returning home he resumed his old trade, which he followed until March 7, 1881, when he was elected superintendent of the County Infirmary of Ohio county, West Va., which position he held until his death, which occurred April 5, 1885, at the age of 67. The captain was a patriotic citizen, a loyal and true soldier, an upright and conscientious man, and was well liked by all who came in contact with him.

CHAPTER III.

LIEUTENANT A. ROLF.

August Rolf is a native of Pollier Province, Hanover Prussia, where he first saw the light August 13, 1828. He came to this country and engaged in business in Wheeling, Va., in 1846. He was first lieutenant of the "German Rifles," a company of Virginia state troops, which was ordered to do guard duty at the hanging of John Brown. Lieut. Rolf enlisted in Company C in May, 1861, and was elected first lieutenant of the company. While lying at Camp Carlisle, he was detached with forty of the men of his company, on special duty at Moundsville, rejoining the company at Beverly. He acted adjutant of the regiment for some time, and commanded the company in the absence of Captain Plankey, up to the battle of Bull Run, and took part in every engagement while he was in the service. At the battle of second Bull Run, Lieut. Rolf commanded Company I, and after that commanded Company E until he resigned in September, 1862, at Arlington Heights. His resignation was accepted by General McClellan. After retiring from the army, he was actively engaged in business in Wheeling, but is now retired, retaining an interest in different manufacturing and insurance companies.

FIRST LIEUTENANT LOUIS P. SALTERBACH.

Louis Philipp Salterbach, of Hachenbourg, was born on the 14th day of February A. D. 1829, Province Nassau, Kingdom Prussia, Germany. When five years old, he was sent to school to be prepared for college. He entered the same 1839, and was graduated in the year 1843. He continued and finished his education at Wiesbaden, frequenting the Gerverbe trade, Technique and Militaire schools.

On the 23d day of November, 1848, Louis Philipp was mustered in the Second Regiment Nassau Infantry, No. 88, 8th Army Corps. This corps was mobilized in January, 1849, to help Schleswig Holstein against Denmark. In this short and brief campaign he took an active part at the celebrated Battle of Dueppel in April, and at several other engagements. He served in all military branches, with the exception of cavalry, until 1854. He received a leave of absence to visit his father and brother in Patterson, New Jersey, U.S. He applied for his discharge in 1855, and received it, and became a citizen of the U.S. He was in the mercantile business until April, 1861. When President Lincoln called for 75,0000 men, Louis Philipp promptly reported, and enlisted as private in the Second Virginia Regiment Infantry at Wheeling, Va. He carried the colors at Cross Keys, Slaughter Mountain, and other battles, and the last time at Bull Run in 1862. He was mustered out as private and promoted second lieutenant, in November, 1862.

In March, 1863, he was commissioned first lieutenant, and afterwards placed in command of Company H, vice Captain Jos. Bushfield. The regiment was changed to cavalry and numbered as Fifth Regiment West Virginia. Salterbach was in nearly every engagement until mustered out at Wheeling, West Va., in June, 1864. He then went to Washington City, stayed there until November, and in said month, he settled his business as commander of Company H with the U. S. government, in the ordinance and quartermaster departments, and with the receipt from auditor "French" in his pocket, he went back to his home at Wheeling, West Va. He is there yet and doing business as notary, insurance and consular agent. He is a worthy man and deserves well at the hands of his adopted country, to which he gave his best service and ability.

LIEUTENANT C. VIERHELLER.

Christian Vierheller was born in Fanerbach, Hessen Darmstadt, near Frankfort on the Main, June 14, 1830. He attended a village school until 1842. At that time his father, Peter Vierheller, concluded to leave his native country, and with his wife and three sons, set sail for America, landing at Baltimore after a long journey. From there they went by the way of Pittsburgh and Wheeling to Monroe County, Ohio, where the family settled on a farm, which was nearly all woods. They began clearing it, but in a short time the father died, and the family was left alone to battle with the world, the subject of this sketch being the oldest of the children, and the only help, but they managed to change the place into a comfortable home. At the age of 19, he went to Wheeling, Va., where he obtained a situation in George Mendel's furniture store, where he remained until shortly before the war, when he engaged in the upholstering business on his own account. About eight years before the beginning of hostilities, he was married, and when he enlisted was a member of the State

CHRISTIAN VIERHELLER,
SECOND LIEUTENANT

Militia. He entered the service as sergeant in Capt. E. Plankey's Company C, Second Virginia Infantry. In the campaign of Gen. Pope, he was commissioned second lieutenant of the company, which rank he held until he retired from the service. In the winter of 1863, while at Beverly, he fell on the ice while returning from duty to camp, fracturing his left knee. The hurt was so severe that after lying in camp a while, he was advised by the surgeons to resign, which he did April 11th, 1863, not being able for further duty. Since then he

CHAPTER III.

has been engaged in farming, and as salesman for furniture stores, his home being now at Wheeling, West Va.

SERGEANT W. F. GRAEBE.

William F. Graebe was born in Germany on the 5th day of April, 1839. His father died when the subject of this sketch was 12 years old, and he came to America when he was 18, locating at Wheeling, Va., where he learned the trade of shoemaker. At the outbreak of the war, he was one of the number that formed Captain Plankey's Rifle Company, which enlisted for three years. After giving his country more than three years of faithful service he was honorably discharged, without having received a wound from the enemy. His narrow escape at Rocky Gap, though, has rendered him unfit for hard work of any kind, being troubled with a weak back. He resumed his old trade at Wheeling, which he followed until 1885. He was prosperous in his business, employing several men all the time, but in 1885 he gave up the boot and shoe business, and entered the Fire Insurance business, and is to-day one of the most successful Fire Insurance men in Wheeling, having acquired a very large business. Sergeant Graebe married Miss Amelia Finsley, daughter of Justice Finsley, of Sherrard, W. Va., to whom have been born six children, four of whom are living. Comrade Graebe is commander of E.W. Stephens G.A.R. post at Wheeling, is a Past officer in the A.O.U.W., and a member of the Improved Order of Red Men, the German Order of Hari Gauri, and the Knights of Pythias. He is a prominent citizen of his city, a man of integrity and honor and a worthy member of society.

WILLIAM F. GRAEBE

JACOB KLEIN.

Jacob Klein had a varied experience, worthy of mention. In the Pope campaign he was detailed to Captain Johnson's battery, where he remained five months, then returned to his company, and remained with it until captured after the Cloyd mountain expedition. He was taken to Lynchburg, thence to Richmond, and then to Andersonville, where he remained until Sherman captured Atlanta. He was then removed to Florence, S. C., then to Wilmington, N. C., then to Goldsborough, then back to Wilmington, about twelve miles from which place, he was exchanged early in March, 1865. With him were Conrad Miller and Ernest Pogmeur of his company, who died from exposure, and Owen Sullivan, who was exchanged with him. He returned to Wheeling by way of Annapolis, where he was sick for six weeks, and was discharged April 24, 1865.

COMPANY D.

On the first Monday after President Lincoln's call for 75,000 troops for three months service, Thomas Gibson, Jr., began to recruit a company in the city of Pittsburgh, Pa.; but not succeeding in securing the full complement of men, the company was not accepted by the Governor. Recruiting was continued, and when the next call for troops came, they again tried to enter the service, but having only fifty men, the company was again refused. But amid the excitement, they determined to mount and equip themselves, and go as an independent organization. While arrangements were being made to that end, word was received from Wheeling, Va., that troops were wanted there, for the protection of the threatened border. The company unanimously decided to go to that city and enter the service there, proceeding by boat, and arriving in Camp Carlisle in May. Captain Gazzam, of Pittsburgh, was there with about the same number of men as Captain Gibson, and by an understanding between the two captains, the two companies were consolidated. On the 14th of June the company was mustered into the service, with the following officers: Captain, Thomas Gibson, Jr.; First Lieutenant, David Ecker; Second Lieutenant, D. D. Barclay.

They furnished themselves with a Zouave uniform, consisting of sky blue pants and red jacket, and were armed with Springfield muskets, and supplied with twenty rounds of ammunition. They were then ordered to Grafton. Several trains had been stopped by the bushwhackers on this route previously, and extra precautions were taken against an attack. Comrades May, Grove, Colmer, and one or two others, rode on the cow catcher under the headlight, so as to be able to see and not be seen, there to watch for the bushwhackers. It was a tiresome ride, and the men reached Grafton weary and hungry, where they received a breakfast of coffee and hard tack, and then proceeded by rail to Clarksburg. Here the company went into camp with companies C and E, and drilled and prepared for active duty. While here the company went out on a scout and captured several citizens, who were accused of bushwhacking and giving aid to the enemy.

One night one of the men of Company D, while out foraging, captured a good sized calf, and at once concluded to take his prisoner to camp. Arriving

CHAPTER III.

near the camp guard, the prisoner became sportive, and being the stronger calf of the two, started on a run for the camp, pulling his captor after him. The camp guard gave the usual challenge, but captor and captive had no time to answer questions, and kept right on. The guard fired his gun and the several companies promptly formed in line of battle. The men being suddenly awakened from a sound sleep, came tumbling out, some only partly clothed. Company C had not received their guns as yet, but like brave men, as they were, they brought into use such weapons as were most convenient, and they fell into line with axes, shovels, etc. A member of one of the companies, with an axe on his shoulder, approached his captain in a quavering voice and said: "Captain, if I should fall in this conflict, I wish you would write home to my mother." This became a byword in the company during its service. On the 5th of July, the three companies started with a supply train of ammunition, etc., for the troops under McClellan and Rosecrans, who were then facing the enemy entrenched at Rich Mountain. After a weary march through a drenching rain and the deep mud, they arrived at Rich Mountain on the evening of July 6th, the day of the battle, in which our troops were successful in dislodging the enemy. Though not in time to participate in the battle, the company felt proud of the honor of doing some little for their country. The companies encamped on the battle field for the night, and on the morning of the 7th resumed the march for Beverly. On the way down the mountain, the little command scattered along the train they were guarding, and passed within less than 100 yards of 600 armed Confederates, who lay in ambush to attack the train, but were afraid to do it. The 600 afterward went in a flag of truce and surrendered. Arriving at Beverly, the company was assigned as company D of the regiment.

The following is the muster out roll, showing list of members and their record. The company was mustered into the U. S. service June 14, 1861, and mustered out June 16, 1864. All the members not otherwise marked, were mustered out with the company. The recruits and veterans were transferred to the Sixth West Virginia Cavalry, when the company was mustered out.

NAMES	RANK	RECORD OF SERVICE
Thomas Gibson	Capt.	Promoted to Major, July 7, 1862
D.D. Barclay	Capt.	Promoted 2d Lt. to 1st Lt. April 17, 1862; to Capt. July 7, 1862; to Major May 1, 1864.
John R. Frisbee	Capt.	Promoted from 1st Sergt Co. F to 2d Lt. Co. D, May 20, 1862; to 1st Lt. July 7, 1862; to Capt. May 1, 1864.

David Ecker	1st Lt.	Resigned April 17, 1862.
Jos. M. Bushfield	2d Lt.	Appointed 2d Lt. April 17, 1862; to 1st Lt. May 30, 1862; transferred to Co. H
A.J. Chambers	2d Lt.	Promoted from 1st Sergt. Co. A, to 2d Lt. Co., July 7, 1862; Resigned Sept. 29, 1862.
Jacob Colmer	2d Lt.	Promoted from 1st Sergt to 2d Lt., Sept. 29, 1862.
James May	Sergt.	
Robert Grove	Sergt.	
Thos. G. Smythe	Sergt.	Discharged for disability, Oct. 25, 1861.
Geo. Nubert	Sergt.	Discharged for disability, Feb. 19, 1862.
Wm. Schmolze	1st Sgt.	Promoted to 2d Lt. Co. F
Jerome Brooks	1st Sgt.	Re-enlisted as veteran, Jan. 5, 1864.
Charles Stark	1st Sgt.	Re-enlisted as veteran, Jan. 5, 1864.
Wm. Steinaker	1st Sgt.	Re-enlisted as veteran, Jan. 5, 1864.
Wm. Gillespie	1st Sgt.	Deserted
Michael Lee	Corp.	Killed in skirmish at Laurel Fork, Aug. 18, 1861.
John H. Heist	Corp.	Killed at Allegheny Mountain, Dec. 13, 1861.
Andrew Listman	Teamster	
John B. Algeo	Private	
David Anderson	Private	Discharged for disability, Oct. 17, 1862.
Jacob R. Ashby	Private	Discharged for disability, March 16, 1863.
Jas. M. Anderson	Private	Re-enlisted as veteran, Jan. 5, 1864.
Chas. Allen	Private	Deserted.
Michael Brubach	Private	Wounded, Droop Mountain.
John Bailey	Private	Discharged for disability, Sept. 11, 1862.
Bonaparte Brooks	Private	Re-enlisted as veteran, Jan. 5, 1864.
Frederick Barth	Private	Re-enlisted as veteran, Jan. 5, 1864.
Washington Black	Private	Re-enlisted as veteran, Jan. 5, 1864.
Michael Burns	Private	Re-enlisted as veteran, Jan. 5, 1864.
Geo. Black	Private	Died at Beverly, Oct. 20, 1861.

CHAPTER III.

Andrew Bernard	Private	Killed at Droop Mountain, Nov. 6, 1863.
Samuel Bowden	Private	Killed at Droop Mountain, Nov. 6, 1863.
Thos. J. Bartlett	Private	Deserted.
Jos. Campbell	Private	
Ira Chase	Private	Killed at Bull Run, Aug. 29, 1862.
Joseph Dowden	Private	Re-enlisted as veteran, Jan. 5, 1864.
Edward Doyle	Private	Killed at Droop Mountain, Nov. 6, 1863.
Chas. Daugherty	Private	Deserted.
Jas. C. Ecker	Private	Discharged May 13, 1863.
Wm. Elkins	Private	Died from wounds received at Laurel Fork, Aug. 18, 1861.
Francis Fitsimmons	Private	
Thos. J. Fennerty	Private	Discharged for disability, Sept. 18, 1862.
James Finlin	Private	Discharged dishonorably at Beverly, Dec. 18, 1863
Thos. Flanagan	Private	Deserted.
Thos. Galvin	Private	
Obadiah Gillespie	Private	Deserted.
Cyrus M. Hane	Private	
John Halpin	Private	Captured Salem Raid, Dec. 19, 1863. Died in Andersonville.
Jno. W. Hastings	Private	Discharged for disability, Aug. 9, 1861
Wm. Harrison	Private	Discharged for disability, Nov. 24, 1861
J.S. Hershberger	Private	Re-enlisted as veteran, Jan. 5, 1864
Wm. Hoyer	Private	Died Aug. 30, 1862, from wounds received at Bull Run, Aug. 29, 1862.
Wm. L. Hughes	Private	Killed at Droop Mountain, Nov. 6, 1863
Danl. D. Haas	Private	Deserted.
Robert Jackson	Private	Discharged for disability, March 17, 1862
Patrick Kearns	Private	In confinement at Fort Delaware
John Kane	Private	
Gabriel Kelley	Private	Re-enlisted as veteran, Jan. 5, 1864

James Little	Private	
Wm. O. Leslie	Private	Wounded at Bull Run. Re-enlisted as veteran, Jan. 5, 1864
Joseph Lehman	Private	Re-enlisted as veteran, Jan. 5, 1864
James Larkins	Private	Deserted.
Adam Moninger	Private	Transferred from Co. A, Aug. 31, 1863
Noah Messenger	Private	
Michael Madden	Private	
J.W. Martin	Private	Discharged for disability, July 8, 1861
Geo. W. Morris	Private	Discharged for disability, Aug. 5, 1861
Mansfield J. Mason	Private	Discharged Oct. 11, 1862, on acct. of wounds rec'd Allegheny Mt, Dec. 13, 1861.
John Moan	Private	Re-enlisted as veteran, Jan. 5, 1864
Wm. Morrow	Private	Re-enlisted as veteran, Jan. 5, 1864
Wm. Miller	Private	Transferred to Capt. West's Cav. Camp, Clarksburg, July 9, 1861
Jacob Musgrave	Private	Deserted.
Robt. Manning	Private	Deserted.
John Morland	Private	Deserted.
Peter McGurgen	Private	Captured Salem Raid, Dec. 19, 1863. Died in Andersonville.
Wm. B. McMurray	Private	Discharged for disability, Aug. 6, 1862
Jno. D. McClelland	Private	Discharged for disability, Dec. 8, 1862
Wm. McGully	Private	Disch. April 27, 1863. Loss of leg in action at Sulphur Springs, Aug. 23, 1862
Peter McMahon	Private	Re-enlisted as veteran, Jan. 5, 1864
James McAleer	Private	Died Aug. 26, 1863, from wounds rec'd in action at Rocky Gap, Aug. 26, 1863
John Neil	Private	
Geo. Newlitte	Private	Discharged for disability, Sept. 18, 1862
Henry Nolte	Private	Died April 13, 1862, Cheat Mountain Summit

CHAPTER III.

John Phillips	Private	
Alonzo J. Powell	Private	Deserted.
James Quest	Private	Killed at Bull Run, Aug. 29, 1862
John Rhodes	Private	Wounded at Cross Keys
Thos. Russell	Private	
Franklin Renforth	Private	
Richard Ryan	Private	Discharged for disability, Jan. 30, 1862
Thos. J. Reed	Private	Re-enlisted as veteran, Jan. 5, 1864
Samuel Ray	Private	Died Sept. 15, 1863, from wounds rec'd in action at Rocky Gap, Aug. 26, 1863
Geo. Reichenacher	Private	Deserted.
Jacob Sawer	Private	
Elias F. Seaman	Private	Promoted to Q.M. Sergt., Sept. 1, 1863
Chas. Stratton	Private	Re-enlisted as veteran, Jan. 5, 1864
Augustus Soles	Private	Re-enlisted as veteran, Jan. 5, 1864
Chas. Sands	Private	Died Sept. 18, 1862, from wounds rec'd at Bull Run, Aug. 29, 1862
John Stilly	Private	Died Sept. 30, 1862, from wounds rec'd at Bull Run, Aug. 29, 1862
W. Stanley	Private	Deserted.
Horner Stevens	Private	Deserted.
Thos. Taylor	Private	Re-enlisted as veteran, Jan. 5, 1864
Patrick Vaughan	Private	
John Wendel	Private	
John Woods	Private	Feet frozen on Salem Raid
Joseph Walton	Private	Prisoner in Libby
Edward Warnock	Private	Captured Salem Raid, Dec. 19, 1863. Died in Andersonville.
Wm. A. Wiley	Private	Wounded at Bull Run. Re-enlisted as veteran, Jan. 5, 1864

CAPTAIN THOMAS GIBSON, JR.

Thomas Gibson, Jr., was born in Allegheny County, Pa., the son of the late Colonel Thomas Gibson, surveyor of the port of Pittsburgh, under the Buchanan administration, and colonel of one of the Pennsylvania militia regiments. His mother's name was Totten, whose father was one of the pioneers in Pittsburgh of the foundry business. Both parents were Irish, and the son

75

inherited the Irish courage and daring. Captain Gibson was a graduate of the Western University of Pennsylvania, at Pittsburgh, and was a gentleman of culture and ability.

LIEUTENANT DAVID ECKER.

David Ecker was a native of Easton, Pa., his parents being what is known as Pennsylvania Dutch. He was a private in a battery during the Mexican war, and an excellent drill master; and to him was due the credit of the efficiency that the company attained in skirmish drill and in the bayonet exercise. He resigned early in 1862, just when the company began to show the training he had given them.

CAPTAIN JOHN R. FRISBIE.

John R. Frisbie was a native of Pittsburgh, Pa., his father being Amos Frisbie, and his mother Eleanor Johnston. His grandfather, John J. Frisbie, at one time lived in the "Old Block House" at the "Point," on the site afterwards occupied by old Fort Duquesne. Capt. Frisbie's parents died when he was a young man, and at an early age he was apprenticed to Messrs. Burke and Barnes, pioneer safe makers of Pittsburgh, and became an expert at his trade, and remained with the firm until about 1859, after which he was running on the river, learning to be a pilot, and was in New Orleans when the secession movement began. The boat started for Pittsburgh, and was thirty-one days in making the trip, owing to the frequent stops and detentions by the Confederate authorities along the river. He enlisted in Captain Alex. Scott's company, known as the "Belmont Guards," which became Company F of the Second Virginia. He was appointed sergeant of the company, afterwards rose to be first sergeant, and on May 20, 1862, was promoted second lieutenant, and assigned to Company D. July 7, 1862, he was promoted to first lieutenant and May 1, 1864, was promoted captain of the company, vice Captain D.D. Barclay, who was promoted major of the regiment. Captain Frisbie served faithfully until mustered out June 16, 1864. The captain was a brave, cool and determined officer, and in the most dangerous and trying places, displayed a coolness not often equaled. At the battle of Waterloo Bridge, August 1862, he was detailed with a squad of volunteers, to set fire to the bridge, a feat which he and his men accomplished under a galling fire of artillery and musketry, and for which he was complimented on the field by General Robert H. Milroy. The captain returned to Pittsburgh at the close of his term of service.

CHAPTER III.

LIEUTENANT JACOB COLMER.

Jacob Colmer was born April 1, 1842 at Duff's Mills, Franklin township, Allegheny County, Pa., his parents being natives of the state. His father, William Colmer, was born in Allegheny County, Pa., and his mother, Lavina Rosensteel, was born near Emsworth, in the same county, and both were descendants of the Pennsylvania Dutch. The son remained at home until he was 18 years of age, working at farming and in the blacksmith shop with his father. On the Monday evening following the call of President Lincoln for 75,000 three months men, Mr. Colmer placed his name as first on the roll of a company of volunteers being recruited by Thomas Gibson, Jr., at a place called Cross Roads, not far from Bakerstown, Allegheny County. After the company had been partly recruited, they went to Pittsburgh, but the quota from Pennsylvania was now filled, and the company was not accepted; but they still held their organization, and when the call came for three years men, they were again doomed to disappointment, so many troops being ahead of them. They then decided to equip themselves as an independent company, and while preparations were being made to this end, word was received that they were wanted at Wheeling, Va., to which place they went. Mr. Colmer was mustered into the service as sixth corporal, but on account of good conduct and attention to his duties, rose step by step until June 17, 1862, he was promoted first sergeant of the company, and held this position until September 29, 1862, when he was promoted to second lieutenant. On several occasions he acted as adjutant of the regiment, and had command of his company on the Salem Raid. On April 27, 1864, he was promoted to first

JACOB COLMER,
SECOND LIEUTENANT

lieutenant, and detailed to the position of adjutant, but declined the position, as he had become so attached to the members of his company that he did not wish to be taken away from them. He served his full term of enlistment and was mustered out with the company. Lieut. Colmer received what education he had by careful attention to studies in the four months per year schooling then in vogue in country districts, and in the summer of 1860, took a course of bookkeeping in Duff's College, Pittsburgh. He was married on December 22, 1868, to Miss Mary E. Scott, of Sharon, Mercer County, Pa., but a native of Allegheny County. The result of this marriage is a family of four bright children, the oldest, William H., now in his 21st year, Alice Scott 16, Lizzie Bell 14, and Charles Stevenson 4 years old. Since the war Lieut. Colmer has served in several responsible positions. For a long time he was clerk in the Pittsburgh pension office; for over 12 years bookkeeper for one large firm in Allegheny City, and is now agent for the Allegheny Insurance Company, of Pittsburgh. He is now serving his 18th year as permanent secretary of Twin City Lodge, No. 241, I.O.O.F., also as trustee of the same lodge during the last 18 years. He also served as secretary of Allegheny Lodge 223, A.F. and A.M., for six years after the close of the war. He now resides at Avalon, Pa., on the P.F.W. & C. Railway, six miles down the Ohio river from Pittsburgh. Lieut. Colmer served his country well and faithfully. He was a brave and accomplished officer, respected as such by all the men of the regiment, and a gentleman held in the highest esteem by all his comrades. As a citizen there are none truer, and he is a worthy and honored son of the country he helped so ably to protect.

LIEUTENANT A. J. CHAMBERS.

A. J. Chambers was born in Allegheny City in 1833, and learned the painting trade, but was engaged a number of years on Ohio river steamers. In April, 1861, he enlisted as corporal in company A in Pittsburgh. He served very creditably in the position, was promoted to sergeant, then to orderly sergeant, and finally, July 7, 1862, his bravery and merit was still further recognized by a promotion to 2nd lieutenant, and he was then transferred to company D of our regiment. After the war he opened up a paint shop in Allegheny and is still following the business. He represented his ward in Common and Select Councils for many years. He was married Aug. 25, 1853, to Miss Caroline A. Dougherty, and their union has been blessed by seven children.

JAMES MAY   JAMES M. ANDERSON

CHAPTER III.

COMPANY E.

Most of the members of this company were from Ohio, having been recruited by Simpson Hollister, Henry G. Jackson, H.B. James and others, in the counties of Monroe and Belmont. A portion of it was recruited by B.F. Bowers, in the counties of Wetzel and Taylor, on the Virginia side of the river, which with a squad of seven from Ritchie County, Virginia, made up the requisite number for organization, which was effected by the election of Simpson Hollister captain, Henry G. Jackson first lieutenant, and B.F. Bower second lieutenant, on the 16th day of June, 1861, at Camp Carlisle. Like the other companies with which its fortunes were linked, it was made up of a great diversity of character, including men of the professions and trades, farmers and business men, all animated by the same spirit of love for their country.

Western Virginia was racked and torn by the conflicts of the contending forces of the Union and its enemies, but there was a large force of loyal men who refused to bend the knee to treason. The little squad referred to, may be taken as a fair average of the loyalty of that section. Thomas and Charles Day, Riley, Wigner, Moats, Adams and French, composed the little band that was the first to represent Ritchie County in the army for the Union. Some of them were Virginians by birth, some were not, but all were in the vigor of early manhood, and being loyal to the heart, each had quietly and soberly decided for himself that duty required from him a prompt response to his country's call, notwithstanding many of their friends and associates held, very different views, and decided to cast their lot with the side of rebellion.

The sentiment for and against the Union cause being pretty equally divided in that region at that time, it was not considered the most healthy thing for either party, to be very demonstrative; so in pursuance of a quiet arrangement, the squad met at Ellenboro station on the evening of June 14, 1861, each with his little package in hand, ready when the shadows grew long, to start on their first night's march to the Ohio River. The march of 16 miles to St. Marys was made without incident worthy of note. The packet Woodside landed the squad at Wheeling, on the morning of the 16th, and they were met by their future captain and 1st lieutenant, and before noon were mustered into the service of their country.

In a short time afterward, this company and four others, were ordered to Clarksburg, where their actual duties as soldiers began. In a short time the movement on Rich Mountain was made, in which engagement a part of this little force took part, and then they proceeded to Beverly, where the company was assigned as company E of the regiment.

The following is the muster out roll, showing list of members and their record. The company was mustered into the United States service June 16, 1861, and mustered out June 16, 1864. All the members not otherwise marked, were mustered out with the company. The recruits and veterans were transferred to the Sixth West Virginia Cavalry, when the company was mustered out.

NAMES	RANK	RECORD OF SERVICE
S. Hollister	Capt.	Resigned Dec. 1, 1862
Thomas E. Day	Capt.	Promoted from sergeant, Dec. 10, 1862. Wounded at Bull Run.
H.G. Jackson	1st Lt.	Appointed adjutant, Aug. 23, 1861
H.B. James	1st Lt.	Promoted from sergeant, June 24, 1861. Killed at Bull Run, Aug. 29, 1862.
Charles H. Day	1st Lt.	Promoted from private to 2d Lt Co. H, assigned to Co. E as 1st Lt., transferred to Co. F, Nov. 9, 1862, to Co. I, May 24, 1863.
John C. French	1st Lt.	Promoted from sergeant to 1st Lt., Sept. 9, 1862. Wounded at Rocky Gap, Aug. 26, 1863.
B.F. Bower	2d Lt.	Resigned Dec. 10, 1861
James B. Smith	2d Lt.	Promoted from private, Jan. 13, 1863
R.H. Wigner	1st Sgt.	Wounded at Bull Run, Aug. 29, 1862
Jos. Riley	1st Sgt.	
D. Danford	1st Sgt.	
John Johnson	1st Sgt.	
John H. Caton	1st Sgt.	
John Fowler	Corp.	
George F. Dillon	Corp.	Wounded at Rocky Gap, Aug. 26, 1863
Henry Deut	Corp.	Wounded at Bull Run, Aug. 29, 1862
William R. Morris	Corp.	
Jas. W. Umstead	Corp.	Wounded at Waterloo Bridge, Aug. 25, 1862
A.Y. Montgomery	Corp.	
M.E. Moore	Corp.	

CHAPTER III.

William H. Foulke	Corp.	Wounded at Bull Run and Rocky Gap. Captured. Died at Danville.
A. McElroy	Corp.	Discharged for disability, Oct. 9, 1861
Isaac S. Rice	Corp.	Discharged for disability, Feb. 28, 1862
Samuel K. Reamer	Corp.	Discharged for disability, Jan. 28, 1863
William T. Bradford	Mus.	Discharged for disability, Feb. 28, 1862
John W.A. Lilly	Mus.	
Samuel M. Ambler	Private	Discharged Nov. 27, 1862, on account of wounds received at Bull Run
Robert M. Adams	Private	Killed at Bull Run, Aug. 29, 1862
Thomas J. Akers	Private	Killed at Droop Mountain, Nov. 6, 1863
James Bear	Private	
James Beatty	Private	Killed at New Creek.
S.A. Bushkirk	Private	Captured at Seneca, Sept. 25, 1863. Died in prison.
Geo. S. Butcher	Private	Killed at Bull Run, Aug. 29, 1862.
George Beach	Private	Deserted June 4, 1863.
James Blair	Private	Deserted Dec. 5, 1862.
D. Castillow	Private	Missing at Winchester, Jan. 1864.
George Castillow	Private	
William I. Cox	Private	
William Clark	Private	Re-enlisted as Veteran, Jan. 5, 1864.
William Cutlip	Private	Captured at Winchester, Jan. 1864. Died in Andersonville.
Christian Conley	Private	Discharged Oct. 29, 1862 on account of wounds received at Bull Run.
Sanford Clark	Private	Discharged for disability, Sept. 1, 1862.
Jacob W. Cox	Private	Killed at Bull Run, Aug. 29, 1862.
George Dent	Private	Wounded at Droop Mountain.
George Dearth	Private	
Israel Dunn	Private	
Asbury S. Davis	Private	Killed at Rocky Gap, Aug. 26, 1863.

Isaac Freeman	Private	
J.C. Frankhouser	Private	
James Fordice	Private	Wounded Bull Run. Re-enlisted as Veteran, Jan. 5, 1864.
Ed. Gaver	Private	
Henry Garring	Private	Captured at Bull Run.
Jas. F. Garrison	Private	Re-enlisted as a Veteran, Jan. 5, 1864. Killed at New Creek, Nov. 1864.
Jasper N. Givens	Private	Dishonorably discharged, May 27, 1863.
William Garroll	Private	Died Nov. 24, 1863, from wounds received at Droop Mountain.
Felix M. Hill	Private	
S.L.D. Hudson	Private	Wounded at Droop Mountain.
John Hess	Private	Killed at Rocky Gap, Aug. 26, 1863.
Elijah Hall	Private	Killed at Bull Run, Aug. 29, 1862.
And. G. Hesselton	Private	Died at Beverly, Dec. 9, 1861, of typhoid fever.
Samuel W. Jones	Private	Discharged Sept. 24, 1863, from wounds received at Bull Run.
R.D. Kelch	Private	Wounded at Bull Run.
D. Kirkland	Private	
James M. Kay	Private	Captured on Salem Raid.
M.L. Lohmire	Private	
Marion Moore	Private	
Robert C. Meredith	Private	
William A. Moffitt	Private	
Andrew Moats	Private	Wounded at Bull Run, Aug. 29, 1862.
William A. Miller	Private	Re-enlisted as a Veteran, Jan. 5, 1864.
Calvin B. Martin	Private	Captured at Rocky Gap, Aug. 26, 1863. Died at Andersonville.
Peter D. Moore	Private	Captured at Seneca, Sept. 29, 1863.
William Messerley	Private	Discharged for disability, Nov. 10, 1862.
John Murphy	Private	Killed at Droop Mountain, Nov. 6, 1863.

CHAPTER III.

Moses Moore	Private	Killed at Droop Mountain, Nov. 6, 1863.
Thos. D. McClary	Private	Re-enlisted after time was out in 6th W.Va. Infantry. Wounded at Winchester.
George H. McGee	Private	Recruit, March 24, 1862.
John McDougall	Private	Discharged for disability, Sept. 8, 1862.
Elijah Pitts	Private	
Samuel B. Pugh	Private	
Cornelius Pittman	Private	Re-enlisted as Veteran, Jan. 5, 1864.
Morgan Rush	Private	Wounded at Bull Run, Aug. 29, 1862, and Rocky Gap, Aug. 26, 1863.
Jas. A. Robinson	Private	
John Reader	Private	Re-enlisted as Veteran, Jan. 5, 1864. Died.
Martin Reader	Private	Re-enlisted as Veteran, Jan. 5, 1864. Died.
Leonard Roberts	Private	Re-enlisted as Veteran, Jan. 5, 1864. Died.
Jacob Ritchie	Private	Killed at Bull Run, Aug. 29, 1862.
John Schoonover	Private	Captured at Bull Run.
S.R. Spencer	Private	
S.B. Smith	Private	
Jacob Smith	Private	Recruit, Dec. 25, 1862.
Jere Sharp	Private	Recruit, July 5, 1863. Died of wounds received at Rocky Gap.
Wm. Sole	Private	
J.W. Stonebreaker	Private	Wounded at Elkwater, 1861. Re-enlisted as Veteran, Jan. 5, 1864.
Fred Schaub	Private	Wounded and captured at Rocky Gap. Died in Andersonville.
Thos. Smith	Private	Killed at Bull Run, Aug. 29, 1862.
Aug. Sponholtz	Private	Died March 10, 1863, at Beverly, of erysipelas.
McKnight Taylor	Private	Wounded at Bull Run. Re-enlisted as Veteran, Jan. 5, 1864.
Thos. B. Tillet	Private	Discharged for disability, Oct. 8, 1862.

John C. Taylor	Private	Deserted July 30, 1861.
Jas. L. Williams	Private	
H. White	Private	Wounded at Rocky Gap.
Levi Waters	Private	
Jasper Wilson	Private	
John D. Webb	Private	
John Williams	Private	Discharged for disability, Nov. 1, 1862.
Jackson Yonking	Private	Re-enlisted as Veteran, Jan. 5, 1864.

CAPTAIN SIMPSON HOLLISTER.

Simpson Hollister, the first captain of the company, was a native of Monroe County, Ohio, and was mainly instrumental in recruiting the company. At the breaking out of the war, he was a member of the Woodsfield bar, and was a delegate to the Chicago convention that nominated Abraham Lincoln for president. Capt. Hollister was a large hearted man, and had his physical condition been good, he could have distinguished himself in the service; but he soon discovered that he was unfit for active campaigning, and after spending some time in the recruiting service, he, from a sense of duty, resigned his commission and returned to civil life. His present home is in Leavenworth, Kas.

CAPTAIN THOMAS E. DAY.

In 1861 when the call was made for three years volunteers, Thos. E. Day was a member of the bar at Ritchie C.H., Va. He was a widower at the time with two very interesting little boys, to whom he was very strongly attached; but notwithstanding his surroundings were not of the most favorable character, he was a Union man from principle, and leaving one of his little treasures with his deceased wife's parents and the other with his father and mother, who then resided at Ritchie C.H., he became one, and rather the acknowledged leader, of the squad of seven who were the first to represent Ritchie Co. in the Union service.

When the squad was enlisted and formed a part of the organization, known afterward in the regiment as Co. E, Thos. E. Day was the only one who received any recognition beyond that of a private soldier, and he was appointed 3rd sergeant. When H.G. Jackson was made adjutant, Orderly Sergeant James was commissioned first lieutenant in his place and Sergeant Day was made orderly sergeant, and on the resignation of Lieut. Bower who left the Co. to take a position in Johnston's Battery, Sergeant Day was commissioned second lieutenant in Jan. 1862. Early in the morning of the first day's

CHAPTER III.

fight at the Second Bull Run battle, Lieut. James was killed while in command of the Co., Capt. Hollister being absent on recruiting service, and Lieut. Day assumed command, but in less than ten minutes received a severe wound in the left arm which disabled him for some time. Having been commissioned first lieutenant, he joined the regiment at Wheeling, when Gen. Milroy's brigade was transferred from the Army of the Potomac, to the Great Kanawha Valley, in Sept. 1862. Capt. Hollister, resigned the captaincy late in the fall of 1862, and Lieut. Day was commissioned to fill the vacancy which he did to the end of our three years' term, with great acceptance to those under his command and with credit to himself.

Capt. Day was a true soldier, and while at times his methods of discipline appeared harsh, and to one who was not well acquainted with him seemed cold and austere, yet he had a kind heart and was true to his friends and his country's cause. His present home is Mexico, Audrain County, Mo.

LIEUTENANT HENRY G. JACKSON.

Henry G. Jackson was a native of the city of Philadelphia, Pa., and having been a soldier in the Mexican war, possessed more knowledge of military affairs than most of his fellow officers of the line, so upon the organization of the regiment, he was made its first adjutant. He was one of the first officers to resign from his position in the regiment, and accepted a captaincy in the 62d Ohio. In this capacity he served for some time, but on account of his failing health, resigned and returned to his native city.

LIEUTENANT H. B. JAMES.

Hamilton B. James was a native of Belmont County, was a carpenter by trade, but at the outbreak of the war, was a clerk in the business house of Hutchinson & Bro., Beallsville, Ohio, and Justice of the Peace. He was chosen as first sergeant of the company, and served as such until the promotion of Jackson, when he was commissioned first lieutenant, and for a considerable time had command of the company. Lieut. James was a quiet, unassuming gentleman, ever faithful in the discharge of duty, and specially interested in the welfare of the men under his command. He was the first man killed in the company at the second battle of Bull Run, August 29, 1862.

LIEUTENANT CHARLES H. DAY.

Charles H. Day was born in New Market, Frederick County, Md., December 25, 1838; attended public school until he was 14 years of age, after which he learned the printing business, and worked at it until shortly before entering the war as a private in Company E. After acting as adjutant for a time during the spring and summer of 1862, he was commissioned second lieutenant and assigned to Company H; was promoted to first lieutenant, September 1, 1862; served as A. A. General of the brigade during the fall and next spring, and as Judge Advocate of General C. M. during the following summer; he was transferred from Company H to E; thence to Company F; thence to Company I, where he was serving at the battle of Droop Mountain, being wounded in the battle; was mustered out March 9, 1864, by orders from the War Department, having been off duty more than three months from wounds received in battle. Re-entered the service as first lieutenant and adjutant to organize the 17th Regiment West Virginia Infantry, August 13, 1864; was promoted to major, September 10, 1864, and to colonel, March 13, 1865, being mustered out June 30, 1865. Since then he has lived in West Virginia and Missouri, and is now on a farm at Occoquan, Prince William County, Va., where he has lived since 1872.

LIEUTENANT J. C. FRENCH.

J. Calvin French is the youngest son of George M. and Mary Porter French, and was born in Washington County, Pa., October 10, 1836. His mother died when he was less than three years old, and much of his early childhood was spent with relatives in Fayette County, Pa. At the age of 12 he returned to his father's home, remained four years, and then became an inmate of the family of Wm. Lindly. He was a boy of all work in the summer and attended school in the winter, but was denied the privilege of a thorough education, which he so much desired. At the age of 19 he accepted a position in the house of R. Porter, at Ritchie C.H., Va. After one year's service here, he associated with three other persons in the hoop and stave trade, on the B. & O. R.R., at points east of Parkersburg. This company erected the first establishment for the manufacture of oil barrels in that region, after the development of the Kanawha field. The war destroyed the business of the company and caused heavy financial losses. In closing up the affairs of the company, Lieut. French found himself possessed of little else save good health and a determination to contribute himself to the cause of the Union. Seeking an interview with persons like-minded, an arrangement was made by which he became one of the seven

JOHN C. FRENCH,
FIRST LIEUTENANT

CHAPTER III.

who first represented Ritchie County in the army of the Union, mentioned in full in the history of Company E. After serving as private, sergeant and orderly sergeant, and having been left in command of the company at Second Bull Run, one of the commissioned officers present being killed and the other wounded, he was commissioned second lieutenant September 9, 1862, and assigned to Company H; then commissioned first lieutenant and assigned to Company E, December 3, 1862. He was assigned to the command of Company B for a short time, while that company was on duty at Belington. While in command of a portion of the skirmish line in advance of the artillery, at the battle of Rocky Gap, he received a severe wound near the left knee, which distorted the joint and has measurably disabled him ever since. Having been rescued by comrades from falling into the hands of the enemy, and conveyed by ambulance to Beverly, he was there kindly sheltered and cared for by Mrs. Jonathan Arnold. When recovered, he returned to his regiment and was commissioned adjutant, and served as such until the regiment was disbanded, but chose to be mustered out with what remained of his company. In August, 1864, he returned to Washington County, Pa., and on September 7th, that year, was married to Miss Sevilla Vaile, in fulfillment of an engagement made in early life. He engaged in merchandizing, was elected Treasurer of the county in 1873, and on the expiration of his term returned to his home in Prosperity, where he has since been engaged in farming. He and family are members of the Presbyterian Church of Upper Ten Mile, and is commander of Luther Day Post, No. 395, G.A.R. Four children have been added to his happy home, Dr. Edward E., of Bentleysville, Pa., Leah Mary, wife of Dr. Booth, Bentleysville, Charles Clinton, who died in infancy, and J. Calvin, Jr., who is acquiring an education. There was no braver officer in the regiment, and Lieut. French deserves special mention for his gallant conduct at the second battle of Bull Run, and for his splendid leadership in the extreme advance, in the dash where he was wounded at Rocky Gap.

LIEUT. B. F. BOWER.

B.F. Bower was a young man about ready to be admitted to the bar in New Martinsville, Wetzel County, Va., in the spring of 1861. When the effort was made to organize a three years' regiment from the loyal element in Virginia, he set to work to recruit a company in Wetzel and Tyler counties, but he found the work somewhat difficult, and finally with about twenty men from the Virginia side of the river, he united with Hollister and Jackson from the Ohio side, and with a few from other quarters, had the required number to form a full company, which according to date of organization was lettered E, and he was commissioned its first second lieutenant. Lieut. Bower only remained with the regiment a short time, but it is but due to him to say that having been overstepped in the way of promotions he did what any spirited officer would have done, viz resign, and take a position elsewhere, which he did in Johnston's Battery of light artillery where his worth was more appreciated. Lieut. Bower is now enjoying a fair practice in his profession at the New Martinsville bar.

LIEUTENANT JAMES B. SMITH.

James B. Smith, a student of Nineteen Summers, left his home in Tyler County, Va., and found his way to Wheeling, in time to enlist in Company E. On account of his youth, size, and bright and cheerful expression of countenance, he was one to attract attention, so that when the Ritchie squad was instructed to select one to increase their number from seven to a mess of eight, Smith was looked after, when the situation was explained to him, and he at once consented to join the mess and ever afterward was identified with the Ritchie squad. His service as a private soldier, was marked for coolness, vigilance and courage. At the Second Bull Run battle in 1862, when Colonel Latham called for volunteers, one from each company, to reconnoiter in front of our lines his lithe form was the first to the front from the company, and among the first of the regiment to return and make an intelligent report of the situation. In November, 1862, he was made a non-commissioned officer, and on March 27, 1863, he was commissioned a second lieutenant, Company E, at this time being about the only one in the depleted regiment that had three commissioned officers. Lieut. Smith was frequently detailed on special duty. On one occasion he was ordered by General Averell to take an escort of three men from the camp at Martinsburg, and reconnoiter the enemy's position at Winchester. Taking with him Anderson of Company H, Castillow and Cutlip of Company E, he proceeded to Bunker Hill, a distance of twelve miles, where he remained until after midnight, when he advanced to a high point overlooking Winchester; here the enemy had a picket of five infantry soldiers, whom Lieut. Smith

JAMES B. SMITH,
SECOND LIEUTENANT

surprised and captured after a little skirmish, gaining valuable information from the prisoners, and also finding himself almost in the presence of a large force of the enemy. He left the main road, not only to bring the prisoners into camp, but to apprise our cavalry out post of the advance of a superior force of

CHAPTER III.

the enemy. The prisoners were given in charge of two of the men while the lieutenant with Cutlip alone undertook to reach the picket post by a country road; this arrangement had hardly been made when the lieutenant was halted, and a dialogue ensued; it was a very dark morning and when the order came from the enemy to advance, the opportunity was made use of to turn and regain the pike, which was done and the two men and prisoners were overtaken and were joined by a small patrol of Pennsylvania Cavalry. The enemy came on with a dash, and all were in a confused mass amid timber and darkness, the prisoners were lost and the three men who had done their part so nobly were carried away by the rush. Lieut. Smith concealed his identity by joining with the enemy in the darkness, until an opportunity was offered to elude them by the roadside, and the force of the enemy turned back and he was left alone. On returning to the outpost alone, and telling his strange experience to the captain commanding, he was regarded with suspicion by that officer, and the question of his being a spy was strongly hinted at; but fortunately at this juncture Maj. Tom. Gibson of the Fourteenth Pennsylvania Cavalry came upon the scene with a detachment from his regiment, and settled all questions of identity.

In March, 1864, Lieut. Smith was appointed an acting assistant signal officer in Department of West Virginia, in which capacity he served until May 13th, 1864, when he and his whole signal corps were taken prisoners by Mosby's Rangers. He was treated with some indignity on account of his being a native Virginian, was taken first to Orange C. H., from thence to Gordonsville, Lynchburg and Danville, Va., and in June, 1864, was sent to Macon, Ga., where he was associated with about one thousand Federal officers. While thus incarcerated in this prison pen, his experience was not different in many respects from that of his fellows. Most of the time was spent in devising plans how they might escape. To relieve the monotony a little hilarity was indulged in, when new recruits were ushered into their dismal prison abode. It was usually known when new prisoners were about to be brought in, and two irregular lines would be formed and the new prisoners were expected to pass between these lines, while a perfect din of shouts would go up in chorus: "Fresh fish! Fresh fish! Don't take his shirt! Leave his haversack," etc. When Lieut. Smith had passed about half way between the two lines, a well-known voice and hearty grasp of the hand caused him to forget all else, as he recognized the tall form and pleasant countenance of that prince of scouts, Charley Smitley, of Company B. About August 1st, Lieut. Smith and about 600 others, were loaded into box cars and started for Charleston, S.C. About 70 of the number escaped from the train while in transit. Lieut. Smith and two others jumped from the cars at Pocotalgo bridge, and secreted themselves in a swamp. After hiding by day and travelling by night for three days, they ventured to the road to consult a finger board, when they were suddenly surprised and recaptured, and forced, half starved, to complete the journey to Charleston, at which place they were placed under fire of the Federal guns while the city was being bombarded, but while thus placed in the jail yard, the "swamp angels" used against the city did them but little harm. In October, 1864, Lieut. Smith, together with a large number of officers, was taken to Columbia, S.C., from which place, November 29th, about 50, through bribery and strategem, effected an escape. Once out of prison they divided into small squads of from three to five and took different directions, some for east Tennessee, others for Sherman's army, while Lieut. Smith and three others undertook to make their way to the coast. After untold privations and narrow escapes from recapture, on the 12th of December, the squad arrived at the coast near McClellanville, where an artillery company had been stationed, but had just left to join Hood's army. All boats had been scuttled to prevent the colored people from escaping. With some difficulty the squad repaired an old life boat, in which they managed to reach a deserted light house, five miles from the main land, called Cape Roman, two of the squad rowing, one steering and the fourth one kept busy bailing out the water with a broken jug. Here they hoped to be able to attract the attention of some passing vessel, but while many were in sight at different times, they failed, and at the end of three days, having no provisions, and failing to catch a cat, which would have been eagerly devoured, nothing was left them to do but return to the main land, which was done after drifting five miles to the northward. Here a new trouble met them. They had been seen by some of the servants, who took them for rebel deserters, and had so reported them. Fortunately, however, the old planter, who met them on their landing and accused them of deserting, was rather easily beguiled by plausible stories and they were let go without being further reported. A faithful colored man was finally secured, who ferried them across both Santee rivers, and through rice swamps to Alligator channel, but the bridge that had connected the main land with the island had been destroyed, so that a rude raft was constructed on which they placed their clothes, and pushing it before them they swam to the island. Not taking time to dress, each one took his clothes under his arms and ran about two miles across the island in time to signal a gunboat before it had got beyond reach. No language can describe the feelings of joy of the half naked and almost famished boys as they noticed the gunboat pull for them, and when taken on board to receive kind greetings from the jolly sailor boys.

After Lieut. Smith's escape he returned to Washington, D.C. His regiment having been mustered out, except that portion that had re-enlisted as veterans, Lieut. Smith was offered and accepted a captaincy in the Sixth W.Va. Cavalry, and received the following complimentary letter from his old commander:

CHAPTER III.

BATH, NEW YORK, 12th Feb. 1865.
To MAJ. GEN. GEO. CROOK, Commanding Dep't of West Va:

GENERAL:-I have the honor to recommend Capt. James B. Smith, Sixth W. Va. Cavalry, as a brave, skillful, and enterprising officer. He formerly belonged to the Fifth W. Va. Cavalry, distinguished himself at Droop Mountain, and afterward at Martinsburg. He has been a prisoner of war since the opening of the summer campaign until the 15th of December, 1864, when he escaped from the enemy at Columbia, S.C. The men of his company are principally veterans, and, I believe, will do good service as cavalry.

I am General,
Very Respectfully, your obedient servant,
WM. W. AVERELL, Bvt. Maj. General.

Capt. Smith went with General Crook's command to the Northwest, and took an active part in the operations of that general's forces in his campaigns against the Indians. The service becoming monotonous and the captain having served his country nearly five years, and having seen service in all its phases, he returned to civil life in his native county, and has since for the most part been engaged in merchandising.

Capt. Smith was married Aug. 19, 1868, to Miss Martha J. Langfitt, of Eagle Mills, W. Va. Three children adorn his home, viz:. Sidney A., Ida L. and Silas M. Smith. The captain and all his family are members of the Christian church.

M. E. MOORE.

M.E. Moore, private of Company E, and one of the veterans of the company, was captured at Greenbrier River, on the return from Cloyd Mt; was in Staunton hospital three months, and had charge of thirteen wounded Union soldiers, during which he saw both the Union and Confederate armies pass through the city. He was started for Andersonville, but having a sore hand and arm, he applied bandages, and when the surgeon examined him he was sent to Richmond, and was exchanged from there. He claimed to have been wounded at Piedmont, which with his sores, saved him a stay at Andersonville. He was discharged at Wheeling, W. Va., May 30, 1866, and lacked only a few days of having served five years. It was the service of a veteran.

COMPANY F.

This company was enlisted in Pittsburgh, Pa., by Alexander Scott, John A. Hunter, Douglass G. Smythe and others, but it has not been possible after an earnest effort, to learn any of the details of the organization of the company.

The following is the muster out roll, showing list of members and their record. The company was mustered into the U. S. service June 24, 1861, and was mustered out June 30, 1864. All the members not otherwise marked, were mustered out with the company. The recruits and veterans were transferred to the Sixth W. Va. Cavalry, when the company was mustered out.

NAMES	RANK	RECORD OF SERVICE
Alexander Scott	Capt.	Promoted to Lt. Col., May 20, 1862
Henry C. Flesher	Capt.	Promoted from 1st Lt., Co. H, May 20, 1862. Promoted to major, Nov. 9, 1862.
Thos. B. Smith	Capt.	Promoted from sergeant. Wounded at Second Bull Run.
John A. Hunter	1st Lt.	Promoted to Capt., Co. A, March 20, 1862
Chas. H. Day	1st Lt.	Transferred from Co. E, Nov. 9, 1862. Transferred to Co. I, May 24, 1863.
Douglass G. Smythe	2d Lt.	Resigned June 17, 1862
Wm. Schmolze	2d Lt.	Promoted from 1st Sgt., Co. D, July 2, 1862
Wm. Broughson	Sergt.	Captured at Rocky Gap, Aug. 26, 1863
Joseph Black	Sergt.	
Wm. Wyble	Sergt.	
Chas. Kirchaffer	Sergt.	
Peter Krouse	Sergt.	Re-enlisted Jan. 5, 1864
Jno. C. Devlin	Sergt.	Discharged for wounds received in action, Nov. 6, 1862.
Isaiah Stephenson	Sergt.	Deserted Aug. 25, 1862
Wm. W. Carney	Sergt.	Killed in action, Rocky Gap, Aug. 27, 1863
Henry Burns	Sergt.	Died at Pittsburgh, Feb. 24, 1864, from effects of a fall

CHAPTER III.

W.H. Silver	Sergt.	Promoted sergeant major, Aug. 1, 1861
Jno. R. Frisbie	Sergt.	Promoted 2d Lt., Co. D, May 20, 1862
Joseph Massy	Corp.	
John Peppard	Corp.	
Geo. McIntyre	Corp.	
Jas. Stewart	Corp.	Died, Jan. 10, 1862, from wounds received in action at Camp Allegheny, Dec. 1861
Jno. Murry	Corp.	Killed in action at Bull Run, Aug. 29, 1862
Ambrose J. Bing	Corp.	Died, Feb. 2, 1864, of disease contracted while a prisoner
James M. Anderson	Private	Deserted May 11, 1863
Michael Burke	Private	
Francis Brecker	Private	
Edward H. Barry	Private	Re-enlisted Jan. 5, 1864
Frank Bannon	Private	Died at Cheat Mountain, Jan. 29, 1862, disease of the lungs
John Cox	Private	
Archibald Campbell	Private	
Richard Carrigher	Private	
John Culp	Private	
C. Chadderson	Private	
Owen Carney	Private	Discharged for disability, Aug. 2, 1862
Bernard Cain	Private	Died at Beverly, Aug. 27, 1861
Peter Cassidy	Private	Killed in action at Bull Run, Aug. 29, 1862
John Daniels	Private	Re-enlisted Jan. 5, 1864
Samuel Drury	Private	Deserted May 8, 1864
Luke Delaney	Private	Deserted March 5, 1863
William Davis	Private	Deserted March 5, 1863
Alexander Dunn	Private	Killed in action at Bull Run, Aug. 29, 1862
Matthew Fanzel	Private	
Richard Ferguson	Private	
Michael Frana	Private	

James Finnin	Private	
John W. Gilland	Private	
John Grant	Private	
Lawrence Gapney	Private	Re-enlisted Jan. 5, 1864
James Gay	Private	Deserted Feb. 23, 1863
James A. Gardner	Private	Killed in action at Waterloo Bridge, Aug. 25, 1862
James Glass	Private	Died March 18, 1864
James R. Henry	Private	
George Hilsdon	Private	
Patrick Hillary	Private	
John Harle	Private	
John Harden	Private	
Marsh. Huntzeker	Private	Discharged April 10, 1863
Joseph Hall	Private	Deserted April 12, 1862
George V. Jones	Private	
Edward Kane	Private	
Francis Lourey	Private	
Thomas Lewis	Private	Deserted July 9, 1861
Michael Loughran	Private	Died March 1, 1864, of disease contracted while a prisoner
Jacob Miller	Private	
Charles Main	Private	
William Matthews	Private	
John Mitchell	Private	Discharged for disability, Oct. 19, 1862
Henry McGill	Private	
Thos. McKeefer	Private	
George McClay	Private	
John McDermott	Private	
Robt. McCormick	Private	Captured at Rocky Gap, Aug. 26, 1863. Died at Andersonville.
L. McMasters	Private	Re-enlisted Jan. 5, 1864
James McLain	Private	Deserted March 29, 1862
Daniel McCay	Private	Died April 27, 1864, at Parkersburg
Frank Nevergold	Private	Deserted Oct. 1, 1862
John Otterson	Private	
Philip Panner	Private	

CHAPTER III.

John Quinn	Private	
John Quillian	Private	
Charles M. Roberts	Private	
Thos. B. Richardson	Private	
Jas. B. Robinson	Private	Re-enlisted Jan. 5, 1864
George W. Snyder	Private	
John Shedden	Private	
John Sheets	Private	
William H. Story	Private	
Daniel Slaven	Private	
Leander Short	Private	
Hugh Smith	Private	Captured at Rocky Gap, Aug. 26, 1863. Died at Andersonville.
Robert Sterling	Private	Discharged for disability, Feb. 22, 1863
Patrick Shine	Private	Deserted Aug. 28, 1862
Thomas Stevens	Private	Died at Beverly, Aug. 20, 1861
Barney Toner	Private	
Martin Walters	Private	
John Werner	Private	
John W. White	Private	
John Walters	Private	Re-enlisted Jan. 5, 1864
Henry D. Ward	Private	Deserted July 9, 1861
Henry Walton	Private	Deserted March 23, 1862
Samuel Watts	Private	Deserted March 5, 1863
Chas. Zimmerman	Private	
John J. Zimmer	Private	

CAPTAIN THOMAS B. SMITH.

Thomas B. Smith is a native of Pennsylvania, being born in Pittsburgh. He assisted in raising the "Belmont Guards"" in May, 1861, and accompanied them to Wheeling, where the company was mustered into the U. S. service. He was mustered in as first sergeant of the company, and was promoted to second lieutenant, thence to first lieutenant, and on the 26th of November 1862, was commissioned captain of his company. Captain Smith was a good officer, and was badly wounded at the second battle of Bull Run, while rallying his men under the severe fire of the enemy, which rendered him unfit for duty for a long time. His career after the war is not known.

LIEUTENANT D. G. SMYTHE.

D.G. Smythe is a native of Pittsburgh, Pa. He received a common school education, but by diligent study and research, he acquired a good knowledge of history and languages, that was of great value to him in after life. He adopted the theatrical profession and played engagements in all of the principal cities in this country, and was a member of the Pittsburgh Stock company at the breaking out of the war, and announced the fall of Sumter to the audience when that event occurred. He at once began to procure enlistments for the army, and in connection with Capt. Alex. Scott and Lieutenant John A. Hunter, recruited the Belmont Guards, Mr. Smythe being commissioned second lieutenant. He served with his company in the battles of Allegheny Mt., Huntersville, and Cross Keys, and in a number of skirmishes. He was correspondent for the Pittsburgh *Dispatch*, writing under the *nom de plume* of "Horatio," giving an accurate description of men and surroundings, which was very readable to the men, and highly appreciated by the proprietors of the paper. He resigned his commission at Mount Jackson, Va., on account of ill health, brought on by exposure during the Huntersville raid. He then visited the southern country for the benefit of his health, and while at Natchez, Miss., was appointed United States Assistant Assessor of Internal Revenue, filling this position for three years. He is now a clerk in the transfer depot of the Pennsylvania Railroad at Pittsburgh, Pa.

PRIVATE JOHN HORLE   LT. WILLIAM SCHMOLZE

CHAPTER III.

COMPANY G.

This company was raised in Pittsburgh, Pa., by Chatham T. Ewing, J. D. Owens, H. A. Evans and others, and was composed of residents of Allegheny and surrounding counties of Pennsylvania, and a few from Wheeling, Va., bearing the name of the "Plummer Guards." John D. Owens was elected captain and Chatham T. Ewing first lieutenant, and the company began to drill. The organization was completed fully on the 15th of May. Joseph Plummer, at the time a prominent shoe dealer on Wood street, in return for the honor of having the company named after him, bought uniforms for the men, consisting of a suit of grey cloth pants, and jackets trimmed with black, very neat and pretty. The quota of Pennsylvania being full, Gov. Curtin declined to accept the company, and the men chafed under their inability to get to the seat of war. At this time the Confederates were becoming active in Western Virginia, and Major Oakes, at Wheeling, came to Pittsburgh to get some troops. The Plummer Guards at once accepted service, going to Wheeling on the steamer John T. McCombs, making their first "camp" on the steamboat Courier, and afterward in Camp Carlisle. They were mustered into the United States service by Capt. Craig, with the following officers: Captain, Chatham T. Ewing; first lieutenant, Alfred Sickman; second lieutenant, Jacob G. Huggins, Capt. J. D. Owens being appointed major of the regiment of which this company was to be a part.

While on the Island, a detail was made from the company, to go to Bethany and get some arms, that were in possession of the military company formed from among the students at the college there, who were nearly all from the south, and in sympathy with that section. The detail consisted of twenty-five men under command of U.S. Marshal Norton, and Sergeant Rook and Corporal Evans. They went to Bethany in omnibuses, reaching there at midnight, surprising and capturing the place, and securing the guns. On the way back to camp, they stopped for supper at West Liberty, where they received an ovation, the citizens meeting them with a brass band, and welcomed them to the town. They reached Wheeling in the night, waking up Governor Pierpont, who made the boys a speech, and told the marshal to take them to a hotel for their breakfast.

Camp Carlisle continued to be their headquarters until July 5th, when the company proceeded to Grafton, thence to Webster, relieving Capt. Tyler, Co. G, Fifteenth Ohio.

From Webster the company went to Laurel Hill, thence back to Webster, and Grafton, thence to Oakland, Md., thence to the "Red House," trying to intercept the retreating enemy after the battle of Corrick's Ford. They double quicked for seven miles, the Twentieth Ohio, Colonel Morton, being close to the company, the most of the time, and captured a few of the gentlemen from the south. Major Walcott of General Hill's staff, ordered the command to halt, when the general made a speech, ending with proposing three cheers for the star spangled banner, which were weakly given by the disgusted men, who were then ordered to retreat. The company then went back to the "Red House," thence to Oakland and New Creek, returning to Grafton, thence to Clarksburg, and by way of Buckhannon went to Beverly, where they met the rest of the companies of the regiment to which they were to be attached, and became Company G.

The following is the muster out roll, showing list of members and their record. The company was mustered into the U. S. service June 13, 1861, and mustered out Aug, 8, 1864. All the members not otherwise marked, except the recruits and veterans, were mustered out with the company.

NAMES	RANK	RECORD OF SERVICE
J.D. Owens	Capt.	Promoted to Major, 2d Virginia Infantry
C.T. Ewing	Capt.	Wounded at Rocky Gap, Aug. 26, 1863
A. Sickman	1st Lt.	Killed in action at Allegheny Mt, Dec. 13, 1861
H. Morton	1st Lt.	Promoted from Corp., Dec. 14, 1861
J.G. Huggins	2d Lt.	Resigned March 22, 1862
S.J. Shearer	2d Lt.	Promoted from Sergt., March 22, 1862
Stephen Ripley	Q.M.S.	
L.F. Fetterman	1st Sgt.	Transferred to 101 Pa., Jan. 6, 1862
A. Boyd Rook	1st Sgt.	Re-enlisted as veteran, Feb. 26, 1864
S.J. Osborne	Sergt.	Chief of first piece
John H. Veach	Sergt.	Chief of second piece.
Adam Brown	Sergt.	Chief of third piece. Wounded at Rocky Gap, Aug. 26, 1863.
Daniel Graham	Sergt.	Chief of fourth piece
Henry A. Evans	Sergt.	Chief of fifth piece. Wounded at Rocky Gap, Aug. 26, 1863.
Robt. Watson	Sergt.	Chief of sixth piece
A.G. Osborne	Corp.	Gunner first piece
W.J. Hawkes	Corp.	Gunner second piece

CHAPTER III.

Joseph N. Powell	Corp.	Gunner third piece. Captured on scout, Jan. 21, 1863. Exchanged.
John Lambie	Corp.	Gunner fourth piece
John Hawkes	Corp.	Gunner fifth piece
John G. Byder	Corp.	Gunner sixth piece
Jere Defibaugh	Corp.	Chief caisson first piece. Captured Salem Raid. Died at Andersonville.
Geo. D. Barclay	Corp.	Chief caisson second piece
Jos. Householder	Corp.	Chief caisson third piece. Re-enlisted Feb. 24, 1864.
John Boles	Corp.	Chief caisson fourth piece
L.G. Marshall	Corp.	Chief caisson fifth piece. Wounded Rocky Gap. Re-enlisted Jan. 2, 1864. Transferred to Batt. B, 5th U.S. Art.
Richard Pudder	Corp.	Chief caisson sixth piece
J.R. Thomas	Mus.	Promoted to Prin. Mus., 2d Va. Wounded at Rocky Gap.
W.L. Edwards	Art.	
J.W. Vangilder	Art.	Captured on scout, Jan. 21, 1863. Taken to Richmond and exchanged.
Alex. Atcheson	Private	
Louis Annington	Private	
Elijah Adams	Private	Captured on scout, Nov. 22, 1862. Exchanged. Re-enlisted Feb. 22, 1864. Transferred to Batt. B, 5th U.S. Art.
Wm. Anshutz	Private	Re-enlisted Jan. 2, 1864. Transferred to Batt. D, 1st W.Va. Art.
Chas. Arbogast	Private	Recruit. Killed at Rocky Gap, Aug. 26, 1863
Geo. W. Arbogast	Private	Recruit. Died in Andersonville prison.
Jno. Bernert	Private	
Michael Bradley	Private	Deserted July 18, 1862
Benj. F. Clawson	Private	Recruit, Oct. 3, 1862
John Casey	Private	
Frank W. Coleves	Private	

H. Campbell	Private	Re-enlisted Feb. 24, 1864. Assigned to Battery D, 1st W.Va. Art.
Wm. Colville	Private	Re-enlisted Jan. 2, 1864. Assigned to Battery B, 5th U.S. Art.
Wm. L. Conner	Private	Discharged for disability, Sept. 1, 1861
W.I. Campbell	Private	Deserted July 18, 1861
Benj. F. Cutlip	Private	Recruit, Oct. 17, 1863
D. Dougherty	Private	
Jeremiah Dufford	Private	
Robt. P. Duxbury	Private	Discharged for disability, Nov. 1, 1861
Rufus E. Evans	Private	
Jno. W. Frazier	Private	
John Fife	Private	Wounded at Rocky Gap, Aug. 26, 1863
Henry Forrest	Private	
Jos. Forsythe	Private	
John Fry	Private	Captured at Beverly. Taken to Richmond, Va. Exchanged.
Wm. Gibson	Private	
Jas. P. Guest	Private	Captured on Salem Raid. Transferred to 6th W.Va. Cavalry, June 22, 1864.
Daniel Garrison	Private	Re-enlisted Jan. 2, 1864
Wm. H. Gregg	Private	Discharged by order General Hill, Co. being above maximum
George Hart	Private	Wounded at Rocky Gap, Aug. 26, 1863
James H. Hall	Private	
James Hastings	Private	
John Hobaugh	Private	Captured Salem Raid
Martin Hope	Private	
Samuel B. Hickman	Private	Recruit
George Huffman	Private	Captured scout, Jan. 21, 1863. Re-enlisted Feb. 24, 1864. Transferred to Batt. B, 5th U.S. Art.
C. McClure Hays	Private	Promoted to adjutant, 2d Va.
Uriah Heaton	Private	Recruit
William Jamison	Private	Re-enlisted Feb. 24, 1864

CHAPTER III.

Andrew Kalor	Private	
Roger Kennelly	Private	
Watson Kilgore	Private	
Francis A. Klein	Private	
Albert Kincaid	Private	Killed in action at Bull Run, Aug. 30, 1862
Jeremiah Leedom	Private	Wounded at Cross Keys, June 1862. Wounded at New Market, May 1864.
Arthur Little	Private	Discharged for disability, Dec. 6, 1862 at Beverly
Samuel Lessig	Private	Killed in action at Rocky Gap, Aug. 26, 1863
Robt. Mansberger	Private	
George C. Martin	Private	
George H. Maxwell	Private	
James Metcalf	Private	Wounded at Rocky Gap, Aug. 26, 1863
John Moan	Private	Killed accidentally, April 26, 1864, on B&O R.R. between Grafton and Clarksburg
Henry W. Martin	Private	Deserted July, 1862
Wm. McCauley	Private	
Alex. McCauley	Private	
Wm. F. McClure	Private	
M.H. McCormick	Private	
Jas. McCracken	Private	
Hugh McCune	Private	
Armstrong McGill	Private	
Far. McGillivray	Private	Captured on Salem Raid. Exchanged.
John McGillvray	Private	
James McIntosh	Private	
William McKee	Private	Re-enlisted Jan. 2, 1864. Assigned to Batt. B, 5th U.S. Art.
James McKendree	Private	Re-enlisted Feb. 24, 1864. Assigned to Batt. D, 1st W.Va. Art.
Alex. McKenzie	Private	Killed in action at New Market, Va., May 15, 1864
David R. Phillips	Private	

George Prentice	Private	Re-enlisted Jan. 2, 1864. Assigned to Batt. B, 5th U.S. Art.
M.V.B. Rodgers	Private	Recruit
Frederick Rowe	Private	Died at White Sulphur Springs, Oct. 3, 1863 of wounds rec'd in action Rocky Gap, Aug. 1863.
John Seibert	Private	
Samuel Shaw	Private	
William Shields	Private	
John W. Sutheron	Private	
Morrison A. Sample	Private	Discharged for disability, Nov. 1, 1861
Jacob Stroble	Private	Discharged for disability, Sept. 1, 1861
John N. Taggert	Private	Wounded at Rocky Gap, Aug. 26, 1863
Joseph Trussell	Private	
Patrick Wallace	Private	Re-enlisted Jan. 2, 1864
Thomas Walsh	Private	Died at Beverly, Sept. 4, 1861
Nathaniel Young	Private	
David R. Yingst	Private	Re-enlisted Jan. 2, 1864
Philip Zeigler	Private	Wounded at Rocky Gap and taken prisoner, Aug. 26, 1863

CAPTAIN C. T. EWING.

Chatham Thomas Ewing was born in New Lisbon, Ohio, January 30, 1839. In the spring of 1852 he, with the rest of his father's family, moved to Pittsburgh, Pa. He united with the Presbyterian denomination when about 19 years of age, under Wm. M. Paxton, who is now pastor in one of the churches in New York City, and was one of the first leaders in the Y.M.C.A. in Pittsburgh, with Wm. Frew, Gilbert McMasters and Wm. Thaw. They held gospel meetings in a room over the Duquesne engine house, and they frequently had the firemen to listen to the services. In the summer of 1860 he was a member of the Pittsburgh Zouaves, a company which afterwards furnished a great many officers for the Union army. At the breaking out of the war, he was in western Kentucky on a collecting tour for some Pittsburgh business houses, and all this time knew nothing of the war; the first he learned of it was on his return when he reached the Ohio river. Hastening home he was greeted with the intelligence of the death and burial of his father, and on the 15th of May he enlisted for the war, becoming captain of Company G.

CHAPTER III.

He was admitted to the bar in the winter of 1861, in his 21st year, and occupied his father's office, with whom had been associated his son-in-law, D.H. Hazen. At the close of the war he practiced law in Pittsburgh until the spring of 1869, when with his family he moved to Des Moines, Iowa. One reason for his moving west was his failing health, the result of wounds and hardships in the war. Finding that the cold winters of Iowa were not beneficial, he removed, in January of 1871, to the healthiest town in Kansas. Having learned the business of printing in New Lisbon, Ohio, he commenced the publication of the *Head-Light* at Thayer, in 1871, and is now plodding away at his old trade, and drawing $12 a month from Uncle Sam. At the age of 25 years, he was married to Miss Ella Wheeler, of Zanesville, Ohio. Four beautiful daughters blessed this union, and John the boy, is now in his sixth year, all alive and self supporting. The income from a country newspaper not being enough to educate them all in a proper manner, one of them is now cashier in a bank, another has a lucrative position as a stenographer, the two younger ones being yet in school. His mother, now 83 years old, is still alive and makes her home with him. Capt. Ewing's record as a soldier, is found in the service of his company, which is an honorable one, and is given in detail in the records of battles and expeditions, in later chapters of this history.

CHATHAM T. EWING,
CAPTAIN

LIEUTENANT ALFRED SICKMAN.

Alfred Sickman was born June 27, 1840, in a farm house in Mifflin township, Allegheny County, Pa. His mother died when he was about 8 years old, and his father, Samuel Sickman, married his second wife, Miss Ann Ailes, about two years later, and removed to California in Washington County, Pa., in the spring of 1858. Alfred attended the seminary there until the breaking out of the rebellion, when he recruited what was later called the "Pike Run squad," and proceeding with his men to Pittsburgh, became a part of the Plummer Guards, and was elected first lieutenant at the organization.

ALFRED SICKMAN,
FIRST LIEUTENANT

He was unassuming, pleasant and considerate, greatly liked by his men. He met every duty as it presented itself, and bravely and conscientiously served his country to the best of his ability. At the battle of Allegheny Mountain, December 13, 1861, while gallantly leading his men, he was shot and fell dead in front of the enemy, dying as a brave soldier should. His remains were left on the mountain side, and were buried by his comrades April 7, 1862, on their way to Monterey. The remains were subsequently removed, and now lie in the beautiful National Cemetery at Grafton.

LIEUTENANT HOWARD MORTON.

Howard Morton was born in Somerset County, Pa., Jan. 2nd 1842. At the age of six years his parents removed to Pittsburgh. His father came from Hampshire County, Mass., and was a descendant of George Morton, the financial agent of the Pilgrims in London. George Morton's son, Nathanial, came over in the "Ann" two years after the "Mayflower", as a member of Governor Bradford's family. Mrs. Bradford was the sister of George Morton. Nathanial kept the records of the colony for over forty years. Three of Major Morton's ancestors, on his father's side, were soldiers. Randall Morton, the father of the subject of this sketch, was a well known educator, and prior to the war was principal of the Fourth ward schools in Allegheny, and now resides with his wife in the Twenty second ward, Pittsburgh, in the enjoyment of his old age. The mother of Major Morton was Miss Crissia Wilson, of Washington, Pa., daughter of William Wilson, and Sarah Clark, who was a daughter Noah Clark, a revolutionary soldier. From the above it will be seen that the major came honestly by his military spirit.

In 1861, the subject of the sketch enlisted in the Plummer Guards, was promoted to corporal and afterward to sergeant, and at the battle of Allegheny Mountain, was promoted to first lieutenant. At Rocky Gap, he was in command, the captain having been wounded in another part of the field. At Droop Mountain, he advanced the guns up the mountain side under the terrific fire of the enemies' batteries on the summit. On the Salem Raid, when penned up by raging waters, by attaching a long rope to the collars of the two lead horses of each gun, carrying it across, and putting a hundred or more men to it, and literally dragging horses and guns

HOWARD MORTON,
FIRST LIEUTENANT

CHAPTER III.

into the raging torrents and through to terra firma, he saved the battery. His defense of Beverly, West Va., in July, 1863, shows his daring and skill. At New Market, Va., Lieut. Morton, in the absence of the captain, commanded the battery, and with such good effect as to call forth letters of praise from Capt. DuPont, chief of artillery, Department of West Va., and from Maj. Gen. Julius Stahel, commanding cavalry.

At the close of his term of service, he was commissioned Major of the 5th Pa. Artillery, and at Salem, Va., commanded the regiment in an engagement with Mosby, in which he out-generaled the famous rebel leader. He was mustered out at the close of the war, and from that time to the present, has been engaged in commercial pursuits, with good success from a financial standpoint. About thirteen years ago be married Miss Mary Bell Reneker, from Cynthiana, Ky., and the union has been blessed with two lovely children, his home being in the East End, Pittsburgh. During the railroad riots at Pittsburgh in 1877, Major Morton went single handed into the camp of the rioters and persuaded them to surrender to him the artillery which they had taken from Breck's battery, and haul it down to the City Hall and deliver it over to the authorities. Gov. Hartranft complimented the Major for his action, and claimed it was the most creditable piece of work that took place during the riots.

LIEUTENANT JACOB G. HUGGINS.

J.G. Huggins, California, Washington County, Pa., was one of the squad that went from that section, and became members of the "Plummer Guards." He was born in East Pike Run township, October 21, 1831, where he lived and worked until he was 20 years of age, after which he worked at boat building until the call for volunteers was made. He received a common school education. When the company was organized for muster, he was commissioned second lieutenant, which position he held until he resigned in March, 1862, at Cheat Mountain summit. Upon his return home he again resumed work at his trade as ship carpenter. He was married February 7, 1863, to Miss Sarah Craft, to whom three children have been born, two sons and one daughter, the latter dying when about two years old. His wife died May 17, 1876.

JACOB G. HUGGINS,
SECOND LIEUTENANT

LIEUTENANT S. J. SHEARER.

Samuel J. Shearer was born in Cumberland County, Pa., in 1836. He was a farmer's son, and up to the age of eighteen, was engaged in the usual farm duties, receiving such education as could be had in the country schools, after which he left his home and found employment with the government, taking part in an expedition fitted out to convey military stores to the troops in Utah. This was attended with great danger, as the wagon trains were at all times beset by hostile Indians. From the Utah expedition, Shearer drifted to Pittsburgh, where he was variously engaged until the breaking out of the war, when he enlisted in Company G. He served as sergeant until the spring of 1862, when he was promoted to second lieutenant, which position he held with credit until the muster out of the company.

Shearer was one of the most nervy men in the regiment and was utterly devoid of fear. He was a magnificent horseman, and the members of the company and regiment, will remember his big black horse which few men beside himself would dare to mount. He was an excellent companion, always cheerful, taking things as they came, without complaint, and was in every respect a thoroughly manly man. In 1867, he married Miss Caroline Zeigler, of Harmony, Butler County, Pa., and lived one year afterward at New Castle, Pa. From there he removed to New Springfield, O., where he has lived for over twenty years, rearing a family of one boy and four girls. He has been engaged in the dry goods and grocery business and farming, to a considerable extent, and with such success as to rank as a successful man in business.

SAMUEL J. SHEARER,
SECOND LIEUTENANT

SERGEANT S. J. OSBORNE.

S.J. Osborne, a native of Westmoreland County, Pa., was born in the year 1837, and lived on a farm until his seventeenth year, when he went to Pittsburgh, where he was engaged until the breaking out of the war, when he enlisted in the company known as the "Plummer Guards." With them he went into service in Western

S.J. OSBORNE

CHAPTER III.

Virginia. He was appointed corporal and afterwards promoted to sergeant, and chief of the first piece, which position he held during the term of service. He was discharged with the company at Wheeling, since which time he has been living in Pittsburgh, and is at present engaged in mechanical draughting in that city.

CORPORAL A. G. OSBORNE.

A.G. Osborne was born in Westmoreland County, Pa., in the year 1833, removing to Pittsburgh to learn the tinsmith trade. On the breaking out of the civil war he enlisted in the company known as the "Jackson Independent Blues," and with them entered the three months service, the company being assigned to the 12th Pennsylvania Regiment, in which he served during his term of enlistment. After his discharge he went to Western Virginia and enlisted in Company G, in which his brother was serving, and when the company was transferred to the artillery service, was appointed corporal and gunner of first piece, in which position he served until the end of the company's service. He was married to Miss Kate Hurst, of Buckhannon, West Va., in 1863, to which place he removed after his discharge, and carried on the tin business, afterwards removing to Emporia, Kansas, where he was engaged in business for several years, from which place he removed to Texas, and is at present living in Dallas, in that state.

A.G OSBORNE

SERGEANT H. A. EVANS.

Henry A. Evans was born in Pittsburgh, Pa., June 30, 1838. His father was born in Huntington and his mother in Allegheny County, Pa. His grandfather Evans, one of the pioneers of the west, built a rolling mill at Connellsville, Pa., very early in the history of that part of the country. His grandfather Henry Burns, was the first white child born west of the Allegheny mountains, whose parents were killed by the Indians when he was an infant, and he was found in the woods by a Mr. Jones, who reared him as his son. Mr. Evans received

HENRY A. EVANS

his education in the public and private schools of Pittsburgh. He chose the profession of medicine, but after studying for a year or more, his health failed and he was obliged to give it up, when he entered a rolling mill and learned to be a heater. He was thus employed when the call to arms came. In a company with a few others he was soon recruiting, and after helping to organize two companies that went into Pennsylvania service, he helped to raise a third, the Plummer Guards, of which he became a member.

Mr. Evans was appointed a non-commissioned officer of his company, and was with it in all the battles in which it engaged, except Droop Mountain and the Salem Raid. At that time he was in the hospital, having been wounded at the battle of Rocky Gap, by a piece of shell striking him on the right side of his head. After being in the hospital three months, he returned to his company, and took part in the battles of New Market and Piedmont, having his hat shot off at the latter and his horse shot in eleven places. While on furlough Nov. 22, 1863, he was married to Miss Sarah Robinson Laing, and they have had seven children, three boys and four girls. On his return to Pittsburgh, at the expiration of his term, he was offered a situation as a heater by Sheed Clark & Co. of Youngstown, O., which he accepted, where he has lived since, except for three years. Mr. Evans was a member of the Board of Education for the city for seven years. Early in his youth he became a member of the M. E. church, and is now an official member of Henrietta M. E. church, Youngstown. He is a member of the Masonic fraternity, belonging to Western Star Lodge No. 21, Youngstown Chapter No. 93, and St. John's commandery No. 20 K. T. He is also a member of Tod Post No. 29, G. A. R. of Ohio.

CORPORAL R. E. EVANS.

Rufus E. Evans was born on the banks of the Cheat river, Virginia, on the fifth day of March, 1841. His father at that time was operating a rolling mill there. At the time the war began, Rufus was learning the trade of nail making in Pittsburgh, but on the call for troops by President Lincoln, he immediately resigned his position, enlisting with the first troops that left for Harrisburg, for three months. While absent, his brother Henry was assisting to raise a company for three years, and Rufus returned and became a member of Company G. He took part in all the engagements his company was in, and remained with it until mustered out. On his return

RUFUS E. EVANS

CHAPTER III.

home to Pittsburgh, he resumed the business which he relinquished to enter the service of his country, and afterwards moved to New Castle, Pa. August 29, 1864, he was united in marriage to Miss Elizabeth Woods, of Washington County, Pa., and has three sons.

JOHN H. VEACH

A. BOYD ROOK

ADAM BROWN

JOSEPH FORSYTHE

JOHN SIEBERT

HISTORY OF THE FIFTH WEST VIRGINIA CAVALRY

COMPANY H.

Company H was recruited at Ironton, Lawrence County, Ohio, by Capt. F.P. McNally, Lieuts. H.C. Flesher and John Combs, June 10, 1861. The company left Ironton for Wheeling on the 23d, on board the steamer Victor No. 3, where they arrived on the 25th, and went into camp at Camp Carlisle. They remained there about thirty days, during which time they were mustered into the service by Capt. Craig. They were then sent to Benwood, four miles below Wheeling, where they did guard duty for a while, and then proceeded by rail to Webster, thence marched to Beverly, where they were assigned as Company H.

The following is the muster out roll, showing list of members and their record. The company was mustered into the U.S. service June 28, 1861, and mustered out June 29, 1864. All the members not otherwise marked, were mustered out with the company. The recruits and veterans were transferred to the Sixth W.Va. Cavalry, when the company was mustered out.

NAMES	RANK	RECORD OF SERVICE
F. Patrick McNally	Capt.	Promoted Major, March 24, 1863
Jos. M. Bushfield	Capt.	Promoted 1st Lt. from Co. D, June 30, 1862. Promoted to Capt., March 24, 1863.
John Combs	Capt.	Appointed 2d Lt., June 10, 1861. Promoted to 1st Lt. & Adj., June 12, 1862. Promoted to Capt., May 1, 1864.
Henry C. Flesher	1st Lt.	Promoted to Capt., Co. F, May 20, 1862
Louis P. Salterbach	1st Lt.	Promoted to 1st Lt. from Co. E, March 24, 1863. Transferred to Co. C, May 1, 1864.
Chas. H. Day	2d Lt.	Promoted 2d Lt. from Co. E, June 13, 1862. Promoted and transferred to Co. I, Sept. 19, 1862.
John C. French	2d Lt.	Promoted 2d Lt. from Co. E, Sept. 9, 1862. Transferred to Co. E, Dec. 3, 1862.

CHAPTER III.

Andrew P. Russell	2d Lt.	Promoted from Private to Sgt., July 13, 1861. Promoted to 2d Lt., Dec. 3, 1862.
Isaac C. Craft	1st Sgt.	
Thos. M. Desilvery	Sergt.	
Michael B. Keeny	Sergt.	Wounded at Bull Run and taken prisoner
Noah Cumpston	Sergt.	
Thos. R. Williams	Sergt.	Wounded at Droop Mountain
Thos. Davis	Corp.	Wounded at Bull Run
John C. McClane	Corp.	
Joshua Kite	Corp.	Wounded at Bull Run
Jas. K. Keeny	Corp.	
Wm. Shirley	Corp.	See Scout article
Geo. Kerns	Corp.	
Jas. B. Parker	Corp.	
Geo. Walters	Corp.	Drowned while bathing in Potomac near Chain Bridge, Sept. 15, 1862.
Reynolds A. Ward	Corp.	Died Nov. 3, 1862
Moses G. Markins	Corp.	Died Sept. 29, 1863, at Beverly, W.Va., from wounds received from bushwhackers Cheat River scout. See article on scouts.
Zachariah Hall	Corp.	Wounded Bull Run. Died at Grafton, April 18, 1864.
Cornelius Collier	Corp.	Re-enlisted as a veteran, Jan. 5, 1864
Chas. Brice	Wag.	
Alfred Anderson	Private	Captured Jan. 1, 1864, near Bunker Hill, Va. Died at Andersonville.
Wm. Argabright	Private	Leg broken
Geo. W. Anderson	Private	Re-enlisted as veteran, Jan. 5, 1864
David Benson	Private	
Reed J. Blackwell	Private	
Chas. Blowers	Private	Insane. Sent home, Sept. 30, 1862, and discharged.

Rowland Brammer	Private	Severely wounded in face at Bull Run, Aug. 29, 1862. Eyesight injured and unfit for duty. Discharged.
John Burksell	Private	Captured on Salem Raid and escaped, Dec. 1863
Wm. Baute	Private	
Jas. M. Bruce	Private	Re-enlisted as veteran, Jan. 5, 1864
Jno. Branimer	Private	Re-enlisted as veteran, Jan. 5, 1864
Martin S. Bazill	Private	Re-enlisted as veteran, Jan. 5, 1864
Jonathan Berry	Private	Killed June 8, 1862, at Cross Keys
Henry Burksell	Private	Killed at Bull Run, Aug. 29, 1862
John Coile	Private	Discharged Nov. 20, 1862
John D. Coates	Private	Deserted June 12, 1862
Chas. Clepner	Private	Discharged Jan. 17, 1863, foot amputated
Martin Cristal	Private	
Terrence Connelly	Private	
Wm. H. Collier	Private	
Louis Cassan	Private	Re-enlisted as veteran, Jan. 5, 1864
Albert F. Call	Private	
John Daugherty	Private	
Wm. Daugherty	Private	
Daniel Dalton	Private	
Absalom S. Douth	Private	
John Dyer	Private	
John Dwyer	Private	Re-enlisted as veteran, Jan. 5, 1864
Martin Elswicke	Private	
Lewis Fisher	Private	
Edmond Freiley	Private	Re-enlisted as veteran, Jan. 5, 1864
Abraham Gaunt	Private	Captured Dec. 19, 1863, on Salem Raid. Died at Andersonville.
John Hope	Private	Wounded Nov. 6, 1863, at Droop Mountain, leg amputated.
Wm. Hope	Private	
Jos. Haney	Private	
Elias Herman	Private	Re-enlisted as veteran, Jan. 5, 1864
Jas. E. Hughes	Private	Re-enlisted as veteran, Jan. 5, 1864
G.W. Hackworth	Private	Re-enlisted as veteran, Jan. 5, 1864

CHAPTER III.

David T. Johnson	Private	
Allen Justice	Private	Died at Elkwater, Dec. 18, 1864
John D. Kidney	Private	Captured
Francis Kirkpatrick	Private	Wounded at Bull Run
Michael Kevill	Private	Killed at Bull Run, Aug. 29, 1862
Geo. Kramer	Private	Killed at Bull Run, Aug. 29, 1862
Saml. Lyons	Private	
Michael Lynch	Private	Re-enlisted as veteran, Jan. 5, 1864
Wm. Morgan	Private	
Jacob D. Mathiott	Private	
Wm. Martin	Private	Re-enlisted as veteran, Jan. 5, 1864
David Martin	Private	Discharged Oct. 18, 1862, for wounds received at Bull Run
Samuel Moore	Private	Deserted Sept. 18, 1862
Theodore Martin	Private	Killed at Bull Run, Aug. 29, 1862
Patrick McNichols	Private	
Michael McCauley	Private	
Daniel McKnight	Private	
H. McGarvey	Private	Re-enlisted as veteran, Jan. 28, 1864
Robt. McGinley	Private	Discharged Nov. 29, 1861, on account of wounds received
Robt. McKnight	Private	Transferred to Veteran Reserve Corps, Dec. 1, 1863
Martin McNamara	Private	Died June 15, 1862
John North	Private	
Abr. Pancake	Private	Re-enlisted as veteran, Jan. 5, 1864
Jno. Robinson	Private	Confined at hard labor at Ft. Del., Oct. 15, 1863, for term of service
Richard Robinson	Private	
John Ross	Private	Discharged for disability, Nov. 10, 1861
Jonathan Roberts	Private	Died May 9, 1862, at Franklin, Va.
Timothy Sharer	Private	Killed by bushwhackers, Bunker Hill, Va. See Scout article.
Geo. W. Sutton	Private	
Albert C. Slater	Private	Wounded at Bull Run. Re-enlisted as veteran, Jan. 5, 1864.
Henry Stratton	Private	Discharged Nov. 17, 1862
Chas. Schmutz	Private	Killed at Bull Run, Aug. 29, 1862

Fritz Strickel	Private	Killed at Bull Run, Aug. 29, 1862
Jas. H. Thacker	Private	
John Tasker	Private	
Geo. W. Thacker	Private	Wounded at Bull Run. Re-enlisted as veteran, Jan. 5, 1864.
Grandville Webb	Private	
Aden Webb	Private	Wounded Rocky Gap and Droop Mountain
Jno. W. Willis	Private	Re-enlisted as veteran, Jan. 5, 1864
James Wilson	Private	Re-enlisted as veteran, Jan. 5, 1864
C.H. Walbert	Private	Discharged Apr. 15, 1863, on account of wounds received at Bull Run.

CAPTAIN JOHN COMBS.

John Combs was born in Burlington, Lawrence County, Ohio, April 1, 1832. He settled in Ironton in 1854, and engaged in the book and stationary business. He enlisted in Company H, and was active in organizing the company, becoming second lieutenant. He was appointed adjutant of the regiment June 9, 1862, and was promoted captain of Company H, May 1, 1864, serving until the end of his term of enlistment. After his muster out, he settled in Ironton, Ohio, where he edited the Ironton *Journal* then changing his politics, he edited the Ironton *Democrat*, then the *Iron Era*. He afterwards went to Chicago, Ill., and engaged in the real estate business, where he lost about all his savings. He returned to Ohio, and is now a reporter on the Columbus "Post."

LIEUTENANT A. P. RUSSELL.

A. P. Russell was born at Russell's Place, Lawrence County, Ohio, December 23, 1841. He worked at farming and tanning until 19 years of age; enlisted as a drummer in the company June, 1861, and was promoted to orderly sergeant in July, 1861. He served as such until in December, 1862, when he was promoted to second lieutenant, and served his term with that rank. He held a first lieutenant's commission, but was never mustered as such. After his retirement from the army, he engaged in the milling business, and has followed that occupation nearly ever since, residing at Russell's Place.

CHAPTER III.

COMPANY I.

This company was organized in Greenfield (now Coal Center) and California, Washington County, Pa., soon after the firing on Fort Sumter. The first Sunday after the news came that Sumter had been attacked, was one of intense excitement. Early in the morning the martial band was brought out, and ere long a crowd was gathered behind it and formed into a procession, which paraded through the two towns. A halt was called on the bank of the Monongahela river in Greenfield, and speeches were made of the most inflammatory character; and the nucleus of a military organization was formed. Other meetings were held, and on April 27, 1861, a company was fully enlisted, and it was named the "McKennan Infantry," in honor of Hon. William McKennan, of Washington, Pa. Notice was sent at once to the Governor of Pennsylvania, that the company had been enlisted and was at his call for duty, and the answer came that our state could not receive us, the quota of three months men not only being filled, but a large number of enlistments ahead. Application was made again and again for our acceptance, but all failed. At last the word came that loyal Virginia was stretching forth her hands, asking the loyal sons of Pennsylvania to come to her help, and we decided to enter the service of that state. The order came for the company to report at Wheeling on July 10. On the ninth the company left for the front, going in wagons to Washington, Pa., where, we stayed over night, and the next day went to Wheeling on the B.&O. railroad, arriving there at 10 a.m., repairing at once to Camp Carlisle. Here we were sworn into the United States service by Major Oakes, the company being officered as follows: Captain, L. E. Smith; first lieutenant, A.A. Devore; second lieutenant, N.W. Truxal.

The company remained in Camp Carlisle until July 22d, when we left Wheeling on the B.&O. railroad, arriving at Grafton on the morning of the 23d, thence to Webster, pitching our tents on the side of the hill, our first camp in the tented field. Here we met a large number of the three months volunteers returning from their victorious campaigns in the front, who heartily cheered us as the "boatmen," because of our coming from the Monongahela river, and many of the men having at one time and another followed that occupation. The regiment often went by that name in the mountains; and partly on that account, early gained the reputation of being a hardy and sturdy force of men. We resumed our march on the 25th, and arrived at Beverly on the afternoon of the 27th, where we joined the other companies of our regiment, and were assigned as Company I.

The following is the muster out roll, showing the list of members and them record. The company was mustered into the U. S. service July 10, 1861, and was mustered out July 28, 1864. All the members not otherwise marked, were mustered out with the company. The recruits and veterans were transferred to the Sixth W. Va. cavalry, when the company was mustered out.

NAMES	RANK	RECORD OF SERVICE
Lewis E. Smith	Capt.	Resigned Nov. 23, 1862. Struck by piece of shell at Cross Keys. Captured Fauquier County, Va., Aug. 1862, taken to Libby prison where his health was broken down.
Norval W. Truxal	Capt.	Promoted from 1st Lt. to Capt., Dec. 27, 1862
A.A. Devore	1st Lt.	Resigned Oct. 10, 1861
D.F. Williamson	1st Lt.	Transferred from Co. K. Resigned.
Jas. K. Billingsley	1st Lt.	Promoted from 2d Lt. Promoted to Capt., Co. C, April 15, 1863. Wounded in ankle at Cross Keys.
Charles H. Day	1st Lt.	Transferred from Co. H
Jas. B. Montgomery	2d Lt.	Promoted from Sergt. to 2d Lt., Dec. 25, 1862
O.M.J. Hutchison	1st Sgt.	Promoted from Corporal to 1st Sgt., May 25, 1863.
Jacob Kent	Sergt.	
Jacob Qualk	Sergt.	Discharged for disability, Dec. 15, 1861
Jacob Hornbake	Sergt.	Wounded in arm at 2d Bull Run
Alexander Latta	Sergt.	
Geo. Underwood	Sergt.	Captured at West Union. Paroled.
John Lopp	Corp.	Discharged for disability, Jan. 22, 1863
Samuel Kent	Corp.	Wounded at 2d Bull Run. Captured at West Union.
John H. Weaver	Corp.	
Jas. T. Bigelow	Corp.	
Robt. Mayhorn	Corp.	Captured at West Union
Elijah Lichteberger	Corp.	

CHAPTER III.

Theophilus Dwyer	Corp.	Wounded at Rocky Gap, Aug. 26, 1863, and captured
Stephen H. Ward	Corp.	
William Garton	Corp.	Captured on Salem Raid, Dec. 1863. Died in Andersonville prison.
Abra'm Leadbeater	Corp.	Discharged for disability, Oct. 21, 1861
Sam'l J. Amalong	Corp.	Discharged for disability, Feb. 18, 1862
James R. Dowler	Teamster	
Jesse Ammon	Private	Captured on Salem Raid, Dec. 1863
John F. Ailes	Private	Killed by the falling of a tree, Nov. 27, 1861
George D. Boyd	Private	
James W. Blair	Private	
Thomas Bee	Private	
W.H. Billingsley	Private	Wounded at Rocky Gap, Aug. 26, 1863. Captured. Died at Savannah.
Jacob D. Billingsley	Private	Re-enlisted as veteran, Jan. 5, 1864
William Bunting	Private	Re-enlisted as veteran, Jan. 5, 1864
Nathaniel Baldwin	Private	Transferred to Invalid Corps, Nov. 1863
Henry Barnhart	Private	Wounded at Beverly, April 24, 1863. Died from wounds.
S.J. Benedict	Private	Deserted
Augustus Clark	Private	Captured at Rocky Gap, Aug. 26, 1863
Joseph W. Chester	Private	
Silas J. Clendaniel	Private	
John H. Connard	Private	
Marion Crumrine	Private	Re-enlisted as veteran, Jan. 5, 1864
David O. Carpenter	Private	Re-enlisted as veteran, Jan. 5, 1864
John N. Crow	Private	Re-enlisted as veteran, Jan. 5, 1864
Geo. W. Clendaniel	Private	Recruit July 5, 1863. Transferred to Co. G, July 19, 1864.

Jehu Dehaven	Private	
Michael Dowling	Private	
Henry E. Devers	Private	
John C. Evans	Private	Discharged for disability, Jan. 1, 1863
Louis M. Freeman	Private	Died of typhoid fever, Feb. 14, 1862
G.H. Fittsimmons	Private	
William Geho	Private	Captured West Union
James H. Gordon	Private	Discharged for disability, May 31, 1862
Dewitt C. Graham	Private	Discharged for disability, Jan. 22, 1863
Andrew J. Harris	Private	Wounded at Bull Run. Discharged Nov. 21, 1862.
Daniel Howe	Private	Killed by guerillas, April 26, 1862
C.S. Hixenbaugh	Private	Captured at Rocky Gap, Aug. 22, 1863
W.H. Hornbake	Private	
Robt. Herron	Private	
Noble Howden	Private	
Samuel J. Howe	Private	
Wm. J. Harris	Private	Captured at West Union
Andrew J. Harris	Private	Recruit, July 5, 1863. Transferred to Co. G, July 19, 1864.
Lemuel B. Howe	Private	Recruit, July 5, 1863. Wounded, captured at Rocky Gap, Aug. 27, 1863. Died at Andersonville.
James Johnson	Private	Discharged for disability, Nov. 15, 1861
William Jobes	Private	Discharged for disability, Sept. 8, 1862
Robert Jobes	Private	Left at Armory Square Hospital, Sept. 25, 1862. There discharged.
Samuel Jobes	Private	
Andrew N. Jobes	Private	
Joseph Jobes	Private	Captured at West Union
Edward Jones	Private	Wounded at Bull Run

CHAPTER III.

Joseph Johnson	Private	
Hugh Lancaster	Private	
Wm. L. Latta	Private	
Allen Moore	Private	
George Marker	Private	Re-enlisted as veteran, Jan. 25, 1864
Jos. E. Mayhorn	Private	Discharged for disability, Jan. 22, 1863
Sansom Miller	Private	Deserted
James P. McCain	Private	Re-enlisted as veteran, Jan. 5, 1864
Jno. C. McLaughlin	Private	Discharged for disability, Oct. 26, 1861
Robt. A. McDonald	Private	
William McCoy	Private	
Robt. A. McCoy	Private	
Isaac S. McCain	Private	Recruit, July 5, 1863. Transferred to Co. G, July 19, 1864.
Albert Norcross	Private	Recruit, July 5, 1863. Transferred to Co. G, July 19, 1864.
William Norcross	Private	
David R. Phillips	Private	
Nathaniel Patterson	Private	Discharged for disability, Jan. 22, 1863
John Peters	Private	Discharged for disability, Sept. 27, 1861
Hiram Qualk	Private	Shot through right lung, May 1864
Frank S. Reader	Private	Captured. See chapter on escape.
Jno. S. Rimmel	Private	
Frederick Rimmel	Private	
Jno. Rimmel, Jr.	Private	Re-enlisted as veteran, Jan. 5, 1864
James Reader	Private	Discharged for disability, Oct. 22, 1861
Chas. W. Sivert	Private	Wounded in leg, amputated, Fauquier White Sulphur Springs, Aug. 26, 1862. Discharged Jan. 9, 1863.

Augustus Shaffer	Private	Discharged for disability, Aug. 8, 1862
Cuthbert Soulsby	Private	Killed at Grafton, July 7, 1863
Wm. Showalters	Private	Deserted
Henry F. Truxal	Private	Recruit, Nov. 15, 1862. Died of typhoid fever at Beverly, Dec. 31, 1862
John W. Truxal	Private	Recruit, Nov. 15, 1862. Transferred to Co. G, July 19, 1864.
Philip Thomas	Private	Recruit, Nov. 2, 1861. Transferred to Co. G, July 19, 1864.
Elihu Underwood	Private	Re-enlisted as veteran, Jan. 5, 1864
Wm. H. Worrel	Private	Re-enlisted as veteran, Jan. 5, 1864
Hiram A. Wells	Private	Re-enlisted as veteran, Jan. 5, 1864
John R. Williams	Private	
Alfred D. Wolf	Private	
Elliott F. Wise	Private	
Abra'm V. Weaver	Private	
Wm. R. Wilkins	Private	
Thos. J. Walker	Private	Wounded in leg at Bull Pasture, while out with foraging party
Thomas Young	Private	
Robert Young	Private	
Nathaniel Young	Private	Transferred to Ewing's battery, Nov. 13, 1861.

CAPTAIN LEWIS E. SMITH.

Lewis E. Smith, a prominent business man of Greenfield, was largely instrumental in enlisting the company, and was naturally looked upon as the proper person to command it. He was a Christian gentleman, observing not only the common moral duties that men owe to one another, but he as well aimed to gain that control of his mind and faculties, by which he could wield a power for good, in whatever position in life he might be placed. He was a grave, earnest man, and was respected by all that knew him. The captain served his country faithfully until failing health compelled him to resign his commission.

CHAPTER III.

LIEUTENANT NORVAL W. TRUXAL.

Dr. N.W. Truxal, of Greenfield, was chosen second lieutenant, the choice being heartily seconded by every member of the company. The Doctor was the very embodiment of good nature and fun, a man of marked ability, and had been for some time editor of the *Monongahela Valley Spirit*, of California, Pa., which ably supported the cause of the Union. He was for years an ardent Democrat, but abandoned that party directly after the Charleston and Baltimore conventions; and when the gathering storm began to darken the Southern sky, his stirring appeals to the people of his section to arm themselves for the impending danger, had the effect of sending into the field quite a number of three months volunteers. An address made by him December 27, 1860, will show the character of the man. He said: "The crisis is rapidly approaching. The people of the North are becoming more and more united in the determination to maintain the Union by vindicating the constitution and the laws. A few arch traitors are occasionally waked up in the north, but they deserve less countenance than the tories of the revolution. The moral leprosy which has infected with its virus every vein of our civil system, and which has so frequently threatened the dissolution of the government, is hurrying us on to a fearful crisis, and when the critical hour comes, if it is found that all the vitals of our body politic are corrupted and depraved beyond the power of recuperating, our once glorious Union is gone forever, and the stupendous galaxy of stars that have elicited the admiration of the world, will reel like drunken men, demoralized, distracted and debauched. But secession must not be tolerated. Revolution must be quelled by the strong arm of the government. Better, far better that a million of brave men perish in defence of the Union, than one state should be suffered to secede. No! No! 'The Union must and shall be preserved,' is the emphatic language of our platform. Millions of brave freemen, who inherit the blood and patriotism of their revolutionary sires, will rush to the field to sustain the Union."

CAPTAIN J. K. BILLINGSLEY.

James K. Billingsley was born January 23, 1836, in Granville, East Pike Run township, Washington County, Pa., and was educated at the California Seminary. He was a public school teacher for eight years. He enlisted as private soldier, was afterward promoted to first sergeant, then second lieutenant, to first lieutenant, and to captain March 5, 1863, and assigned to Company C. He was wounded at Cross Keys, but served until the regiment was mustered out. He was appointed U. S. storekeeper November, 1868, and served until 1875; was elected to the Penna. House of Representatives for the sessions of 1875-6-7-8 and 1881-7-9. Was Justice of the Peace in California from April 6, 1883 to August 16, 1883 and resigned; was appointed Postoffice Inspector

August, 1883, and served to July 1, 1885; was re-appointed September 3, 1889, and resigned January 31, 1890. He is now a resident of California, Pa.

LIEUTENANT J. B. MONTGOMERY.

James B. Montgomery was born near Brownsville, Fayette County, Pa., October 10, 1834. He learned the trade of millwright, which he followed for a while, and afterward engaged in merchandizing in 1860, and was appointed postmaster of Pike Run P.O. He was married June 7, 1858, to Miss Mary C. Reeves, daughter of Van Buren and Margaret Reeves. When the McKennan Infantry was organized, Mr. Montgomery became one of the members of the company, as a private. After the organization of the regiment, he acted Q.M. sergeant for about a year, and at his own request was relieved, that he might return to his company, as fifth sergeant. He was never off duty, while in the service, and was in all the engagements of his regiment, and always in the front. In the second battle of Bull Run, he acted as orderly sergeant, and was with the company in the terrific fire, when the enemy attacked them from the railroad cut. Fortunately for the company, it lay so close to the cut, that the fire of the enemy went over their heads, and the men thus escaped the heavy loss that must otherwise have occurred, and that befell some of the other companies. In the second day's battle he planted our flag on the edge of the cut in the road, and there it remained in the hot fire that followed. He did good service in this battle, which led to his appointment as second lieutenant of the company, a promotion he richly deserved. When the regiment

JAMES B. MONTGOMERY,
SECOND LIEUTENANT

was mounted, he gave many instances of his gallantry, on scouts and in battle, holding a specially important place on the Salem raid, being in the command of his company, in the advanced and most perilous positions. He was ordered to clear the ford at one place, and with his gallant company he performed the duty required, to the entire satisfaction of the general, but was left behind, and was not able to rejoin the brigade until Greenbrier river was reached. When the heroic scout, M.G. Markins, was shot at the Gum road, Lieut. Montgomery and his men went to rescue him from the enemy, and was the first company to reach the place. After the battle of Cloyd Mountain, Lieut. Montgomery was among the number that joined General Hunter at Staunton, and went with his army to the fight at Lynchburg. He had charge of the remnant of

CHAPTER III.

the regiment, acquitting himself with great credit. In a hard fight in front of Lynchburg, our forces lost several pieces of artillery, and General Averell ordered Lieut. Montgomery and his little command to charge the captors and retake the pieces. They did so and recovered all of the pieces but one. Upon his retirement from the army, the lieutenant again engaged in merchandizing, but lost all in the panic of 1873. Since then he has been fireman and engineer in the Atlas Paint and Color Works, Pittsburgh. Lieut. Montgomery was a brave soldier and a good officer, is a useful and honored citizen, and enjoys the respect and confidence of all the men of the old command, and is eminently worthy of both.

FRANK SMITH READER.

The subject of this sketch was born in Greenfield, November 17, 1842. His father, Frances Reader, was born in Warwickshire, England, in 1798, and with his parents, removed to Washington County, Pa., in 1802; his mother, Ellen Smith Reader, was the daughter of a farmer in Union township, same county, and was of Scotch descent. He worked at farming and carpentering, and acquired at the schools at his home and elsewhere, an academic education. He was one of the first to enlist in his company, and served over his full term of three years. He took part in all the campaigns that his company was in except Allegheny Mountain, Salem Raid and Cloyd Mountain and participated in Averell's advance on Lee's left flank in July, 1863, and New Market and Piedmont campaigns in May and June, 1864, that the company was not in. While at Woodville, Va., August, 1862, he was externally poisoned by some vines, and afterwards suffered severely from diarrhoea, his only sickness while in the service, from which he did not recover until the return to West Virginia in October, but kept with his company and on full duty. On July 1, 1863, he was detailed by special orders for duty at Gen. Averell's headquarters; in May, 1864, for duty at Gen. Sigel's headquarters, and afterward at Gen. David Hunter's, serving as orderly in the campaigns. After the victory at Piedmont, June, 1864, he was one of the first Union soldiers to enter Staunton, and there had charge of paroling 500 wounded Confederates. He was captured on this expedition, and made his escape, of which see account in a later chapter of this book, and was discharged of date with his company, so broken in health that further service was impossible. He taught school that winter, pursued a course of bookkeeping in Iron City College the next spring, and in July, 1865, accepted a position in the Internal Revenue service, 24th collection district of Pennsylvania, where he served at different periods for over 10 years, and was Chief Deputy Collector nearly 8 years.

December 24, 1867, he was united in marriage to Miss Mame F. Darling, of New Brighton, Pa., to whom two sons have been born, Frank E., and Willard S.

Reader. He attended Mount Union College, Ohio, in 1867; and in the spring of 1868, entered the North Missouri Conference of the M. E. Church, as preacher in charge of a circuit of nine appointments, but his voice so completely failed, that he was compelled to retire after one year's service. May 22, 1874, with Major David Critchlow, 100th Pennsylvania Regiment, he established the *Beaver Valley News*, at New Brighton, Pa.; on January 1, 1877, he bought the Major's interest in the paper, and on February 4, 1883, began the publication of the *Daily News*, in which business he has continued ever since. He was secretary of the Republican county committee for several years; while in that office prepared and presented to the legislature the first law enacted in the state for the government of Republican primary elections; was alternate to the Chicago convention that nominated Blaine in 1884; served in council and school board of his borough, and has held other positions of trust at the hands of his neighbors. He has been a member of the M. E. Church for 25 years, being an active worker in the church for over 23 years of the time, and for over 15 years has been superintendent of the Sunday school in New Brighton, now comprising more than 550 members. It is a work in which he takes special delight, and gives to it his best energies, ability and time.

COMPANY K.

This company was organized in large part, at Parkersburg, W. Va., as Company A of the Home Guards, by Dr. John W. Moss and J.P. Kiger, about the first of April, 1861. The object of the organization at that time, was to protect the city, and to take possession of 400 flint lock muskets and two pieces of artillery, which were sent to Parkersburg at the time of the John Brown insurrection, and were stowed in the jail building. The sheriff and many of the city officials sympathized with the seceding states, and were making boxes to ship these arms to Richmond, when about sixty men of this company quietly assembled at the city hall, one afternoon about the 15th of April and marched to the jail, headed by John Jackson, and demanded the arms. The demand was refused, when the company with axes and crowbars broke into the jail, and took the arms out, and put them in the city hall, where they were guarded day and night for two weeks, when the Fourteenth Ohio, three months men, came in and took possession of them, which were the first troops that entered Parkersburg, coming by boat from Marietta, O. The company knew that this regiment was coming, and intended to be at the landing to receive them, but were a little late getting started from camp, so that when they were within three squares of the wharf, they heard the boat coming. Capt. Kiger then started his company on the double quick, and they were not seen by the troops on the boat, until they

CHAPTER III.

turned a corner at the wharf. Before coming into view, the color bearer of the company fell, hurting himself somewhat, and their handsome silk flag, a present from the loyal ladies of Parkersburg, fell out of ranks and out of sight. The soldiers of the boat seeing the troops approaching the river so rapidly, and not being able to distinguish who they were, supposed it to be an attack by the enemy, and the greatest confusion followed. The long roll was beaten on the boat, officers gave sharp and quick commands, and ramrods were rattling as the men loaded their guns. Captain Kiger took in the situation at a glance, halted his company, who waved their hats, and cheered the approach of the boat, and quiet was soon restored.

Previous to this little episode, when the company had the arms safely deposited in the city hall, they marched to the court house, where Jackson mounted a store box and began to make a speech to the company. By that time a large crowd of Southern sympathizers had collected, and General Moorehead, who was at the time commander or the militia of Virginia, rushed up to Jackson and demanded the return of the arms that had been taken. But few words passed when Jackson struck the general over the head with his cane, when stones and brickbats were hurled among the company from every side. The affray lasted about ten minutes, during which knives, stones and fists were freely used. Many were badly hurt, but the company came off victorious, and Jackson finished his speech.

Soon after the street fight, a call was made for three months volunteers, and all of the company, numbering sixty-eight, enlisted, except four, one of whom was too old, and the other three were so badly hurt that they could not go, but the three enlisted afterwards in the three years service. The number was increased to eighty men, under command of Captain John Kiger, and went into camp at Wheeling. The quota not being full, the mustering officer refused to muster them into the service. About that time Andrew Grubb was raising a company for an Ohio regiment, in Bridgeport, O., and he agreed to fill out the quota, supplying twenty men for that purpose, and he was elected first lieutenant of the company, and the company was mustered into the service July 21, 1861, for three years. At once they repaired to Beverly, where they became Company K of the regiment.

The following is the muster out roll, showing list of members and their record. The company was mustered into the U. S. service July 21, 1861, and was mustered out August 20, 1864. All the members not otherwise marked, were mustered out with the company. The recruits and veterans were transferred to the Sixth W. Va. Cavalry, when the company was mustered out.

HISTORY OF THE FIFTH WEST VIRGINIA CAVALRY

NAMES	RANK	RECORD OF SERVICE
John P. Kiger	Capt.	Resigned Jan. 8, 1862
Andrew Grubb	Capt.	Promoted to Captain, Feb. 19, 1862
Arthur J. Weaver	1st. Lt.	Promoted to 1st Lt., Feb. 19, 1862. Killed in action at Droop Mt., Nov. 6, 1863.
David A. Jennings	2d. Lt.	Resigned, Jan. 22, 1863
Daniel K. Shields	2d. Lt.	Promoted from Sergeant, Co. B
D.F. Williamson	2d. Lt.	Promoted Adjutant
George A. Quimby	Sergt.	Wounded in neck at Cross Keys and in side at Kelly's Ford
Wm. R. Stewart	Sergt.	Wounded at Bull Run
Geo. H. Eddleman	Sergt.	Wounded Cross Keys. Re-enlisted as veteran, Jan. 5, 1864.
Edward Wells	Sergt.	Re-enlisted as veteran, Jan. 5, 1864
Daniel A. Roels	Sergt.	Transferred to V.R.C., Dec. 18, 1863
Robert Gaddis	Corp.	See Scout article
George W. Brown	Corp.	
Julius P. Ford	Corp.	
Thos. Donley	Corp.	
Chas. E. Chaddock	Corp.	Re-enlisted as veteran, Jan. 5, 1864
Chas. Metur	Corp.	Re-enlisted as veteran, Jan. 5, 1864
Marquis D. Kenny	Corp.	Died Nov. 11, 1863, from wounds received at Droop Mountain
Edward C. Maley	Corp.	Died Nov. 9, 1863, from wounds received at Droop Mountain
Geo. W. Golden	Corp.	Died of fever, July 24, 1862, Woodville, Va.
John Merricks	Corp.	Discharged May 4, 1863, on account of wounds received at Bull Run
Lafayette Bawyer	Corp.	Re-enlisted as veteran, Jan. 5, 1864
Eli Roberts	Bugler	
James L. Wilson	Bugler	Recruit. See his sketch.
Dewitt C. Heaton	Bugler	Discharged for disability, Oct. 24, 1862
David Arnett	Wagoner	
Jas. Eddleman	Blacksmith	Re-enlisted as veteran, Jan. 5, 1864
Arthur M. Anderson	Private	Wounded Winchester, Feb. 10, 1864

CHAPTER III.

Geo. D. Ashworth	Private	Re-enlisted as veteran, Jan. 5, 1864
Charles L. Broy	Private	Re-enlisted as veteran, Jan. 5, 1864
Samuel J. Byard	Private	Discharged for disability, April 3, 1862
John C. Cain	Private	Thumb shot off accidentally
James A. Craven	Private	Re-enlisted as veteran, Jan. 5, 1864
Benj. F. Clark	Private	Re-enlisted as veteran, Jan. 5, 1864
G.M. Chichester	Private	Re-enlisted as veteran, Jan. 5, 1864
Patrick Clary	Private	Discharged for disability, May 24, 1862
Thomas Comstock	Private	Deserted July 3, 1862
Patrick Dougherty	Private	
Jeremiah Deems	Private	Captured on Salem Raid. Died in prison.
John W. Dougherty	Private	Re-enlisted as veteran, Jan. 5, 1864
Adam Davis	Private	Deserted April 11, 1864
Robert Dyson	Private	Recruit, Oct. 3, 1862
Chris. Detrick	Private	Killed in action at Waterloo Bridge, Aug. 25, 1862
Franklin Diddler	Private	Discharged for disability, July 24, 1862
William Fowler	Private	Re-enlisted as veteran, Jan. 5, 1864
George W. Grimes	Private	Sentenced by G.C.M. to work out service with loss of pay
James Gardner	Private	Killed in action at Waterloo Bridge, Aug. 25, 1862
Jas. Goggins	Private	Transferred to V.R.C., July 18, 1863
Noah Hoover	Private	
Geo. W. Huggins	Private	
John H. Heaton	Private	Wounded in action at Bull Run, Aug. 29, 1862. Captured and died in prison.
James Hart	Private	Re-enlisted as veteran, Jan. 5, 1864
Jas. F. Huff	Private	Re-enlisted as veteran, Jan. 5, 1864
Henry Hanes	Private	Re-enlisted as veteran, Jan. 5, 1864
Thomas Hunter	Private	Re-enlisted as veteran, Jan. 5, 1864
A. Hollingshead	Private	Wounded in action at Cross Keys. Leg amputated. Discharged Aug. 22, 1862.
James Hanes	Private	Discharged for disability, Dec. 3, 1862

HISTORY OF THE FIFTH WEST VIRGINIA CAVALRY

Stephen G. Jones	Private	Re-enlisted as veteran, Jan. 5, 1864
Chas. Knox	Private	Re-enlisted as veteran, Jan. 5, 1864
Saml. B. Knox	Private	Re-enlisted as veteran, Jan. 5, 1864
James Kelley	Private	Deserted Aug. 9, 1863
Jno. D. Landermilk	Private	Re-enlisted as veteran, Jan. 5, 1864
John Lagan	Private	Discharged for disability, Nov. 17, 1862
Benj. F. Muks	Private	Re-enlisted as veteran, Jan. 5, 1864
John Maidens	Private	Re-enlisted as veteran, Jan. 5, 1864
James Miller	Private	Re-enlisted as veteran, Jan. 5, 1864
W.H. Mail	Private	Killed in action at Cross Keys, June 8, 1862
Michael Maloney	Private	Died Feb. 19, 1863
Edward Melvin	Private	Transferred to V.R.C., July 18, 1863
Owen Megan	Private	Discharged for disability, March 2, 1863
Isaac Millstead	Private	Discharged for disability, April 17, 1863
Thos. W. McClunen	Private	
Robt. McClennon	Private	
Thos. McConkey	Private	Died from wounds received in action at Droop Mt., Nov. 6, 1863
B.W. McGraw	Private	
Winchester McAtee	Private	Recruit, July 5, 1863
Richard H. McAtee	Private	Died Sept. 11, 1861, at Beverly
Danl. McConaha	Private	Discharged for wounds received at Cross Keys
Peter McGovern	Private	Deserted July 30, 1863
Miles McDonough	Private	Deserted Oct. 18, 1863
Franklin Nelson	Private	Re-enlisted as veteran, Jan. 5, 1864
Hiram Nelson	Private	Discharged for disability, Oct. 1, 1861
John Oaks	Private	Killed in action at Rocky Gap
Augustus Ryman	Private	Re-enlisted as veteran, Jan. 5, 1864
Calon M. Reed	Private	Re-enlisted as veteran, Jan. 5, 1864
Harmon Statter	Private	
Lindley Sexton	Private	Captured at Salem Raid
Thos. M. Smith	Private	Wounded at Bull Run
Frederick Shaffer	Private	Re-enlisted as veteran, Jan. 5, 1864
Saml. A. Sams	Private	Re-enlisted as veteran, Jan. 5, 1864

CHAPTER III.

Harvey Stewart	Private	Re-enlisted as veteran, Jan. 5, 1864
Josiah B. Smith	Private	Re-enlisted as veteran, Jan. 5, 1864
John Sallyards	Private	Re-enlisted as veteran, Jan. 5, 1864. Wounded at Droop Mt.
Irvin M. Smith	Private	Discharged for disability, April 3, 1862
Israel Taylor	Private	Transferred to V.R.C., Jan. 15, 1864
Thomas C. Traman	Private	Discharged for disability, Aug. 23, 1862
Timothy Valentine	Private	Re-enlisted as veteran, Jan. 5, 1864
Thomas F. West	Private	Captured on Salem Raid. Died at Millen, Ga.
W.L. Wickham	Private	Re-enlisted as veteran, Jan. 5, 1864
Alex. Waters	Private	Re-enlisted as veteran, Jan. 5, 1864
Isaac Wilt	Private	Re-enlisted as veteran, Jan. 5, 1864
Geo. W. Wakefield	Private	Re-enlisted as veteran, Jan. 5, 1864
Joseph Yearian	Private	
Jos. S. Yearian	Private	Died March 19, 1864

CAPTAIN J. P. KIGER.

John P. Kiger was born in Winchester, Va., in 1822. At the age of 21 he made Parkersburg his home, and followed merchant tailoring until the war. He married at the age of 25, at Parkersburg, and had one son and one daughter. He was well educated, took a deep interest in politics and military affairs, and held various offices in the State Militia. He was drill master for years of the militia in his county, and was considered the best drilled officer in Wood County. His ambition was to be a soldier, for which he seemed to be specially adapted, in personal appearance, courage and skill. The War of the Rebellion afforded the opportunity, and he had the honor of leading Company K to the front. He was well liked by his company, and he took great pride in equipping and drilling the men, bringing them to a high state of efficiency. He resigned in the fall of 1861, on account of the ill health of his wife, and remained with her until her death. He resumed business in Parkersburg until 1875, when he removed to the valley of Virginia, and is now making his home with his son, near Washington, D.C.

CAPTAIN A. GRUBB.

Andrew Grubb joined Company K at Wheeling, with a squad of men from Ohio, and became first lieutenant. Upon the retirement of Capt. Kiger, he became captain, which position he held until the company was mustered out. He was an efficient, brave and faithful officer, and the men had a good leader in him. He was always ready for duty, and no service was too severe for him to fulfill to the best of his ability. After retiring from the army he lived in Bridgeport, O., until his death, which occurred 1889. The captain was held in high esteem by his comrades, as a patriotic, courageous man.

LIEUTENANT A. J. WEAVER.

Arthur J. Weaver ranked among the bravest and best soldiers of our regiment. We are indebted to Sergeant G.A. Quimby of his company, for the following facts in regard to him: He resided in Parkersburg for two or more years before the war, his parents living in Frederick, Md. He was born in the south, place not known, in 1837, and was unmarried. He seemed to have a presentiment from the time he enlisted, that he would be killed. He was often heard to say that should it be his lot to fall, he wanted the world to know that he freely gave his life for the best government in the world. He was of a genial, cheerful disposition, and in camp freely mingled with the men, joining in their sports. On the march, he would cheer the men, and make their burdens as light as possible, often helping to carry the guns of any who were worn out. He was never absent from the company, or sick a day, during his service, and was on every march and in every engagement until his death, never complaining or finding fault with his condition. On the Huntersville raid December, 1861, in the severe cold, and heavy rain, with no shelter of any kind, he spread his blanket over his own and Quimby's shoulders, on which a gum blanket was laid, and playfully said, 'we will play horse and sleep standing,' sharing all he had with his comrade. He was very fond of scouting, and in this way did some good work, and gained valuable information. Just before the Droop Mountain battle, the men were eating a meal, and he told them to eat heartily as they had hard work before them. Turning to Quimby's mess he joined them, and said to Quimby, "It may be, 'Buddy,' this will be the last meal you and I will eat together": then followed the battle, the heroic charge, and Lieut. Weaver in his best spirits, happy and cheerful, gave up his noble life for his country.

LIEUTENANT D. A. JENNINGS.

David A. Jennings was promoted to second lieutenant from private February 19, 1862, and resigned January 22, 1863. No date is available to give a sketch of his life. When he enlisted he was 20 years of age.

CHAPTER III.

SERGEANT G. A. QUIMBY.

G.A. Quimby was born in Washington County, Ohio, August 6, 1841, of English descent, and remained on a farm until 13 years of age, when he was apprenticed to learn the brick mason trade at Marietta. His parents died in 1847, leaving four boys and three girls, George being but 6 years old. He had no school privileges, reading being the only branch that he learned, until he was taught to write by his comrades, George Brown, J.P. Ford and W.R. Stewart, after they were in the field. He drifted from place to place, working at his trade, making Parkersburg his home in 1859. At the age of 13, he united with the Baptist church at Marietta, Ohio, and was always active in church duties. Quimby was one of the first to join the company, and his record was that of a good soldier, never shirking duty, in his place on the march and in the battle, and missed but one fight in which the company was engaged, Allegheny Mt. He was then stricken down with typhoid fever. When his time was out, he enlisted for one year in Company G, Second W. Va. Cavalry, and was in the third brigade, third cavalry division, commanded by General Custer. He was in the battles under Sheridan in the valley, and at Petersburg, engaging in all that his brigade had a part in, until the surrender of Lee at Appomattox. At the close of the war he made Dayton his home, then married and moved to Columbus, O., where he engaged in contracting and building until 1880, when his health gave way under the effects of diseases contracted in the army, and is now a bookkeeper. He is a member and deacon of Hildreth Baptist church, was Sabbath school superintendent for several years, and is an active member of McCoy Post No. 1, G. A. R.

G.A. QUIMBY

CORPORAL G. W. BROWN.

George W. Brown was born in Lancaster County, Pa., and left home at an early age and traveled through the west, learning cigar-making, which he was following in Kentucky, when the war broke out. Like many thousands of loyal men in the south, he was compelled to seek safety, and traveled through the woods until he reached the Ohio river, thence to Parkersburg, where he sought an opportunity to "get even" with his enemies, and he joined Company K. He was lively and agreeable, a favorite with his comrades. His courage in battle could not be surpassed. After the war he settled in Parkersburg, where he was married and made that his home since.

LIEUTENANT J. L. WILSON.

James Lewis Wilson is the son of the late Capt. Daniel Wilson, of Company B, and was born at Philippi, Va., December, 1848. He claims to be the youngest regularly enlisted soldier from West Virginia, who served during the war of the rebellion, being less than 14 years of age when he was mustered into the service as drummer of Company K. When he joined, Lieut. Weaver took him into his tent, and he shared with this brave officer his bed and board, until the lieutenant was killed. At the reorganization of the regiment in the fall of 1864, when the recruits and veterans were consolidated with the Sixth West Virginia cavalry, and took the latter name, and while at New Creek, and the mounted and available part of the command was in the field, the place was surprised and captured by Gen. Rosser's command. Nearly all the men were captured, and among the rest the young bugler. The men were hurried by hard marches through the mountains, without food or suitable clothes, or blankets, as everything had been taken from them, to Staunton, thence to Richmond, where they were confined in Pemberton prison. In the building with 600 other unfortunates, he spent the winter of 1864-5, where they were all subjected to the hardships and privations incident to southern prisons. There he celebrated his sixteenth birthday. The heartless remark of "Old Boots," the jailor, that "here is a boy that would like to see his mother," as he with other officers passed along the line taking the names of those who could not stand the treatment much longer, will not soon be forgotten. A few days later, however, all in the building were paroled, placed in a vessel, steamed to City Point, thence north, where he joined his regiment. The regiment soon after went west, and saw service in Kansas, Nebraska, Colorado and Wyoming, against the Indians. His term of service expiring December, 1865, he was sent to Omaha for discharge, after three years and four days service. Just 17 years of age, he found himself on the then borders of civilization, far from home, with a few hard earned dollars in his pocket, a great deal of experience, and no education. He returned to his home in W. Va., started at once to a select school, then to Morgantown,

JAMES L. WILSON

CHAPTER III.

where he was a cadet at the Agricultural college, remaining one year. He then began the study of medicine under Dr. A.H. Thayer, his old surgeon. By the advice of Capt. Blue, one of his old regiment, he came before the Examining Board at Morgantown, in competition with others of the district, for admission to West Point. He was successful and was appointed in June, 1869, by Hon. J.C. McGrew, and entered that famous military school in June, 1870. He was graduated No. 5 in a class of forty-one, in 1874, joining his regiment, the Fourth U. S. Artillery, in California. He was graduated at the U.S. Artillery school in 1876, took part in the campaigns against the Sioux Indians in 1876, the Nez Perces in 1877, the Bannocks in 1878, and the Apaches in 1881. He was professor of Military science and tactics, and of Mathematics, at the W. Va. University 1884 to 1888. He completed the course of submarine mines and torpedo service, at the school of application for Engineers, at Willetts Point, N.Y., 1889. Lieut. Wilson was united in marriage with Miss Camilla Zantzinger, niece of Admiral Farragut, at the residence of the admiral in New York City, November 10, 1874, and has two daughters, Virginia Farragut, and Mary Augusta. He is now first lieutenant of the Fourth Artillery, and is located at Jackson Barracks, New Orleans, La.

CHAPTER IV.

THE QUARTERMASTER'S DEPARTMENT.

A regiment to be efficient, and to do its best service, must have a well equipped quartermaster department, administered by an intelligent, strong officer. Without this its strength will be sapped and its usefulness impaired. Such a department the regiment had, and it was a rare occasion when the men suffered from lack of supplies, and then never through the fault of our own quartermaster. Lieut. Webster A. Stevens was the first quartermaster of the regiment, who had the duty of organizing the department, and putting it in shape for good work. The command had been in active service less than one year, when he resigned the office, and on July 7, 1862, Lieut. Alex. J. Pentecost was commissioned and appointed to the office. He had been in the department for a few months, and was acquainted with its duties, and when he took charge new life and vigor were infused into it. It was not a work that was entirely congenial to the lieutenant's taste, but he took hold of it with his usual energy, and became one of the best officers that served in our command. Prompt, vigilant, reliable and intelligent, he met every demand made upon him, and was a model quartermaster. His choice was an active command, and at the head of a troop he would have been a dashing, brave officer, and would have won great renown. But at the request of his superiors he accepted this office, and there did a work that was, perhaps, of more benefit to the men he directly served, than if he had commanded a company or a battalion. For his faithful work, the men honor him. Associated with him were George H. Kirkpatrick commissary sergeant, and E. F. Seaman quartermaster sergeant, who were valuable aids in the onerous and responsible duties of the position, and Thos. S. Eichbaum, of Company A, was the lieutenant's clerk.

LIEUTENANT A. J. PENTECOST, R. Q. M.

Alexander J. Pentecost was born November 18, 1835, at Pittsburgh, Pa. When five years old, his father died, and in 1845 his mother moved to Allegheny. Since that time he has been a resident of the latter city. At the age of twenty years, having served an apprenticeship at the machinist's trade, he became a member of the firm of Pentecost, Graham and Bole, engine builders, Allegheny. He disposed of his interest in this business, and three years later, when the discovery of gold at Pike's Peak created so much excitement, started west in search of fortune. Going by way of Leavenworth, Kansas, and across the plains, he arrived at a point about fifteen miles from the base of the "Rockies" in the month of June, 1859. Here he found an Indian lodge, and met General William Larimer, a Pittsburgh banker, who had taken up his abode in an old log hut near-by. Upon this spot the beautiful city of Denver, Colorado, has since arisen. Continuing their journey to the mountains, young Pentecost spent several months exploring the "wild west" and prospecting for gold, and returned home in the spring of 1860.

When Sumter was fired upon, and President Lincoln's call for troops was issued, Mr. Pentecost was among the first who responded to that call. It was his intention to recruit a company at Neville hall, but the city guards, under the command of Colonel Alexander Hays, had taken possession of the hall, and his plans were frustrated. Pentecost then enlisted with the Washington Rifles, afterward Company A, being recruited at old Lafayette hall. This company, in response to a call from Governor Frank H. Pierpoint, of Virginia, went to Wheeling and entered the service of Virginia. They were ordered into service soon after muster, taking charge of the B. & O. railroad. At this juncture Corporal Pentecost was detached from the regiment to assist in organizing a quartermaster's department at Grafton, Virginia. In September, 1861, he was ordered

ALEXANDER J. PENTECOST,
FIRST LIEUTENANT AND
BREVET CAPTAIN U. S. V.
MAJOR N. G. P. 1873

to the Kanawha valley, and returning to Wheeling in December, reported to Governor Pierpont. The latter desired him to assist Colonel Harris recruit the Tenth Regiment of Virginia Infantry at Clarksburg; but preferring to remain with his regiment, which was then in winter quarters on Cheat Mountain, he immediately reported at regimental headquarters, was assigned to the quartermaster's department, and July 7, 1862, was commissioned first lieutenant and regimental quartermaster, *vice* Lieutenant W. A. Stephens, resigned.

Lieut. Pentecost rendered active and efficient service in the following, and several other notable battles: Rich Mountain, Gauley Bridge, McDowell, Cross

CHAPTER IV.

Keys, Cedar Mountain, Kelly's Ford, White Sulphur Springs, Waterloo Bridge, Gainesville, Second Bull Run, Beverly, Rocky Gap, Droop Mountain, Cotton Mountain, Cloyd Mountain and Jackson River. He is the possessor of numerous commendatory letters, complimenting him upon his valor on the battlefield, from which the writer has selected the following on account of its brevity:

PITTSBURGH, PA.
A. J. PENTECOST, ESQ.

SIR:-- It affords me great pleasure to say, that while you were under my command in West Virginia, acting as Regimental Quartermaster of the Second Virginia Infantry, you discharged your duties with energy and marked ability, and that at the battle of Droop Mountain you participated in the action with great gallantry, contributing much to the success of your regiment, although your legitimate duties might have been a reasonable excuse for not taking part therein. The reports of your regimental commander, Lieutenant-Colonel Scott, were always most complimentary to you.

Wishing you every success in civil life, I remain,
Your Obedient Servant,
WM. W. AVERELL, Late Brig. Gen'l, U. S. V.

He comes of a military family, being the great grandson of Colonel Dorsey Pentecost, who took active part in the revolution, commanded the military forces of Washington county in 1781, was one of the first justices of the peace at old Fort Pitt, a member of the supreme executive council of Pennsylvania 1781 to 1783, and president-judge of court of common pleas of Washington county. Colonel Dorsey was also the great grandfather of Colonel Jos. H. Pentecost, commander of the One Hundredth Pennsylvania Volunteers, who was killed in battle at Fort Steadman, March 25, 1865.

In civil life, Mr. Pentecost has occupied numerous positions of public trust, and has been most successful in business. He is a member of the Masonic Fraternity on the retired list, having been made a mason at Allegheny City in 1867. March 13, 1865, he was brevetted captain, U. S. V., by the President of the United States for gallantry and meritorious conduct during the war, and in 1867 was commander of Post 91, G. A. R., department of Pennsylvania. October 31, 1873, he was commissioned major and aid-de-camp of the National Guards of Pennsylvania, by General John F. Hartranft, and assigned to the Eighteenth division. In 1888, at the annual meeting of the Society of the Army of West Virginia, held in Columbus, Ohio, he was elected one of the vice presidents, and in 1887-89 was appointed treasurer of his regimental association. He was a member of Allegheny city councils in 1874, has at different times held the offices of president and treasurer of the third ward, school board, and in 1887-'89, was a member of the high school committee, and member of the board of school controllers of Allegheny City for twelve years.

Mr. Pentecost has been married twice and has four sons and four daughters now living. April 2, 1863, he wedded Miss Virginia H. Andrews at Pittsburgh. Three children, Grant Meigs, Alexander J., and Daisy V., were the result of this marriage, but the mother and daughter both died.

His second, and present wife was Miss Emma P. Marcy, a relative of the late General R. D. Marcy, and of Mrs. General George B. McClellan. They were married in Allegheny City in January, 1874. The children of this marriage are three sons, Howard M., Dorsey D., Frank Pierpont, and five daughters, Nellie S., Adelia R., Bessie B., May B., and Emma D.

He has a beautiful and happy home in Allegheny City, ranks among the most successful real estate dealers in Pittsburgh, commands the honor and respect of all who know him, either in business, public or social life; and his many old comrades who peruse this volume will be glad to know that in health and physique he is perfect. A most entertaining and witty conversationalist, he can relate innumerable interesting anecdotes of both the sorrowful and amusing phases of a soldier's life, as well as of the bravery and endurance of the "boys in blue."

E. F. SEAMAN, Q. M. SERGEANT.

E. F. Seaman was born in Zelionople, Butler county, Pa., December 26, 1842. His parents were both natives of the state, and his grandparents were Germans. Mr. Seaman received a common school education, and at the age of 15 years left his home, and went to Pittsburgh, Pa., where he worked at gardening a few miles below the city. Shortly before the war broke out, he began to learn the trade of roll turning, which he followed until the call to arms, when he enlisted as a private in Company D. Not being able to enlist in any of the many companies forming in his city, on account of his youth and slender build, he boarded the

ELIAS F. SEAMAN,
QUARTERMASTER SERGEANT

steamer McCombs for Wheeling, Va., where the rules were not so strict, and joined the company then being formed on Wheeling Island. This company was composed almost wholly of men from Pittsburgh and vicinity. He remained with his company, participating in all the battles in which the regiment took part, until July, 1863; and when it was mounted, he was promoted

CHAPTER IV.

to quartermaster sergeant of the regiment, in which capacity he served until his term of enlistment expired. Returning to Pittsburgh, he again took up the trade of roll turning, and served his apprenticeship. He has had charge of the roll turning department at the Black Diamond Steel Works, of Park Bro. & Co., Pittsburgh, for the last twenty years, and it is the largest works of the kind in the country. On December 24, 1865, he married Miss Carrie Sold, of Allegheny City. Their union has been blessed with five children, three boys and two girls, the oldest and youngest being the latter, aged respectively 23 and 9 years. Comrade Seaman is a well preserved man of 47 years, in the prime and vigor of health. He is a prominent member of the Union Veteran Legion, as well as other societies, and is the life of whatever company he may join. During his service he was brave and true, always at his post, and a comrade that had the love and respect of all his associates. He was very thoroughly tried on the great Salem Raid, when he was one of the party commanded by Lieut. Pentecost in the retreat, and he was of invaluable service on that occasion. It required courage of the utmost staying quality, and Sergt. Seaman displayed his full share of it. In all other positions in which he was placed he was just as brave and true. In his official capacity, he was very efficient, and rendered full service to his country. In the regimental association and Society of the Army of West Virginia, he is a whole host in his good nature and entertaining qualities, and is the life and spirit of the gatherings. In the work of preparing the regimental history, and placing his command in its proper place before the people, he has been of invaluable aid to the Historian, and much is due to him for the completeness of the work. Comrade Seaman is one of the best types of American manhood, and very properly enjoys the respect and confidence of all that know him.

GEORGE H. KIRKPATRICK,
COMMISSARY SERGEANT

THOMAS S. EICHBAUM,
CO. A.

HISTORY OF THE DEPARTMENT.

For the following history of the Quartermaster's department, the Historian is indebted to Lieut. A. J. Pentecost, its able head. The reports, official orders, etc., are exact copies of the originals, and the anecdotes, and incidents of battle, are told in Lieut. Pentecost's own language, as follows:

"During the winter of 1861-2, while in winter quarters on Cheat Mountain, and for some time afterwards, provisions were plentiful enough; requisitions approved by regimental commander and signed by commander of the company, would procure all the rations and clothing required, and officers had the privilege of purchasing provisions from the department at cost of same. In April, 1862, we were ordered to the front, and on May 13th our headquarters were at Franklin, Va., where we joined General Fremont. Then followed Fremont's campaign, his resignation and the advance of the army under General Pope.

The following order was issued soon after this:

HEADQUARTERS, 1ST CORPS, ARMY OF VIRGINIA, Aug. 4, 1862.
Special Order, No. I:
Quartermasters of regiments and batteries will make requisition for ambulances, horses and harness, and send them to chief quartermaster's office without delay. Each regiment is entitled to three two-horse ambulances and one transport cart. The ambulances now in use by regiments and batteries, will be deducted from the number allowed, as above, by the respective quartermasters.

By Command of MAJ. GEN'L SIGEL,
Per F. A. MYSENBERG, A. A. G.
To A. J. PENTECOST, 1ST L'T and R. Q. M.

At the time this order was issued, we were camped near Woodville, transportation was excellent, and there was an abundance of clothing, camp equipage, etc., but this prosperous state of affairs did not last long. During the next few days the following official orders were issued:

HEADQUARTERS INDEPENDENT BRIGADE, CAMP NEAR WOODVILLE, Aug. 7, 1862.
Special Order, No.3:
Private Charles Stratton, Company D Second Regiment Virginia Infantry, is hereby relieved from duty as clerk in Provost Marshal's office of this brigade,

CHAPTER IV.

and will report for duty to Lieut. A. J. Pentecost, Quartermaster Second Regiment Virginia Infantry, as clerk in his department.

By Order of BRIG. GEN. R. H. MILROY.
HENRY C. FLESHER, Captain and A. A. A. G.

HEADQUARTERS MILROY'S BRIGADE, CAMP NEAR WOODVILLE, Aug. 8, 1862.
Special Order, No.4:

The Quartermaster Sergeant will remain with the train during the march.

By Order BRIG. GEN. R. H. MILROY.
FIELDING LOWERY, Captain and A. Q. M.

We had now received orders to move to the front and on the evening of August 9, arrived at Cedar Mountain. That night and the following day there was some skirmishing. We were holding a flag of truce. The offices on both sides were riding around conversing with one another. A Confederate officer approached me and inquired what state I was from. I replied: 'From Pennsylvania.' 'Indeed!' said he, 'So am I. I am from Monongahela city. I am Captain Dushane, General Ewell's chief of staff.' 'I was very sorry to witness the death of Colonel S. W. Black, an old Pittsburgher. He was killed in a battle near Richmond a few days ago.' After a little further conversation Dushane rode away. I hardly believed it possible, in the excitement of battle, for him to have seen Colonel Black killed, but when we got to camp, and received our mail, letters from Pittsburgh corroborated his statement. On this same day Generals Stonewall Jackson and Stuart, Confederates, Generals Sigel and Milroy, Union, were riding over the field, when some officer would ask, pointing to one of the latter: 'Can you tell me who that officer is?' The question would, of course, be answered by one of our men; and it was all wrong, for General Milroy being a very large man, and General Sigel rather small, it gave Confederate sharpshooters an advantage they should not have had. It was stopped as soon as discovered by the officers. I recollect going over the battlefield and examining some wagons Stonewall Jackson had left behind in his retreat. They were built like scows, and fashioned after the old Conestoga wagons used in Pennsylvania fifty years ago.

    Our trains were from one-half to three-fourths of a mile in length, and I had a desperate time that night trying to keep the teamsters awake. In riding along the line to see that all was right, I would suddenly discover a break in the column, which was invariably caused by some one of the teamsters falling fast asleep on his horse. While on our march that led to the battle of Bull Run, I received the following orders:

HEADQUARTERS INDEPENDENT BRIGADE, WARRENTON, VA, Aug. 26, 1862.
Special Order, No.5:

During the temporary absence of Capt. Fielding Lowry, Lieut. A. J. Pentecost is detailed as A. A. Q. M. Qf this brigade.

By order of GEN. R. H. MILROY,
HENRY C. FLESHER, A. A. A. G.

CAMP CEDAR RUN, VA., Aug. 27, 1862.
Special Order, No.7:

LIEUT. A.J. PENTECOST, Quartermaster Second Regiment Virginia Infantry: You will at once hold, subject to my order, three four-horse, or mule, teams, even if you have to empty the aforesaid wagons, and destroy the property when necessary.

By order of COL. R. E. CLARY, Chief Quartermaster Army of Virginia.
FIELDING LOWRY., Captain and A. Q. M.

On this march I was with Gen. Milroy almost constantly, and well remember, when we reached Manassas Junction on the evening of the 29th, he said: 'We must take Jackson before night.' We lay on our arms that night, and were in such a position that we could see all along Gen. McDowell's line of battle. He was trying to prevent Longstreet's forces from joining Jackson's, and the continuous flash from the muskets of both lines, presented the appearance of a canal, or river, of fire. Gen. Schenck was with us for a short time during this memorable scene, and became so impatient that he finally exclaimed 'Can't we go and help them?' Although reminded that we dare not move from the position we were then in, he persisted in his desire to move up and pitch in to the rebels. We were so close to the Confederates that night, we could hear their voices. Gen. Milroy was in the saddle next morning at daybreak, and saluted us with the remark, 'We must take them before breakfast.' The boys did not seem to appreciate this mode of warfare, but preferred to replenish the inner man first. After riding to the top of a small hill and being fired at by the Confederates, the general returned in haste, and gave the order to the boys to make coffee. He had hardly finished speaking, when down went the

CHAPTER IV.

fences, rail by rail, until there wasn't one left. The general rode around among the men, and seeing one of them had his coffee almost made, requested him to let him try it. He evidently did not like the quality, however, as he made a very wry face over it. During the engagement which followed, a company was sent out on our left. Colonel Latham and I were sitting on our horses together when he inquired: 'Where has that company gone?' I replied I did not know, but would find out, and rode off in the direction indicated. I had not gone far when an orderly rode up to me and said: 'General Milroy wishes to see you, on our extreme right.' I at once rode over to the general, who said: 'You are making an unnecessary sacrifice of your life this morning. I want you to go, as quickly as possible, to Alexandria, where I understand all the lame and lazy are, and bring them all here.' This I considered a scheme to keep me off the battlefield for that day, at least; however I, of course, obeyed his orders, promptly. Upon arriving at Alexandria I procured all the surgeons I could find, had them examine a lot of men who were feigning sickness, and finally succeeded in getting quite a good command back to the scene of action, which we reached some time that afternoon. I rode up in the direction of the railroad cut, and there witnessed a scene beyond the powers of description. The enemy had taken a position behind this cut. Many of our men were lying in the cut, either killed or wounded, and every time one of the latter would attempt to rise from the ground, the rebels would fire. Both sides having ceased firing, our handful of men were again placed in line ready for an emergency, but remained inactive until about five o'clock. At this time, as Lieutenant-Colonel Scott and I were riding over the field, we noticed General Fitz John Porter, and his division, at the edge of a piece of timber. An orderly rode up to the general with a message, and, just as he was reading it, the Confederates opened a deadly-fire from a cornfield on our left. They were fairly mowing swathes in Porter's ranks, when the latter began to return their fire; and it was at this juncture General Milroy showed his foresight and bravery. Although our regiment had been so greatly reduced in numbers, we gained a point known as Bald Knob, and the general seeing the Pennsylvania Bucktails lying in reserve, shouted to them to follow him, which they did with a will. By going in with a rush we held the enemy's right. By this move the entire rebel advance was held, and an immense number of our men saved from absolute slaughter. During this sharp skirmish I was on my horse, when some one reminded me I was making a target of myself, and had better dismount. I was saved the trouble, however; for just at that moment a shell plowed a furrow under my noble steed, and down he went without the slightest warning.

Immediately after, we went into camp at Fort Ethan Allen, to recruit our shattered command, many of the men being greatly in need of clothing and medical attention; and while at this fort I received the following order:

CAMP NEAR CHAIN BRIDGE, VA., Sept. 6, 1862.
Special Order, No.8:
LIEUT. A. J. PENTECOST, Q. M. Second Virginia Infantry:

You will retain six (6) of your best teams, or as many as you may need for the transportation of five (5) days provision for the regiment. All other teams must be immediately sent to Col. D. H. Rucker, Q. M., Washington, D. C., who requires the service of 300 teams. If the first army corps cannot furnish 300 teams, under the above directions, the provision teams must be reduced. The regimental baggage must be unloaded and stored, and an agent with guard of infantry will proceed to Georgetown, store and guard the baggage at that place, or Washington, D. C., which ever may be most desirable. It is desirable that you at once proceed to get your trains ready. When so, please report.

By order of D. W. LOOMIS, Chief Q. M., First Army Corps.
FIELDING LOWRY, A. A. Q. M.

We were now ordered to West Virginia, and on the way passed through Washington, where our regiment was reviewed by President Lincoln, in front of the White House. This was by his own request, made on one of Gen. Milroy's visits to him after the battle of Bull Run. From Washington we went to Point Pleasant, West Va. This trip furnished many amusing incidents, such as a number of the boys taking French leave by jumping off the train, while crossing the Allegheny mountains. Among these leave takers was an old man named Fitzsimmons, a private in Company D, and it was reported that he had been killed by his jump from the cars. One evening in the following October, Col. Latham and I were sitting out in front of our quarters, when Fitzsimmons approached the colonel with the usual military salute. 'Is that you, Fitz?' said the colonel. 'It is, colonel,' replied Fitzsimmons. 'Why,' said the colonel, 'I heard you were killed when you jumped off the train, coming over the mountains.' 'I heard that myself, colonel, when I got to Pittsburgh, but I knew it was a lie as soon as I heard it,' was Fitz's droll reply. We were now camped at Buckhannon and like Fitz, the boys had all reported for duty. The following orders were issued:

HDQRS. SECOND VIRGINIA VOL. INF., BEVERLY, VA., Oct. 30, 1862.
Special Order, No. 12:

The following soldiers are hereby detached as teamsters, and will be enrolled as extra duty men, from the dates opposite their names, by Lieut. A. J. Pentecost, regimental quartermaster: J. McCrea, Co. A, Antony Cristy, Co.

CHAPTER IV.

C, Jefferson Reed, Co. D, Oct. 12, '62; Marion Moore, Co. E, Oct. 21, '62; John Sheets, Co. F, Oct. 25, '62; H. Schott, Co. C, Oct. 21, '62; H. McGarvey, Co. H., John Rimmel, Co. I, Oct. 12, '62; Calon Reed, Co. K, Jas. Wilson, Co. H, Robt. A. McCoy, Co. I, David A. Castillow, Co. E, Nov. 1, '62. Private Jos. Black, Co. F, is hereby detailed regimental blacksmith from Oct. 12, 1862.

The following are hereby detailed as extra duty men, and will report for duty to Lieut. A. J. Pentecost, provided with one ax each: Wm. Dever, Benj. F. Kurtz, Co. A; Thos. B. Richardson, Matthew Fanzell, Co. F; I. G. Martin, John N. Leese, Co. B; Jackson Yonking, Wm. I. Cox, Co. E; S. G. Jones, Isaac Wilt, Co. K; R. Bowman, H. Emmerig, Co. C; D. F. Johnson, Cornelius Collier, Co. H; Bonaparte Brooks, John Woods, Co. D; Henry Devers, Wm. McCoy, Co. I.

By Order of A. SCOTT, Lieut.-Colonel.
(Signed) J. COMBS, Adjutant.

HEADQUARTERS CHEAT MOUNTAIN DIVISION, BEVERLY, VA., Nov. 15, 1862.
Special Order, No. 96:

Lieut. A. J. Pentecost, R. Q. M. 2d Va. Infantry, is hereby appointed A. A. Q. M. for the Post at Beverly, until further orders, and as such will be obeyed and respected. He will also have charge of all the duties properly belonging to the Q. M. Dep't. at this Post.

By Order of BRIG. GEN. R. H. MILROY.
HENRY C: FLESHER, A. A. A. Gen.

HEADQUARTERS NORTHERN BRIGADE, BUCKHANNON, VA., Feb. 16, 1863.
Special Order, No. 27:
Captain Comley, C. S., U. S. A., Clarkburg, Va., is hereby ordered to turn over all commissary stores and property at Beverly, Va., to Lieut. A. J. Pentecost, A. A. Q. M. and A. C. S. at that Post.

By Command of BRIG. GEN. MOOR.
N. GOFF, A. D. C., A. A. A. Gen.

POST HEADQUARTERS, BEVERLY, W.VA., March 10, 1863.
LIEUT. A. J. PENTECOST, A. A. Q: M.:

You will furnish Capt. Thomas E. Day transportation for the corpse of A. Sponholtz, late of Company E, Second Regiment Virginia Infantry to Fetterman, on the B. & O. R. R.

By Comand of A. SCOTT, Lieut. Colonel Commanding Post.
J. COMBS, Post Adjutant.

POST HEADQUARTERS BEVERLY, VA., April 9, 1863.

Capt. D. D. Barclay, 2d Reg't Va. Vol. Inf., Capt. H. H. Hagans, Co. A, 1st Va. Cavalry, and James B. Montgomery, 2d Va. Vol. Inf., are hereby appointed a Board of Survey, and will report to Lieut. A. J. Pentecost, at 2:30 o'Clock p.m. this day.

By Order Of LIEUT. COL, A. SCOTT, Commanding Post.
J. COMBS, Adjutant.

Nothing of interest occurred here until the 24th of April, 1863. It was a dismal day, raining at intervals, and a heavy fog, or mist, overhung the valley near Beverly. I was seated in my office, when I was told Col. Latham, who was commander of the post, wished to speak to me. Upon going to the door I found the Col. seated on his horse. He said there was something wrong at the picket lines, and requested me to go with him to investigate the trouble. I at once ordered my horse, and we started in the direction of a bridge which crossed the river near Huttonsville, taking with us an Ohio company of cavalry. A short distance from the bridge, we found Frank Ferris, of Beverly, lying on the ground. As I looked down at him he said, 'Here is my pistol, lieutenant, I am shot.' He appeared to be very weak. I took the pistol, and leaving him in charge of the guards at the bridge, we continued on our way. A little further on, Col. Latham called my attention to a long line of cavalry on the other side of the river. On account of the fog, it was impossible to tell to which army they belonged, and I remarked that they were probably a company of cavalry sent out as an escort, with one of my trains during the morning. Riding on in the direction of Huttonsville, we posted guards, and returning to the bridge, had barely reached the end of it, when we heard the sound of horses' hoofs. Upon looking around we discovered our guards coming back on a double quick, evidently pursued by a large force of Confederate cavalry. I succeeded in checking our men when they reached us, and got them into a little flat near by. The guards at the bridge now began to get alarmed and wanted to know how they were to defend themselves against a whole regiment. Col. Latham ordered them to climb to a point of rocks near the bridge, and hold the latter at all hazards. Seeing another large body of Confederates

CHAPTER IV.

moving toward Beverly, the colonel said we had better notify our men who were in camp there. Putting spurs to my horse, I complied with the colonel's suggestion as quickly as possible, and had barely arrived at camp when the Confederates began throwing shells from the mountain peaks as fast as they could load. It soon became apparent that we were at the mercy of a force, very much our superior in numbers, under Gens. Imboden and Jones. Our men fought bravely but were driven back, inch by inch, into the town of Beverly. As quartermaster and commissary at Beverly, I had a large amount of stores in my charge, and feeling certain we would finally have to leave the town, I began preparing the warehouses for destruction. Our commissary stores were in charge of Com. Sergt. Geo. H. Kirkpatrick, who built flues of candle boxes, and strewed lines of powder across the floors, so that when the signal was given the whole thing would go like a flash. About the time these preparations were completed, I received the following telegram:

BUCKHANNON, VA., April 24, 1863.
To COL. GEO. R. LATHAM, Beverly, Va.:

Destroy all the stores you cannot take with you.

B. S. ROBERTS, Brig. Gen.

I certify that I promulgated the above order to Lieut. A. J. Pentecost, during the engagement at Beverly, Va., April 24, 1863.

GEO. R. LATHAM, Commander.

When the bullets began whizzing close to our heads, and I saw retreat was inevitable, I rode out on the main street and threw up my hand as a signal to set the match to the stores. In a few moments the store houses were no more, and they were the last the government ever built at that place. I shall never forget the expression depicted on the faces of our boys as they looked back at the camp, and saw the rebels ransacking the tents. Just as we were at the edge of the town a Confederate regiment came sailing through the woods, and charged on us, and we returned their charge in such a vigorous manner, it nearly took their breath away, and they left us in hot haste. We camped that night just outside the town, at Leading creek, and although all was perfectly quiet, Maj. McNally dreamed we were again attacked and waked me up by shouting at the top of his voice, 'Fall in boys, fall in!' The next morning we proceeded to Clarksburg, from there to West Union, and finally went into camp at Buckhannon. From Buckhannon we returned to Beverly, were made mounted infantry and placed under command of the celebrated Gen. Averell, an officer from the Army of the Potomac. The following orders were issued:

DIVISION QUARTERMASTER'S OFFICE, WESTON, VA., May 24, 1863.
LIEUT. A. J: PENTECOST, Q. M., Second Virginia Volunteer Infantry:

SIR: - By order of Brig. Gen. W. W. Averell, commanding Independent Division, you are requested to furnish me with following information immediately. Make a report in writing. Number of days rations and forage on hand; number of shelter tents in regiment and any required; any clothing needed and what quantity.

J. N. RUTHERFORD, Capt. and Q. M., U. S. A., and Div. Q. M.

ASSISTANT QUARTERMASTER'S OFFICE, WESTON, Va., May 26, 1863.
LIEUT. A. J. PENTECOST, Q. M. Second Virginia Volunteer Infantry:

SIR: - By order of Brig. Gen. W. W. Averell, you are requested to furnish me the following information immediately:
What number of public horses, public mules, private horses, two horse wagons, four horse wagons, and ambulances, belonging to the regiment, and the condition of transportation,

Very Respectfully, Your Obedient Servant,
J. N. RUTHERFORD, Capt., and A. Q. M., U. S. A.

HEADQUARTERS FOURTH SEPARATE BRIGADE, BEVERLY, VA., June 14, 1863.
Special Order, No. 13:

Lieut. A. J. Pentecost, R. Q. M., 2d Reg't Va. Vol. Inf'ty, is hereby relieved from duty as acting assistant quartermaster of the Post at Beverly. He will turn over the public property pertaining to the so-called Post at Beverly, for which he is accountable, to the R. Q. M., of the 10th Va. Vol. Inf'ty.

By Command of BRIG. GEN. AVERELL.
C. F. TROWBRIDGE, Captain and A. A. A. Gen.

CHAPTER IV.

HDQRS. SECOND VIRGINIA VOL. INF., GRAFTON, VA., June 24, 1863.
Special Order, No. 26:

Privates Robert McCoy and Jos. Chester, of Co. I., C. M. Roberts and C. Kirchoffer, of Co. F, Second Regiment Virginia Volunteer Infantry, are hereby detailed as extra duty men, and will report to Lieut. A. J. Pentecost, forthwith, for duty.

By Command COL. G. R. LATHAM.
J. COMBS, Lieut. and Adj't.

June 23d, we were in camp at Grafton, and drew horses for the entire command. Shortly after this we were sent to Buckhannon. Provisions and clothing were plentiful and nothing of importance transpired until the month of August. In that month we were on the march with Gen. W. W. Averell commanding, and Col. Geo. R. Latham commanding regiment. On August 26th we fought a battle at Rocky Gap. When on the march, after I had the trains fully under way, it was my custom to ride with some officer. On the morning of August 26th, I was riding beside Capt. C. T. Ewing, and while we were chatting on various subjects, we noticed a man, mounted on a gray horse, descending a hill. As soon as he saw our advancing column, he turned and tried to avoid us, but Ewing and I, putting spurs to our horses, soon overtook and captured him. In reply to Capt. Ewing's questions, he stated he was a quartermaster in the Confederate army, and was out purchasing supplies. Seeing something bulky in his pocket, the captain asked him what it was. He replied, 'It is Confederate money,' and pulled out a large package of 10, 20 and 50 dollar bills, and of which Capt. Ewing promptly relieved him. The quartermaster then said he must account to his government for the money, and would like to have a receipt. Ewing referred him to me, saying, 'This is our quartermaster and he will give you a receipt,' and handing me part of the money, he rode off without further ceremony. By this time the column had arrived on the scene and our prisoner was handed over to the guard.

A few minutes after this little episode, General Averell and I were riding at the head of a column, when we heard the sound of artillery ahead of us. Knowing that Captain Ewing was in advance with the guns, we at once concluded he had met the enemy, and opened fire. We started for the scene of action on a double quick, and arriving there found Ewing badly wounded. We were on a pike road and the general immediately deployed the Second Virginia and Fourteenth Pennsylvania cavalry to the right, Third and Eighth Virginia to the left, Ewing's battery in the center. We made a number of charges during the day, but neither side seemed to gain any advantage. Toward evening General Averell came and told me we would make the final charge, and requested me to pass the word along the line. I, in turn, requested Lieut. Colmer to do so. The signal for this charge was the raising of dust by the horses of the Fourteenth Pennsylvania cavalry, commanded by Captain R. Pollock. The moment the dust appeared, we charged; but it was a vain attempt, for our ammunition gave out and we had to fall back. During the charge I was swinging a sabre with all my might, and Major McNally and Sergeant Carney, who were almost by my side, were both killed. It was now getting dark, and although Lieut. John R. Meigs and myself had promised to meet the general after this charge, we concluded to try to get a little rest, if possible.

Lieut. Meigs, General Averell's Chief Engineer, was a graduate of West Point, and son of Maj. Gen. M. C. Meigs, Q. M. Gen. U. S. Army. He was a gallant officer, and displayed great courage in this battle, and at Droop Mountain and on the Salem raid. He was murdered by bushwhackers in the Shenandoah valley, and Gen. Sheridan threatened general destruction in the valley in retaliation. In the first charge in the morning, I recollect being on the left of our regiment, when I came shoulder to shoulder with Col. J. M. Schoonmaker, who was on the right of his regiment, the 14th Pa. Cavalry. We were not successful, and as we fell back to the foot of the hill at a maple grove, I stood behind the men when they fell back, and found myself near a tree. I heard some of our men calling to me, but could not make out what they meant, but on looking across a rail fence, I discovered a Confederate taking aim at me, who had been there for some time, whose firing had caused pieces of bark to fall over me, but I had not noticed it particularly until I saw the marksman. I immediately moved nearer our own forces. The following day we began a retreat, lapping the trees across the road to prevent the enemy from following us.

Upon reaching Beverly, we went into camp, and while there the following orders were issued:

HDQRS. QUARTERMASTER DEP'T, FOURTH SEPARATE BRIGADE, Sept. 22, 1863.
LIEUT. A. J. PENTECOST, R. Q. M. Second Virginia Infantry:

You will report to these headquarters by 11 o'clock this morning, the exact number of horses required by your command, to make it completely effective.

By Order of BRIG. GEN. AVERELL.
G. H. NORTH, Lieut. and A. A: Q. M. 4th Sep. Brig.

CHAPTER IV.

HDQRS. Q. M. DEPT., FOURTH SEPARATE BRIG., BEVERLY, W. VA., Oct. 6, 1863.
Circular:

The general commanding directs that hereafter all regimental quartermasters in his command, in foraging in the surrounding country, will in no case take all the hay from Union men, but leave enough to winter their stock. Regimental quartermasters will be held responsible for violation of this order by the trains in their charge. When fodder can be obtained, it is directed that it be used to make up the deficiency in hay, giving receipts for same, to be accounted for by the brigade quartermaster.

HEADQUARTERS FOURTH SEPARATE BRIGADE, BEVERLY, W. Va., Oct. 15, 1863.
Circular:

All officers will turn over tomorrow morning, to regimental quartermasters, for transportation and storage, all baggage in excess of the following allowance:
To each officer a small valise, or carpet bag, and small mess kettle. These articles will be carried on the two wagons allowed to each regiment. All officers' tents will remain standing until further orders.

By Command BRIG. GEN. W. W. AVERELL
L. MARKBREIT, A. A. A. Gen.

HEADQUARTERS FIRST SEPARATE BRIGADE, BEVERLY, W. VA., Oct. 18, 1863.
Special Order, No. 4:

Lieut. A. J. Pentecost, R. Q. M., 2nd Regt. Va. Mounted Inf., is hereby ordered to proceed to Clarksburg on business connected with the quartermaster department of this brigade.

By command of BRIG. GEN W. W. AVERELL.
L. MARKBREIT, A. A. A. Gen.

HEADQUARTERS FIRST SEPARATE BRIGADE, BEVERLY, W. VA., Oct. 20,1863.
Special Order, No. --:

Leave of absence is hereby granted to the following named officer: Lieut. A. J. Pentecost, R. Q. M., 2nd Regt. Va. Mounted Inf., for five days.

By command of BRIG. GEN. AVERELL.
WILL RUMSEY, Capt. and A. D. C.

During the illness of Capt. W. H. Brown, Gen. Averell's chief quartermaster, I was chosen to act as quartermaster for the division on the Droop Mountain expedition.

The following is a copy of receipts given on the Droop Mountain expedition, by order of Gen. W. W. Averell, commanding division:

ON THE MARCH NEAR LEWISBURG, VA., Nov. 7, 1863.
THE UNITED STATES,
TO JOHN SMITH, Dr.

    Rails burnt by troops - $25
    Five tons of hay, $6.00 - $30
    Total -- $55.00

I certify that this account is correct, and that the above items were taken for the good of the service, and recommend the payment of said claim, should the said John Smith prove loyal to the close of the war.

By order BRIG GEN. W. W. AVERELL, Commanding Div.
A. J. PENTECOST, 1st Lieut. and A. A Q. M., Cav. Div.

    December 1, 1863, we left New Creek and started on the Salem raid, which was, perhaps, one of the most hazardous and exciting expeditions of the war. Everything went well until we reached Jackson river on our return. On account of bad weather, and worse roads, our transportation was not of the best and progress was rather slow. The trains were guarded by the Fourteenth Pa. cavalry, under command of Lieut. Col. Blakely, and were a considerable distance behind the rest of the command. We were finally cut off from them entirely by the burning of a bridge. Capt. W. H. Brown, Commissary Serg't George H. Kirkpatrick, and I started down the road to investigate the trouble, and on our way met a detachment of Confederates who had captured some of our ambulances, and fired on us. We returned to camp, and there found several Confederate officers standing around the fire, holding a conversation with our own officers. They informed us that we were their prisoners, and taking charge of us would be merely a matter of form. I expressed my opinions pretty freely, and after some sharp words they departed. The air

CHAPTER IV.

was very cold that night, but we had to sleep at a distance from our fire to avoid being shot at. Morning came at last, and Captain Powell and myself were ordered to command the advance. The fire of the enemy's artillery from the mountain tops began to have a telling effect and we finally concluded to burn the trains, which was successfully accomplished under the direction of my Quartermaster Sergeant Elias F. Seaman, who deserves much credit for the manner in which he conducted it. We were now forced to fight or cross the river, and discovering a fording a short distance up the stream, we started for it, hotly pursued by the enemy. Just as we reached the ford Lieut. Colonel Blakely came up and shouted: 'Volunteers, step out and defend this fording under command of Lieut. A. J. Pentecost.' He was promptly obeyed, and assured me he would remain near at hand with reinforcements. We held the fording for some time and finally succeeded in joining our command on the mountains near Calahans. When we arrived there the boys shouted themselves hoarse, they were so rejoiced at our escape. The march was continued, we defeated the Confederates at several points, and the tearing up of the Virginia and Tennessee Railroad ended the great Salem raid.

The following order speaks for itself:

WAR DEPARTMENT, ADJ'T GEN'L'S OFFICE, WASHINGTON, Dec. 30, 1863.
Special Order, No. 578:
[EXTRACT.]

The quartermaster's department will issue gratis, to each man of Gen. Averell's command, one pair of shoes, and a suit of clothing, to replace those lost and worn out in his recent expedition.
By order of the Secretary of War,

(Signed), E. D. TOWNSEND; Ass't Adj't Gen.
Official copy: WILL RUMSEY, A. A. G.

The following orders were issued at Martinsburg:

HDQRS. FOURTH DIVISION DEPT. W. VA., MARTINSBURG, W. VA. Feb. 6, 1864.
Special Order No. 31:

Lieut. A. J. Pentecost, R. Q. M., 5th Regt. W.Va. Vol. Cav., will proceed to Webster and Clarksburg, W.Va., to attend to business connected with the Ordinance Department of his regiment. He will return as soon as practicable.

By command of COL. J. M. SCHOONMAKER
HENRY N. HARRISON, A. A. A. G.

HDQRS. FOURTH DIVISION DEPT. W. VA., MARTINSBURG, W. VA. Feb. 22, 1864.
Special Order, No. 46:
[EXTRACT.]

Lieut. A. J. Pentecost, R. Q. M., 5th W. Va. Cav., will proceed to Clarksburg and Wheeling, W. Va., to transact business connected with the Ordinance Department of this Division.

By command of BRIG. GEN. W. W. AVERELL.
WILL RUMSEY. A. A. G.

HDQRS. THIRD BRIG., FOURTH DIV., DEPT. OF W. VA., MARTINSBURG, VA., March 10, 1864.
General Order, No. 6:

Lieutenant A. J. Pentecost, R. Q. M., Fifth W.Va. Cav., is hereby announced as acting assistant quartermaster of this brigade, and will be obeyed and respected accordingly.

By order of LT. COL. F. W. THOMPSON, Commanding.
J. W. CARE, A. A. A. G.

HDQRS. FOURTH DIV., DEPT. OF W. VA., MARTINSBURG, W. VA., March 15, 1864.
LT. A. J. PENTECOST, R. Q. M, Fifth W. Va. Cav:

This command will at once be put in condition to take the field. The officers' baggage and the men's kits will be kept packed when not in use. Arms, ammunition and equipments to be kept in good order. Three days' rations and one day's forage will be kept in possession of the troops. Surplus equipage, arms and stores of all kinds, excepting tents, will be immediately packed and held in readiness for transportation, and proper reports will be made to the A. Q. M., to inform him fully upon all matters in his department. Condemned harness will be turned over to the A. Q. M. Regimental drills will be faithfully carried on, and all officers and men must be constantly in fighting condition.

CHAPTER IV.

By command BRIG. GEN. W. W. AVERELL.
WILL RUMSEY, A. A. G.

HDQRS. FIFTH W. VA. CAVALRY, PATTERSON'S CREEK, W. VA., March 22, 1864.
Special 0rder, No. 10:

Lieut. A. J. Pentecost, R. Q. M., 5th W. Va. Cav., is hereby authorized to issue orders on the B. & O. R. R. company, for transportation from Patterson's creek station, W. Va.

By command of Col. Geo. R. Latham.
J. COMBS, 1st Lieut. and Adjutant.

Our trip by railroad and steamboat from Patterson Creek to Charleston was without accident or anything of interest to the reader. From here we went to Dublin Depot and fought the battle of Cloyd Mountain, under command of Maj. Gen. George Crook, in which we were victorious. We then returned to the Kanawha valley and from there continued our march to Wheeling.

June 14, 1864, our term having expired, we were mustered out at Wheeling. There was much excitement and some funny things occurred. I remember, as I was standing in front of a hotel, on Water street, gazing at the pedestrians, a number of them gave me the regular military salute. I was much puzzled over it for some time, but finally discovered the cause. The boys were being paid off, and as soon as they received their money they cast aside their uniform and dressed in citizen's clothes. This made such a change that I failed to recognize them.

In closing this paper, I wish to express my appreciation of the service of my commissary and quartermaster sergeants, who were capable and true in their work and animated by the highest sense of duty for their country. They did their whole duty, as soldiers, and when they retired to private life became citizens of which any country might well be proud. The country owes a debt of gratitude to them for their faithful service, and I recall their devotion to duty as one of the most pleasant recollections of my service. My clerk, Thomas S. Eichbaum, was efficient and attended to his duties with marked ability."

CHAPTER V.

THE CHAPLAIN AND HIS WORK.

Religion and war, though at variance in principle, were closely associated in the War of the Rebellion, perhaps more so than in any war of modern times. While it was the function of the latter to kill and destroy, it was the duty and work of the former to minister to the wounded and care for the dead, though the fallen ones may have been foes in the conflict. How it may have been in other regiments the writer cannot say, but in our favored command there was no officer who did his duty more faithfully than the Chaplain, and no department of the military life that was more vigorous and useful. Rev. J.W.W. Bolton was the chaplain of our regiment in the whole of its service, so that he and his work were one, and so inseparably connected that a description of the work is a sketch of the noble officer who had charge of it.

Rev. James W. W. Bolton, D.D., M.D., was born November 7, 1834, in Harrison county, Va., (now W. Va.) He is a son of John and Sarah I. Bolton - the father a native of Rockingham county, Va., and the mother of Franklin county, Pa. His paternal grandfather, Abraham Bolton, served in the war of 1812, and his maternal grandfather, James O'Hanlon, served throughout the Revolutionary war, under Gen. George Washington. The subject of this sketch was brought up on a farm, in Tyler county, Va., now Pleasants county, W. Va., near the town of Hebron, and received such schooling as the

REV. JAS. W. W. BOLTON,
D.D., M.D.

times afforded, being a close student from his early boyhood. His parents taught him from childhood, by precept and example, the importance and obligations of the Christian religion. He was industrious, and obedient to his parents. The books that most deeply interested his young mind were the Bible and the life of George Washington. He had a great desire to acquire knowledge, and made rapid progress in his studies, having an excellent memory. While a boy he often committed to memory, during the week, a chapter, and sometimes more, of the New Testament, and recited the same at Sunday school. As he grew up he often engaged in debates, in societies for that purpose, in his neighborhood and the surrounding country. He delivered his first Fourth of July oration in 1848. He united with the Methodist Episcopal Church, at Hebron, in 1854, under the ministry of Rev. John B. Hill, now of the Iowa Conference, and was by him licensed to exhort in 1855. He was licensed to preach, in 1856, by Rev. A. J. Lyda, D.D., then Presiding Elder of the Parkersburg District, by order and in behalf of a Quarterly Conference of the Harrisville Circuit. He was engaged in teaching in Virginia and Ohio from 1854 to 1857, and was admitted to the Western Virginia Conference of the M. E. Church (now the West Virginia Conference) in the spring of 1857. His first appointment was the Williamstown Circuit, his colleague being Rev. James W. Latham, brother of Col. George R. Latham. This circuit embraced fifteen appointments which were met by each preacher once every four weeks. In 1858 and 1859 he had charge of the Murrayville Circuit. In December, 1858, he engaged in a four days' theological debate, at Belleville, Va., which gave him a great reputation as a polemic; and the debate was a very useful one to the Church. He was ordained Deacon in April, 1859, by Bishop Thomas A. Morris, at Parkersburg, Va. In 1860 he was stationed at Weston. He was ordained Elder in March, 1861, by Bishop Osmon C. Baker, at Wheeling, Va.

From the firing on Fort Sumter to July, 1861, Dr. Bolton was active in preaching, making Union speeches, in flag raisings, and in the organization of the Home Guard at Hebron. This was an important work, resulting in great and lasting good to that section, and to the state. The Union men were in constant peril, and sacrificed and endured much for their country, a service that cannot be fully appreciated except by those intimately acquainted with it. On July 4, 1861, he delivered an oration at a celebration at Hebron, and the next day went to Clarksburg, Va., where he preached to that part of the Second Virginia Volunteer Infantry Regiment remaining there after July 5th. He was appointed chaplain, and ordered by Colonel John W. Moss to join the regiment being concentrated at Beverly, Va., which he did on August 2, 1861, and was commissioned chaplain of the Second Regiment Virginia Volunteer Infantry, and at once entered on his duties. During the encampment at Beverly, the regiment had no stated place of worship, but frequent services were held in the open air. The first service was held there on Sunday evening, August 4, 1861, when the

CHAPTER V.

regiment was gathered in front of the colonel's tent. The chaplain introduced the services by reading the hymn, the first stanza of which is as follows:

"How sweet the name of Jesus sounds
In a believer's ear!
It soothes his sorrows, heals his wounds,
And drives away his fear."

After the singing of the hymn, he offered a fervent prayer. He then announced as the text, the following: "Therefore if any man be in Christ, he is a new creature: old things are passed away; behold, all things are become new." 2 Corinthians, 5th chapter, 17th verse. It was a beautiful evening, and there was a hush and quiet not usual in a military camp. The men not long from home, with its priceless blessings yet fresh in their minds, felt the solemnity and sacredness of the hour; and there were but few that were not touched by this new phase of service as soldiers. The sermon was clear, forcible and eloquent. The greatest interest was manifested by all, and the service, so sacred and beautiful, was of great benefit to the men, who evidently greatly appreciated it.

During the stay of the regiment at Beverly, the chaplain was busy visiting the sick, burying the dead, and administering to the men; and the services were very laborious. At Elkwater frequent services were held, and of necessity all were out of doors. The regiment had no buildings until near the close of our stay there, when some small ones were erected for winter quarters, and during the stormy months there the open air was the only tabernacle. One of these services will be remembered, held near the breastworks, when the chaplain used one of the cannons for his desk, on which he laid his books. He preached with his usual spirit and fervor, and while the sermon was in progress a heavy snow storm swept down the valley. The chaplain was not in the least discomfited, but continued the services, the men remaining with him to the last. As they had not been in the habit of fleeing from the enemy, they refused to be driven back by the elements. When the exhausting and dangerous raid, beginning December 31, was made to Huntersville, the chaplain went along, and was in the front, exposed to the dangers of the trip, and deported himself with true soldierly bearing, setting a worthy example of bravery and cheerful endurance. The next three months, January to April, 1862, were passed on Cheat Mountain Summit. Here the chaplain rendered a service that was of great value to the men. Very little preaching could be done, except in the company quarters, where occasionally the men were treated to a discourse of great power. The most of the religious work was done in a quiet way in the organization of Bible classes in most of the companies, which were attended by many bright minds, and the discussions that followed the truths brought out, were of incalculable value to all who took part. Preaching out of doors was impossible. Snow storms, heavy drifts, furious winds, and a general warfare of the elements prevented service of that kind. To attempt it was for the preacher to invite a tornado to catch his breath and fill his mouth with snow. But the debates, the sharp criticisms and the close study of the Bible laid the foundation for good and successful work afterward. On the 22d of February, when the anniversary of Washington's birthday was celebrated, the elements harmonized with the occasion, and much and good oratory from Col. Moss and Surgeon Hazlett followed. The exercises of the day were appropriately opened by the chaplain, who devoutly invoked the Divine blessing.

Then followed the active and perilous campaign of the Mountain Department. The troops were almost constantly in motion, but religious services were not omitted on that account. At Monterey, McDowell and Franklin meetings were frequently held, generally out of doors, though the weather at times was very rough. At the battle of McDowell, May 8, 1862, the chaplain asked and obtained permission to join our forces on the mountain, that were fighting so furiously, and kept to the front, rendering what service he could. The campaign up the valley followed, the battle of Cross Keys was fought, and in the latter part of June the brigade was in camp at Strasburg, getting ready for another and more severe campaign. On the 4th of July, Gen. Milroy had a brigade meeting to celebrate the day, on which occasion he made a speech to his admiring and delighted men, who came about as near idolizing him as ever men did a brigade commander. The general made a special request that Chaplain Bolton should open the services with prayer, which he accordingly did. The general had great confidence in the chaplain, and lost no opportunity of showing it. Preaching services were held whenever practicable, and with our chaplain that meant when it was not impossible. In the Pope campaign, and until the order to return to Western Virginia, religious services were held as frequently as possible. After crossing the Blue Ridge, and while in camp at Woodville, the chaplain preached to the regiment, and omitted nothing that could be done for the spiritual benefit of the men. At Cedar Mountain, the day after the big fight, and while our forces were yet contending, services were held, the bullets coming uncomfortably near the improvised pulpit, but not interrupting the services. In the exciting campaign that followed, services were held as often as circumstances permitted, but there was very little time, for some days, for anything but fighting. After the retreat to Washington, while lying in the defences at that city, regular services were held for the remnant left of the regiment, and continued until the order came for our return to Western Virginia.

Upon our return to Beverly, we were again in position to hold regular religious services. The Presbyterian Church had been used by the quartermaster department, and the seats were all gone and the building in very bad

CHAPTER V.

condition. The chaplain asked permission of the trustees to use the building for religious services, which was cheerfully granted. He then called for volunteers to put the church in proper condition, when men of all the trades needed offered their services, and seats were made, flues built, and the house was thoroughly cleaned and everything put in good shape for occupancy. The church was opened with Thanksgiving services in November, and used until we were compelled to leave in April, 1863. A protracted meeting was held lasting about two months, during which Chaplain Bolton did all the preaching, except two or three sermons by a Presbyterian preacher. The revival was one of great power, deep and lasting in its work, resulting in about fifty conversions, and the strengthening of many believers. Many who gave their hearts to God in this meeting, afterward fell in battle, and they died as true soldiers of the cross, as well as of their country. The meetings were characterized by great power, with the choicest singing, the very best of order and the highest respect for the place; and were attended by a fine, noble appearing class of men, who reverently took part in the services and helped materially in them. The church was packed, audience room and gallery, and there was preaching every night, and sometimes during the day. When the revival services were not in progress, regular services were held on Sunday and prayer meetings during the week, which were attended by the soldiers and many citizens; among the latter Mrs. Arnold, the Bakers, Harts and others. After the retreat from Beverly, Thanksgiving and other services were held at Buckhannon. There were services in camp at New Creek, the latter part of November, 1863. During the series of raids by Gen. Averell, to January, 1864, the chaplain was along doing whatever he could, and always at the front, but there were but few public services. He helped the surgeons, prayed and talked with and cheered the men, and proved himself to be what he always was, a true, noble, brave man, ready for whatever duty fell to his hands. Our command lay in camp at Martinsburg, West Va., over two months from January 1, 1864, one of the most trying places in its history. Here services were held regularly, and during the time a revival of great power was enjoyed. The meetings were held in the Lutheran Church, and were conducted by Chaplains Bolton, Osborn, 14th Pennsylvania Cavalry, and Pomeroy, 18th Connecticut, and lasted about six weeks. Chaplain Bolton preached each alternate night. At first the singing did not go smoothly, and there was some concern about it. Chaplain Bolton took hold of it, and with his strong, musical voice started a familiar old Methodist hymn. That night a large number of his regiment was present, and the boys understood at once that they were to help, and scores of voices joined the chaplain's. The regiment had in it an unusual number of good singers, and when these grand voices joined in, there was no longer any doubt as to the singing. The charming old hymn was sung with a will, the church fairly ringing with the melody, to the great delight of Chaplain Pomeroy and the gallant

Connecticut boys, who were evidently not used to such singing. It was a glorious series of meetings, and many were converted. Other services were also held. Chaplain Bolton went to Hedgesville, where a portion of our regiment was in camp, among the number, Maj. Barclay, Lieut. Colmer and others, and preached one Sunday to them. The last services he held in the regiment, were at Charleston, in the Kanawha valley, before entering on the expedition that led to Cloyd Mountain.

The duties of the chaplain were varied and many, and the office was not one of leisure, but of continual and severe work. In time of battle he was called to minister to the wounded and dying, and in the hospitals to comfort the unfortunate inmates of both armies. He had particularly heavy duties at Second Bull Run and Rocky Gap. While at Washington many days were spent in visiting the hospitals and ministering to the sick and wounded. Chaplain Bolton was severely wounded at the battle of Cloyd Mountain, Va., May 9, 1864, being shot in the right ankle by a musket ball. He was taken to Charleston, West Va., on May 23, and remained there till June 15, when he was removed to the General Hospital at Parkersburg, West Va., where he entered June 17, 1864. The trip from Cloyd Mountain to Charleston, in all 14 days, was very painful and exhausting. He was taken in ambulance, by way of Dublin, Union, Meadow Bluff, Sewell Mountains and Gauley bridge, to a point on the Great Kanawha river, about 20 miles above Charleston; and from that point by boat, to the last named place. The roads were very rough and mountainous. He was very much prostrated when he reached Charleston. From there he was taken by boat to Parkersburg. When he reached there he was very much reduced in health and strength, by reason of his wound. The Rev. Thomas H. Monroe, of the West Virginia Conference of the M. E. Church, was the chaplain of the hospital. While there Chaplain Bolton sometimes preached to the boys, but he had to sit down while preaching. Soon after he was able to sit up, he was invited by Chaplain Monroe and others to preach. All were anxious to hear the wounded chaplain. It was arranged for him to preach on Sunday evening, about the first of September. When the hour came, some of the boys placed him in an armchair and carried him into the chapel, which was filled to overflowing with brave soldiers who had experienced hard service in the army and had stood in the front of battle, but who, on account of wounds or diseases were then inmates of the hospital. In the congregation were some who had heard him preach when he was strong and could stand. Although he was weak and in pain, he preached to the great delight and edification of the audience. The Lord helped him, and Chaplain Monroe and the brave soldiers encouraged him with their sympathies and prayers. The audience was very much affected. Brave men wept while he preached. The ball was extracted from the wound on February 3, 1865, by Surgeon W. A. Banks, U. S. A., assisted by Drs. C. D. Safford and J. C. Clemmer. The operation was difficult and painful, but the

CHAPTER V.

brave chaplain endured it like a hero. He was discharged from the hospital at Parkersburg on March 21, 1865, and was mustered out of the service March 24, 1865, at Wheeling, West Va. He suffered intense pain, and the wound has greatly hurt him ever since, making him very much of a cripple for life.

He was appointed by Bishop E. S. Janes, in March, 1865, to Ellenboro and Harrisville, an appointment made by the kind Bishop for the special benefit of the heroic chaplain, as he had attended to his ministerial duties on crutches. He entered on the duties of the charge on the first of April, though weak and suffering. He had to be helped on his horse to ride to his appointments. He used his crutches for months after being mustered out of the service, and has had to use a stout cane from that time on. Until the spring of 1885, the wound continued to break out, at intervals, and discharge pieces of bone; and since that time there have been, at times, indications of re-opening of the wound. He is never free from pain, and at times suffers greatly from the wound. He may yet have to undergo amputation of the wounded limb. In 1866, be was appointed to Fairmont Station, where he did good service for the church, although suffering daily in consequence of his wound. Having studied medicine, he entered on the practice of the same in the spring of 1867, and continued the practice until the summer of 1870. He had charge of the Sistersville circuit in 1869-70. In 1871 he was stationed at Parkersburg, remaining there until 1874. While he was there a fine church and parsonage were built. In the spring of 1874 he was appointed Presiding Elder of the Clarksburg district, and remained until the fall of 1877, the time of the Conference having been changed from spring to fall. He was then appointed Presiding Elder of the Morgantown district, and served till the fall of 1881. He was elected delegate to the General Conference in 1876, and served on the Committees on Episcopacy and Revisals, and participated in the debates of the Conference. He was appointed on the Publishing Committee of the Pittsburgh *Christian Advocate*, to serve from 1870 to 1880. On account of the severity of his wound, Dr. Bolton was compelled to take a supernumerary relation from 1867 to 1869, also from 1881 to 1885, and from 1888 to 1889, though often preaching while in this relation.

In 1881 his wound opened, causing great pain and discharging pieces of bone. He then concluded to attend medical lectures, which he did at the University of Maryland, Baltimore, Md., in the fall and winter of 1881, the spring of 1882, and the fall and winter of 1882, and he was graduated in March, 1883, with the degree of M.D., and was authorized to practice in West Virginia by the State Board of Health, and then resumed the practice of medicine, continuing in the same till the fall of 1885, when he again entered the active work of the ministry, and was appointed to Short Creek and Liberty, 1885 to 1887. In the fall of 1887 he was appointed to Oakland, Md., and to Fairmont Station in 1889. In the year 1879, he was honored with the degree of D.D., by Allegheny College, Meadville, Pa.

Dr. Bolton was married on September 26, 1865, to Miss Eunice C. Buckley, daughter of Harrison W. and Eliza J. Buckley, near Worthington, Marion county, W. Va., by Rev. A. J. Lyda, D.D., then presiding elder of the Clarksburg district. The parents of both Dr. Bolton and wife were strong Union people, together with their families, and endured much for their country. It was at times at the peril of their lives that they maintained and expressed their loyalty to the old flag and the Union, but they never wavered, for a moment, in their duty. They were active in every possible way to help maintain the Union, and did their full share in stemming the tide of disunion that threatened at one time to overwhelm Western Virginia. It was owing to loyal people like these, that this noble young state threw off the shackles of the pro-slavery power, and emphatically and early declared for the Union. Too much honor cannot be awarded them for their patriotic and brave services. Dr. Bolton is a man of strong intellect, highly educated, of a high order of ability, and an accomplished gentleman. He has been a very useful man in his conference. He showed signal ability as a presiding elder. He has succeeded well in all departments of ministerial work. Since the war he has often been called on to dedicate churches, and in that work he has always succeeded grandly. He commands large congregations; and those who hear him once, desire to hear him again. He is most loved and respected by those who know him best and have been longest acquainted with him. He is often requested to preach funeral sermons in memory of old friends in the country where he was brought up, and elsewhere. On these occasions vast crowds of people, old and young, come to hear him. He is also often called on to deliver lectures and addresses on special occasions and select subjects. He has been frequently called on to preach the annual sermon in memory of our deceased soldiers, and to deliver the address on Decoration day. He at one time read quite an extensive course in law, though not with the intention of practicing the profession of law. He is well informed in medicine, theology, the sciences, and general literature. He is a skillful physician and an able minister. He has a good knowledge of the dead languages, and reads, with facility, the Bible in the original tongues. He has a kind heart and is very benevolent to the needy. He is a man of strong convictions, and has the courage to avow and follow them.

  He was chosen chaplain of the Society of the Army of West Virginia in 1886, 1887 and 1889. The late General George Crook was President of the Society of the Army of West Virginia at the time of his death. He and the Chaplain were very warm friends. When General Crook was buried at Oakland, Md., Chaplain Bolton attended and participated in the services. The present year (1890) is one of the most successful in his ministry. During the past winter he conducted revival services in Fairmont, with great success. The church there is in a very prosperous condition, and is increasing in numbers and spirituality. He is much loved and admired by the people of his charge, and he

CHAPTER V.

reciprocates their affection. The relations of pastor and people are mutually pleasant. Dr. Bolton is a true friend of the old soldiers, and is warmly attached to the members of his regiment.

CHAPTER VI.

IN CAMP AT BEVERLY, 1861.

The demoralized remnants of Pegram's and Garnett's commands were hovering around our lines, bushwhacking our supply trains and scouting parties. The three months volunteers had cleared the field from the Ohio river to Elkwater and Cheat Mountain Summit, and ours was the army of occupation; but these fragments of a proud army organized themselves into predatory bands, with the view of preying on the tempting booty of government stores that every day lined the Staunton pike from Webster to Cheat Mountain, a distance of 67 miles. To protect our lines and the government property, scouting parties were frequently sent out to break up the bands of bushwhackers. Soon after our arrival at Beverly, Lieut. Devore, of Company I, and Lieut. Smythe, of Company F, were ordered out with a squad, to look after some of these bushwhackers, in the direction of Corrick's Ford. They returned the same day, and after taking a hasty supper, Lieut. Devore was again sent out with twenty of his own men, to intercept a Confederate mail carrier. The detachment lay out all night, watching a bridle path on the side of Cheat Mountain. It was a dark, dreary night, and the pelting rain fell without cessation, making the situation an exceedingly uncomfortable one. The party returned to camp in the morning without any knowledge of the mail carrier, but with the proud consciousness of having done some severe duty.

On the 18th of August, a detachment of the Second Virginia and Sixth Ohio, numbering 50 men, was sent to the Laurel fork of the Cheat river. They followed an old road across Shaffer Mountain, and as they approached the river the road became very marshy, and the heavy pines and thick laurels stood like a wall on either side of the road. A body of the enemy lay in ambush on the opposite side of the narrow stream, and as our party were wading through the water, unconscious of a foe in such close proximity, they were startled by the sharp report of a rifle, followed quickly by another and another, and two of the party lay dead and one other mortally wounded. The detachment was helpless, the enemy being secure amid the dense laurel thickets, which were so thick that man or beast could be so completely hidden in them that no eye could detect their presence, while our forces were open to their view, and closely within the range of their muskets. Resistance was useless, and our men hastily retreated through the narrow defile. Hurriedly gathering up the dead and the wounded, they retraced their steps as rapidly as possible, carrying the wounded man to a rude cabin on Shaffer mountain, where they were obliged to leave him, while they tenderly wrapped the bodies of their dead comrades in their blankets and buried them in the mountain. When they returned to camp, the report of their expedition created a great excitement, and Col. Bosley, in command of the post, immediately ordered out a detachment of one hundred men from each of the two regiments, under command of Maj. J. D. Owens, of the Second Virginia. They found the wounded man, and upon arriving at the place where the other party had met such disaster, they were also fired into, but fortunately no one was hurt, and the command proceeded across Cheat and Shaffer mountains to the foot of the Alleghenies. After emptying their rifles this time, the bushwhackers fled, leaving their horses and saddles, which were captured by our men. To provide against surprise and ambushes, Lieut. Devore was directed at one place to take twenty men and go around a foot hill and fall in with the advance guard on the other side. The advance had not been apprised of this movement, and as the squad was approaching the road through the underbrush, the bullets of the advance began to whistle around their ears, much to their discomfort, but the mistake was fortunately discovered before any damage was done. At the foot of Shaffer mountain, two of Company I being in the advance, created quite an alarm by shooting two fat sheep, but before the rear could come up on a double quick, the sheep were skinned. This was a flagrant breach of orders, but the officers were pacified and a general compromise effected, by building a fire and cooking the mutton, which afforded a rare feast. On the third day the detachment returned to camp, having traveled almost uninterruptedly more than one hundred miles.

The scouting, and sentinel duty, were necessarily very heavy, and the new soldiers were soon inured to the hardships and privations that were afterward to be a part of their every day life. The discipline was rigid, and whenever the rain would permit, the troops were thoroughly drilled in the manual of arms, and in company and regimental evolutions. Everything that went to make up the soldier's life was experienced and nothing was omitted that would fit the troops for the stern realities of war, that came to us shortly afterward. Pages could be written of the pleasant scenes, the hours of relaxation and enjoyment, that came to brighten the soldier's life; and the weeks at Beverly had many bright spots and hours. The lack of veneration for officers in high command,

CHAPTER VI.

coupled with the controling desire to serve faithfully our country, led to many absurd and ludicrous situations. While the colonel or the captain might still be John or Jim in the affections and expressions of the men, yet an order in the line of duty from these same officers, would be carried out regardless of results.

Jack Halpin, of Company D, was well known throughout the regiment. He was from the Five Points, N.Y., and was a "case," yet good hearted and obliging. Just after the battle of Rich Mountain, Jack paid a visit to the village, and while on his way back to camp, saw an individual who wore a slouch hat, and who pulled from his pocket a large plug of tobacco and took a chew. The command had received no pay as yet, and the men were run down financially, so that tobacco was one of the luxuries. Jack thought he would improve the opportunity, so he stepped up to the stranger, and said: "Give us a chew, Cap." The individual addressed looked Jack over and replied, "I guess not." The crushing reply of Jack was, "Go to the D----l," and he went on his way to camp. Shortly afterward, there was a rush to the road on the side of the camp, to see some one pass, and among those that went over was Jack. The person passing was General Rosecrans, who happened to be the same person that refused Jack a chew of his tobacco. Jack related what had happened, and quietly remarked that be would get even. That night Jack was detailed on guard duty. The countersign had just been issued, when a horseman came dashing through the darkness up to the post where Jack was stationed. The night was a beastly one, the rain falling in torrents, and the mud ankle deep. Jack halted the horseman and ordered him to dismount, and advance with the countersign. General Rosecrans, for it was he, told Jack who he was, and said that the mud was so deep that he would ride up and give him the countersign. But Jack knew his business, and here was his opportunity to get even, so he said, "Get off that horse and come forward, or I will put a hole through you." Jack didn't get his chew when he wanted it, but the general was nearly swamped in the mud before he was permitted to pass.

Every road and path had its picket, and the camps were strictly guarded. It was while the guards were under the most stringent orders to pass no one at night without the countersign, that the biter was bit, or, in other words, that Col. Bosley was subjected to an exceedingly practical joke, if such it was. About two miles from town, on the road that passes from Beverly over Rich mountain to Buchannon, there was a tavern kept by a Mr. Baker, who, by the way, was a good Union man, and kept everything in first-class order. There was a picket on the bridge that spans the river close to Beverly on this road. One afternoon, Col. Bosley, with his staff, crossed the bridge and rode out to the tavern. Here they dined and were detained until after dark. The officer of the day had made his rounds, and the pickets made acquainted with the countersign. Night had fully set in and it was as dark as erebus. Charley

Hixenbaugh, of Company I, was on post at the bridge, and was on the alert for anything in his line of duty. Presently he heard the clatter of horses' hoofs. Near and nearer they came, when, ringing out sharp and clear on the night air, was heard the voice of the faithful sentinel:

"Halt! who comes there?"

The answer was immediate:

"Col. Bosley and staff."

"Dismount one, advance, and give the countersign," demanded the sentinel.

"Well, but we haven't the countersign," said the colonel; "my name is Col. Bosley, commander of this post."

"Don't care a d--n," said Charley; "my name is Charley Hixenbaugh, of Bellevernon, and you can't pass;" and there the Bellevernon boy held the colonel until the arrival of the sergeant of the guard, who decided that the colonel and his belated escort might pass into town.

Shortly after entering the service, Dr. Hazlett was temporarily promoted to the position of brigade surgeon, and when new recruits with their medical officers arrived, it was his duty to instruct the latter how to proceed. Surgeon A., of the --- Cavalry, had come, more splendidly arrayed than Solomon, elegantly uniformed, sword and sash, military hat and plume, gauntlet gloves, etc. Calling at the surgeon's headquarters, which were at the foot of a tree, he inquired how he was to obtain medical supplies for his battalion. Being informed that they would be forthcoming upon a requisition, he desired to know what that was. When enlightened, he inquired where he could procure an ambulance. The answer to that was by a requisition upon the quartermaster. "But," he replied, "we have no quartermaster;" and before time was given to answer him, he struck an attitude and said, "I have it, *I'll make a requisition for a quartermaster*," and off he strutted. Surgeon Hazlett met him sometime afterward, sword, sash, hat and plume gone, unkempt and unshaven, his whole outfit would not have brought 75 cents. The surgeon drily remarked in regard to it; "In his dilapidated state, I had not the heart to ask him about the requisition, but mostly for the reason if I had done so, he would have trounced me."

When the regiment went to Elkwater, a few of the men were left behind to guard the post. S.J. Clendaniel relates an incident that shows their fidelity, if not their sagacity, as soldiers. Capt. Otto was in command, things began to look dangerous, and orders were very strict. One night a picket shot was heard, and the posts all fired in turn, creating consternation in the camp. The guards were ordered to fire at anything they saw move, and they carried out orders to the letter. Geo. E. McCloy, of Company F, was posted beyond the Methodist Church near the river, when he was discovered by the bridge guard, who opened fire upon him. McCloy returned the compliment, and the firing became general throughout the camp. Capt. Otto came to the rescue and

CHAPTER VI.

saved bloodshed between the contending forces. He double quicked his men down to the Court House, followed the road some distance, when bang went a gun, and a regular fusilade followed. It looked as if a real fight was now on the hands of the boys, and they were ordered to fall back to the jail. The officer in command there inquired the cause of the firing. The captain stated some one had discovered a black stump and fired upon it, creating an alarm that almost resulted seriously. The same night Clendaniel's gun went off accidentally, the bullet almost hitting a drill master who was near, lodging in the weather boarding just over his head. It was an eventful night of alarms, but fortunately no one was hurt. But the awkward recruits of Beverly, soon learned better the arts of war, and in after days were as efficient as they were brave and true.

During August the troops at Beverly suffered severely from typhoid fever, dysentery and diarrhea, and many of them will remember with gratitude all their lives the kind words, the careful attention and the refreshing delicacies from the good women of that town. One in particular deserves honorable mention, Mrs. Jonathan Arnold, a sister of the Confederate Gen. "Stonewall" Jackson, who was lavish in her offices of kindness. Her fragile form was almost ubiquitous in the hospitals, and with her own tender hands she soothed the aching temples of many a dying soldier boy, far away from the loved ones at home. She was as an angel of mercy among the sick, and did all in her power to render less arduous and irksome the lives of the country's defenders. She was ardently attached to the Union cause, notwithstanding the devotion of her distinguished brother, and other relatives, including her husband, to the Confederate cause. Of this noble woman, Dr. Hazlett, surgeon of the regiment, speaks in the most glowing terms. He was in position to see her work of love, and says: "Many incidents of her loyalty and courage are personally known to the writer. Almost alone, amidst a disloyal community, she unflinchingly declared her devotion to the flag, not only by word but act. Her house was an asylum for the sick soldier, and faithfully she ministered to his wants. Her resources were often taxed to their utmost, and many were her regrets that she was unable to do greater good. On more than one occasion have I found her the sole watcher at the bedside of a disabled soldier. We have never heard that she received one farthing from the government, for her generous and loyal outlay, and have reason to believe that she never made application; but if there is one deserving soul in the great army of patriots that merits special recognition at the hands of the republic, it is Mrs. Jonathan Arnold."

CHAPTER VII.

RELIEF OF CHEAT MOUNTAIN.

General R. E. Lee was now in command of the "Army of Northern Virginia," advancing to retrieve the losses of Gens. Floyd and Wise. The predatory bands were called from their fastnesses in the mountains of Western Virginia, and reorganized with large additions at Staunton and Lynchburg. Having fully completed his arrangements, early in September Lee ordered the advance with 11,000 men. As he approached Cheat Mountain he divided his forces into two columns, sending one along the Staunton pike to attack Col. Kimball, of the 14th Indiana, with his 300 men on the summit of the mountain, and leading the other in person by the Huntersville road toward Elkwater. His object was to get to the left and rear of the latter post. Four companies of Indiana troops, however, held the whole force in check, and forced them to the rear and right of Cheat Mountain, completely hemming in the 300 who held the summit. This event was sprung so suddenly and unexpectedly upon Reynolds' outposts, that the only wonder is that they were not captured without firing a gun. But the word surrender was not in the vocabulary of the beleaguered Indiana boys, who stood firm to their posts and held the attacking troops completely at bay until relief came to them.

On the 12th of September, the Second Virginia and Sixth Ohio Infantry, were ordered up from Beverly on a forced march, starting at 3 o'clock in the afternoon, leaving behind a small detachment of the Second for camp and garrison duty at Beverly.

The regiments arrived at Huttonsville after dark, and waited there long enough to take a good rest, when they pushed rapidly on to Elkwater. The mud was fearful, being in many places axle deep, rendering travel hard and difficult. The march from Huttonsville was through intense darkness, rendered doubly so by the lowering clouds, the lofty mountains about us,

173

and the thick forests of pine that stood like blackened walls on either side the column. As we marched along, ever and anon would be heard a smothered exclamation from some comrade, whose foot had haplessly caught in a root or laurel bush, tripping him and sending him headlong into the abyss of mire. It was fun for the rest of the comrades, but a very grave matter for the mud bespattered boy. Thus we marched for twelve weary miles, but the men stood it bravely, the cheering prospects of a brush with the enemy banishing all grumbling and discontent. We made no secret of our march. The shouts of the teamsters as they plunged along through the mud; the shouts of laughter when some comrade met a muddy fate, commingled with the war whoops of the men and the loud commands of the officers, reached the ears of the rebel force that lay along the base of the mountain on the opposite side of the valley through which the narrow river ran, striking them with terror, and no doubt aiding in inducing them to abandon their contemplated capture of the gallant 300 men on the summit of Cheat mountain, who were now completely surrounded. The two regiments arrived at Elkwater about midnight, having marched twenty-five miles in less than nine hours. They were greeted with loud cheers by the small garrison at Elkwater, and the tired and mud-covered troops soon found repose on the wet ground where, without shelter, they slept till the *reveille* called them to duty. After partaking of a hasty and meagre breakfast, the Second Virginia and the Third Ohio, which took the place of the Sixth Ohio, started for the work that was before them - to help drive Lee's army of 11,000 back across Cheat river, and thus relieve the little garrison on Cheat mountain. The Second Virginia, with Col. Moss at its head, was ordered to take the advance. The boys stripped for the fray, and arriving at the swollen river, dashed through it waist deep with a cheerfulness that was prophetic of certain victory. The Third Ohio catching the inspiration, followed with a bound, and the dripping column moved rapidly forward.

    The enemy had taken position on the side of a foot hill of Cheat mountain, his right resting at Becca creek, a small mountain stream running down a gulch in the mountain three or four miles from the summit. The pickets at the base of the foot hill were soon discovered, but taking alarm at the bold front of the advancing column, they fled to their camp and gave the alarm. The two regiments now came up on the double quick, charging over the rocks and through the bushes up the mountain, with the prospect of finding the enemy somewhere in line of battle; but in this they were disappointed, for they soon reached his camp, which was found to be deserted, and the morning meal of hot corn and coffee was left smoking by the lonesome looking camp fires. The troops picked up haversacks, guns, pistols, etc., besides nearly 700 blankets, and took a hasty lunch of the hot corn and coffee. The enemy continued his flight with such celerity that pursuit from that point was deemed useless, and Gen. Reynolds gave orders to hold the position at all hazards, as that was the

CHAPTER VII.

key to the camp on the summit. The enemy's line had extended along the base of the mountain, a distance of some four miles south of Becca creek, and parallel with the river, his left resting a short distance above the mouth of Elkwater; and while the stirring events referred to were occurring, Lee's forces made an attack on Reynolds at Elkwater, but were repulsed, and he hastily fell back and took position above the mouth of the creek. The next day, rallying his disheartened army, he made another desperate effort to carry our position at Elkwater, and simultaneously made an attack on Cheat river bridge, but was again repulsed with a severe loss, and retreated ten miles.

In the memoirs of Gen. Robert E. Lee, pages 122 to 126, an account is given of this campaign, as follows:

The possession of the pass (Cheat mountain) was of great importance to the Confederates, as the Parkersburg turnpike was the principal line over which operations could be successfully carried on in northwestern Virginia.

Early in September, Gen. H.R. Jackson reported to Gen. Loring that Col. Rust, Third Arkansas regiment, had made a reconnaissance to the rear of Cheat mountain pass, and had discovered a route, though difficult, by which infantry could be led. Soon after Col. Rust reported in person, and informed Gen. Lee of the practicability of reaching the rear of the enemy's position on Cheat mountain, from which a favorable attack could be made.

Another route was in the meantime discovered, leading along the western side of Cheat mountain, by which troops could be conducted to a point on the Parkersburg turnpike about two miles below the Federal position in the pass. This being the information that Gen. Lee had been most desirous of obtaining, he determined to attack the enemy without further delay. The opposing forces at this time were about equal in numbers. Loring's force was now 6,000, Jackson's about 5,000 strong. Reynolds' force had been increased to about 11,000 men; of these, 2,000 were on Cheat mountain and about 5,000 in position on the Lewisburg road in front of Loring. The remainder of Reynolds' force was held in reserve near the junction of the Parkersburg turnpike and the Lewisburg road.

Lee determined to attack on the morning of the 12th of September. The plan was that Col. Rust should gain the rear of the Federal position by early dawn and begin the attack. Gen. Anderson, with two Tennessee regiments from Loring's command, was to support him, while Jackson was to make a diversion in front. Cheat Mountain Pass being carried, Jackson with his whole force was to sweep down the mountain and fall upon the rear of the other Federal position; Gen. Donaldson with two regiments was to gain a favorable position for attacking the enemy on the Lewisburg road in flank or rear; and Loring was to advance by the main road on the Federal front. In case of failure, Anderson and Donaldson were to rejoin Loring, and Rust was to find his way back to Jackson. The troops gained their designated positions with remarkable promptness and accuracy in point of time, considering the distance and the difficulties to be overcome. Col. Rust's attack on Cheat Mountain was to be the signal for the general advance of all the troops. It was anxiously expected from early dawn throughout the day.

The Tennesseeans under Anderson became so impatient that they requested to be led to the attack without waiting for Rust, but Anderson thought that he must be governed by the letter of his instructions and declined granting the request of his men.

Anderson and Donaldson, finding that their situation was becoming critical, being liable to discovery and between two superior forces, rejoined Loring on the 13th. On the same day Col. Rust reported in person his operations, which amounted to this: He had heard nothing of Anderson; he passed the day watching the Federals, who were in a state of unconscious security, and then retired, his presence not having been suspected.

A council of war was then held, in which it was decided that the position of the Federals was too strong to be attacked in front with any reasonable prospect of success, and that a flank attack was now out of the question, inasmuch as the Federals had been aroused by the discovery of the danger which had so recently threatened them. The troops were therefore ordered to resume their former positions.

In a letter to Governor Letcher, dated September 17, Gen. Lee wrote as follows about his failure:

I was very sanguine of taking the enemy's works on last Thursday morning. I had considered the subject well. With great effort the troops intended for the surprise had reached their destination, having traversed twenty miles of steep, rugged mountain paths, and the last day through a terrible storm, which lasted all night, and in which they had to stand drenched to the skin in the cold rain. Still their spirits were good. When morning broke I could see the enemy's tents on Valley river at the point on the Huttonsville road just below me. It was a tempting sight. We waited for the attack on Cheat mountain, which was to be the signal, till 10 a.m.; the men were cleaning their unserviceable arms. But the signal did not come. All chance for surprise was gone. The provisions of the men had been destroyed the preceding day by the storm. They had nothing to eat that morning, could not hold out another day, and were obliged to be withdrawn. The party sent to Cheat mountain to take that in in the rear had also to be withdrawn. The attack to come off from the east side failed from the difficulties in the way; the opportunity was lost and our plan discovered. It is a grievous disappointment to me, I assure you. But for the rainstorm I have no doubt it would have succeeded. This, Governor, is for your own eyes. Please do not speak of it; we must try again.

The garrison at the summit, magnified into 2,000 by General Lee, consisted in fact of 300, which may be taken as a fair indication of Lee's estimate of our

CHAPTER VII.

forces, and of the reasons that led to his utter rout in the mountains. The facts are that he was out generaled and outfought, and that by a force less than his own. The forces so completely routed and driven from their stronghold, were under the eye of General Lee, and to our regiment is due, in part, the honor of administering the first defeat to General Lee.

Colonel Moss, of the Second, who was senior officer, in command of that little army at Becca Creek, immediately turned his attention to the relief of the 300 men on the summit. It was necessary that communication be opened without delay, as the force he had just driven from their camp near Becca creek, would probably make a hasty march back to the Staunton pike on the other side of the mountain, and unite with the force at the Cheat river bridge, for the purpose of capturing Colonel Kimball on the summit, or with their whole force combined, they might return with the view of routing Col. Moss' command.

The Fourteenth was spent in scouting and adjusting the picket lines. One of the guards fired at our own men, which brought the entire command into line of battle. On the 15th a scouting party of twenty men from Company I, was ordered to open communication with Kimball's camp on the mountain. They followed a bridle path along the side of the mountain and reached the pike about three miles west of the summit, where they met a scouting party from the garrison who, supposing our boys to be rebels, prepared to give them a warm reception, but fortunately two of Col. Kimball's men were with the latter acting as guides, who were recognized. Two dead rebels were found lying near where the path strikes the pike, who had been killed the previous day while engaged in action with Kimball's forces, and left unburied. Colonel Sullivan with the Thirteenth Indiana regiment, had marched from Huttonsville the day before, and assisted Kimball in clearing the pike. They had a brisk fight with the enemy at or near the junction of the path and pike, in which the latter were repulsed with a severe loss, the woods being strewn with their guns and clothing in large quantities. The force on the summit were at work unceasingly, and felled acres of heavy pines on the eastern slope of the mountain, so as to sweep the bridge that spans the river less than a mile from the summit, where the Confederates were making repeated efforts to cross, with a view of taking the garrison by storm. Then Colonel Moss deemed it necessary to fortify his position on Becca creek, with the expectation that Lee would pay the camp a flying visit, and breastworks were thrown up capable of giving protection to the two regiments, being yet all the troops there. The path leading to the pike was picketed and patroled day and night, and every precaution taken to guard against surprise. We were ordered to hold this position at all hazards, and this too when reduced to half rations, compelled to live and sleep in the open air, without the shadow of a tent, while the rain poured down in torrents, drenching everything susceptible to water.

On the night of the 20th the pickets began firing, when the command was hastily formed behind the breastworks, ready to repel the anticipated attack of the enemy. Guns were carefully examined and every preparation made for the scene of carnage momentarily expected. The officers passing along the line, cautioned us not to fire until the command was given, and then to fire low. We patiently waited for that command, shivering in the cold night air, but it never came. Ere long quiet reigned in the valley, the guards were again posted, and we were ordered to sleep on our arms. It has not been learned to this day what the pickets fired at. Morning came, and Capt. Plankey with one party, and Capt. Smith with another of 20 men from his own company, scouted through the surrounding country, but failed to find the enemy. Capt. Smith's party went about five miles and returned with two fat ground hogs as the fruit of their expedition. A great deal more scouting was done, and energy wasted, during our stay in the lonely valley. On the 22d a supply train reached us, and our hunger was relieved. The Sixth Ohio and an Indiana regiment passed through the valley to the summit of Cheat Mountain, thus relieving us, and we returned to Elkwater on the 23d pretty well worn out. The long, forced march of the men on the night of the 12th from Beverly to Elkwater; their plunging through the river on the morning of the 13th; their incessant scouting, picketing and scouring the mountains in drenching rains without shelter, and living on half rations for eleven days and nights, spoke volumes for their powers of endurance, and an iron constitution could not endure much more. Gen. Reynolds complimented the officers and men for their gallantry in charging over those rugged steeps and dislodging the enemy, for their promptness in executing every command, and also for their bravery and tenacity in holding a position of such vital importance, constantly menaced by a force five times their own, without shelter and almost without food, heedless of the pelting showers that daily and nightly fell for those eleven days. But the work was done and well done. Lee had been held in check at Cheat Mountain and Becca Creek, and repulsed at Elkwater, and was disheartened. Lee, who subsequently distinguished himself as the great military leader of the Confederates, had come to retrieve the disasters of Floyd and Wise, and was himself repulsed. But his great disaster in this campaign, compelled him to relinquish his hold on this western region, and we may well imagine his chagrin, as he led his defeated army away from before the bristling bayonets and guns of Cheat Mountain and Elkwater.

CHAPTER VIII.

IN CAMP AT ELKWATER.

About this time the enemy was organizing camps for the enlistment and drill of recruits at various points near our lines. One of these was at the base of Elk mountain, at a place called Mingo Flats, one at Huntersville, and another at Lewisburg. To break up these camps, and capture or destroy their supplies was a desideratum, inasmuch as the inclement season was coming on, and it was important for us to render such posts untenable and thus put an end to enlistments.

On the 6th of October, Gen. Reynolds ordered out the 2nd Virginia, 3d Ohio, 6th Ohio, Baum's battery and one battalion of cavalry, the colonel of the 3rd Ohio being placed in command. About 3 o'clock in the afternoon, the expedition left Elkwater. The heavy rains had rendered the narrow road almost impassable, and the mountain streams were swollen bank full; but the column moved forward, and when night fell on that wild and dreary region, they found themselves in a deserted rebel camp, where they remained without shelter, on the wet ground, until morning. It was a fearful night. The rain fell almost in torrents, seeming to ooze from the evergreens over our heads, and as the drops fell on the weary bodies of the soldiers, they cut like icicles, chilling one to the very heart. Any who could were glad to seek shelter under a pile of brush, or under the friendly protection of a fence or pile of stones. The next morning the command was out bright and early, ready for the day's work. The line of march was taken up, and by noon we arrived at Mingo Flats, but the enemy had heard of the approach of the column, and hastened to Huntersville. The cavalry was sent in pursuit and after following them a few miles, found the tents, wagons, guns, etc., of the Confederates all in a pile burning, and their cartridge boxes strewed along the way, while several boxes of cartridges were soaking in a stream near by. This, aside from the empty honor of having been bushwhacked, was the sum total of our whole work, and we prepared to return to camp. The column started back, slept on the wet ground that night, and reached camp the next day, wading through the swollen streams more than a dozen times in the one morning.

On the twentieth of the month the detachment of the Second, which had been detained at Beverly for post duty, rejoined the regiment at Elkwater, and the joy of meeting was unbounded. The severe campaigning through which we had just passed had tested the capabilities of the men for the hardships incident to a soldier's life. Many of the men of the regiment were broken down and disabled, and a number were discharged, leaving a body of hardy and brave men, fitted for the most onerous duties of the hard service in the mountains. The regiment was now fitted out with new guns, the best make of Minie muskets. The old muskets were turned back to the government without the shedding of a single tear. It is true the venerable weapons had seen some very active service; some of them had poured forth their contents into the ranks of the enemy, and kicked back about as hard into the shoulders of the men manning them, but these considerations failed to evoke much sympathy. We were tired of carrying howitzers. The order was now given to build winter quarters, and every day the clanking axe could be heard on the hill sides felling trees. Drilling, building quarters and recuperating were the order of the day. Many foraging expeditions were made into the more fertile parts of the valleys and hills to get hay and corn for the use of the horses, and sometimes for something palatable for the men.

On November 11th a party of eighty men went from the Second, scouring the country in the direction of Huntersville, scaring away Confederate recruiting officers and soldiers who were on furloughs to their homes. A few prisoners were captured and a large number of cattle brought into camp by them. The regiment had inspired such terror among the bushwhackers that not so much of that warfare was indulged in. Though not a thousand strong, by their skill as marksmen and their indomitable courage, the regiment had become a terror to all the enemy in the Cheat and Elkwater section, and were masters of the whole region.

November 13th Company G of the regiment was detached for transfer to the artillery arm of the service, forming afterward battery G of the First West Virginia Light Artillery. They entered upon their new and untried duties as the only battery we now had in that section, the others having been ordered away. The service of this gallant battery was so intimately connected with that of our regiment, that its history will form a part of that of the regiment, its presence being noted in order of time, in all the battles in which it was engaged.

On the 5th of December a small detachment of the regiment was ordered out with two days' rations, to capture some rebel mail carriers near Roaring Creek on the Buckhannon pike. They brought into camp two rustics in

CHAPTER VIII.

butternut suits, claiming to be peaceable farmers. Under the butternut coats were Confederate uniforms, and in their shirt bosoms were important letters from prominent citizens to the Confederate Gen. "Bill" (Mudwall) Jackson, giving him full details of our forces and operations. Many of these old mountaineers were rebel in sentiment, and we were kept constantly on the alert, to prevent them from giving information to the enemy.

On December 13th, an expedition consisting of 250 of our regiment, 650 of the 9th Indiana, 400 of the 25th Ohio, 300 of the 13th Indiana, 130 of the 32d Ohio and 30 of Bracken's cavalry, attacked the camp of the enemy on the summit of the Allegheny mountains, generally known as Camp Baldwin. The camp was in command of Gen. E. Johnson of Georgia. The 2d left its camp at Elkwater on the 10th of the month, taking the path over Becca creek to Cheat Mountain summit, arriving there about 9 o'clock at night. They remained there until the morning of the 12th, awaiting the arrival of the rest of the troops from Beverly and Huttonsville. The line of march was taken up that day, the command reaching Greenbrier camp about 9 p.m., remaining here until about 11 o'clock, when the march was resumed. Here the force was divided, the 9th Indiana and the 2d Va., taking the Green Bank road to the right, while the rest of the command followed the Staunton pike, under command of Brig. Gen. Robert H. Milroy, who kept on in the darkness until he came within half a mile of the enemy's camp when he halted. Hastily reconnoitering his position, he began the ascent of the mountain. Though weak and worn by their long night's march, the soldiers pressed forward, and at early dawn they reached the summit. They were to wait here for the attack of the other column, but they came upon the enemy's pickets, who fell back on their camp. Col. Jones, in command of the advance, seeing that his approach would be known, ordered Lieut. McDonald of the Thirteenth Indiana to pursue them, the regiment pressing over the rocky ground until it came to the edge of the woods in full view of the camp. The enemy was expecting them and was in line of battle. McDonald immediately deployed his men and the battle began, and after a few rounds the enemy retreated in great confusion leaving their dead and wounded behind them. Their officers succeeded, however, in rallying them, and they advanced with great determination, when the contest raged fiercely. The enemy was repeatedly driven back to his cabins, but as often returned to the fight, until after three hours fighting, the ammunition being nearly exhausted, McDonald ordered his men to fall back. This was made the more necessary, from the fact that the other column did not make its appearance. Col. Moody in command, found the march more difficult than he expected, the hill being very steep, and for three miles his men had to toil up the hillside, covered with trees felled by the enemy. The combined attack was to have been made before daylight, but the first column did not reach the summit of the mountain until daylight, and the other not until 8 o'clock, or just after McDonald had fallen back. Thus Col. Moody's division had also to encounter the whole force of the enemy. This they did in the most gallant manner, advancing with cheers, and driving the enemy back to within 200 yards of their camp. The Confederate fire then became so destructive, that our troops were compelled to take shelter behind the logs and trees, where their fire was so effective, that the enemy was unable to dislodge them. Majors Milroy and Owens maintained their position here for a long time against three times their number, when seeing no prospect of being supported by the other column, they too fell back. The loss of our command was 137, while our regiment lost 9, among whom was Lieut. Alfred Sickman of Company G, who was instantly killed. Lieut. Sickman was a cool, brave and gallant officer. He ascended the mountain in a meditative mood, as if he apprehended the danger into which he was about to rush, and when the charge was made, he went into it with undaunted courage.

The official report of the Confederate commander, Gen. E. Johnson, shows his forces to have been 1,200, and their loss a heavy one, including some of their best line officers. Under the adverse circumstances, with the enemy's camp fortified, it was a well fought battle, and reflected great credit on the gallant men who bore the brunt of the fighting, which lasted at the several points from 7 o'clock in the morning until 2 o'clock in the afternoon, inflicting a much heavier loss on the enemy than was suffered by our forces. Maj. Owens complimented highly the men of his regiment for their brave conduct on the field. The regiment then returned to its camp at Elkwater.

Several scouting parties were sent out during the rest of the month to break up marauding parties of the enemy, and clear the country of the bands sent to harass our lines. The service of this kind, and constant and severe picket duty, were so heavy that but little rest was given the men. Neither weather nor the numbers of the enemy, deterred the expeditions that covered almost every foot of the surrounding country. Settled in our winter quarters, behind a line of fortifications, we had no fear of the enemy even in greater numbers than our depleted regiment, which was now left alone to protect the Elkwater valley and hold the outposts of our entire army. Deep snow added to the discomforts of the situation, but it brought a new amusement to the troops, that of hunting, which was freely indulged in by those who liked the sport. The report was soon circulated that deer were being killed, which created considerable excitement, as many of the men had never seen the animal at freedom in his native wilds. The origin of the report was in a hunting expedition of Serg'ts. D.F. Williamson and G.A. Quimby, who, after tramping over the hills for several hours, brought down a fine young animal, which they thought would make very good eating. It was soon reported in camp that they had shot a deer, and the demand for it exceeded far the supply, the fortunate hunters selling it out at twenty-five cents per pound. Several of the officers were supplied, and the general verdict was that it was a fine specimen of deer. It was a long time

CHAPTER VIII.

before the sergeants dared to tell the purchasers of their game that their deer was nothing more than a common calf. It is believed that more deer of this kind were caught than the native and genuine article. The sport was stimulated by this capture and afforded a great deal of fun, if nothing more substantial.

One cool morning in December, a scouting party was sent out to the mountains, there being a slight fall of snow, and the streams high. They headed for "Windy hollow," wading the river, crossing a ridge and then followed a road that ran along a stream, until they reached a hill which they climbed. On top of the hill they went into camp, building good fires, around which they tried to rest for the night. The snow had melted, and the ground was very wet, making a cold, disagreeable resting place. They lay so close to the fire that nearly everyone of them burned their clothes, and S. J. Clendaniel, of Company I, nearly burned his shoes off his feet, while Billy Bowser, of Company A, lay with his back to the fire, and his suit was burned so that nothing was left but his drawers, and he wore a standing flag of truce. Sam. Kent, Sam. Howe, "Hop" Lancaster, Jehu Dehaven and "Graball," of Company I, were among others on the scout, some of whom received the seeds of disease that never left them. The party returned to camp without accomplishing anything.

Shortly before the battle of Allegheny Mountain, another party was sent out, many of the same men being on it, and were attacked at Elk Mountain, one of the men being wounded by bushwhackers. John Oaks, of Company K, was sent to camp for reinforcements, and Serg't Black, of Company A, with a number of men, went to the relief of the party that had been attacked. They went on to the Little Meadows, arriving there at daylight, thence to Big Springs. Another detail was sent out, making three in all for this one scout. The roads were fearfully rough, in some places impassable, and the men were greatly fatigued and broken down. The return to camp was made without any incidents of special note, and without accomplishing anything of real value.

The frequent tramps out on the hills brought some very queer experiences. One that afforded a good deal of amusement at the time, was the fright received by a member of Company G. An old man lived on the mountains near camp, who had his coffin ready made and in his room, into which he would get when anyone approached the house. On one occasion a member of Company G went to the house, when the old man softly stole into his coffin, and pretended that he was no longer of the land of the living. Company G stepped into the house where all was quiet, and saw a watch hanging on the wall. Further investigation revealed the old man at rest in his narrow wooden house. Said the visitor, "Well, the old man is dead, and I will take his watch, he will not have any further use for it," and went to get it, when a groan from the depths of the coffin, arrested his progress, and, to his horror, he saw the old fellow rise as if from the dead, and get out of the coffin. Horror struck, the intruder jumped through a window, badly cutting his arm on the glass, and hastily made his way to camp.

Every device imaginable was called into service, to while away the hours, and there was no lack of fun and amusement such as the ingenuity of soldiers alone could make and enjoy, with the limited resources at their command. The contact with the mountaineers occasioned a good deal of interest and enjoyment, and sometimes experiences that were not pleasant. Thus the month were away, and the stirring events of war had almost been forgotten, when the news came that C3onfederate officers were enlisting and gathering troops up the valley, and the word was passed to put a stop to it.

On December 31st a detachment of 400 men of the Twenty-fifth Ohio, and 38 of Bracken's cavalry from Huttonsville, and 300 of the Second Virginia, under command of Maj. Webster, of the Twenty-fifth, went to Huntersville to break up the force concentrating there. Shortly after leaving Elkwater they were followed by the rest of the two regiments. It was a severe march, in the dead of winter, with the roads blockaded, and drenching rain and sleet, making a distance of 102 miles in a little less than six days, penetrating the enemy's country thirty miles further than any of our troops had before gone. The expedition was a very successful one, resulting in the complete dispersion of the enemy, who Maj. Webster believed, consisted of 400 cavalry and several hundred of mounted militia, and two companies of infantry. The regular force was stated by Gen. E. Johnson, in command of the rebel troops at Monterey, to be 250. Our force in action consisted of about 700 men, which Gen. Johnson magnified into a force of from 4,000 to 5,000. The contest was a spirited one, but with very little loss on either side, one man of the Twenty-fifth Ohio being wounded; the loss of the enemy not being known. The men were eager for action and charged upon the rebel forces in the town with great impetuosity, driving everything before them. A large quantity of rebel stores was captured, estimated to be worth $30,000, all of which was destroyed by fire. In his report of the expedition, Maj. Webster specially mentions Maj. Owens, Capts. Planky, Gibson and McNally, and Lieuts. West, Ecker, Day, Hunter, Smyth, Huggins and Weaver, of the Second, for the prompt, efficient and gallant manner in which they performed their duty on the march and in action. Of the men, he says: "Too much praise cannot be awarded. They at all times cheerfully submitted to necessary discipline. For one hour and a half in which they were engaged in driving the enemy from cover to cover, a distance of two miles, not a man flinched." Upon our return to camp, the word was passed that we would change our quarters to Cheat Mountain, and all was bustle and excitement over the matter.

Severe work was also being done in other portions of Western Virginia. Confederate Gen. Henry A. Wise was superseded by Gen. John B. Floyd early in August, who, under the influence of the inspiring news from Bull

CHAPTER VIII.

Run, determined to gain possession of the Valley of the Kanawha, resulting in some spirited fighting during the fall. In the latter part of August, a body of Confederate cavalry under command of acting Col. Jenkins, was ambushed at Piggott's Mill, and the demoralization was so complete, that Gen. Wise in his official report says he met men with their subordinate officers, flying at 5 miles distance from the enemy, and so panic struck, that even there they could not be rallied or led back to look after the dead and wounded.

An ambuscade and skirmish between Wise's forces and a small force of Union troops occurred September 4th, with a small loss, and no definite results.

On the last day of August, Gen. Rosecrans advanced southward over Krutz and Powell mountains to Summersville, drove back the enemy's advance posts, and pushed on by a forced march of seventeen miles and a half toward Gauley river, finding the enemy on the heights over looking Carnifex Ferry. The march of Rosecrans was through the broken country, and on the difficult and well nigh impassable roads of the mountains. Climbing the rugged mountains and dragging their heavy cannon after them, was but a part of the work of these brave men. Crossing the summit of the mountains, they encountered on the other side a body of cavalry which was driven before them. They were soon on their way to Summersville, and hearing firing ahead, they double quicked to the scene of conflict, in time to see the rebels fleeing along the hillsides beyond. Pressing forward they soon came upon the enemy's pickets, and the firing of the advance commenced. Having now arrived in presence of the main body of rebels, Gen. Benham was sent forward to reconnoiter their position. The brigade went forward and while laboring up the hill with the artillery, suddenly a prolonged and terrific roar of musketry was heard in the woods directly in their front. These severe and terrible volleys of the rebels were met in an instant, by the well directed and deliberate volleys of the gallant brigade. Ere long the artillery opened, making grim music among the mountains. The 12th Ohio was ordered up. Charging along at double quick with thundering cheers, they dashed into the thicket out of which the volleys rang. Cannon and howitzers followed heavily after, and directly McCook's German brigade was ordered to charge the rebels' entrenchments. It was just what they desired, and the colonel galloped along the lines, telling the brave boys what work was before them. Cheer after cheer rent the air at this announcement and they moved steadily forward as on parade, to do their dreadful work. A part of them had charged almost to the enemy's works, when they were recalled. Night was coming on and it was not deemed prudent to storm the works in the dark. Gallantly had they fought for four long hours and now they lay down to sleep resting on their arms, a part of them within two or three hundred yards of the fort. When morning came, the enemy was gone, leaving behind them large quantities of ammunition and stores, and hastily crossed the Gauley river and destroyed the ferry boat so that our troops might not follow. We lost about 120 killed and wounded, Col. Lowe, of the 12th Ohio being among the killed. The rebels retreated to Meadow Bluff.

In the northeast of Western Virginia, Gen. Kelley, who held and guarded the Allegheny section of the Baltimore and Ohio railroad, started from New Creek on the night of the 25th of October, advanced rapidly to Romney, the capital of Hampshire county, driving out a rebel battalion. It was a very spirited dash, well worthy of the gallant boys who were guarding that portion of the state. Placed against anything like equal numbers, they were well nigh invincible, and when they came upon the rebels, on this occasion, they swept upon them like a tornado, capturing two cannons, sixty prisoners, several hundred stand of arms, with all the camp equipage, provisions and munitions of war. It was a severe blow to the enemy and for a time cleared this portion of the state of rebels.

On the 10th of November, just after 7 o'clock in the evening, 150 men of the Ninth Virginia Infantry, a new regiment just being formed, was completely surprised by 700 cavalry, under command of Colonel Jenkins, the guerrilla chief, all being killed or captured, except fifty or sixty who escaped. The place was held by Jenkins until the next morning, when Col. Zeigler and his brave Fifth Virginia boys came upon the scene, accompanied by a number of the Home Guards of Lawrence county, Ohio, and the Confederates were driven from the place on the double quick. The Home Guards were so incensed at the secession citizens of the place who, it was claimed, encouraged Jenkins, that they set fire to the town, and a large portion of it was burned.

Rosecrans, who was now in command of all the troops in Western Virginia, had posted himself at Gauley Mountain on New river, three miles above its junction with the Gauley river. Floyd and Wise, after Lee's departure, took position on the southside of the river and employed themselves in intercepting and cutting off the Union teamsters engaged in supplying our troops. To put an end to this petty warfare Rosecrans advanced against Floyd. The attack in front was duly made on November 12th and Floyd retreated, and on the 14th Floyd's rear guard of cavalry was attacked and driven by Benham, its colonel, St. George Croghan, being killed. No further pursuit was attempted. Floyd retreated to Peterstown, more than 50 miles southward. Floyd was then ordered with his brigade to Tennessee, and Wise's brigade went to Richmond, from which place it was sent to Roanoke Island.

On the 29th of December, Sutton garrisoned by Rowand's company of the First Virginia cavalry, was attacked by 135 rebel guerilas, and the company was compelled to retreat to Weston, when the guerillas burned the town. Col. Crook, with four companies, went in search of the same gang from Summersville, encountered them in Clay and Braxton, killing six, the rest being chased into the mountains. On the 30th Col. Anisansel, with three companies

CHAPTER VIII.

of the First Virginia Cavalry, and three of the Third Virginia Infantry, marched to punish the marauders, and killed 22, thus breaking up their nest in the Glades. There was another conflict with guerillas at Guyandotte, January 14, 1862, which closed operations in Western Virginia, until the grand movement of our armies in the spring.

CHAPTER IX.

CAMP AT CHEAT MOUNTAIN SUMMIT.

On the 7th of January, 1862, our regiment was ordered to pack up and march to the camp on Cheat Mountain Summit, and relieve the Ninth Indiana, which was sent to Kentucky. We left our winter quarters in the picturesque little valley with some regret, and with many misgivings as to the comfort that would attend us on top of the mountains. Two days march and we were in camp amid the towering pines, where we remained until April 5th, almost three months cut off entirely from all forms of civilization, except that of our own isolated lives, and with no contact with the active world that lay below us miles away. Our stay on the bleak summit of Cheat Mountain, was one devoid of much interest, and it required all the ingenuity of the soldiers in the quarters, to provide amusements and pastimes to while away the long winter months. There was a great amount of picket and guard duty, but not sufficient to employ the time of the men, who had been used to such an active life for the past six months. Heavy guards were thrown out on the dismal posts and the weary hours hung heavily on the hands of the faithful sentinels; but they regarded neither the storms, the hardships nor the dangers that beset them, but bravely met the demands of duty, content to serve their country in whatever form the call to duty came.

On the 22d of January, 1862, the men of the regiment were gladdened by the appearance of Company B, this being the first time the company had been with us since the organization of the regiment. After the regiment had been formally organized at Beverly in July, Company B was ordered to Belington, on the pike between Beverly and Philippi, where it was entrusted with the protection of twenty-five to thirty miles of mail and transportation on the

Fairmont, Morgantown and Beverly roads, and served as scouts, pickets, patrols and escorts against the rebel guerillas that infested the mountains, and with whom they had many collisions. While they missed the stirring events through which the rest of the companies passed, in the period referred to, their services were no less valuable on that account, as they did a work that was essential to the safety of their comrades in front. They endured many hardships and had all the dangers that surround a small command, in a country where bushwhacking was the favorite method of warfare by the enemy. In all those six months the communications of our army with the source of supplies were kept open and clear.

Our location was such that we were compelled to carry wood fit for fuel a long distance, and chop it from the trees before it could be carried. It was an almost hourly scene to see some one of the messes, ankle or waist deep in the snow, chopping the beech and birch, and then slowly and laboriously carrying great loads of it to their quarters. It was hard work, but had the merit of giving that form of exercise to the men which was no doubt beneficial, but not in the least enjoyed. Cutting and carrying wood in the deep snow, and in the fierce and bitterly cold winds of the summit, was not a pastime, and had no pleasures comparable to those of the more exciting and dangerous work incident to our stay in Elkwater Valley.

CAMP ON CHEAT MOUNTAIN SUMMIT

But when off duty, after the day's routine, when the tender flapjack, the juicy mess pork and the fragrant coffee had done their work of mellowing our moods, and filling our stomachs, more gentle and agreeable hours filled our barracks with pleasure. The sound of revelry and mirth greeted the ear, and strange contortions of the body greeted the eye. One of our furloughed boys returned from civilization and brought with him a violin, a flute and several jewsharps. A tambourine was made and a bayonet used as a triangle, and an orchestra was formed that made as merry music as ever willing feet moved to. Who can forget those scenes of rare enjoyment? Who would forget them if he could? They were oases in a life that had so much of desert, and many a choice spirit, languishing for home, tired, despondent, utterly cast down, was given renewed life by the merry souls that were always on the lookout for the bright side of even the most gloomy life. Our life on Cheat Mountain

CHAPTER IX.

is a precious memory, but it is saddened by the untimely death of a few of our noble comrades who, far from home and loved ones, gave up their lives for country.

In the three months we were here in camp, numerous scouting parties were sent out, and there was scarcely a day that some of the men were not out in the wilds of the mountains, or in the depths of the valleys, making it lively for marauding parties of the enemy, and very uncomfortable for the rebel garrison on Allegheny heights, but a few miles away, and in plain view of our camp. No matter how fierce the mountain storms, or severe the cold, the details were sent out; and in many cases it seemed a hardship that might be spared, but no duty was omitted. The several scouting parties, foraging expeditions, reconnoisances, forays, their destination and their service, made up of themselves a work that cannot be described in words, or computed in the language of figures. This was the outpost of all that vast and dangerous mountain region. That comparatively small band stood alone to protect our long extended line, while within sight of us, across the valley on the Alleghenies, was the outpost of the Confederates, a force larger than ours, watching our every movement, and threatening us all through the winter. Back of them was the active energy of the enemy, planning for the spring campaign, and getting ready to gain a stronger hold on the state, and get nearer to the Ohio river. In all the campaigning of that winter, there was no other service like this, and none which could be compared with it in severity, in any department of our army. We were literally above the clouds, and in full sweep of the terrific wind storms that raged often day and night. The camp was on the summit, and was nearly, if not quite, 4000 feet above the level of the sea, the highest Union camp during the war, and perhaps the highest camp of either army, where a command was quartered any length of time. The camp of the enemy on Allegheny Mountain was not quite so high, though there was not much difference. Often without vegetables, with nothing but hard crackers and the thickest of mess pork, fat and juicy, to eat, we were subjected to considerable sickness; and among the rest a mild form of scurvy, with jaundice and fevers. The strongest constitutions were severely tried, but when that hard winter was over, there remained a body of hardy men, that stood the succeeding campaigns as but few men could, and were among the strongest and bravest of the Union forces. Opportunities for improvement were also given those who desired them, and for those who cared for literary work, there was enough time to con many a valuable text book, and read many a valuable and interesting work, in the realms of theology, literature and science. On the 22d of February, a meeting was held to celebrate Washington's birthday, and it was one of great interest to every soldier there. Amid the booming of cannons, and the cheers of the patriotic men of the regiment, fervid speeches were made, extoling the virtues of the Father of his Country, and pledging ourselves to fidelity to the Nation which we had sworn to defend against all its enemies.

In the early part of March, Lieut. A. J. Weaver, of Company K, with 63 picked men from the companies of the regiment, was sent to destroy a lot of Confederate supplies at Green Bank, about 35 miles from camp, between which place and Cheat Mountain Summit, was the camp of the enemy on Allegheny Mountain. The route of the detail was a circuitous one, through the bleak mountains. They reached Green Bank at 2 o'clock the next morning. When they reached the outskirts of the town, Lieut. Weaver sent Sergt. Quimby, of Company K, with ten men ahead to reconnoiter, and instructed him to return within half an hour. This detail stopped at the first house they came to, and there learned that there were only about half a dozen Confederate soldiers in Green Bank, and that they were sleeping in a church. After short consultation, the detail concluded to go ahead and surround the church and capture the sleeping enemy. They had just got inside the churchyard, finding the church vacant, when they saw in the dim moonlight a squad of men coming down the street toward the church. They of course thought them to be the Confederate soldiers, so they dropped down behind the fence, intending to fire on them. Just as the sergeant was ready to give the command to fire, he heard Lieut. Weaver's voice, which undoubtedly prevented some sad work. After firing a building containing large quantities of stores, the party returned to camp, arriving there after dark, nearly exhausted.

In the latter part of March other troops began to arrive on the summit, preparatory to an advance on the enemy camped on Allegheny Mountain. Large quantities of provisions, tents, camp equipage, etc., were brought up, and the word given that ere long active service in the field would again begin. On April 4th word was received that the rebels in Camp Allegheny were evacuating the place, and immediate preparations were made to advance by our command. On the 5th the line of march was taken up, and we left Cheat Mountain summit never again to camp on its inhospitable heights. The forces were under the command of the brave brigadier general, Robert H. Milroy, a brief account of whose life and service is here given.

MAJOR GENERAL R. H. MILROY.

Robert Huston Milroy, son of Gen. Samuel and Martha Milroy, was born in Washington county, Ind., June 11, 1816, about seven months before the territory was admitted as a state. His father was a hard-working, successful farmer, was a member of the first constitutional convention of Indiana, and afterward for a number of years was a member of the legislature of that state, and at one time speaker of the House. The son aided the father in all the hard work of the farm until his 25th year. Prior to this he had received only a country schooling,

CHAPTER IX.

but for years had been strongly desirous to secure an education at West Point, or at some college. But his father being a self-educated man, refused this desire of the son, for the reason that he believed that a collegiate education was more injurious than beneficial, and pointing to his fine library told Robert to educate himself. During the winter of 1840-41, his father sent him to Pennsylvania to visit two half uncles, and to collect from them a balance of $200 due from his grandfather's estate, which his father told him to appropriate to his own use in visiting the large eastern cities. But on receiving the money Robert determined to use it in obtaining his highest desire, a collegiate military education. He had heard favorably of Norwich Military University at Norwich, Vt., Capt. A. Partridge, formerly superintendent at West Point, president, and went there and entered for study. By intense application to study, almost day and night, for two years and seven months, he was graduated with the degrees of Master of Military Science, Master of Civil Engineering and Bachelor of Arts. After vainly trying to get a commission as lieutenant in the regular army, he returned home in the spring of 1844 and began the study of law. In the spring of 1845 he went to Texas, took the oath of allegiance to "The Lone Star," and voted for its annexation to the United States. In the fall of that year he returned home on account of the death of his father, and resumed the study of law. On the breaking out of the war with Mexico, he promptly raised a company of volunteers and was mustered into the service of the United States for one year as captain of Company C, First Indiana Infantry, a part of the Indiana brigade of Brigadier Gen. Joe Lane. When the year was up, Capt. Milroy recruited another company for the war, but it was not accepted. After the muster out of his company, Capt. Milroy returned to his home in Delphi, Ind., and again resumed the study of law. He attended a course of instruction in the Law Department of the Indiana State University during the winter of 1848-9, and was graduated with the degree of Bachelor of Law.

In May, 1849, he was married to Miss Mary Jane Armitage, of Delphi, and was admitted to the practice of law soon thereafter. In the fall of that year he was elected a member of the convention to remodel the constitution of his state. In 1852 he was appointed circuit Judge, and upon the expiration of his term, in 1854, he moved to Rensselear, Ind., where he continued the practice of law, until the breaking out of the rebellion in April, 1861. Seeing clearly several months prior to that event, that war was inevitable, Judge Milroy, on February 4, 1861, issued a stirring call for the prompt organization of volunteer companies all over the state, to be ready with the volunteers of other states, to crush the coming rebellion in its infancy, and requested that all men qualified for military service, who desired to join such a company at Rensselear, to give or send their names to him, and as soon as a sufficient number of names was received, a meeting would be called for the election of officers, which was done. This was the first call made for volunteers for the great war. When war came, Indiana was called on for 60 companies of three months troops, and Capt. Milroy at once tendered his already organized company, which was mustered into the service April 24, 1861, as a part of the Ninth Indiana Infantry, of which Capt. Milroy was elected colonel. He soon received an order to report with his regiment to Col. B.F. Kelley, at Grafton, Va., and crossed the Ohio river into Virginia, May 30, reporting to Col. Kelley, June 1. He took part in the battle of Philippi, the first of the war, and his regiment was in the advance in the pursuit of Gen. Garnett, who was killed at Corrick's ford. The three months regiments then returned home.

Colonel Milroy went home with his regiment, but before disbanding, requested them to re-enlist for three years, and by September 12th, he had his regiment filled to the limit. He was appointed brigadier general to date from September 3d, but was not assigned to the command of a brigade until October 10, remaining with his regiment. He reported to General Reynolds at Elkwater on September 19th, and took part in all the campaigns of that section. On December 10, General Reynolds was transferred to another field, and Gen. Milroy was left in sole command of the Cheat Mountain region. He fought the battle of Allegheny Mountain December 13, and directed the expedition to Huntersville December 31, after which the troops went into quarters for the winter. The history of Gen. Milroy from this time until the return to Western Virginia, after the Second Bull Run, is that of our brigade, which he led in every battle and on every march. The full account may be seen in the succeeding chapters, all of his official papers that can be reached, being quoted almost in full.

November 7, 1862, Gen. Milroy left our brigade, and went to New Creek, where he had eight regiments of infantry, two batteries and three cavalry companies under his command. On December 11, he moved his command from New Creek to Petersburg, and while there sent out scouting parties to Franklin, Brock's Gap settlement and Wardensville, and captured a number of prisoners. On the 21st he sent Gen. Cluseret with his brigade to Strasburg, which he captured, and then to Winchester which he occupied December 25, where Gen. Milroy went January 1, 1863. Here the general received his commission as major general, to date from November 29, 1862, and was presented with a very fine sword by the officers of his command, as a mark of their confidence and esteem. He was very active while here and did good service.

As there has been a great deal of criticism of the action of Gen. Milroy at Winchester from June 12 to 16, 1863, it is but just to state briefly some facts relating to it. In volume 7 of the "Rebellion Records," will be found Gen. Milroy's report and letter relating to the affair, which the survivors of the old Second Virginia, will do well to read, as a vindication of their beloved general, whose memory has been aspersed without cause. Gen. Milroy had a positive order to remain at Winchester, and never received orders to evacuate it. In

CHAPTER IX.

obedience to the order he remained there, until he demonstrated the impossibility of remaining longer without being annihilated, or compelled to surrender. The former was not demanded for the good of the service, and the latter with him was impossible. He had less than 7,000 effective men, and with that small force would not have deemed it his duty to await the approach of Lee's army, had he known they were coming that way. He had a right to expect that if Lee's army advanced against him from Hooker's front, that he would be informed of it by the general-in-chief, through Gen. Schenck, but no such information was ever received. Gen. Milroy knew nothing of the presence of Lee's army until the end of the second day's fighting, when he captured some prisoners from whom he learned he was fighting Lee's army, which then had him surrounded. He fought them till 8 o'clock on the evening of the third day when his ammunition and provisions, and all hope of succor, being exhausted, he cut his way out at daybreak on the fourth day, June 15, 1863, and got through with over 6,000 effective men, who were on duty in July, as was amply proven before the Court of Inquiry called at his request in August, 1863. As soon as the general-in-chief, Halleck, learned that Milroy had arrived at Harper's Ferry, he telegraphed Gen. Schenck in terms very insulting to Milroy, to give him no command at that place. By orders from Gen. Schenck, he then proceeded to Baltimore, thence to Bloody Run in Bedford county, Pa., where some 3,000 of his command were, that had come through by way of Hancock. He was actively employed, and was preparing to move to the attack on a considerable rebel force in McConnelsburg, where he received an order on the 26th, from Gen. Couch, in whose department he was then acting, to turn over his command to Col. Pierce, Twelfth Pennsylvania cavalry, and report at once to Gen. Schenck in Baltimore, which he did, when by order of the general-in-chief, he was placed in arrest. Thus it was for doing his duty, and staying the advance of Lee's army of 60,000 men for four days, which delay enabled Gen. Meade to gain time and interrupt Lee's march, and choose the ground to fight the great pivotal battle of the war at Gettysburg, he was placed in arrest like a felon, and his command by his absence greatly crippled in its efficiency, and he made the victim of malice. There being no charges or causes assigned in the order of arrest, and none being furnished after repeated demand, Gen. Milroy demanded a court of Inquiry, to investigate and report upon the evacuation of Winchester. This court was ordered August 4, 1863, and completed its labors September 7, and by its findings and report, and the opinion of President Lincoln thereon October 27, Gen. Milroy was wholly exonerated from all blame. It was an astounding affair, and an act of injustice to a brave and patriotic general, that the exigencies of the service could not excuse.

On May 13, 1864, after being out of command 10 months and 17 days, he received orders to report to Maj. Gen. Thomas, at Nashville, Tenn., for duty, where he arrived on the 22d. While Gen. Milroy was in command in Tennessee, his time was occupied in guarding the various lines of transportation, and occasionally in heavy skirmishing with guerillas. In September he had several engagements with Gens. Williams and Wheeler, and later fought Gens. Forrest and Bates. On December 7th he had a desperate encounter with Bates, near Murfreesboro, in which Bates and Forrest were defeated with heavy loss. This was the last regular battle Gen. Milroy was in, though he remained in command at Tullahoma and Nashville till July 1865, and resigned on the 18th of that month, and was mustered out July 26, 1865. Gen. Forrest said of him that Milroy was the only Union general that ever defeated him in a fair fight.

After leaving the service, he remained in Tennessee for some time and then returned to his old home in Delphi, Ind., where he resumed the practice of law. In July, 1872, he was appointed superintendent of Indian affairs for Washington Territory, and moved his family to Olympia, where he resided up to the time of his death. He held this office for two years, when it was abolished. Afterwards he was appointed United States Indian agent for the Yakima agency, and held this office till President Cleveland removed him in September 1885, for "offensive partisanship." After this he practiced law up to the time of his death, which occurred at Olympia, March 29, 1890, aged 73 years, 9 months and 18 days.

Gen. Milroy was one of the bravest and noblest men of our country. The writer, and the other members of the Second Virginia, had ample opportunity to see the general's bravery tested, and every one will unhesitatingly agree that he was the bravest and coolest man they ever saw in the storm of battle. No braver warrior than Gen. Milroy ever buckled on a sword. His fame is fixed in the annals of his country and in the hearts of his soldiers, all of whom loved him as a father, and followed him wherever he called with implicit faith in his judgment and courage. An experienced officer, and thoughtful writer of the Union army, who knew from personal service under Milroy at Winchester, what kind of a commander and fighter he was, has written the following: "Had Gen. R.H. Milroy been put in command in a place where his genius and ability fitted him to fill, he would have been the Murat of America. There was not an officer in the army of the Union that excelled him in dash and true native courage."

Gen. Milroy was a profoundly religious man. He was cast on the sea of doubt and skepticism for a number of years, but returned to his early faith and became a member of the Presbyterian church, under the ministry of Rev. J.R. Thompson, of the State of Washington.

The Second Virginia Infantry never served under a general for whom the men had so great an affection. It was the regard of men for friend, and that he was their friend is the testimony of every member of the old regiment. The affection was returned by the noble general, who spoke of them as "my boys,"

CHAPTER IX.

and to whom he had but to speak and they would follow him into the very jaws of death. In a letter to the Historian from one of the general's family, the writer says: "It seems to me that father spoke more frequently of the Second Virginia Infantry than he did of all the other regiments he commanded. There seemed to be more persons in it that he individually remembered and thought a great deal of." When the general was requested to write some of the early events of his life for this history, though very feeble, he expressed a desire to do so, "because," as he said, "the old Second Virginia Infantry asked for it," and his son said he was willing to do anything he could for the old regiment, "for there was time when he knew the regiment would do anything he asked them to do."

CHAPTER X.

MOUNTAIN DEPARTMENT.

March 11th, 1862, President Lincoln issued War Order No. 3, directing "That the country west of the department of the Potomac, and east of the department of the Mississippi, be a military department, to be called the Mountain Department, and that the same be commanded by Gen. John C. Fremont." Gen. Fremont assumed command of the department on March 29th, and prepared at once for aggressive operations. Included in this department were the forces of the Cheat Mountain District, under Brig. Gen. Robert H. Milroy, of which the Second Virginia formed a part.

Under date of March 16th, Gen. Milroy had recommended to Gen. Rosecrans a plan of operations, which included in its scope the capture of the forces on Allegheny Mountain, thence a rapid march on Staunton. Whether this recommendation was favorably considered by Gen. Fremont, the records do not show, though it may be inferred that it was, from a communication to the Secretary of War, April 3d, in which Gen. Fremont says: "We have lost an opportunity to capture the force at Camp Baldwin (Allegheny) for want of horses to move the batteries under Gen. Milroy." Gen. Milroy had expressed a fear of such a result in his terse statement: "Fear that game I have watched so long will escape me at last." On April 4th Gen. Fremont addressed the Secretary of War, reciting the bad condition of his mountain army in the way of transportation, and closed by saying that "Last night Gen. Milroy was ordered to advance, with the intention of occupying Allegheny, and generally now it seems that on our part movements in advance have become necessary."

According to estimates made by Gen. Fremont, his whole available force, ready for active service, amounted to but 18,807 men, with which to guard a frontier of 350 miles, 300 miles of railroad and 200 miles of water communication. The Cheat Mountain district, under Gen. Milroy, comprised 6,084 of these forces. Before leaving the summit, a scouting party, under command of Capt. George R. Latham, consisting of eighty men, from Companies B and K, went in the direction of Monterey. They camped the first night about three miles east of the Staunton pike, at the foot of the Allegheny Mountains; the next day they traveled hard through the heavy timber to the summit of the Alleghenies; thence they descended the mountain and quietly entered the town of Monterey, which they held until the arrival of the regiment, being the first troops to enter the place.

All preparations were completed, and the order to advance was given. We left camp on Cheat Mountain summit at 2 o'clock p.m. on Saturday, April 5, 1862, and marched that day to Camp Greenbrier, a distance of twelve miles, where we camped for the night on the banks of the beautiful river that runs through the valley. It was our first night for three months in the valley, and to us it was one of the most delightful of our army life. The first faint approaches of spring were to be seen, and we lay down to rest under the clear sky of an April night, with just enough frost to make huge camp fires very comfortable, which were made from the fences that were near the camp.

Early on the morning of the 6th, we continued our march and before noon we were in Camp Allegheny, where all winter hundreds of Confederate troops had been in camp, that were now retreating southward. The distance to the camp was nine miles, but it was all up hill, and once again we were on the mountain top. It was a strongly fortified point, commanding all the approaches, and it was easily seen why our brave men failed in their attempt to capture it the December previous. We remained here through the night, and a dreary, dismal place it was. On the 7th we marched to Monterey, a distance of about sixteen miles, and it was one of the roughest and most disagreeable marches we had yet experienced. The snow fell continuously and melted as it fell, forming a bed of mud that was almost impassable, while overhead we had all the comforts of a snow storm, and cold enough to make us miserable. Upon our arrival in Monterey we found Capt. Latham and his party in charge. The following day other troops came in, and soon a fair-sized army was ready for duty. On the 8th a scouting party was sent out from our regiment, which came in contact with the enemy, but no loss was sustained. At night our pickets and some of the enemy's scouts had a fight, but no one was hurt on our side. April 21st, Capt. Ewing was directed to take twenty-five of his men toward Clover Lick, Huntersville and Green Bank to ferret out, and capture or kill all mail carriers or guerrillas he might meet, especially to capture, if possible, Jacob Beveridge, residing on Clover Lick, and if he resisted or attempted to escape, his life must pay the forfeit. They were to take coffee and sugar rations for four days and the rest of the rations to be furnished on the way. The captain and his squad went on their delightful service of meeting guerrillas and killing them, if they tried to get away. They went to Beveridge's house, but that

CHAPTER X.

individual was not at home. Finding a big iron kettle Serg't Osborne prepared a novel supper, the recipe for which the captain gives as follows: Twenty-three chickens, a large handful of salt, a bucket of water, and balls made of Indian meal. It was a great success and highly enjoyed. Finding that Beveridge was determined not to come home and be captured, the party returned to camp.

The life in Monterey was one of unusual interest, and had enough of danger in it to give it spice and variety. We were quartered in the empty houses that were available, and though crowded beyond comfort, it afforded a life particularly dear to the soldier. When off duty, the fun and frolic that pervaded every company and every mess, were of the most hilarious character. Here the true art of foraging, in all its varied aspects, was learned by the boys, and they were apt pupils. For the first time we were in the enemy's country where there was something to eat, and other duties kept the officers and guards from scrutinizing too closely the mysterious movements of some of the men, who seemed to be unusually active in the service of their country. The farmers in the neighborhood could explain everything but they did not, and meanwhile the soldiers lived on the best that the country afforded.

On the night of the 11th, companies C, F and H of the Second and a few cavalry, went out on the pike toward McDowell, to reconnoiter, and had a skirmish with the advance of the enemy. Toward morning they charged the enemy, ran them into their camp, and were treated to a lively return of bullets, in which two of the cavalry were hurt and one of Company F slightly. This led to an attack on our camp the next day. About 9 o'clock on the morning of the 12th, skirmishing began on our outposts, but the pickets were able to hold their own until almost noon, when the advancing force threatened their capture. About 12 o'clock the long roll was beaten, and all the troops in the place fell quickly into line. Our regiment, and the 32d and 75th Ohio regiments, took position on the right of the town, and the 25th Ohio and battery took position on the left of the town. Reinforcements were sent to the pickets, consisting of two companies of the Seventh Ohio, Companies B and D, Second Virginia, two companies of the Twenty-fifth Ohio, two of the Thirty-second Ohio, one company First Virginia Cavalry, and one gun of Capt. Hyman's battery, under command of Maj. Webster. The skirmishing was quite brisk for a short time, but the enemy were put to flight and pursued to their camp near McDowell. Our loss was three men badly wounded in the Seventy-fifth Ohio. The force of the enemy was about 1,000, with two cavalry companies and two pieces of artillery, and their loss was quite heavy.

On the 13th a false alarm caused the sending of the Second in the direction of Crab Bottom, marching about two and a half miles before it was discovered that our own troops, and not rebels, were the party that created the alarm. On the same day a heavy scouting party went to McDowell, and found the enemy fortifying on Shenandoah mountain. On the 16th, Company I, of the

Second, some other infantry and a company of cavalry, went in the direction of McDowell to reconnoiter, and were the first troops to enter McDowell, the Second Virginia again taking the lead. They drove in the enemy's pickets, and prepared the way for the advance of other troops, which immediately went to the place, and they returned to Monterey on the 18th.

On the 24th a foraging party, consisting of 26 wagons, with a guard of ten men, was sent out to Bull Pasture, about 15 miles from McDowell, for forage. Near Williamsville, the train became water bound, the rain falling in torrents. In pulling away from the edge of a stream that was rapidly rising, they had to pass a clump of laurels, from which the bushwhackers fired on the train, and William Howe, teamster of Company I, but not enlisted, was shot through the head. Soon after this his father, Daniel Howe, Company I, was also shot in the head, both killed, and T. J. Walker, of the same company, son-in-law of Daniel Howe, was struck in the left ankle by some missile, or stray shot, and falling severely hurt himself, but was able to get back to camp. Two of the guards were killed and two mortally wounded, and the teams were all captured and the wagons burned, 80 horses and mules being taken by the enemy. It was a disastrous affair to the party, and created intense excitement in camp. Gen. Milroy at once took measures to suppress the guerrillas, and they were so effective as to receive the commendation of Gen. Fremont, who said in a dispatch to Gen. Milroy: "Your efforts in suppression of guerrillas approved. The commanding general takes this occasion to say that he has been gratified with the good conduct and gallantry displayed by your command since entering the Monterey Valley, and requests that as much be conveyed to them through your headquarters." The "efforts" of Gen. Milroy were effective, and there was less of this kind of warfare thereafter.

On the 29th the Second left Monterey to take part in the general movement that was soon to be made under the leadership of Gen. Fremont. The three weeks' stay at Monterey was one of considerable hardships, plenty of hard work as well as pleasure, such as the soldiers could have in their rough and exposed life. The weather was very severe at times, snow having fallen to a depth of ten inches in the latter part of the month, while rain, mud, storm and cold were of such frequent occurrence as to make our stay at times very disagreeable. The service was hard in picket duty and scouting, and bore heavily on the troops, but they endured it as became good soldiers.

On April 28th Capt. Ewing was ordered to hire or press all the teams necessary to forward to Monterey all the guns of the battery formerly in charge of Capt. Johnson at Elkwater, consisting of six guns. They started without a single horse to walk back thirty-two miles to Elkwater to bring six guns, six caissons, the battery wagon and forge into the prospective fight at McDowell. Some of the boys never had walked thirty-two miles before that day, but Milroy's order was imperative, and they reached Elkwater in good

CHAPTER X.

shape. The company went to work with a will to press horses into the service of Uncle Sam. They found the horses and moved the battery for the first time in their lives. They had all kinds and descriptions of horse flesh and harness. Later on when they struck Blenker's Division at Franklin, they styled them the "Western Virginia Bushwhackers." They reached McDowell on the 7th and had nearly all night to get ready for the fight, the first real hard battle that they had ever been in, with their old plow harness, their colts that had never been broken, broken down old mares going on three legs, and ran the guns up and unlimbered them in the face of the enemy, and fired away until Gen. Schenck came at night with his division.

Our stay at McDowell was a very exciting one, closing with a stubborn fight. The Second was kept in active service nearly the whole of the time. On the 30th Companies F and I were sent out on a scout, and at the same time Company B returned to camp from service of the same kind. The former party returned on May 4th, bringing with them a train of wagons loaded with flour. It was a welcome addition to the commissary department. Amid scouting and heavy picketing the force, consisting of Milroy's own command, passed the time, the demands on the strength and endurance of the men being very severe, but there was no conflict with the enemy until the 7th. On that morning the alarm was given and the forces of the command were placed in position for receiving the assaults of the enemy. The alarm was created by an attack on the 32nd Ohio and some of Shuman's cavalry, which were posted on the Shenandoah mountains about five miles from McDowell. Our little force was compelled to retreat, losing their tents, camp equipage, etc., and about twenty of the regiment were captured on picket duty. Shuman's cavalry cut their way through a portion of the enemy's forces, with a small loss. This was merely the prelude to the stubborn fight of the next day, when our forces, small in number, met the heavy forces of the rebels, and were compelled to retreat.

On the morning of the 8th Gen. Schenck arrived with about 3,500 men, and though the senior of Gen. Milroy, permitted Milroy to conduct the battle. The enemy was discovered on Bull Pasture mountain, one and three-fourth miles from McDowell, on our right and front. Our battery commenced to shell them to ascertain their numbers, and Maj. Long, of the Seventy-third Ohio, and Company B, of our regiment, engaged them, skirmishing from about 10 o'clock until 3 in the afternoon, when Capt. Latham, of Company B, informed Gen. Milroy that the enemy were endeavoring to plant a battery upon the mountain, which would command our whole encampment. Aside from the efficient service rendered by Company B, the Second was not engaged in the battle, but was drawn up in line in full view of the fight, where it was held to support the artillery, and advance if needed. It was an unenviable situation and the men were anxious to go forward and take part in the exciting and dangerous conflict, but their duty was to await orders. From our position we had a splendid view of the whole scene, and it was one of grandeur and splendor, particularly after nightfall, that human eyes are not often permitted to see. About 3 o'clock the Twenty-fifth and Seventy-fifth Ohio attacked the enemy in front, and though but little over 900 in number, without any shelter from the fire of the enemy, they advanced up the precipitous mountain side upon a force of fully twice their own, protected by entrenchments and the natural formation of the mountain, and maintained the position unaided for one and a half hours. About 4 o'clock the Eighty-second and Thirty-second Ohio and the Third Virginia regiments were ordered to turn the right flank of the enemy, which they obeyed with the greatest alacrity, and kept up a destructive fire, causing the enemy to waver several times. The action then became general and bloody, lasting until after 8 o'clock. Capt. Ewing's battery, with the guns of Johnson's battery, was called into service, and gave good support until the forces came into close contact. The flashing of the guns after nightfall on the mountain side and crest, amid the trees, was indescribably grand and beautiful, and no one witnessing it can ever forget it. At times sheets of flame shot from the angry mouths of the guns, lighting up the whole mountain side, and again the flash from one or a few muskets made a scene of particular beauty and animation. A few minutes after 8 o'clock the firing ceased, and both sides rested, our men retiring to camp in good order, bringing with them their dead and wounded. The actual forces engaged in the battle under Gen. Milroy, were the regiments named, numbering 2,268 men, and their loss was 26 men killed, 227 wounded, and 3 missing, in all 256. Companies B and D, of the Second Virginia, were ordered out as pickets on the Staunton pike, and held the road, remaining as a rear guard, until the troops and supplies were safely on the road to Franklin, when they retired, protecting the rear of our column.

The report of the enemy was made by Gen. T.J. (Stonewall) Jackson, whose account is not very dissimilar to that of Gen. Milroy, as to dates and general plan of action. The rebel forces were under the command of Gen. E. Johnson, and consisted of his brigade, that of Gen. Taliaferro, and Col. Campbell, in all twelve regiments and one battalion, numbering more than twice as many as Gen. Milroy led against them. Their losses are officially reported, as follows; Killed, 16 officers and 59 men; wounded, 38 officers and 385 men, a total of 498 killed and wounded, almost twice as many as in our forces, showing that though at a great disadvantage in numbers and position, our men fought with great courage and effectiveness. Gen. Johnson, two colonels and two majors were among the wounded, and one colonel was killed, of the Confederates.

Early next morning, under orders from Gen. Fremont, our forces retired in the direction of Franklin, where the troops of the Mountain Department were being concentrated. The line of march started at 4 o'clock, stopping for the night about eight miles from Franklin. During the day's march we were constantly harassed by the enemy, and at noon were drawn up in line of battle

CHAPTER X.

to repel their approach, but they fell back. The following day we reached Franklin, where we went into camp. The guerillas were busy during the night, but with disastrous results to them. On the 11th or 12th we were ordered into line several times, but no serious fighting occurred, the enemy being content to wage bushwhacking without giving us the opportunity to meet them fairly in battle.

The arrival of Gen. Fremont and staff on the 13th, created intense excitement in camp. They brought with them eight regiments and four batteries, followed the next day by six regiments and two batteries. There was the greatest curiosity to see the gallant general, and his handsome presence and military bearing, gave great confidence to the troops now directly under his command. He was welcomed with military honors and by the plaudits of the thousands of soldiers encamped in the place. We were no longer annoyed by the forays of bushwhackers, the enemy having retired from our immediate front, but a more dreaded enemy threatened us, that of hunger. On the 17th the supply of bread of all kinds was exhausted, and the only food left the thousands of men in the camp was fresh beef, and not even salt had we with which to season it. For some reason our supply trains were delayed, and for three days, and in some cases longer than that, there was not a pound of bread for the thousands of weary and hungry men, but unsalted beef was the only rations. In this time we were subjected to the exposure of heavy rains, and were required also to help in the erection of fortifications; the unfit food, and heavy labor, making such a draught on the endurance of the men, that the forces were greatly weakened. Diarrhea, dysentery, etc., were the common lot of all, and it was in this condition we were found, when the order of march came on the 25th.

It was about this time that the famous brigade under Gen. Milroy was formed, consisting of the Second, Third and Fifth regiments of Virginia infantry, the Twenty-fifth Ohio infantry, and Ewing's, Hyman's and Johnson's batteries.

On the 21st, Col. Moss and Lieut. Col. Moran resigned their commissions, and Capt. George R. Latham was appointed colonel, but was not commissioned until the 24th. On the same day that he was appointed colonel, Capt. Latham was sent to Seneca, in charge of 500 men, to disperse or capture the notorious Bill Harper and his gang of bushwhackers. Upon arriving at their destination, Capt. Latham and party met Harper, whom he killed, and three of his men, besides wounding several others, and capturing a large quantity of stores. It was an expedition of great value, resulting in clearing out this notorious gang of bushwhackers. Maj. J. D. Owens was left in charge of the regiment, commanding it until the return from the battle of Cross Keys, where he did good service with his gallant men.

Gen. Fremont gives the following graphic account of the condition of affairs at Franklin: "The streams at my rear were swollen by the incessant rains, and the roads had become almost impassable. Not so much as one quarter forage was got forward, and except an incomplete ration of bread, no rations had been got up for the men. For days together, fresh beef, with a little salt, was the only provision on hand for issue. Coffee, so essential and desirable in the field, was becoming a luxury almost unknown. Sick lists were largely on the increase, and such was the demoralization induced by privations endured, that demonstrations among the men, amounting almost to open mutiny, had in instances to be put down with a strong hand."

The line of march was taken up May 25th, and the weary tramp to Strasburg was to try the strength and spirit of the troops. The roads were horrible, delaying the column, the wagons and the artillery almost swamping in the mud. Our brigade reached Petersburg on the 27th, and resumed the march the next morning, stopping for dinner at beautiful Moorefield, amid the lovely and picturesque scenery about it. We marched nine miles further and camped for the night in the Lost mountains. During the next day we marched a few miles and rested for the night in the forest of this wild mountain region. On the 1st of June we arrived within five miles of Strasburg, striking the rear of Jackson's retreating army. The latter part of the march was through drenching rains, falling in torrents on the men, who had but little protection from thorough wetting, and as the excitement of the firing in front reached us, we dashed through streams and double quicked to the scene of firing, forgetting our weariness and discomfort in the hope of a fight with the enemy. Then began the famous campaign in the Shenandoah valley, in which the forces under Fremont, worn down by hunger and fatigue, forced to battle the command of Stonewall Jackson, and in the language of President Lincoln, addressed to Gen. Fremont June 13th, "You (we) fought Jackson alone and worsted him." The following account of our rapid march up the valley to Harrisonburg, not equalled to this time by any campaign in the war, in rapidity of action or severity and hardships, is from the official report of Gen. Fremont:

"With the arrival of the rear, the leading corps of my command again stretched forward, taking the road to Strasburg. At 7 o'clock in the morning of this day, June 1st, my advance, under Lieut. Col. Cluseret, first touched Jackson's main body, driving in the advanced pickets of Gen. Ewell's brigade. Pressing forward and encountering and driving stronger bodies of skirmishers, the column within a short distance came upon cavalry and a battery in position, which immediately opened fire. About noon the enemy's batteries ceased fire, and my troops were ordered to encamp. Our cavalry, being pushed forward, found the enemy withdrawing and a strong column of infantry just filing past our front. A reconnoissance by Col. Cluseret with the 8th Virginia, pushed to within 2 miles of Strasburg, showed the enemy

CHAPTER X.

withdrawn, and at nightfall this officer, with his brigade, accompanied by a battalion of cavalry and a section of artillery, was ordered to move forward upon Strasburg and determine the position of the enemy. The day closed with one of the most violent rain storms I have ever seen, with really terrific lightning and thunder, and the night being very dark, and Col. Cluseret being without guides or knowledge of the country, his troops passed the town of Strasburg, and marching to the light of the enemy's fires, about 11 o'clock came into contact with Ashby's cavalry, which occupied the road forming the rear of Jackson's position, about two miles beyond Strasburg, on the road to Woodstock. Having ascertained the position of the enemy, Col. Cluseret withdrew his men and returned to camp. The reconnoissance showed the enemy in retreat. With daylight of June 2nd, my command moved in pursuit. Closely pressed by my advance, the enemy at about 10 a.m., turned to make a stand. After determined resistance for an hour the enemy were driven from position and again pursued. Repeatedly during the day they faced about and were as often compelled to relinquish the fight. The pursuit was rapid, not less than 18 miles being made in the space of 5 hours. In one instance scarcely a hundred yards separated my advance from the enemy, the latter, however, gaining a small bridge and unlimbering rapidly upon a rocky rise beyond. By sunset the enemy had reached for the night the higher points beyond Woodstock. The retreat was reckless. Over 500 prisoners fell into our hands. Several hundred stand of small arms cast away or left in stacks by the rebels were also gathered. Of gray-coated stragglers at least a thousand were in the woods and country adjoining. Broken ambulances, clothing, blankets, and articles of equipment strewed the route. Our loss was small. At the last stand made by the enemy, he lost 7 killed. His total loss during the day must have been considerable. At about 5 o'clock in the afternoon Gen. Stahel's brigade occupied Woodstock.

Although much fatigued by the forced march of the day previous, my command at an Early hour of the morning of June 3, were upon the road to resume pursuit. Again the rear guard of the enemy turned to cover his main body, or to gain time for placing obstacles, tearing up the road, or destroying culverts and bridges. The fire of the opposing batteries was mutually brisk, with, at intervals, an accompaniment of the dropping shots of small arms. Strenuous effort was made by the rebels to destroy the bridge over Stony Creek, at Edinburg, about five miles out of Woodstock. A portion of the planks were torn up and the timbers so far cut that the structure sank, partially broken, about midway of the current. So prompt, however, were my advance troops that the party left by the enemy was compelled to retreat in haste without further execution of its design. A ford was found at a short distance up the stream, and, with some difficulty, cavalry and artillery were gotten across. By noon my command were mainly upon the farther bank and again in rapid motion. The bridge over Cedar (Mill) Creek at Mount Jackson was saved nearly intact by the celerity with which the enemy was overtaken. The rebel Gen. Ashby barely escaped capture at this point by Capt. Conger's company of Third Virginia Cavalry. This company, pressing forward under their persevering leader, were in season to come on a body of the enemy about to fire the largest and more important bridge beyond Mount Jackson, crossing the north fork of the Shenandoah. A gallant charge was made, but the volleys of grape and musketry drove back the small command. The bridge was successfully fired, burning rapidly, with thick volumes of flame and smoke.

The pontoons procured by me at Pittsburgh, having been kept well up with the column, were now ordered to the front, and preparations immediately made to gain passage by rebridging the Shenandoah. A heavy rain set in, but operations were continued throughout the night. By six in the morning the bridge was made available for crossing and a force of infantry and cavalry gotten over. Suddenly, however, the river began to rise, to a yet greater height. In the space of four hours, flooded by the storm and its mountain tributaries, it had gained fully twelve feet, with a current correspondingly turbulent and swift. The drift borne down was working great mischief and several of the boats were swamped. To save the bridge from utter destruction the ropes were cut and the pontoon swung round to the northern shore. The troops already across being well posted and amply covered by our batteries upon the bluffs, little apprehension was felt as regarded their immediate safety. Toward night the stream, as suddenly as it had risen, began to subside, and parties at work renewed their efforts. Their task was arduous, and it was not until 10 a.m. of the next day that the bridge was again in condition for crossing.

On the 5th of June, then, crossing safely the bridge of pontoons, my column, with scarcely more than half the numbers of the enemy in advance, retook the trail and pushed steadily forward. A lapse of more than thirty hours since the burning of the main bridge over the Shenandoah had given the enemy an advantage he proved not slow to use. He was not overtaken upon the 5th, and having made eighteen miles and passing on the way the enemy's fires still burning, my command was bivouacked beyond New Market, the enemy's camp being but a few miles ahead.

On the 6th I was enabled by an early and rapid march to restore the lost contact. Our progress was a little retarded by the burned and blazing culverts which had been fired by the enemy along the road, but sharp artillery and cavalry skirmishing was renewed during the forenoon, and at about 2 o'clock my advance drove his rear guard through Harrisonburg. The direction taken by the main force of the enemy being uncertain, my troops were ordered into camp around the town. Later in the afternoon the First New Jersey Cavalry, with a battalion of the Fourth New York Cavalry, came suddenly upon the enemy's camp in the woods several miles to the southeast, and was driven out with serious loss. A little before sundown Gen. Bayard entered the woods

CHAPTER X.

with four companies of Kane's Rifles (Bucktails) and the First Penn'a Cavalry. Almost immediately after getting into the timber, the Rifles encountered a regiment of cavalry with artillery and a regiment of infantry, from which they received a very damaging fire. A very severe engagement of half an hour followed, during which the Rifles lost upward of forty in killed, wounded and missing. Col. Cluseret coming up with his brigade to the support of the Riflemen, the enemy retreated in disorder, leaving him in possession of their camp. On their part, the enemy in this sharp affair suffered still more severely, losing among the killed Gen. Ashby, who, up to this time, had covered their retreat with admirable audacity and skill.

On the 7th a reconnoissance in force was sent out under General Milroy in the direction of Port Republic. We left Harrisonburg at 2 p. m, traveling about six miles, through fields and woods, striking Jackson's force but avoiding bringing on an engagement. We found that Jackson had turned in the direction of Port Republic, and that he was about to turn in force to dispute our advance. We returned to camp to rest for the conflict of the morrow. On the morning of the 8th, Sunday, the march was resumed, the command taking the road leading directly through the woods to Cross Keys. About 8:30 our advance under Col. Cluseret, struck the enemy at a point near Union church and immediately engaged him. The rebels were driven back about a mile, when they were drawn up in line of battle, and Gen. Fremont ordered his troops into position with a view to a general attack. Our line of battle was as follows: Milroy's brigade formed the right wing, with Schenck in reserve; left wing, Stahel; center, Cluseret; reserve to Stahel and Cluseret, Bohlen, and Fourth N. Y. cavalry extreme left, with cavalry watching our right and rear.

Of Jackson's position Gen. Fremont says: "The enemy occupied a position of uncommon strength, commanding the junction of the roads to Port Republic. His main line was advantageously posted upon a ridge, protected in front by a deep declivity, and almost entirely masked by thick woods and covered by fences. Near his center, and on the summit of an abrupt ascent, bordered at the base by the high perpendicular bank of a marshy creek, he had massed, in addition to his guns elsewhere, three of his best batteries. From superiority of numbers his flanks both at the right and left considerably overlapped mine."

Judging the enemy's right to be his strategic point, the general decided to press him from this side. It resulted in a fierce fight, in which the German troops in General Blenker's division were severely punished, but they resolutely held their ground, resisting with great gallantry the repeated bayonet charges of the rebels. General Milroy's brigade on the right was doing effective service, steadily driving the enemy, advancing his lines fully a mile. In our front were Generals Early and Elzey, and though they obstinately disputed every foot of ground, they were forced to retire before the forces of General

Milroy, whose brave and impetuous leadership was almost irresistible. The Second was in the hottest of the fight, and responded to every command and order with the precision and heroism of veterans. While hurrying into line the enemy's shells fell thick and fast about us, but not a man wavered. It was a serious time, but neither danger nor noise could check the flow of the spirits of the men, and they went into the conflict confident, courageous and cheerful.

At first our regiment was placed in position along a fence with the batteries of our brigade in front. The batteries opened on the rebels, when the courtesy was returned, and the shot and shell flew thick and fast into our lines, giving the boys some idea of the realities of war.

The position of our regiment was then changed, and we lay in a ravine with our batteries to the rear of our position, and here we were treated to the music of the screaming and hissing shells, which seemed to us to be as thick as the leaves of Vallambrosa, but the softness of the ground, into which scores of shells sank, saved us from serious injury. Again we were moved, this time into a ravine where we were in line between our batteries in the rear on an elevation, and the rebels in front. We were then permitted to witness an exciting artillery duel, which was rendered terrible by the screaming of the horses that were wounded, and far more by the men of the regiment who were shot. The battle was fully on, and we were ordered to the right and front to resist the enemy who were attempting a flank movement. A brisk and severe musketry fight was the result, with considerable loss to our brigade, and a much heavier one to the opposing forces, who were compelled to give way before the gallantry of our troops.

Gen. Fremont, acting on information from Gen. Shields that he could hold the bridge at Port Republic, and prevent Jackson crossing the river, determined to defer a renewal of the battle until morning, reform his lines, and give the men a needed rest, as they had been marching and fighting since early morning, without any chance to rest or take food. The command was directed to bivouac, and the night was busily spent in preparations to have the command in readiness for a general advance in the morning. But Gen. Shields failed to burn or hold the bridge, Jackson drove him from his front, and escaped across the river. In the morning when Gen. Fremont advanced he found no enemy in front, but the enemy's dead in great numbers lay upon the field. Advancing toward the river, a black column of smoke, rising about five miles in advance, showed the Port Republic bridge on fire, and soon afterwards the sound of cannon and white wreaths from rapidly exploding shells along the line of the river, showed an engagement in progress in the vicinity of the bridge. A single brigade sent forward by Gen. Shields to hold the bridge had been cut to pieces, and Col. Carroll in command, had for his own reasons failed to burn the bridge, and the result was before us, while Jackson was on his way to Richmond. Thus ended the battle of Cross Keys, and the

CHAPTER X.

advantages were certainly with General Fremont who, with a force of 10,500, met the whole command of Jackson, of at least 18,000, consisting of Jackson's division of three brigades of eleven regiments, one battalion and six batteries; Ewell's division of four brigades of sixteen regiments, one battalion and five batteries, and two regiments of cavalry and a battery. The loss in our command was 114 killed, 443 wounded, 127 missing, total 684.

The loss in Jackson's command incomplete reports, was 58 killed, 402 wounded, 47 missing, total 506, taken from reports of Jackson and Ewell. Our brigade lost in this battle 23 killed, 122 wounded, 14 missing, total 159, of which the Second lost 3 killed, J. B. Kelly Co. A., J. Berry Co. H., and W. H. Mail Co. K., and 19 wounded, with 2 missing; total 24.

General Fremont has the following relative to his troops, in his report: On the evening of the 7th, preceding the battle of Cross Keys, it was ascertained that less than one full ration in any form remained for issue, and it was only upon the certainty of a fight the next day that the council assembled decided for any plan to move forward. These circumstances cannot but forcibly illustrate the physical condition of my men four days after Cross Keys, on their return to Mount Jackson. It was, indeed, less a matter of surprise that their fatigues and privations had begun unmistakably to tell upon the most robust than that the mass had been got forward at all. More than 200 had, up to this time, after careful examination by a board of surgeons, been discharged for disabilities incident to their hard service, while the remaining sick and wounded, brought along mainly in army wagons owing to want of ambulances, upward of 1,000, were now at Mount Jackson. The heroism, the uncomplaining patience with which the soldiers of my command endured the starvation and other bodily sufferings of their extended marches, added to their never failing alacrity for duty against the enemy, entitle them to my gratitude and respect. For their good conduct on the march and on the field, I take this opportunity to thank them as well as their officers, regretting that within the limits of this report I cannot dwell upon the many single cases of individual merit that came under my notice.

The energetic movements made by the general and his excellent treatment of his troops, greatly endeared him to the command, and he was popular to a wonderful degree. Firm and rigid in discipline, he saw that all fully attended to their duty, but in personal contact with his men he was kind and considerate, and made due allowance for their fatigued condition.

In this campaign we marched 200 miles in 115 hours of marching, it being 432 hours from the time we started until the close of the expedition. We walked in column nearly two miles an hour, a record sufficient to attest the endurance of the men and their fidelity to the cause they so well served. For about six weeks they were without tents or shelter of any kind, and on the 24th of June, when the command had returned to Strasburg, they received, for the first time since they started on the campaign, full rations, a period of considerably over a month, and previous to that time, they had became exhausted for want of food. Our regiment came out of the campaign with less than 300 men fit for duty. Our march back to Strasburg was uneventful, and we arrived in that old town on the 20th. We had been in camp for several days at Mount Jackson, a section of country of rare beauty, but like all the rest of the valley, devastated by the ravages of war.

On the 22d our whole regiment went out on an expedition, returning at night, without seeing anything of note. On the 24th all the troops left Strasburg and went to Middletown, except our brigade, which was left to keep a watch on the valley. We were camped on a beautiful spot, out in the edge of a woods, where we had all the delights of country life, and had an enjoyable time, so far as that was possible under the circumstances. On the 26th our regiment went out on another scout, returning the next day, having accomplished nothing. While in camp at Strasburg a large number of the men of our division were discharged for disability, this being particularly true of the German regiments in Blenker's division, on whom the expedition told particularly hard. Upon arriving at Middletown, Gen. Fremont's troops effected a junction with those of Gens. McDowell and Banks. On the 26th an order was issued by the President placing Gen. Pope in command of the troops under these generals. In regard to this Gen. Fremont says: "Having the conviction that consistently with a just regard for the safety of my troops and what was rightfully due to my personal honor, I could not suffer myself to pass under the command of Gen. Pope, I asked to be relieved from the duty to which I had been assigned under him. On the 27th of June, having been relieved of my command by direction of the President, I proceeded to New York to await further orders."

CHAPTER XI.

THE ARMY OF VIRGINIA.

Under date of June 26, 1862, President Lincoln issued an order that "the forces under Maj. Gens. Fremont, Banks and McDowell, including the troops now under Brig. Gen. Sturgis, at Washington, shall be consolidated and form one army, to be called the Army of Virginia." Maj. Gen. John Pope was appointed to the command of the army, and Gen. Fremont's forces became the First Army Corps. Upon the declination of Gen. Fremont to accept the command, Maj. Gen. Franz Sigel was appointed to the command of the corps, and assumed command on June 30th. The "Independent Brigade" of Brig. Gen. Robt H Milroy, formed a part of the First Army Corps. It was composed of the Second, Third and Fifth Virginia Infantry, the 82d Ohio Infantry, companies C, E and L, First Virginia Cavalry, and the 12th battery Ohio Light Artillery. In the new organization of our brigade, we lost our old comrades of the gallant 25th Ohio, with whom we had braved many dangers, and whom we had learned to trust as the bravest of the brave in our little army. They remained in the corps, but in another brigade, the brave 82d Ohio taking their place with us. Independence day was duly celebrated by the brigade. The firing of cannon was the signal to form in line, and the brigade was drawn up to take part in the exercises of the day. The celebration was begun with music by the bands, after which a number of the members of our regiment sang, when the Divine blessing was invoked by the chaplain, Rev. Bolton. Maj. Webster, of the 25th Ohio, read the Declaration of Independence, and then followed a speech by brave Gen. Milroy, which wrought the command to the highest pitch of enthusiasm, and evoked rounds of applause. It was a lovely day, most fittingly observed.

Under date of July 4th, Gen. Pope issued an order directing Gen. Sigel to march to Sperryville by the way of the Luray valley. In reply to this order, Gen. Sigel forwarded to Gen. Pope, July 5th, his order organizing his corps into divisions, etc., among which is named the "Independent Brigade, Gen. Milroy; *this will be the advance brigade.*" It can be said with all truthfulness, that this part of the order was strictly carried out, as we were always kept next to the enemy; in the front when we advanced on the enemy, and on the rear when we retreated. We broke camp on the 5th and started on our long weary march, not to end until we reached Washington. Our march up the valley to Luray was an uneventful one, except the suffering from intense heat, as we trudged along hour after hour, with very little rest. Nearly half the regiment gave out from heat and exhaustion. We reached the little town of Luray on the 9th, marched over the Blue Ridge, and on the 11th went into camp near Sperryville, at the eastern base of the mountains. Passing through Luray, before reaching the mountain slope, great excitement was caused by some one firing out of the windows on our regiment. Inquiry developed the fact that the fire arm that hurled the deadly bullet, was in the hands of a woman. This was an incident a little out of the usual order, though we had become accustomed to the bushwhacking that greeted us on every march and from every hillside. The march over the beautiful range was an interesting one, though severe, and was made a joyous occasion by the happy spirited men of the regiment. A band of German singers in Company C enlivened the march by their singing, their strong and musical voices filling the woods, and giving new life to the men so weary from their fatiguing march. We remained at Sperryville until the 22nd, when we went to Woodville.

A report of the condition of our brigade while here, showed that we had present for duty 110 officers and 2,397 men, and in our entire army 2,473 officers and 49,328 men. We were now fully in the field ready for duty, with a small but courageous army, anxious to advance against the enemy. The men had the utmost confidence in Gen. Pope, and believed that a campaign of victories awaited them. On the 14th of July he formally addressed the officers and men of his army, in the celebrated letter which has been so much criticized.

We lay near Woodville until the 9th of August, preparing for the general advance that was soon to take place. July 18th we had a brigade drill, the first our regiment ever took part in, the brigade being commanded by Gen. Milroy, and July 29th we had a division drill under direction of Gen. Sigel. It was so novel to the men that they really enjoyed it, a fact that could not be stated of drilling in general, so far as it related to our regiment. A "war meeting" on the 27th, and a pole raising at brigade headquarters on the 31st, gave the occasion for a good deal of oratory. A speech from Gen. Milroy was always a treat to the men, as he was nearly as popular as an orator, as a fighting general. On the 5th of August, General Sigel led us in a sham battle, and it was exciting enough to arouse the enthusiasm of the most sluggish. August 7th we were reviewed by Gen. Pope, who was enthusiastically cheered by the men, to his evident delight.

CHAPTER XI.

We broke camp on the evening of August 8th, taking up the line of march at 11:30, arriving at Culpepper Court House next morning. We lay at this place until evening of the 9th, listening to the sounds of battle that came from Cedar Mountain, where a fierce battle was fought between Gen. Banks' corps, and the rebel forces. We waited anxiously for marching orders to proceed to the scene of action, but strangely enough we were kept in camp, unemployed, until night, when we were hurried to the front. In his official report Gen. Pope states that Gen. Sigel failed to march promptly from Sperryville as directed, and he was several hours late, rendering it impracticable for his corps to be pushed to the front as intended. The corps not being provided with rations before starting, had to be supplied from Gen. McDowell's provision train at Culpepper, rendering another delay necessary, so that our corps failed to get into this battle, as was designed. Had we been on time, no doubt a brilliant victory would have resulted, instead of a drawn battle.

Our approach to the field of conflict at night was one of the most picturesque scenes we had ever witnessed. At intervals along the way were camp fires shining brightly; the signal officers were transmitting their signals by lights, the beautiful colors gracefully waving in the air like fairy wands, while in front the booming of cannon, with the flash that accompanied the fatal missiles lighting up the night, made a scene ever to be remembered. It was beautiful, and the animated scene was further enlivened by the rude sounds of war that came to us from the front. The long column marched steadily forward to the mountain, where they encamped for the night. The firing of cannon ceased about midnight, when the weary troops lay down on their arms to rest, ready for the carnage that they believed the morrow would bring. Alarms were frequent during the night, but no serious collisions took place. During the night Jackson withdrew his troops about two miles from our front, and in the morning Milroy's brigade pushed forward and occupied the ground, and for some time had quite heavy skirmishing with the enemy. The day was exceedingly hot, and ere long there was a cessation of hostilities. The next day was spent by both armies, under a flag of truce, in burying the dead, for which duty our regiment was detailed. The men of the two armies mingled freely together and talked over the results of the battle. It was a strange, though not unusual, scene, and the friendliness expressed was one of the inconsistencies of the war. During the night of the 11th, Gen. Jackson evacuated his position in front of us and retreated across the Rapidan river, leaving many of his dead and wounded on the field, to be taken care of by our army. The next day our brigade and the cavalry started in pursuit of the retreating Confederates, following them to the Rapidan, where we rested. Our whole army was pushed to the front on the 4th, our right, under Gen. Sigel, resting on Robertson's river.

Before a week had elapsed, Gen. Pope became assured that nearly the whole of the Confederate army, at Richmond, had left there and were concentrating in his immediate front, with the intention of overwhelming him before he could be joined by any part of the army of the Potomac. He then fell back beyond the Rappahannock, and by the 19th his army was posted for eight miles along the north bank, from Rappahannock station to Warrenton Springs. Across the river was Lee with 85,000 men, being the whole of his army except D.H. Hill's and Holmes' divisions, opposing the 45,000 of Pope's command. On the 19th our brigade received orders to march, and on the evening of the next day, we went into camp at the Sulphur Springs, where we lay until the next morning, when we marched to Kelly's Ford, a few miles from Rappahannock station. An almost continuous artillery fire had been kept up between the two armies since the morning of the 20th. Lee made repeated efforts to cross the river at various points, and along the whole line of eight miles the firing was kept up, but with little loss on either side. At the Ford we met the enemy, but failed to bring on an engagement the first day. We watched the enemy closely and prevented them from doing any damage to any part of our lines. On the 22d there was more serious work, and after an engagement of some hours, we drove the enemy and took possession of the field. The loss was slight, but the work, was severe and trying. This engagement is referred to as Freeman's Ford in General Milroy's report. In this battle, so vividly referred to by Gen. Milroy, ours was one of the regiments that lay in the woods, as reserve for our batteries. While we received but little injury, it was a place of the most trying character, lying so long under the fire of the enemy's batteries, yet not permitted to respond. The bursting shells that were hurled into the woods, sent pieces whirling and whizzing in every direction, so much so, that there was a constant feeling of uncertainty as to injury that might follow. It was no uncommon thing to see one of the men pick up one of these pieces, which he watched as it lazily made its way among the branches of the trees, and then fell to the earth, sometimes too much spent to inflict damage, while again with force enough to destroy life, if any unfortunate came in its way. Yet amid all this danger and confusion, with our own gallant batteries hurling death and destruction at the enemy, it was a common sight to see weary men lying behind logs or sitting behind trees, sleeping as soundly and sweetly as if in the quiet, and safety of camp. But how those messengers of death screamed as they sped, and shook the very air as they exploded, in that historic wood! This tested the courage of men often more than the exciting charge, or the steady fire in column. Milroy's veterans were equal to any demand made upon them, and their hard service in the battle field, their skill in the bush with the guerrillas, and their undaunted and untiring forays on scouts, gave them the kind of endurance and courage, that made even this kind of warfare tolerable. There was no flinching and where the order came for more active work, they were alert, active and vigilant, and as brave as the most noted soldiers in history. We held our position undisturbed during the night.

CHAPTER XI.

On the morning of the 23d we left Kelly's Ford, our brigade bringing up the rear of the corps, marching toward Sulphur Springs, where we engaged the enemy. Our battery began shelling them, and then our infantry opened a brisk fire on the infantry of the enemy, who were soon forced across the creek and were compelled to retire behind their batteries. The Confederates had torn up the bridge, thus preventing our advance, except the few cavalry that crossed over, and, darkness coming on, Gen. Milroy encamped his brigade a short distance back from the banks of the creek. The next day was a more stirring one, bringing with it some of the severest fighting we had yet experienced. Our brigade opened the ball in the morning, and was under fire nearly the whole of the day. On the 24th an incident occurred out of the regular order, that caused great fun afterward, but was exceedingly dangerous at the time. The Second and Third Virginia regiments were marched up near where the Confederate artillery had been doing good service, and ordered to fire into the woods where the artillery had been posted. Not being able to elicit any response to our attack, the regiments began to cheer, and gave three old-fashioned cheers, followed by three groans for Jeff Davis. Before the groans had fairly been uttered, there was a storm came out of that woods that discouraged all further cheering. We fell hastily back, and it was not often that any troops ever were subjected to such a raking from grape and canister as we then had. Fortunately we got under cover of the trees, and as shot after shot was fired into us, we dropped behind the logs and trees and escaped injury, except in the case of Charles W. Sivert, of Company I, who was shot in one of his legs, which was amputated, and Wm. McGully, of Company D, who lost his right leg by one of the grape shots striking him in the knee, and severing the leg all but the muscles in the rear part of the knee. Dr. Hazlett afterwards amputated it.

The artillery engagement mentioned in Gen. Milroy's report, of this day, was the greatest of the war to our brigade, and it was certainly one of the grandest sights that man ever witnessed. It was in fact a tremendous artillery duel, in which the skilled gunners of both sides exerted themselves to the utmost. Our regiment lay in the rear of our batteries, and though somewhat exposed, viewed the scene with an absorbed interest. We lay back of the brow of the ridge, and as the thunder and roar of the artillery seemed to shake the very earth, we could see the belchings of the enemy's guns, and notice to some extent, the effect of the good work of our gunners. How the shot and shell flew and shrieked through the air above and about our lines! What excitement stirred the hearts of the brave men who calmly went at their work, as if it were mere play! It was a hard and a gallant fight, but the guns of the enemy after a while became quiet, and the victory rested with the batteries of the Union army.

The same evening we received orders to proceed to Waterloo Bridge, arriving there about 5 o'clock, where we immediately went into action, the artillery doing good service, and the skirmishers preventing the enemy from gaining any advantage. Even after night had closed over the scene, the enemy kept up the firing, at times opening furiously on us with small arms, which we returned to their satisfaction. The next day, the 25th, the action was resumed with all the fury of demons. The artillery was at times deafening, while the steady crack of the musketry showed where the battle was in progress. There was glorious work performed at Waterloo Bridge, enough of itself to immortalize the brave men that took part in it, and it was one of the most dangerous places in the campaign of Pope. Those of the men not engaged, or while at rest, found but little safety anywhere. It seemed as if the Confederates had a full range of the whole field, and that there was no place too remote for their deadly bullets, whose zip at unexpected places, kept the boys in a state of uncertainty and doubt. Still there was no shirking, and when the call came for active duty, and that of the most desperate kind, it was performed well. Lieut. John R. Frisbee, of Company D, with a squad of men, was ordered to fire the bridge, which duty he performed with a courage of the most exalted character. With the fierce firing between the opposing forces, that on the part of our brigade to divert the enemy's attention from the squad at the bridge, and on their part to prevent this action, it made the situation an exceedingly trying one to the brave men, but the bridge was doomed from the moment the order came to our regiment to destroy it, and though it burned slowly, and it seemed like an age almost until it was useless for its purpose, there was no faltering on the part of any.

The men in squads, of their own accord, at one time, went to an exposed point where, as sharp-shooters, they did an immense amount of damage to the enemy and made him observe a caution that must have been galling and trying. Dark put an end to the conflict, and after nightfall we retired from the scene of danger. We left about 9 p.m. and arrived at Warrenton next morning at daylight. It was a hard march after our severe campaigning, and many a comrade fell by the wayside, worn out, and so exhausted that further advance was impossible. But not long after the command was at rest in camp, the weary men rejoined their companies, again ready for the arduous and dangerous duties before them. We lay at this place until the 27th, when we marched toward Gainesville and had an exciting day of it. Upon arriving at Broad Run, four miles from Gainesville, the bridge was found to be on fire and the Confederate cavalry and artillery drawn up on the opposite side. Maj. Kreps, commanding the cavalry detachment of our brigade, immediately charged the enemy and put them to flight. The pioneer corps was at once set to work and in fifteen minutes the artillery crossed the bridge. On the 28th we marched toward Manassas Junction, arriving within a mile of the Junction at noon. In the afternoon the brigade joined the corps near Groveton, where it rested until

CHAPTER XI.

morning. During the evening, and until about 9 o'clock, the firing was very heavy and severe, but our brigade was not engaged in it.

The following is Gen. Milroy's report of the operations of his brigade to this time: On the 19th we marched all day, passing through Culpepper, and encamping at midnight about four miles north of that place, on the Sulphur Springs road. On the 20th at daylight resumed march toward Sulphur Springs, reaching there at 5 p.m., without any signs of the enemy in our rear. Started on the morning of the 21st with brigade in advance of corps, in the direction of Rappahannock station, and reinforced Banks and McDowell, who had thus far prevented the enemy from crossing the river at that point, and found a heavy artillery engagement going on. We arrived about noon, and were ordered to rest near Gen. Pope's headquarters until a position in the field could be assigned me. About 2 p.m, I was ordered to advance toward the river and take position on the right of King's division. After advancing about a half mile my brigade was divided, yourself, General, (Sigel) taking two regiments along the road, myself moving with the other two through the fields, a small squad of rebel cavalry, who had been watching our movements from the edge of the woods in front of us, fleeing at our approach. Upon arriving at the edge of the woods I halted my column and allowed the sharpshooters and skirmishers some five minutes in advance. I then started my two regiments, crossed the woods, about a quarter of a mile in width, and halted, finding ourselves on the right of the line of skirmishers then engaged, established by Gen. Patrick of King's division. Remaining here some two hours, the enemy making no demonstration, I fell back to the fields, in the rear of the woods to rest for the night. In the meanwhile you, General, had placed my infantry and battery in position near the road on my right. Thus disposed of, we rested until the following morning.

On the morning of the 22d I was ordered early to take the advance in the direction of Freeman's Ford, about one and one-half miles in front and to the right of us, where the enemy had massed the night previous, and were then holding the ford. When within a quarter of a mile of the ford, in order to reconnoiter and select position, I hurried forward, accompanied by my cavalry, being screened in my approach by a long belt of pines bordering on the river. Arriving at the edge of the pines I halted my cavalry and, accompanied by my staff, crossed the road and ascended an eminence commanding the ford. Scarcely three minutes had elapsed when the enemy opened upon me from two batteries with grape and shell. I immediately hurried my cavalry across the road to a safe position, and ordered my battery, under Capt. Johnson, forward on the double quick. In less than five minutes after receipt of the order he had his pieces in action amid a perfect shower of shot shell and canister from three of the rebel batteries, and in ten minutes after had silenced their heaviest battery. He continued engaging the enemy for about two hours, compelling them to constantly change the position of their guns, when, his ammunition giving out, I asked for another battery. Capt. DeBeck's battery of McLean's Brigade, was sent me, he in turn being relieved by Capt. Buell, of the reserve artillery, in about two hours. The enemy ceased firing about 3 p.m. My infantry, which at the commencement of the action I had placed under cover of the woods on either flank of the battery, had suffered but little, some two killed and 12 or 13 wounded by canister and shell.

About 3 p.m., wishing to ascertain the cause of the enemy's silence, I determined to cross the river, and accordingly sent for my cavalry, numbering about 150 effective men. I then crossed the ford, sending a company of sharpshooters across and deploying them, ordering their advance up the hill occupied in the morning by the enemy's batteries, myself with my cavalry in the meantime going around by the road. Arriving at the summit of the hill, I discovered the greater part of the enemy's wagon train, accompanied by their rear guard, moving up the river in the direction of Sulphur Springs. Their cavalry, upon discovering us, gave the alarm, hurrying off their teams and stragglers in the greatest confusion. I posted a platoon of cavalry as videttes, at the same time throwing forward 20 of my sharpshooters, who commenced skirmishing with the rear guard. Being merely reconnoitering, and not having sufficient force to pursue their trains, I ordered my two remaining companies of cavalry into line, under protection of the hill. The remainder of the sharpshooters I deployed as skirmishers, ordering them to feel their way into the woods on my left. They had scarcely entered the woods when they met the enemy's skirmishers, and from their number and the length of the line I inferred that they had a large force to back them. Shortly after they opened a heavy fire to my left and rear beyond the woods I had thrown my skirmishers in, which I afterward learned was the attack of the enemy upon Bohlen's brigade, which had crossed the river below me. It now being sundown, and not being allowed to bring any force across, I returned, my brigade resting for the night without change of position.

At 7 a.m., 23d received orders to move in the direction of Sulphur Springs, my brigade bring up the rear of the corps. When a short distance *en route* I was directed to take a road on my left, a rougher but shorter route to the Springs, the main body of the corps having continued on the main road. Upon coming into the main road again I found myself in advance of the corps. When within a mile of the bridge across Great Run I found our cavalry in line of battle behind the woods. Upon inquiring the cause, I was informed that the enemy were in force at and across the run and had fired on them. Upon this information I passed them with my brigade, and finding the rebel guns in position across the creek, I placed my battery in a commanding position on this side and commenced shelling them, at the same time throwing my infantry into the woods, who soon found and opened a brisk fire into the rebel infantry in front

CHAPTER XI.

of them on our side of the creek, my men being exposed from the commencement to a cross fire of grape and canister from a masked battery across the creek. But notwithstanding all these odds we soon forced them across the creek and to retire for protection behind their guns. The enemy having torn up the bridge, and it now being dark, I encamped my brigade for the night a short distance back from the banks of the creek.

Next morning, 24th, a strong pioneer force having been put to work on the bridge to repair for our artillery to cross, I crossed my infantry upon the sleepers, not waiting for my cavalry or artillery. I deployed a strong skirmishing party and was soon on the track of the enemy, who had fallen back during the night to their main body, which had crossed the river by the bridge at Sulphur Springs, my skirmishers advancing as far as the Springs. As soon as my infantry appeared on the heights commanding the bridge across Hedgeman's river, the enemy, who were in position, opened fire from the opposite shore. I sent back for my battery and returned this fire. The other batteries of the corps soon coming up, a general artillery engagement ensued, which resulted in our driving their gunners away, leaving their pieces very temptingly displayed. Wishing to take advantage of this unexpected opportunity in securing their guns, I had just crossed the bridge, with one of my regiments following close behind, and when nearly in reach of the prize found myself in a hornet's nest. As if by magic the hills and woods became alive with the enemy; the deserted batteries were suddenly manned and a semi-circle of guns, nearly a mile around us, commenced pouring a steady stream of shell and canister upon the bridge. I called to my regiment, which was then crossing, to retire, which it did in very good order and rapid style. Our batteries immediately responded to their fire, thus drawing their attention away from us. In a moment the air was fairly alive with shot and shell, and I took advantage of their elevation to join my command. At this juncture I received orders to take the advance of the corps in the direction of Waterloo Bridge, six miles above Warrenton Springs. I got my brigade in motion and arrived at the bridge at about 5 p.m. I placed Dieckmann's battery in position on a commanding eminence on the left of the road and near the bridge, immediately opening fire upon a rebel battery across the river, at the same time throwing my skirmishers down near the bridge and along the bank, where they were soon engaging the rebel skirmishers. Thus matters stood when darkness partially put an end to the firing, but the enemy opened on us furiously several times during the night with small arms, which was promptly replied to.

On the morning of the 25th the batteries on both sides opened again and continued through the day without serious loss to us. About 3 p.m. I received orders to burn the bridge at once at all hazards, and to this end brought forward my four regiments of infantry to engage the enemy's infantry, concealed in the woods near the bridge on the opposite bank. By keeping up a steady artillery and infantry fire, I succeeded in covering a party firing the bridge, which, being of heavy oak, burned but slowly, and it was not till dark that the bridge was entirely consumed. We then received orders to march to Warrenton, my brigade to bring up the rear of the corps. We left about 9 p.m. and arrived at Warrenton next morning at daylight. Here we remained in camp until the morning of the 27th, when we received orders to take the advance in the direction of Gainesville.

My cavalry, upon arriving at Broad Run, within four miles of Gainesville, found the bridge on fire and the rebel cavalry, with one piece of artillery, drawn up on the opposite side. Maj. Kreps commanding my cavalry detachment, immediately ordered a charge, and after two successive charges succeeded in putting them to flight. By this time my infantry had arrived and I set the pioneer corps to work repairing the bridge, which was executed with such promptness that in fifteen minutes after we were enabled to cross our artillery. Meanwhile I had pushed ahead with my cavalry and infantry in the direction of Gainesville. When within two miles of Gainesville, I sent a platoon of cavalry with a regiment of infantry and a section of my battery to hold the road leading to Hay Market station. With the rest of the brigade I continued on the main road, and upon approaching Gainesville found we had intercepted Longstreet from joining Jackson, Ewell and Hill, who had just passed up the railroad toward Manassas Junction. At Gainesville we took some 200 prisoners, stragglers from Jackson's army. There received orders to halt my brigade for the night.

SECOND BULL RUN.

This historic battle was opened on the morning of August 29th, by Milroy's brigade, and some fierce fighting was done. The Confederate forces were in position from Groveton to Sudley Ford, Jackson's left, under Hill, stretched northward toward Sudley Ford on the Bull Run; then came Ewell's division under Lawton, in the centre; then Jackson's own division, now commanded by Starke, on the right, resting near the little hamlet of Groveton. His force lay mainly behind an abandoned railroad, whose deep cuttings formed a strong intrenchment, and the ground was thickly wooded. The Confederate artillery was mainly massed in on low ridges in the rear of the right. Jackson's front fell back about half a mile until they reached the abandoned railroad, where a fierce combat ensued. Gen. Milroy's brigade formed the centre of the corps, and took possession of an elevation in front of the "Stone House" at the junction of the Gainesville and Sudley Springs roads. Gen. Schurz formed the right and Gen. Schenck's division the left. Our brigade was thus again placed face to face with the old Stonewall forces, whose bravery and prowess we had to meet in a most sanguinary conflict. It seemed to be our fate to fight this

CHAPTER XI.

gallant command. Our first experience was at McDowell, then at Cross Keys, and now at Groveton, on the historic fields of Bull Run. The Confederates had the advantage of being sheltered by the railroad cut, equal to breastworks, where they could meet our assaults, and be in less danger than we were. In the order of battle named, we advanced from point to point, taking advantage of the ground before us, until our whole line was involved in a terrific artillery and infantry contest. For four hours, 6:30 to 10:30 a. m., our whole force was hotly engaged, our brigade and Schurz' advancing one mile, while Schenck advanced two miles. The Confederates being driven behind the embankment, the order was given to drive them out if possible, when Milroy and Schurz charged fiercely upon the entrenched forces of the enemy, but were driven back with great loss; the charge was repeated and again repulsed. The enemy then threw forward large masses of infantry against our right, but was driven back three times by the troops of Milroy and Schurz, who stood like veterans, but were now so hard pressed by the overpowering numbers hurled against them, and so weakened by losses and exhausted by fatigue, that reinforcements were sent to them; and the attacks of the enemy were quieted for a time. At 2 o'clock in the afternoon, some regiments were sent forward to relieve Milroy's brigade, which had maintained their ground for 8 hours against greatly superior numbers, and suffered great loss in dead and wounded.

The second day's battle was as fierce as the first, in which our brigade took a prominent part. Sigel was informed by Pope that it was his intention on the 30th, to "break the enemy's left," and that he, with the First Corps, should hold the center, with Gen. Reno on the right, and Gen. Reynolds on the left. Sigel's corps took position behind Groveton, on the right of the Gainesville turnpike. In our immediate front was massed apparently the whole force of the enemy. Gen. Reynolds on the left, was in a heavy fire of musketry and artillery, while Gen. Porter went to the front, into the woods where our corps lost so heavily the day before, and became engaged with the enemy who were sheltered behind the same old railroad cut. At the same time the enemy opened with shell and solid shot against our center and left wing. Thus the battle continued, and about 5 p.m., Gen. Sigel received a dispatch through Gen. McDowell, and written by Gen. Porter, requesting McDowell to "push Sigel forward," and the latter immediately made arrangements to comply with the order. While executing his movements Gen. Porter's troops came out of the woods in pretty good order, bringing a great number of wounded with them. In reply to a question from Gen. Sigel why they were retiring so soon, they said they were out of ammunition. Sigel then held his troops well together to prepare for any movement of the enemy. Incessant volleys of musketry betrayed the enemy in great force on our left, and Milroy was sent there to assist McLean's brigade. The fighting became terrific, constant and furious. Gen. Milroy, with his brigade, and some other regiments, which he had brought forward, repulsed the enemy on the left with great loss, the General having his horse shot under him. Our forces on the left, who had met the furious assaults of the enemy, were overpowered and came rushing out of the woods, panic stricken and demoralized, leaving Milroy to face the advancing and exultant foe, who followed our men to the edge of the woods. The official report of Gen. Milroy, relates in graphic language the fight that then took place between his forces and the enemy. A better contested line was not maintained in the battle, and despite the superior numbers against us, we held our ground until the attack at that point ceased. The battle on this evening was one of the most furious and determined of the war, and only the superior strength of the enemy, prevented a complete and glorious victory by our troops. The whole field seemed to be alive with the bursting and screaming shells, which filled the air with missiles of destruction, and a dense smoke, the incarnation of the horrors of war. Amid all that destruction, in the very presence of death, with men falling in every direction, our brave boys stood to the work, and none more nobly than our own regiment.

In this destructive battle, the loss of the enemy in killed and wounded was 8,400, while our total loss in killed and wounded was over 10,000. The loss of our brigade was 70 killed and 286 wounded, being tenth in the order of losses, dead and wounded, out of 46 brigades that took part in the battles, and eighth in the order of the number killed. The total number of our brigade in the campaign was 2,507, and many of these were sick and unable for duty long before the ten days' fighting began, and not over 2,000 were actively engaged, showing a loss of fully 18 per cent in this brief campaign alone. It was a severe, hard campaign, and our brigade was handled with a skill and bravery not excelled by any brigade in the entire army. Both Gens. Pope and Sigel referred in the highest terms of praise, to the gallant conduct of Gen. Milroy's brigade, and great credit was given it for the excellent work done by it. In the terrible and unequal light on the 29th, when the Second was sent to support the Fifth Virginia and Eighty-second Ohio, the regiment lost fully one-fifth of all its members present, killed and wounded, in a very few minutes, and yet the next day the brave boys left took their places, and with the rest of the brigade, now scarcely more than a regiment, held in check the force of rebels that had turned the left flank of our army, which is reported fully in Gen. Milroy's report. The men of the regiment had fully proved their bravery, skill and tenacity of purpose, and if they had never fought a battle afterward, they would have had glory enough for one regiment. The fighting on this day was as severe as any that our regiment ever experienced, and those who were in the vicinity of that left flank on that occasion, will never forget it as long as memory lasts. The panic stricken, stampeding forces, that we were sent to reinforce, were fairly mowed down by the rebel batteries, and had our brigade not been protected as it was, the carnage must have been horrible.

CHAPTER XI.

The losses in our brigade were as follows: Third Virginia, 8 killed and 31 wounded; Fifth Virginia, 13 killed and 62 wounded; Eighty-second Ohio, 24 killed and 99 wounded; battery, 1 killed and 4 wounded; Second Virginia, 24 killed and 90 wounded. Our regiment sustained more than one third of the losses of the brigade. The following are the names of the brave men who were killed in our regiment: J. B. McMillan, Company B; August Davis, John B. Wiley, Company C; Ira Chase, James Quest, Company D; Lieut. H. B. James, Geo. S. Butcher, Rob't M. Adams, Jacob W. Cox, Elijah Hall, Jacob Ritchie, Thomas Smith, Company E; John Murry, Peter Cassidy, Alex. Dunn, James A. Gardner, Company F; Henry Burskell, Michael Kevill, George Kramer, Theodore Martin; Charles Schmitz, Fritz Strickel, Company H; Chris Deitrick, James Gardner, Company K.

The following is Gen. Milroy's report of the work of his brigade in this battle: Next morning, 28th, I took the advance toward Manassas Junction, arriving within a mile of the Junction at noon. I halted to await further orders. I accordingly turned my infantry aside into the shade of the woods and sent my artillery ahead as far as the Junction, there being no water for them nearer. Upon visiting the railroad station at the Junction I found an immense amount of government stores in cars, which were yet burning, having been set on fire by the rebels the night previous, after having helped themselves to all they could carry off. At 3 p.m. I received orders to join the rest of the corps, then marching in the direction of New Market. I accordingly moved across the country and soon overtook them. After marching about an hour skirmishing commenced in front. I was ordered to go forward and take position on Schenck's left, and pressed forward through the woods and underbrush in the direction of the rebel firing, which seemed to recede as I advanced. It finally grew dark, but I pushed forward in the direction of the firing, which had gradually grown into the thunder of a desperate battle. It becoming so dark, and the nature of ground not admitting of my battery being pushed forward, I left it in charge of two companies of infantry and started forward with my four regiments in the direction of the heavy firing, which suddenly ceased with great shouting, indicating, as we judged, a victory by the rebels. It being now 9 o'clock, and the darkness rendering the recognition of friend or foe impossible, I withdrew to my battery, which was on a line with the front of the corps, then fully a mile in my rear, resting my brigade here for the night.

On the following morning, the 29th, at daylight, I was ordered to proceed in search of the rebels, and had not proceeded more than 500 yards when we were greeted by a few straggling shots from the woods in front. We were now at the creek and I had just sent forward my skirmishers, when I received orders to halt and let the men have breakfast. While they were cooking, myself, accompanied by Gen. Schenck, rode up to the top of an eminence, some 500 yards to the front to reconnoiter. We had no sooner reached the top than we were greeted by a shower of musket balls from the woods on our right. I immediately ordered up my battery and gave the bushwhackers a few shot and shell, which soon cleared the woods. Soon after, I discovered the enemy in great force about three-quarters of a mile in front of us, upon our right of the pike leading from Gainesville to Alexandria. I brought up my two batteries and opened upon them, causing them to fall back. I then moved forward my brigade, with skirmishers deployed, and continued to advance my regiments, the enemy falling back.

Gen. Schenck's division was off to my left and that of Gen. Schurz to my right. After passing a piece of woods, I turned to the right, where the rebels had a battery that gave us a great deal of trouble. I brought forward one of my batteries to reply to it, and soon after heard a tremendous fire of small arms, and knew that Gen. Schurz was hotly engaged to my right in an extensive forest. I sent two of my regiments, 82d Ohio and Fifth Virginia, to Gen. Schurz's assistance. They were to attack the enemy's right flank, and I held my other two regiments in reserve for a time. The two regiments sent to Schurz were soon hotly engaged, the enemy being behind a railroad embankment, which afforded them an excellent breastwork.

The railroad had to be approached from the cleared ground on our side through a strip of thick timber from 100 to 500 yards in width. I had intended with the two regiments held in reserve, Second and Third Virginia, to charge the rebel battery, which was but a short distance from us over the top of the hill to our left, but while making my arrangements to do this I observed that my two regiments engaged were being driven back out of the woods by the terrible fire of the rebels.

I then saw the brave Cols. Cantwell and Zeigler struggling to rally their broken regiments on the rear of the forest out of which they had been driven, and sent two of my aides to assist them and assure them of immediate support. They soon rallied their men and charged again and again up to the railroad, but were driven back each time with great loss. I then sent the Second Virginia to their support, directing it to approach the railroad at the point on the left of my other regiments, where the woods ended, but they were met with such a destructive fire from a large rebel force that they were soon thrown into confusion and fell back in disorder. The enemy now came on in overwhelming numbers. Gen. Carl Schurz had been obliged to retire with his two brigades an hour before, and then the whole rebel force was turned against my brigade, and my brave lads were dashed back before the storm of bullets like chaff before the tempest. I then ordered my reserve battery into position a short distance in the rear, and when five guns had got into position, one of the wheel horses was shot dead, but I ordered it unlimbered where they were, and the six guns mowed the rebels with grape and canister with fine effect. My reserve regiment, Third Virginia, now opened with telling effect. Col. Cantwell, of the

CHAPTER XI.

82d Ohio, was shot through the brain and instantly killed while trying to rally his regiment during the thickest of the fight.

While the storm was raging the fiercest Gen. Stahel came to me and reported that he had been sent by Gen. Schenck to support me, and inquired where he should place his brigade. I told him on my left and help support my battery. He then returned to his brigade, and soon after, being attacked from another quarter, did not again see him during the day. I was then left wholly unsupported, except by a portion of a Pennsylvania regiment, which I found on the field, and stood by me bravely during the next hour or two. I then rallied my reserved regiment and broken fragments in the woods near my battery and sent out a strong party of skirmishers to keep the enemy at bay, while another party went forward without arms to get off as many of our dead and wounded as possible. I maintained my ground, skirmishing, and occasionally firing by battalion, during the greater part of the afternoon.

Toward evening Gen. Grover came with his New England brigade. I saw him forming a line to attack the rebel stronghold in the same place I had been all day, and advised him to form line more to the left and charge bayonets on arriving at the railroad track, which his brigade executed with such telling effect as to drive the rebels in clouds before their bayonets. Meanwhile I had gathered the remnant of my brigade ready to take advantage of any opportunity to assist him. I soon discovered a large number of rebels fleeing before the left flank of Grover's brigade. They passed over an open space some 500 yards in width in front of my reserved regiment, which I ordered to fire on them, which they did, accelerating their speed and discomfiture so much that I ordered a charge. My regiment immediately dashed out of the woods we were in, down across the meadows in front of us after the retreating foe, but before their arriving at the other side of the meadow the retreating column received a heavy support from the railroad below them, and, soon rallying, came surging back, driving before their immense columns Grover's brigade and my handful of men.

An hour before the charge I had sent one of my aides back after a fresh battery - the ammunition of both my batteries having given out - which arriving as our boys were being driven back, I immediately ordered them into position and commenced pouring a steady fire of grape and canister into the advancing columns of the enemy. The first discharge discomposed them a little, but the immense surging mass behind pressed them on us. I held on until they were within 100 yards of us, and having but a handful of men to support the battery, ordered it to retire, which was executed with the loss of one gun. I then rallied the shattered remnants of my brigade, which had been rallied by my aides and its officers, and encamped some three-quarters of a mile to the rear.

The next morning, 30th, I brought my brigade into position assigned them, and remained in reserve until about 4 p.m., when I threw it across the road to stop the retreating masses which had been driven back from the front. I soon received an order to move my brigade off to the left on double quick, the enemy having massed their troops during the day in order to turn our left flank. I formed line of battle along the road, my left resting near the edge of the woods in which the battle was raging. Soon our troops came rushing, panic stricken, out of the woods, leaving my brigade to face the enemy, who followed the retreating masses to the edge of the woods. The road in which my brigade was formed was worn and washed from three to five feet deep, affording a splendid cover for my men. My boys opened fire on them at short range, driving the rebels back to a respectful distance. But the rebels, being constantly reinforced from the masses in their rear, came on again and again, pouring in advance a hurricane of balls, which had but little effect on my men, who were so well protected in their road intrenchment. But the steady fire of my brigade together with that of a splendid brass battery on higher ground in my rear, which I ordered to fire rapidly with canister over the heads of my men, had a most withering effect on the rebels, whose columns melted away and fast recoiled from repeated efforts to advance upon my road breastwork from the woods. But the fire of the enemy, which had affected my men so little, told with destructive results on the exposed battery in their rear, and it required a watchful effort to hold them to their effective work. My horse was shot in the head by a musket ball while in the midst of the battery cheering on the men. I got another, and soon after observing the troops on my left giving way in confusion before the rebel fire, I hastened to assist in rallying them, and while engaged in this the battery took advantage of my absence and withdrew.

I had sent one of my aids shortly before to the rear for fresh troops to support this part of our line, where the persistent efforts of the rebels showed they had determined to break through. A fine regiment of regulars was sent, which was formed in the rear of my brigade, near the position the battery had occupied. The rebels came around the forest in columns to our right and front, but the splendid firing of the regulars with that of my brigade, thinned their ranks so rapidly, that they were thrown back in confusion upon every attempt made.

Shortly after sunset my own brigade had entirely exhausted their ammunition, and it being considered unsafe to bring forward the ammunition wagons where the enemy's shells were constantly flying and exploding, and the enemy having entirely ceased their efforts to break through this part of the line and had thrown the weight of their attack still farther to the left, I ordered my brigade back some one-half of a mile to replenish their ammunition boxes and there await further orders. I remained on the field.

Feeling certain that the rebels had been completely checked and defeated in their attempt to flank us and drive us from the field, I felt we could now

CHAPTER XI.

securely hold it until morning, by which time we could rally our scattered forces and bring up sufficient fresh troops to enable us to gain a complete victory on the morrow. I felt certain that the rebels had put forth their mightiest efforts and were greatly cut up and crippled; I, therefore, determined to look up my little brigade and bring it forward into position, when we would be ready in the morning to renew the contest. I left the field about 8 p.m. in possession of our gallant boys, started back in the darkness, and was greatly surprised, upon coming to where I expected to find my brigade, with thousands of other troops, to find none. I kept on a half mile further in painful, bewildering doubt and uncertainty, when I found you, general, and first learned from you, with agonizing surprise, that our whole army had been ordered to retreat back across Bull Run to Centreville.

On the 3d of September, the brigade was in the defenses at Washington, and the army of Virginia, which had fought and suffered so heavily, was merged into the army of the Potomac. We were so used up by our campaigning, that we were left in the defenses, while fresher troops met Lee in Maryland, and defeated him at Antietam. We lay here until the 29th of September, drilling, recuperating, and enjoying occasional visits to the capital, when we were ordered to return to Western Virginia.

BATTERY G.

On the 25th of July, Capt. Ewing received orders to turn over his guns at Warrenton, and the company was virtually disbanded, the men being divided among other batteries, Buell's and Dieckmann's batteries receiving the main portion. On the first of August Capt. Ewing was detailed as ordinance officer on Sigel's staff. Lieutenants Morton and Shearer were in West Virginia with a part of the battery, and had no part in this campaign. Orderly Sergeant Rook with one sergeant and eighteen men, was placed in charge of the four caissons, battery wagon and forge, and ordered to report to Capt. Buell, who had command of Sigel's artillery reserve corps. Stephen Ripley and two or three others were with the captain at Sigel's headquarters, handling ordinance and acting as aids on the general's staff. Sergeant H. A. Evans was assigned to Capt. Buell's staff, and was a witness of that gallant officer's death, receiving his death wound on the 22d at Kelly's Ford. Gen. Milroy's graphic report of the work of the artillery that day, tells in an interesting way of the hard fighting, and of the discomfiture of the enemy. While Capt. Buell's guns were sending hot shot into the ranks of the Confederates, Sergeant Evans rode up to the captain to make a report, when a shell screamed through the air, struck and passed through the captain's horse, and striking and mortally wounding the gallant captain, who died from the wounds the next day. Sergeant Evans then returned to Buell's battery, now commanded by Lieut. Hill, and took command of the right piece of the left section, to which he had been formerly assigned.

Dieckmann's battery, to which a part of Battery G men were assigned, is specially mentioned in Gen. Milroy's report of the engagement at Waterloo bridge, where for parts of two days they made things lively for the enemy. They were near the bridge, and vigorously shelled the opposing forces, while Lieut. Frisbee and his brave men were burning the old bridge. Before the advance to Waterloo bridge, Milroy's forces had a severe fight, which tested the endurance of the men, and showed the skill of our gunners.

The bloody work was continued, and at Bull Run the batteries with which our boys were connected, won imperishable renown. Buell's battery on the first day was actively engaged, the section in which Battery G boys served, being sent to Gen. Heintzelman, and were put in Gen. Kearney's division, where they had to meet and repel the attack of the Confederate cavalry, firing all their ammunition, and then falling back to the rear. They refilled their caissons, and on the second day the section was ordered to the left, and had only got into position when Sergeant Davis of Buell's battery was shot, and the command of the section devolved on Sergeant Evans of Battery G. This was the end section on the left, and when the Confederates made their charge on the batteries, it was one of the tightest places of the battle. Good work had been done by the gunners, and the forces of the advancing, exultant enemy were considerably punished, as they charged forward, but despite all the hard fighting, they could not be stayed, and they broke through our lines. The section was out of ammunition except some canister, when the order was given to fall back. One of the guns was loaded to the muzzle with the canister, and when the Confederate infantry came steadily forward in a solid mass, with bayonets fixed and with the determination to sweep all before them, and when within fifty or sixty feet of the gun, our men fired right into their faces, with terrible destruction. They did not stop for an instant, nor did they fire a shot, but pressed forward. The battery immediately started for the rear, and the Confederate officer gave the command to fire, when the air seemed to be fairly blue with the explosion, the bullets whistling and singing, carrying death with them, three gunners and two drivers being killed, among the rest being Albert Kincaid of Battery G, a brave, noble young man, loved by all his comrades. The sections were reunited at Arlington Heights, and went with Milroy's brigade back to Western Virginia.

CHAPTER XII.

RETURN TO WESTERN VIRGINIA.

We boarded the cars in Washington and arrived at Pittsburgh at midnight, September 30th. Here we were taken in charge by the sanitary commission, and given such treatment by the noble women of that grand organization, as we had not had since we left our homes at the beginning of the war. We were received in old city hall, where the patriotic women fed and cheered the tired and worn men, and rendered such service that it was an inspiration to us for future dangers and hardships. No words too strong have ever been written or uttered, in commendation of the cheerful services of these loyal, Christian women, aided and backed by the noble work of the churches and organizations. So long as life lasts, and memory recalls the past, so long will the loyal soldiers of our country who passed through Pittsburgh, remember and bless these staunch and loyal supporters of their country. October 1st the Pennsylvania companies of the regiment were granted a furlough of two days, and they separated for a brief visit to their homes, the other companies going to Wheeling. At the close of our brief visit home, our companies were sent to Wheeling, thence to Parkersburg, and then started on a march to Point Pleasant, opposite the mouth of the Big Kanawha, where the regiment had gone. We met them on the 15th near the Point, returning to Parkersburg, and joined them, arriving at Parkersburg on the 17th. Thence we went to Clarksburg, where we were supplied with an outfit of winter clothing, ready for the arduous work before us. We left here on the 21st, arriving at Buckhannon on the 22d, where we lay in camp for a few days. We resumed our march on the 28th, arriving in Beverly on the 29th, where we laid out a camp and settled down. On the 4th of November, Company B was ordered to Belington, and Company H to

Leading Creek, to guard the road over which our supplies were to come. By the middle of the month all the troops were taken from Beverly except the eight companies of our regiment, and we were ordered to drill about four hours per day, besides watching the counties about us, and doing our utmost to checkmate General Imboden, one of the boldest of the partisan rangers in Western Virginia. We were left undisturbed by him until the night of December 3d, when the regiment was called into line of battle, and rested on their arms until daylight. Our discovery of his approach, thus preventing a surprise, caused Imboden to retrace his steps, and the quiet of camp life was renewed. While at Leading Creek, Samuel Lyons, Richard Robinson and two or three others of Company H, were sent over on Cheat River on a scouting expedition, and when there camped in a farm house. Not posting their pickets at every avenue of approach, they were surprised to see three rebels stalk into the house, who were unaware of the presence of any Yankees. Our boys were wide awake, however, and at once covered the intruders with their guns, compelling them to surrender, and brought them prisoners into camp.

While located here, we were detached from Gen. Milroy's command, much to the grief of the men. He was placed in command at Winchester, and promoted to major general of volunteers, in recognition of his efficient services. Our regiment at once passed a set of resolutions, congratulating the general on his well deserved promotion, to which he responded with the following characteristic letter:

HEADQUARTERS SECOND DIVISION EIGHTH ARMY CORPS
WINCHESTER, VA., March 31, 1863
LIEUT. COL. SCOTT, et al., Second Virginia Regiment.

Gentlemen: Your favor of the 10th, congratulating me on my promotion to the rank of major general in the volunteer service of the United States, was duly received. To say that I thank you for your friendly congratulations and your expressions of feeling toward me, but poorly expresses my emotions, coming, as the congratulations do, from the Second Virginia Volunteer Infantry, one of the oldest of the West Virginia regiments in the present war, and one of the many West Virginia regiments that I have had the honor to command - a regiment justly entitled to be called veterans, for long, arduous and faithful service, through winter storms and summer suns, through pitiless cold, and rain, and mud, through burning heat and stifling dust, through the thunder and din of battle - always on hand for the march or scout, skirmish or battle - a regiment to whose valor I am much indebted for the honorable promotion recently conferred on me by our government; congratulations from a regiment who have so long known me, followed me, and became endeared to me

CHAPTER XII.

by a companionship of dangerous trials and privations, excite feelings which can be better appreciated than described. I thank you for the very flattering mention made of me in connection with the noble and patriotic resolutions you have adopted, which meet my most hearty approval. Please give my most heartfelt greeting to your brave boys, and say to them that I much regret that our temporary separation has been so long and unpleasantly extended; but I hope for its termination soon and to have the pleasure of the company of brave old Second Virginia with me in the coming campaign.

ROBERT H. MILROY, Major General.

We lay in camp in this place for six long months, but found it no easy duty. Nearly the whole of the time not over six hundred men formed our command, Capt. Ewing's battery being with us most of the time. We fixed up our tents into winter quarters with the help of some boards, as best we could, and had as comfortable homes as could be expected under the circumstances. While the weather remained pleasant, the drilling was almost continuous, but it was child's play to the severe scouting in which we were almost constantly engaged, during the whole of the winter. In January, 1863, Brig. Gen. Moor was placed in command of our brigade, which was known as the "Northern Brigade."

Surgeon Hazlett relates the following incident: "On a crisp morning in November, the colonel, myself and an orderly, mounted, and armed with Spencer rifles, went to Shaffer mountain to hunt deer. Near the base of the mountain we were joined by W, an old hunter, a typical Virginia mountaineer, thoroughly familiar with the habits of the game we were after, a quiet, unobtrusive man. The colonel and orderly went along the base of the mountain, and W and I followed a bridle path to the crest of the mountain. While walking along I questioned my companion on the subject of buck-ague. Yes, he had heard of it, he missed his first deer in that way. I desired W to give me the first shot, and I would disprove the existence of buck-ague, to which he agreed. We soon reached the top, where we secreted ourselves to wait until the report of the colonel's gun should startle the herd. Soon the reports of two gun shots notified us that the colonel had found game. With eager expectation I braced myself in the stirrups, raised the lock hammer of my carbine, which was charged with an ounce ball and cartridge, and awaited the comer. 'There he comes,' said W, and looking up the crest there came a fine buck. 'Don't fire until I give the bleat,' said W, who stood almost behind me. This cry, very similar to the bleat of a sheep, W. uttered, when the deer was about fifty yards from us. 'Shoot,' cried W, which I did, and down dropped the buck. Elated with my success, I proudly announced that I had aimed for the left foreshoulder. On reaching the deer, W cut its throat, and pointing to the left fore-shoulder, said there was where the bullet struck. I was in an ecstasy of delight, and I remarked that he would find that my ball had passed entirely through the deer. I rubbed my hands and declared I had 'busted' the buck-ague theory. The animal was examined but no trace of my bullet could be found, but a small bullet, not much larger than a buck shot was taken out. W was silent, gazing steadfastly at the bullet. He then remarked: 'Mighty curious thing this buck-ague. I never knew it to fail; every fellow misses his first deer sure, and if you think you hadn't the buck-ague, just look at your gun.' I did so, and found the hammer of the lock raised and the charge not exploded. W had shot the deer and the report of his gun I mistook for my own. I besought and implored W not to expose me, humbly acknowledging that I had it bad, and he kept my secret."

November 4, 1862, Col. Latham issued orders to Capt. Ewing, as follows: "You will have as many of your men as arms can be obtained for ready to march at a moment's notice, without tents or camp equipage, but all mounted, as they will be used for cavalry." The next day Gen. Milroy issued the following orders to the captain: "You will immediately send out eighteen men, in different directions, for the purpose of hiring transportation, etc." Ten days later, the general ordered: "Capt. Ewing's Company G, Second Regiment Virginia infantry, will report to the regiment for duty, and are hereby detailed to act as artillerists until further orders." The captain remarks drily that there were very few companies in the army that were required to be infantry, cavalry and artillery all at the same time.

On February 10th, an expedition consisting of sixty cavalry and seventy-five infantry, commanded by Capt. C. T. Ewing, was sent to Pocahontas county to capture Confederate recruiting parties and stores. They secured 13 prisoners, 152 head of cattle, 15 horses and mules, and a large number of arms without any loss or accident on our side. April 18th, an expedition was sent to Franklin, taking it by surprise, capturing a few prisoners. Our loss was two men wounded, but not of our regiment. These are but a few of the many scouting parties sent out, the work being almost incessant and of the most exhausting character. The picket duty was also heavy, and the service throughout was very severe.

On March 12th an election was held in the regiment for the erection of Western Virginia into a separate state, and all the qualified voters performed their duty, giving an overwhelming majority in favor of the new state. About the 1st of April, Brig. Gen. Benj. S. Roberts was placed in command of our brigade, to try his fortune in the peculiar warfare of the mountain region.

On the 24th of April, our little command, consisting of less than 900 men, was attacked by a large force of Confederates, consisting of infantry, cavalry and artillery. In the morning Frank Ferris, sheriff of Randolph county, was out on some business, and was shot through the breast by the advance of the

CHAPTER XII.

Confederates. He rode to our pickets, in charge of Sergeant Wm. F. Graebe, Company C, and gave the alarm, the first intimation we had of the approach of an enemy, and they were then but eighteen miles distant. The last, heroic act of the sheriff, was to apprise the small garrison of its danger, and then yield his life. (Author's note of correction: Frank Ferris recovered from his severe wounds, and is yet living near Beverly.) We hastily prepared for defense, but before we were ready to make the best of our circumstances, the Confederates came down the valley in force, on both sides of the river, evidently intending to cut off our retreat and capture us. As soon as they came within range, our artillery opened on them, and soon skirmishing was begun on our left, which was kept up briskly for some time. The force of the enemy on the right stopped behind some timber, and Company F was sent to engage them. But our men were unable to stem the strong force they met, and it being ascertained that the enemy were endeavoring to surround us, our colonel deemed it wise to withdraw, which was done in good order, the enemy being baffled at all points in their efforts to cut us off. We left the town about 3 o'clock in the afternoon, after firing the commissary stores, which were burned by order of General Roberts, to prevent them from falling into the hands of the enemy. While making our way to Leading Creek, just as we were crossing a little stream that crossed the road, the Confederate cavalry charged us, and several shots were fired, resulting in the wounding of Henry Barnhart, Co. I, who was shot through the body and mortally wounded, dying on the 28th. Some of our men were captured in the charge. About four miles further we were again charged upon, the enemy being repulsed with such vigor and dash, that they then let us alone, not deeming it prudent to follow us so closely. We marched to Leading Creek that night, where we remained until morning. Two more of the regiment were captured here while out on a foraging expedition. We continued our march to Belington, where it was our intention to make a stand, and endeavor to force the enemy to battle, but we received orders from General Roberts to join him at once at Buckhannon. That night we camped at Philippi, and the next evening, the 26th, we arrived at brigade headquarters, and were at once ordered into line of battle, but no enemy appearing, we went into camp. On the 27th we ambushed for a force of rebel cavalry, but they kept at a respectful distance, and we resumed our march, arriving at Weston in the evening, where we camped for the night. Before leaving this place we destroyed all the commissary stores, consisting of a large quantity of flour, beans, rice, sugar, etc. The next morning we continued our march, reaching Clarksburg about 10 o'clock at night, almost worn out. During the 29th and 30th we were constantly on the alert for some forces of the enemy that kept annoying us, but we could not get near enough to them to measure strength. Their policy was to worry us by persistent and unexpected assaults, and not to come to battle. The following is the official report of the fight made by Col.

Geo. R. Latham, who was in command of the forces at Beverly, to General Roberts:

On April 24th, about 9 a.m., I received notice that the enemy was in force at Huttonsville, eleven miles distant, and advancing. I immediately proceeded to the front with two companies of cavalry, advancing on both roads leading up the valley toward Huttonsville. Having proceeded about five miles, we met their advance guard on both roads. We fell back slowly, worrying and impeding the progress of the enemy wherever an advantage could be gained. At 12 M., the enemy being within two and a half miles of Beverly, I repaired to the town to see that the troops were properly disposed the most successfully to meet the attack, as I was satisfied, from their steady and determined advance, and the rumbling of artillery in the rear, that they were in very considerable force, though from the thick fog, an estimate was yet impossible. My force consisted of seven companies of the Second Virginia Infantry, numbering for duty 400 men; five companies of the Eighth Virginia Infantry, 289 men; Capt. Frank Smith's Independent Company of Ohio Cavalry, 98 men; Capt. Hagans' Company A, First West Virginia Cavalry, 59 men; one section, consisting of one 10-pounder Parrott gun and a 6-pounder brass smooth bore, of Ewing's battery, 32 men, a total of 878 men, rank and file. I took a strong position on the south side of the town, commanding the entire valley and the turnpike above, but flanked by back roads on each side. In this position I placed the Parrott gun and the Second Virginia, holding the detachment of the Eighth Virginia and the brass gun in reserve to watch the flanks. About 2 p.m. the action was opened with artillery and infantry, skirmishing at long range. A large force of the enemy's cavalry and part of his artillery was now seen advancing on the back road west of the valley toward the road leading from Beverly to Buckhannon and effectually turning our right. This movement it was impossible for us to counteract, though with the river intervening we were not in much danger of an actual attack from this force. The object of this movement was to prevent our retreat toward Buckhannon. Three regiments of his infantry were at the same time advancing cautiously through the woods, pressing back our skirmishers toward our front and left, his artillery playing directly in front, with two regiments of infantry in reserve. At 3 p.m. the action had become quite brisk along our whole line; our skirmishers were driven in on our front and the enemy had advanced to within canister range. The commands of his officers could be distinctly heard, and he was pressing well beyond our left. Shortly after this I received your order to fall back. I immediately set my train in motion, destroyed the public stores of all kinds, and about 5 p.m. drew off my forces. The movement was executed in perfect order, and though the enemy pressed our rear for six miles, and twice charged us with his cavalry, there was no confusion, no hurry, no indecent haste. His cavalry charges were handsomely repulsed, and he learned to follow at a respectful

CHAPTER XII.

distance. We marched this evening nine miles, and having gained a safe position, rested for the night, our pickets and those of the enemy being about one mile apart. In this affair we lost 1 man, believed to be killed, 2 wounded (1 of Second Virginia), and 14 prisoners - 10 from the Second Virginia, 2 from the Eighth Virginia and 2 from Capt. Smith's company.

Brig. Gen. J. D. Imboden, in command of the Confederate forces, in his official report, gives the number in his own immediate command about 1,825 men, and the number from Gen. Saml. Jones' command about 1,540, giving him an entire force of about 3,365 men, of which about 700 were mounted. He lost two men killed, three wounded and 11 prisoners, in all 16, at Beverly.

When our forces were attacked, and it was seen that we were overpowered, Sergt. Geo. Jones and privates Martin Walters, Hugh Smith, William Weible and Thomas B. Richardson, of Company F, were detailed to guard the ford over the river. They held their position until the regiment was driven from the town, when they found that they were surrounded by the enemy, and that it was out of the question to rejoin their company. Surrender seemed to be the only way out of the difficulty, but a consultation was held, and the boys determined that they would not surrender, but keep in hiding until an opportunity presented itself for escape. They lay in the bushes for two days and one night, and when the second night came, they were so hungry that another council of war was held, when it was decided to make a break for liberty; that they would proceed separately, to meet again at a place designated. They were successful in their efforts, and met as agreed upon. They then traveled together for about 15 miles, keeping in the woods, to make a distance of six miles; and then after all their care and maneuvering, they ran into the Confederate pickets, who fired upon them, but, fortunately hurt no one. They made good their escape from this danger, and after about two weeks more of rough traveling, and hiding in caves and in the woods, they reached the regiment at West Union, but little the worse for their rough experience. Evening of the 4th we boarded a train of cars, and were run to West Union, where we arrived about 2 o'clock in the night. The rebels had already burned several bridges, and we were sent to this place to protect the railroad and bridges. On the 6th a force of 1,400 cavalry charged our pickets, capturing 16 of them, and charged down the valley, but halted before they came within range of our regiment, which was drawn up in line of battle, and they retreated as hastily and as quickly as they came. We pursued them at once, but no trace of them could be found. It was a brilliant dash, and as we had no cavalry we could not successfully follow the bold rangers that attacked us. On the 11th we left West Union, and arrived at Weston May 13th, where we remained in camp a few days, and where all our force was concentrated, ready for any emergencies that might arise. We left here on the 19th of May, marching through Buckhannon, reaching Beverly at noon on the 21st. The men captured at West Union returned to us on the 22d, and reported to their companies.

A telegram was sent to the commanding officer in the valley, after our return, by Col. Harris, of the Tenth Virginia, that a force supposed to be a detachment from the Confederate army, had visited Upshur county, had succeeded in capturing a number of fine horses and made their escape into the mountains. There was no cavalry in this section at the time, and it was at once decided to make the attempt to intercept the raiders in the Elk river district, with infantry, an undertaking that did not promise great success, but all were anxious to try it. Fifty men were at once detailed, under command of Capt. Hall, of the Third Virginia, with Lieut. French, of the Second, as second in command. The detail left Beverly in the evening, and went fifteen miles before camping, starting again at early morn, and by rapid marching most of the way over exceedingly rough country, they succeeded in reaching Elk river a little after nightfall, camping in and about the cabin of a backwoodsman, who scarcely knew that there was a war on hands. He was the possessor of but little besides a wife and three stands of bees. In the morning he was the possessor of a wife only, for at the first peep of day the boys carried the hives to the river bank and shook the bees into the stream, securing to themselves a delightful breakfast, which they took care to flavor with wild onions, which had grown in abundance. Following the tortuous stream they came to the county seat of Webster county; thence they advanced to reach the junction of the two branches of the Elk river. When within two miles of this place a moccasin track was noticed in the wet sand, and the inference was that the presence of the Union troops was being heralded by some mountaineers to the marauders who were being followed. Here the roads forked, one branch leading over a rugged spur of the mountain while the other followed the stream, coming together at the junction of the branches of the river. The command was divided into two equal parts, Capt. Hall crossing the spur while Lieut. French followed the stream. Though the latter went on the double quick, he failed to overtake the owner of the moccasins, and when he reached the hamlet at the junction of the branches, not a living soul was to be seen. But a few minutes later they saw the captain and his men emerging from the thick undergrowth on the mountain point, and with them a squad of prisoners and a number of fine horses. The owners of the moccasins had accomplished their purpose, had apprised the marauders of the approach of the Union boys, and they had stealthily secreted themselves in the timber until they found the river route was being followed, and, as they supposed, by the entire force. They then took the mountain road, intending to leave the blue coats in the rear, but as they began to descend the hill the captain halted them so suddenly and unexpectedly that resistance was useless. Sergeant Wigner, of Company E, Second Virginia, was the first to discover the legs of the horses under the drooping branches,

CHAPTER XII.

before the body of the leader was visible, and with his gun leveled on him called a halt and demanded a surrender. The whole party was captured, and it was discovered that the leader was a famous "partisan ranger," as they styled themselves, by the name of Watt Cool. The captain talked strongly of inflicting summary punishment upon him, but at the suggestion of the lieutenant a better use was made of him. The command had successfully accomplished their object without the shedding of a drop of blood, but they were about sixty miles from any Union force and without any proper knowledge of the country. The captain proposed to the old guerilla that if he would faithfully act as guide for us to Buckhannon his life would be spared, and he promised, and kept his word, all arriving at Buckhannon tired, footsore and hungry. The stolen horses were restored, and Cool and his party were sent to Camp Chase, where he died.

We remained at Beverly until ordered to Grafton to be mounted. In this time we were kept busy drilling, except when out on scouting parties, which were so frequent that it was difficult to keep run of them.

CHAPTER XIII.

FOURTH SEPARATE BRIGADE.

May 23, 1863, Brig. Gen. W. W. Averell was assigned, by special order No. 133, headquarters Middle Department, Eighth Army Corps, to the command of the Fourth Separate Brigade, and assumed command on the 24th. The general had won renown as a dashing cavalry officer in the Army of the Potomac, and came to the western region with the prestige of success. He was one of the ablest cavalry officers of the army, and handled a brigade or division with a skill and bravery, that won him the honor he deserved. He was more than a match for any Confederate general that he encountered in West Virginia, with anything like equal numbers. At Droop Mountain he defeated superior numbers intrenched on the mountain, and on the Salem raid he outgeneraled the officers commanding many times his force. The Fifth West Virginia Cavalry always had a great liking for the dashing general and admired his high courage and ability. We give herewith a brief sketch of his life:

MAJOR GENERAL W. W. AVERELL.

William W. Averell was descended from New England families. His father was a pioneer of western New York and his grandfather a soldier of the Revolutionary War from Connecticut. His great grandfather wedded a daughter of Josiah Bartlett, the first governor of New Hampshire under the constitution, whose name appears second on the Declaration of Independence. His grandmother was a Turner of Mayflower memory, and his mother a Hemmenway, a name borne by one of the oldest New England families. His father hewed a farm out of the wilderness in Steuben county, N.Y., early in the century, and the first postmaster and the first magistrate in the town of

Cameron, which offices he held for many years, rearing a family of five children, and died in 1887, aged 92 years. William had the benefit of an academic education, and taught school during two winter terms when he was 15 and 16 years of age, and surveyed lands and roads during the summer. In 1851, at the age of 18, he entered West Point, and was graduated in 1855. While he maintained a fair standing in his class, he devoted all his spare time to a comprehensive course of reading, which the great library at West Point permitted him to enjoy. Fond of athletic sports, he excelled in horsemanship, and stood at the head of a class of five riders. On graduation he was assigned to the regiment of mounted riflemen, now the Third United States Cavalry, whose colonel was then W.W. Loring. He was ordered to the cavalry school at Jefferson Barracks, Mo., whose superintendent was Col. Charles A. May, of the Second Dragoons. The school was removed to Carlisle Barracks, Pa., in December, 1855, and Lieut. Averell remained with it as adjutant until August, 1857. Fitzhugh Lee, W. H. Jackson, D. H. Maury, C. H. Tyler and many other dashing cavalry officers, served at the school while Averell was adjutant. In the autumn of 1857, he joined his regiment in New Mexico, and assumed command of a company, of which both his senior officers were absent; the captain, Andrew Porter, on leave in Europe, and the first lieutenant, Gordon Granger, on recruiting service. An incursion of Kiowa Indians into the valley of the Rio Grande in December, 1857, gave Averell his first chance in an Indian fight, which he embraced by destroying the band and capturing the chief in a hand to hand encounter. For this exploit he was honorably mentioned in general orders from General Scott, commander-in-chief of the army. The outbreak of the Navajo tribe in 1858, opened an active field for "The Rifles," as his regiment was familiarly called, and Averell was engaged in about twenty-five combats with that powerful tribe, and was

WILLIAM W. AVERELL,
BRIGADIER GENERAL AND
BREVET MAJOR GENERAL

mentioned in general orders several times for his gallant conduct. His frontier experience was terminated by a wound received in a night attack of Navajoes on his camp, October 8, 1858, which resulted in the fracture of his left thigh, and put him upon crutches for nearly two years. In 1861, Lieutenant Averell went to Washington to see Mr. Lincoln inaugurated, and witnessed the struggles of many of his old southern comrades and friends, to escape the social

CHAPTER XIII.

and political toils which drew them into secession and rebellion. Although still on sick leave, and an invalid and lame, when Fort Sumter was fired upon, he at once reported for duty, and was selected by General Scott as bearer of dispatches to Col. W. H. Emory then in Northern Texas and the Indian nation, commanding the first regiment of cavalry and the first regiment of infantry, the only portions of our little army in that region which had escaped the disgraceful surrender of Twiggs. Emory's command was isolated by the intervening turbulence of secession in Southern Missouri and Arkansas, and a special messenger was decided upon as the only means of communication. Making his way through these states with a variety of adventures, young Averell reached Fort Smith to find it in the hands of a rebel force under Col. Boreland from Little Rock, and our troops some hundreds of miles out on the wild and perilous frontier. Purchasing a horse, he escaped from the town, swam the Poteaux river, which was booming, and the bridge burned. He was pursued and captured fifty miles out on the Wachita trail, escaped to the San Bois Mountains which he crossed to the north, was again pursued on the Arbuckle trail, but escaped at the expense of becoming lost for forty-eight hours, but constantly making his way westward. In a blind ride through a savage country, infested with wild beasts and murderous men, for over 260 miles, he found the command he was seeking to the southeast of Fort Arbuckle, surrounded by Texans and frontier secessionists. The anxieties of the command were dispelled and its march taken up to the northward. Averell parted with the command on reaching Kansas and hastened to Washington. He was employed in mustering in volunteer regiments until recalled to become adjutant general of the regular brigade at the first battle of Bull Run, and after that adjutant general to the governor of Washington, and provost marshal of the Army of the Potomac. In August, 1861, he was appointed colonel of the Third Pennsylvania Cavalry, and shortly after had the Eighth Cavalry added to his command, forming the first brigade of cavalry organized in the war. He led the advance into Manassas, March, 1862, and served with the cavalry during the Peninsula campaign. He was promoted to brigadier general United States volunteers, September 26, 1862, and served in the Army of the Potomac until he was appointed to the command of the Fourth separate brigade in West Virginia, May 16, 1863. Our command served under his leadership until our regiment was mustered out, in which time his history is that of the gallant brigade which he commanded. He served after that time in the severe battles of the Shenandoah Valley. He was breveted brigadier general United States army, March 13, 1865, for gallant and meritorious services in the field during the rebellion, and breveted major general United States army, March 13, 1865, for gallant and meritorious services at the battle of Moorefield, Va., and resigned May 18, 1865, and since has resided at Bath, Steuben county, N. Y.

On May 25th, Gen. Averell sent official notice to Company G of the permanent transfer of the company to the First Regiment of West Virginia Light Artillery, in accordance with the following order:

WAR DEP'T ADJT. GENERALS OFFICE, Washington, May 18, 1863
Special Order No. 221. [Extract.]

Company G, Second Virginia Volunteer Infantry, now serving as a battery, is hereby permanently detached from that regiment and will hereafter form part the First Regiment Virginia Light Artillery as a gun battery. The Governor of Virginia is hereby authorized to recruit a company to replace it in the Second Virginia Infantry,

By order of the Secretary of War,
E. D. Townsend

It may be well to state in this connection, that the company thus authorized to be recruited, never became a part of the regiment. It was organized late in the spring of 1864, did not even join the regiment, but upon the muster out of the regiment in the summer, with the veterans and recruits, became a part of the Sixth West Virginia Cavalry. The Second Virginia Regiment had but nine companies from the time Company G was made a battery.

The new brigade formed for Gen. Averell was composed of the Second, Third and Eighth Virginia Mounted Infantry, the Fourteenth Pennsylvania Cavalry, Gibson's Battalion of Cavalry and Battery G. The intention was to organize a force that would be able to meet the Confederate partisan rangers on their own ground, and as our regiments were so intimately acquainted with all the ins and outs of the warfare of the mountains, they were selected for this exceedingly difficult, arduous and dangerous service. On June 15th our regiment left Beverly for Grafton, arriving at the latter place on the 17th. Horses were distributed to the command on June 21st, and from that time until fully organized for active duty in the new line of service, we were kept constantly busy learning to ride and manage our horses, and doing such drilling as we were capable of. We were known for the time as "Mounted Infantry," and did service in either arm of the service, as occasion required. We received our equipments of arms and accoutrements on July 2d.

On the 2d of July, Battery G was at Beverly, and while the orderly sergeant was making out his morning report, half the horses being let out to grass, and a dreamy listlessness was over everything, a citizen who lived in the immediate vicinity came along, and asked the men if they were not afraid of the rebels, and informed them that the whole valley above was full of them, and

CHAPTER XIII.

he had walked ten miles to come and tell them. While discussing the matter, Harmon Snyder came along and confirmed the first report, when Capt. Ewing had bugler Phillips blow "boots and saddles." They got enough horses together to move the guns, and soon enough to supply the whole battery, and by nine o'clock were ready for duty. A few minutes later some of Captain Frank Smith's Independent Cavalry Company of Cincinnati, came riding in, and reported that most of their company were captured; that the Confederates had slipped around between them and Beverly, built a fence across the road, and surrounded them, a few only making their escape. About the same time Col. Harris held a consultation in regard to what was best to be done. The baggage wagons with commissary stores, etc., had been ordered out on the road toward Webster, but it was soon found that the roads were all occupied by the enemy under Gen. W. L. Jackson. Our troops went up to the hill just a little northeast of Beverly, and about 2 o'clock the enemy opened on them with their artillery about four miles away, and then advanced within a mile and a half, doing no harm, and evidencing no real desire for close and warm work. They kept firing occasionally all night, and Ewing returned the courtesy by throwing a shell at them every two or three minutes. Capt. Ewing sent John McGilvery with another man in the direction of Webster for reinforcements, who continued until they opened communication with General Averell. On the morning of the 3d the little garrison was still surrounded, but early in the day Major Gibson's battalion came to their relief. A strong and rapid fire was then opened on the enemy, when the rest of the Fourteenth Pennsylvania cavalry and the Third and Eighth Virginia came up, and the Confederates fled precipitately. Our forces followed them in the morning, General Averell now in command, skirmishing a little at Huttonsville, after which they fled beyond our reach. The command returned to Beverly, and the part belonging to Gen. Averell's brigade, returned to Webster on the 10th.

On July 7th the Second Virginia went to Buckhannon, remaining in camp there until the 15th, when they marched to Beverly during the night, in a heavy rain. On the 17th, six companies of the regiment went on an expedition in the direction of Huntersville, but did not encounter any of the enemy. Companies E and K went to Cheat Mountain Summit, D remained at Beverly and B at Buckhannon. The expedition returned to Beverly on the 18th, in a drenching rain, and the next day the regiment resumed their camp at Buckhannon, remaining there until the 20th of August, when they joined the brigade at Huntersville on the 23d. On the 4th of August Company B went on a scout, and on the 6th Companies E and I were sent out, and other scouting parties were constantly keeping a close watch on the front, ready for the forays of the enemy. While here the time was mostly taken up in drilling, the men learning readily the duties required of them in their new arm of service.

On July 7th, Gen. Averell, with all his brigade except the Second Virginia, was ordered east to harass the lines of Gen. Lee, in his retreat from Gettysburg. While not permitted to take a part in that memorable battle, the brigade rendered efficient service on Lee's flank, causing him considerable trouble and loss. Gen. H. W. Halleck, in his report to the Secretary of War, November 15, 1863, thus concisely states the services of our department in that campaign:

"The operations of our troops in West Virginia, are here referred to as being intimately connected with those of the Army of the Potomac. The force being too small to attempt any important campaign by itself, has acted mostly upon the defensive, in repelling raids and breaking up guerilla bands. When Lee's army retreated across the Potomac in July last, Brig. Gen. Kelley concentrated all his available forces on the enemy's flank, near Clear Spring, ready to co-operate in the proposed attack by Gen. Meade. They also rendered valuable services in the pursuit, after Lee had effected his passage of the river."

The troops were forwarded as rapidly as possible, but arrived too late at Williamsport, Pa., to do any service there, Lee's army having crossed the river and was on its way south. Gen. Averell with his brigade hastily retraced his steps, aiming to reach the valley and attack Lee's forces in that locality. On the 18th we captured a number of prisoners, and on the 19th found the enemy on the Martinsburg road, having some severe skirmishing and driving them before us, capturing many more prisoners. The next day a large force of the Confederates attacked us and we were compelled to fall back, with considerable fighting during the night. On the 24th we again advanced and continued our forward movement until we reached Winchester on the 30th, camping and reconnoitering at various intermediate points. During our stay here a great many Confederate deserters came to our lines, who were sent to the rear, and a large number of prisoners were paroled. It was a part of the writer's duty in camp to look after paroling of prisoners, care of deserters and to hear the complaints and woes, and request for passes, of the citizens of the surrounding country. At this point the number of exceedingly and obtrusively "loyal" people that annoyed Gen. Averell's headquarters, might have led to the belief that that part of the beautiful valley was the home of all the loyalty of Virginia; but the loyalty was not of the kind to inspire confidence, and the utmost care was required that no advantage was secured by the enemy by means of passes. The command lay here until the 5th of August.

While here, one of those pleasant affairs, so full of good cheer to all concerned, took place, which explains itself in the following letter:

CHAPTER XIII.

BUCKHANNON, W. VA., August 3, 1863.
TO THE MEN AND OFFICERS OF COMPANY G:

I have received through your captain a beautiful sword, with "Col. George R. Latham, Second Virginia Volunteer Infantry, from the men and officers of Company G," engraved on the scabbard. I accept this as a token of friendship, and as such regard it above all price. Unexpected and unsolicited, it must be the offering of those whose friendship knows no mercenary motive. I accept it and prize it more highly, as a token of confidence in my public and representative character. Not in pride but in humble thankfulness, I thus highly appreciate your estimate of my public services, coming as it does from those with whom I have longest served and who can best judge of my merits. Finally, I accept it as a most expressive emblem of your appreciation of the situation. All that is good, noble, desirable and praiseworthy - the secret admonitions of heaven; the patriotic promptings of our own hearts; the yearning for freedom by the oppressed of foreign despotisms, and even an ardent desire for the peace of the world - plead for the vigorous prosecution of the existing war, and the final and complete crushing out of the rebellion; and the sword is the most appropriate and expressive emblem of the present purposes of every American patriot. Please accept my best wishes and sincere assurance of high regard. Hoping that your future may be even more brilliant than the past, that you may all live to see our country again happy, in the restoration of an honorable peace, that as citizens you may be beloved of all your fellows and honored by high Heaven, and that future generations may rise up and call you blessed,

I remain your most obedient servant,
GEO. R. LATHAM.. Col., 2d Va. M't'd, Inf.

CHAPTER XIV.

ROCKY GAP EXPEDITION.

On the 5th day of August the command moved to Capon Springs, and the next day to picturesque little Moorefield, clamoring over the mountains to reach this beautiful little valley. We had a lively bout with some rangers on the 5th, and on the night of the 6th they killed one and wounded four men of the Fourteenth Pennsylvania cavalry. On the 9th we marched to Petersburg, remaining there until the 19th. During our stay here we were annoyed a great deal by the bushwhackers, killing one of the Fourteenth Pennsylvania. The "Swamp Dragons," a company of about fifty Union natives, who operated in the mountains, were doing a good work, and were able to meet the guerillas on an equal footing, being more than a match for their foes. August 19th the line of march was resumed, reaching Franklin that day, burning the Saltpetre works, and capturing the men that were operating them. The next day, we marched to Monterey, capturing a few prisoners. We reached Huntersville on the 22d, after a very dangerous and exciting march. We had considerable skirmishing, and our wagon train was attacked on the 21st, two of our men being wounded and several horses killed. The next day one of our command and two of the enemy were killed.

The brigade was joined at this place on the 23d by the Second Virginia and Tenth Virginia and two pieces of Capt. Keeper's battery. The Second Virginia left Buckhannon on the 20th of the month and made the march direct to Huntersville to join their command, meeting with the hidden enemy in the bushes and on the hillsides, not knowing what moment the last call should come to a brave comrade. The march was a hard, dangerous and severe one, but on rejoining their brigade the gallant boys forgot their fatigue and were anxious to meet the enemy now massing in their front under Gen. W. L. Jackson. The command resumed the march on the 24th, reaching Warm

Springs shortly after dark, a distance of twenty-five miles. During the day the front of the column was severely bushwhacked, wounding a number of the command. We punished the enemy slightly in the same manner and captured on the march over one hundred saddles and bridles, which we burned, and at Warm Springs we captured a number of sabres, guns, etc. The next day we went about twenty-five miles in the direction of Lewisburg, having considerable skirmishing and making some unimportant captures. On the 26th we advanced thirteen miles, to within three miles of White Sulphur Springs, and at about 8 o'clock found our advance opposed by Gen. Jones at a place called Rocky Gap.

The enemy were strongly entrenched, with a clearing and corn field in their front. The Third and Eighth Virginia were dismounted and thrown out to the left of the road, and our regiment and a portion of the Fourteenth Pennsylvania cavalry, dismounted, moved to the right of the road. Ewing's battery was ordered to take position on a slight elevation to the right of the road. Lieut. Shearer's section dashed into position quickly, followed by Lieut. Howard Morton with the remaining guns. A severe fire of canister greeted them from the enemy's guns, which were unmasked at point blank range, and in the few seconds required to get into action, a number of the battery were disabled, and a few of the horses were killed or disabled. Capt. Ewing, while seeking a better position for the battery was wounded, and carried from the field, leaving the battery in command of Lieut. Morton. Notwithstanding the terrible odds against them, the battery was worked with such telling effect, that the enemy's guns were soon rendered comparatively harmless for the rest of the action. Battery G had an accident happen to one of their pieces, that was out of the usual order. After the fight had begun, the battery was ordered into position, and went on a trot to the place designated. One of the pieces ran off the road alongside another one, and just then the Confederates fired vigorously, frightening the horses, which were new to the work. They reared and broke the pole and the limber got fast on a stump, so the men could not unlimber the gun. Sergeant Evans then ordered the drivers to turn and pull the piece down on the road, so as to be on the level. Just as they did this, Charles Arbogast, the middle driver, was shot through the breast and fell from his horse. His brother, George Arbogast, who drove the wheel team, jumped off and caught his brother Charles, pulling him out of the way. As soon as the horses found they were not controlled, they made a jump and landed on the road, with the piece upside down. The lead driver, David R. Yingst, held on to the horses, and they lay in the middle of the road in full view of the enemy. The horses were then raised to their feet, after great difficulty, by the efforts of Sergt. Evans, Yingst and Billy Gibson, while one of their own pieces was firing grape right over them and a Confederate battery was firing close to them. There was a rail fence near and the shots from the enemy struck the

CHAPTER XIV.

rails, throwing the pieces all over the men. After they got the horses up, a new pole was put in and the gun was put to work trying to make up for lost time. Gen. Averell was near by and complimented the men on their good work in righting the gun under such difficult conditions. The battery lost heavily in this battle. Capt. Ewing was severely wounded and left in the hands of the enemy, together with the killed and other wounded of the battery. The captain relates that when he found himself outside the protection of the old flag, he could not keep back the unbidden tear, and all the prisoners shared in the feeling. Samuel Lessig and Charles Arbogast were killed and Serg'ts. H. A. Evans, Adam Brown, and S. J. Osborne; W. F. McClure, Lawrence Marshall, John N. Taggart, Fred Rowe, George Hart, Phillip Zeigler, John Fife and James Metcalf were severely wounded. Sergt. Evans was struck on the right side of his head by a piece of shell, which exploded just over him, and all that saved him was it striking the hat band, which turned it out. He was knocked senseless and the bone badly shattered, seventeen pieces being taken out and it now troubles him severely.

While the battery was doing such effective work, the rest of the brigade were gallantly charging all along the line. Our regiment, supported on the left flank by one-half of the Fourteenth Pennsylvania Cavalry, advanced through the cornfield, meeting with a murderous fire from the enemy, safely posted behind their breastworks. We pressed onward, however, almost up to the fortifications, but were there met with such a withering fire that human endurance could stand it no longer, and we fell back a short distance, taking position in a gully, or dry creek bed, where we were partially sheltered. In that severe charge some of our bravest officers and men fell. Among the rest, the brave McNally, of our regiment, foremost in the line, waving his sword and cheering his men. The major had taken hold of one of the Confederates and captured him, when they both fell at once, the Confederate being instantly killed by his own men. The position of our regiment in the gulley was a very exposed one now, being far in advance of our line. Gen. Averell, who was directing movements from the center of the line, near Ewing's battery, ordered the part of the Fourteenth Pennsylvania Cavalry that was mounted, to make a diversion by charging down the road toward the enemy's fortifications. This brave body of men made one of the most daring charges of the war, not only facing a murderous storm of leaden hail from the front but also, to their surprise, received an enfilading fire along their flank from a large body of infantry concealed in a cornfield to the left of the road. On they dashed, regardless of death and danger, and reached the breastworks of felled trees and fence rails thrown across the road. While endeavoring to force their way through, they were surrounded by the force upon their flanks and were nearly all killed, wounded or captured. During the excitement of this heroic charge, the survivors of the Second were withdrawn from their exposed position in the gulley to a safer position on the ridge in their rear. The Third and Eighth Virginia had also met a largely superior force of the enemy posted in their front, and although they struggled gallantly, were unable to dislodge them. After the heroic charge of the Fourteenth Pennsylvania down the road, had disclosed the presence of the enemy hid in the cornfield to the left of the road, Lieut. Morton, of Battery G, changed front with four guns and swept the cornfield with canister, causing the enemy who were massed there, a greater loss in men than from any other source during the battle. Night put an end to the conflict, and both armies rested during the night.

Upon the approach of daylight the battle was resumed, and General Averell tried his best to break the enemy's line, but in vain. About 10:30 a.m. he discovered that the ammunition of both the battery and other troops was almost exhausted, and he reluctantly gave the order to withdraw, retiring in good order, traveling all day, that night, and the next day until 3 p.m., when we arrived at Huntersville, a distance of fifty miles. It was a fearful march, without rest, and constantly harassed by the bushwhackers, who seemed to be in every wooded place, whence they sent into our columns the death dealing bullets. There was not the slightest opportunity to defend ourselves, and it was warfare that was devoid of the excitement of the battle field, hence the harder to bear. The same evening we marched to Marlan's Bottoms, where we rested for the night.

A great deal of execution was done by parties of sharpshooters of our command that gained advantageous positions and struck the enemy at every opportunity. As an instance of this, there was one party composed of Charley Hixenbaugh, John N. Crow, Hiram Qualk, T. Dwyer and Silas J. Clendaniel, of Company I, with Jacob Simon of Company C, and some others, that gained the top of the ridge and there did good work. A singular thing is related by one of the boys relative to the three wounded men of Company I and their horses. The men were W. H. Billingsley, T. Dwyer and Lemuel Howe, who were also captured. Their horses, supposed to be in a comparatively safe place, were wounded and had to be shot.

The corps of pioneers plied their axes with good effect upon many large trees near the road, cutting them nearly in two. As the troops were withdrawn, Battery G, with their guns double shotted with the last canister they had, grimly waited the expected advance of the exultant foe. As they came on with their usual yell, the battery boys let them have it red hot, and then limbering up their guns, with the new horses they had procured during the night, pulled out in a trot. The pioneers made their final cuts and the trees fell across the road, completely blocking it; as the Confederate cavalry dashed up they were greeted with a volley from the rear guard lying behind the fallen trees, and who then galloped after the retreating column. Company C formed part of the rear guard, and on the morning of the 28th, in going around a steep hill, were

CHAPTER XIV.

fired upon by the enemy, who were concealed in the rocks above. Lorenz Turk was killed and Henry Myer was severely wounded. The company was then about two miles behind the column, and immediately put spurs to their horses to regain our forces. The road in some places was only about ten feet wide, with a deep ravine below. It was with difficulty that the horses could be ridden past and over the fallen body of Turk and of the horses that were also killed, and when Sergt. Graebe's horse came to the place he shied and went over the side of the road into a deep wash-out, striking on his head, with the sergeant beneath him. His comrades supposed he was killed and passed on. Though bruised considerably, the horse was able to get up after awhile, when Graebe mounted him and soon rejoined the company, to their great surprise. We continued our march on the 29th, arriving at Big Springs by evening, but did not stop, marching all night and the next day until evening, when we reached Huttonsville, a distance of forty-five miles. It was a hard, trying march, and we were mercilessly bushwhacked, going into camp weary and sore, but with hope and courage for the future. In a little over three days we had marched over one hundred miles, about fifty hours of which were in line of march. On the 31st we returned to Beverly, where we went into camp and remained until November.

The Confederate papers in their comments on the battle, said: "The Yankees, under the great raider Averell, took a summer jaunt to the White Sulphur Springs for the benefit of their health, and met with such a warm and cordial reception that many of them concluded to remain and take up their bounty land, but were satisfied with six feet of ground instead of a quarter section." They had little to boast of, however, for the retreat was a most orderly and well conducted one, we bringing off all our guns, wagons and ambulance, leaving behind our dead and those so badly wounded that they could not be moved, while the loss of the enemy was very great.

The losses of the brigade were 26 killed, 125 wounded and 67 captured -- total, 218. The losses of our regiment were as follows:

Killed--Rudolph Armstrong, Lorenz Turk, Company C; Asbury S. Davis, Company E; W. W. Carney, Company F; John Oakes, Company K.

Wounded--Major F. P. McNally, G. W. Miller, Sergt. Maj., John R. Thomas, Principal Musician, W. H. Graham, Company A; James Callahan, Kidd S. Simpson, Company B; James McAleer, Samuel Ray, Company D; Lieut. John C. French, G. F. Dillon, Calvin B. Martin, Morgan Rush, Fred Schaub, Company E; Hugh Smith, Company F, Aden Webb, Company H; T. Dwyer, W. H. Billingsley, Lemuel B. Howe Company I.

The following order was issued by Gen. Averell upon reaching Beverly:

HEADQUARTERS FOURTH SEPARATE BRIGADE, BEVERLY, W. VA., Sept. 1, 1863.
Special Orders, No. 45:

The brigadier general commanding desires to express to the officers and men of this command who took part in the recent expedition into the country occupied by the enemy, his high appreciation of the fortitude and gallantry they have displayed. You sought the enemy in his strongholds and drove him in confusion from his camps, destroying his military resources throughout a vast region. Relying upon the cooperation of other forces, which had been promised you, but which did not come, you attacked a superior force of the enemy with an impetuosity which dislodged him from his first position, and success was dawning upon your arms, when lack of ammunition obliged you to pause. Even then you stood fast, witnessing the fall of many noble comrades with a fortitude that the approaching reinforcements of the enemy could not disturb. When directed to withdraw, you retired with the dignity becoming soldiers baffled but not beaten. You have encountered cold and hunger, and the murderous shots of lurking cowards have been met with the indifference of tried courage. The combined efforts of the enemy failed to made us relinquish our purposes or prevent our return. Let the grief which fills our hearts for our fallen friends, render them stout in a just cause. Prepare at once for greater undertakings.

By command of BRIG. GEN. W. W. AVERELL.
C. FRED TROWBRIDGE, Capt. and A. A. A. G.

The following is General Averell's report of this expedition, the best account of the raid and battle that the writer has ever seen: On August 5, I left Winchester and marched over North Mountain to Wardensville, twenty-eight miles. A lieutenant and ten men of Imboden's command were captured on the way by Capt. Von Koenig who led the advance during the day. I arrived at Moorefield with my command at 8:30 p.m., on the 6th, after a tedious march of thirty miles over a difficult road. At Lost river a company of the Fourteenth Pennsylvania was sent to Moorefield, via Harper's Mills, where it captured a lieutenant and a party of the enemy, but subsequently falling into an ambush after dark, lost its prisoners and thirteen men captured. Four of the Fourteenth Pennsylvania were wounded, and three of the enemy were killed and five wounded. On the 9th, I left Moorefield and marched to Petersburg, eleven miles, leaving Gibson's battalion on the South Fork. My command was at this time badly in want of horse shoes and nails, clothing and ammunition, requisitions for which had been made by my quartermaster, at Cumberland, on the 7th. The order of Brig. Gen. Kelley to move was received on the 15th, at

CHAPTER XIV.

Petersburg, but it was not until noon of the 17th that horse-shoe nails arrived. Some ammunition for Ewing's battery was also received, but I was unable to increase my supply for small arms which amounted to about thirty-five cartridges to each man. This was sufficient for any ordinary engagement, but we had a long march before us entirely in the country occupied by the enemy, and I felt apprehensive that the supply would be exhausted before the expedition should be ended. It was my opinion that the delay, which would ensue by awaiting the arrival of ammunition, would be more dangerous to us than undertaking the expedition with the supply we had. Therefore on the 18th, Col. Oley, of the Eighth West Virginia, was sent with his regiment up the North Fork of the South Branch of the Potomac, and Gibson's battalion up South Fork, and on the morning of the 19th I moved with the Third West Virginia, Fourteenth Pennsylvania cavalry and Ewing's battery nearly to Franklin, sending forward two squadrons to destroy the Saltpeter works, five miles above.

On 20th, I proceeded up the South Branch to Monterey, over a rough road, the Eighth West Virginia and Gibson's battalion joining the column on the march. A few guerrillas were captured on the road. At Monterey the quarterly court was found in session. Upon my arrival it was adjourned and the principal officials arrested. It was learned that Imboden had been there the day previous to hold a conference with Maj. Gen. Samuel Jones, upon the subject of attacking me at Petersburg. The road to Huntersville was taken on the 21st, as far as Gibson's store, my advance, conducted by Lieut. Rumsey, aide-de-camp, driving about 300 of the enemy before it, during the march, to within five miles of Huntersville. Our casualties during the day were only four wounded and six horses killed and disabled, although constantly annoyed by shots from guerrillas who infested the bushes along the way. Learning, during the night of the 21st, that the enemy had assumed a position in a ravine, about three miles from Huntersville, which was difficult to carry on account of the precipitous character of the sides, I made a false advance on the 22d with Gibson's battalion, while the main body taking a by-road to the right, reached Huntersville without meeting resistance, rendering the position of the enemy useless to him, and causing him to retire in haste toward Warm Springs. Col. Oley, with the Eighth West Virginia and one squadron of the Third West Virginia, was sent after the retreating enemy and overtook his rear guard at Camp Northwest, from whence it was driven several miles. Camp Northwest was burned and destroyed, with commissary buildings and stores, blacksmith shops, several wagons, a number of Enfield rifles, gun equipments and a quantity of wheat and flour at a mill close by. A large number of canteens, stretchers, and hospital supplies fell into our hands.

The 23d was spent at Huntersville awaiting the arrival of the Second and Tenth West Virginia. The Tenth and a detachment of about 350 of the Second West Virginia and a section of Keeper's battery arrived during the day from the direction of Beverly. The Second had 40 rounds of ammunition per man, with 1,000 rounds additional, which were transferred to the Third West Virginia. During the day a reconnaissance, under Lieut. Col. Polsley, Eighth West Virginia, was made toward Warm Springs. One lieutenant and five men of the enemy were captured, and 12 killed and wounded. Our loss was only five horses shot. On the 24th the march was resumed toward Warm Springs, through which Jackson and his forces were driven over the mountains east of that place toward Millborough. Our losses during the day were two men severely wounded, some slightly hurt and a few horses shot. Captured many arms, saddles, and other stores from the enemy. The forces under Jackson having been driven out of Pocahontas county too soon to permit them to form a junction with any other bodies of the enemy, and the prospect of overtaking him being very small, I determined to turn my column toward Lewisburg, hoping that my movement up to the Warm Springs had led the enemy to believe that I was on my way to his depots in the vicinity of Staunton. I relied also on some co-operation from the direction of Summerville. I therefore sent the Tenth West Virginia back to Huntersville, and on the 25th made a rapid march of 25 miles to Callaghan's, in Allegheny county, destroying the saltpeter works on Jackson's river, on my way. Arrived at Callaghan's, reconnoitering parties were sent to Covington and Sweet Springs. Some wagons of the enemy were captured near Covington, and the saltpeter works in that vicinity destroyed.

At 4 a.m. on the 26th my column was formed, enroute to White Sulphur Springs. The road crossed two mountain ranges before 10 miles had been traveled over. About 9:30 a.m., when about 12 miles from Callaghan's, a message from Capt. Von Koenig was received by me at the head of the column, that the enemy were resisting his advance, and desiring reinforcements. A squadron of the Second was sent on at a trot, and a squadron of the Eighth ordered forward. A few minutes elapsed when the enemy's cannon announced his purpose of disputing our farther progress and indicated his strength. I at once started the column forward at a rapid gait down through a narrow pass, which soon opened out into a little valley a mile long, inclosed on each side by rugged rocky heights, covered with a stunted growth of pine, oak and chestnut trees. At the opening, the projectiles from the enemy's cannon first struck the head of our column. A jutting cliff on the right afforded protection for the horses of the Second and Eighth, and the dismounted men of the Second were at once ordered to the summit of the ridge on our right, and the squadron of the Eighth dismounted to the hill on our left. A section of Ewing's battery was brought up rapidly and planted on the first available position, where it opened briskly and with great accuracy. The squadron of the Eighth, ordered to the left, mistook the direction in some way, and found itself on the right with the Second West Virginia. The main body of the Eighth West Virginia, led by Col.

CHAPTER XIV.

Oley, however, soon made their way to the crest on our left. The Third West Virginia and Fourteenth Pennsylvania were ordered forward, and came to the front, dismounted very soon. I beg to call your attention to the fact that my column of horses, nearly four miles long, was now in a narrow gorge, and that during the time necessary for the Third West Virginia and Fourteenth Pennsylvania to arrive at the front, it was necessary that Ewing, supported only by the advance guard, should maintain his position against an attack of the enemy's artillery and infantry combined. The Second on the right and the Eighth on the left, afforded some support, but Ewing's battery, with canister, not only resisted the approach of the enemy, but actually advanced upon him, in order to obtain a better position, and held him at bay until the arrival of the Fourteenth Pennsylvania and Third West Virginia, which were at once deployed to the right and left of the road, thus filling up the gap in my line. The enemy gave away his position to us and endeavored to assume another about half a mile in rear of the first, with his right resting upon rugged prominence, his center and left protected by a temporary stockade, which he had formed of fence rails. I resolved to dislodge him before he should become well established, and then if possible, to rout him from the field. One of the guns of Ewing had burst, and the other five were advanced to within 600 yards of the enemy. Capt. Von Koenig was sent to advance the Third and Eighth, orders were sent to the right also to advance. Gibson's battalion was thrown into a house and the surrounding enclosures which stood in front of the enemy's center. The enemy clung tenaciously to the wooded hill on their right, and Gibson's battalion was driven from the house by a regiment of the enemy, which at that moment arrived upon the field. I immediately caused the house to be set on fire by shells, which prevented the enemy from occupying it. The right was able to gain only a short distance by hard fighting. It then became an affair of sharpshooters along the whole line at a distance of less than 100 yards. The effort which my men had made in scaling a succession of heights on either hand, had wearied them almost to exhaustion. A careful fire was kept up by small-arms for three hours, it being almost impossible for either side to advance or retire. During this time I reconnoitered the position, going from the hills on the right to the left. At about 4 p.m. I determined to make another effort to carry the position. A squadron of the Fourteenth Pennsylvania, which had not been dismounted, was brought up and instructions sent to the commanders along the line that a cavalry charge was about to be made on the enemy's center, and directing them to act in concert. The charge was splendidly made by Capt. Bird, of the Fourteenth Pennsylvania cavalry, who led his men until he came to a stockade which the enemy had thrown across the road. Orders had been given to the officers commanding the regiments on the right, to press forward at the same time and endeavor to gain the Anthony's Creek road, which came in on the enemy's left. The order to the Second to advance was conveyed by Lieut. Combs, the adjutant of that regiment, who delivered the order to that portion of the regiment nearest him. Maj. McNally on the right, and Lieut. Combs on the left, of the regiment, with less than 100 men, advanced on the enemy's line and drove them out of the stockade, leaving Maj. McNally mortally wounded in the hands of the enemy. The effect of the cavalry charge was to cause about 300 of the enemy to run away from the stockade, exposing themselves to a deadly fire from the Fourteenth Pennsylvania, Col. Schoonmaker, but their position was soon regained by their reserves. No united effort was made to attain the road on the extreme right, as directed. Reports soon reached me from all parts of the line that ammunition was falling short. The slackened firing of the enemy evidently indicated that his supply was not plentiful. The night came with no change in position, and no tidings from the west, whence Gen. Scammon was expected. During the night all the ammunition in the wagons was brought up and equitably distributed, and every available man was brought to the front. It was quite evident to my mind that if the resistance of the enemy was kept up, I could go no farther in that direction. It was impossible to retire during the night without disorder, and perhaps disaster. By remaining until morning two chances remained with me; first, the enemy might retreat, and, second, Scammon might arrive. The morning showed us that both chances had failed, that the enemy had received ammunition, and that re-enforcements were coming to him from the direction of Lewisburg. The battle was renewed, but every arrangement made in rear for a prompt withdrawal. The ambulances loaded with wounded, the caissons, wagons, and long columns of horses were placed in proper order upon the road, details made for the attendance of the wounded, trees prepared to fall across the gorge when our artillery should have passed, and commanding officers received their instructions. The enemy's re-enforcements arrived and attempted to turn my left about 10 a.m. At 10:30 o'clock the order to retire was given, and in forty-five minutes from that time my column was moving off in good order, my rear guard at the barricades repulsing the enemy's advance twice before it left the ground. Successive barricades were formed and my column reached Callaghan's about 5 p.m., where it was halted, fires built, and the men and horses given the first opportunity to eat for thirty-six hours. After dark the fires were left burning and the column took the road to Warm Springs. A scouting party of the enemy in front of us had left word with the citizens that Jackson was at Gatewood's, with a strong force. This shallow attempt at deception did not deter us from marching to that point, where we arrived at daylight on the 28th. At 9 a.m. the march was resumed to Huntersville, without interruption, but with considerable annoyance from guerrillas. At evening we marched to Greenbrier Bridge, or Marlin's Bottom, where Col. Harris, with the Tenth West Virginia was posted. The ensuing day the command moved to Big Springs, where it was

CHAPTER XIV.

ascertained that a party of the enemy had entered the road before us for the purpose of blockading it. At 2 a.m., on the 30th, we were again en route, and at daylight came upon a blockade, half a mile long, made by felling large trees across the road. While delayed in cutting it out the animals were fed and a strong blockade made in rear. The command arrived at Beverly on August 31, having marched, since June 10, 636 miles, exclusive of the distance passed over by railroad, and of the marches made by detachments, which would increase the distance for the entire command to at least 1,000 miles. This command has been mounted, equipped and drilled; marched over 600 miles through a rugged mountainous region, fighting the enemy almost daily; had one severe battle; destroyed the camps of the enemy; captured large amounts of supplies and 266 prisoners, in less than eighty days. The strength of the enemy opposed to me in the engagement at Rocky Gap was 2,500, as near as could be ascertained by observations and from the reports of prisoners, and also from statements of rebel officers. I did not have 1,300 men in the front the first day.

The following is the report of Maj. Gen. Sam. Jones, commanding the Confederate forces of the battle: On the evening of August 23 I received information from Col. Wm. S. Jackson that Brig. Gen. Averell, U. S. Army, with a force estimated at over 4,000 men, consisting of cavalry, mounted infantry and artillery, was in motion from the direction of Moorefield. So far as I could ascertain, Gen. Averell was on a raid toward Staunton. He had driven Col. Jackson from Hightown and his camp near Huntersville, and he later had fallen back to Gatewood's on Back Creek, on the road from Huntersville to Warm Springs. I had a few days previously ridden over that road, Col. Jackson accompanying me part of the way, and from my own observations and his representations, believed that he could detain the enemy on that road long enough to enable me to send a force to his assistance or place it in the rear of the enemy. I accordingly ordered the First Brigade of my command, Col. George S. Patton, commanding, to move by the Anthony's Creek road. I joined the brigade myself on that road on the 25th. On the morning of that day I received a dispatch from Col. Jackson, dated at 9 o'clock on the previous day, at Gatewood's. He informed me that he had driven back the enemy's skirmishers to his old camp near Huntersville. The tenor of the dispatch induced me to believe that he could not only check the opposing force at Gatewood's but could move up and join the First Brigade at the intersection of the Anthony's Creek road from Huntersville to Warm Springs. I dispatched him, informing him of the movement of that brigade, directed him, if possible, to join it at the junction of the roads above mentioned. I have reason to believe that he never received my dispatch, and that it was intercepted by the enemy. While on the march on the 25th information was received, which I deemed reliable, that the enemy had not only driven Col. Jackson from Gatewood's but had forced him beyond Warm Springs. Still remaining under the impression that the destination of the enemy was Staunton, the First Brigade was ordered to turn off from the Anthony's Creek road and take a shorter route to Warm Springs. After 10 o'clock that night information was received which satisfied me that the enemy had abandoned the pursuit of Col. Jackson. and that while the First Brigade was marching toward Warm Springs, Gen. Averell was advancing from Warm Springs to Callaghan's. I immediately ordered Col. Patton to return on the Anthony's Creek road in the hope of intercepting the enemy on the road from the Warm to the White Sulphur Springs. By a night march our advance guard reached the intersection of the latter named road at the same instant that the head of Averell's column debouched from the defile through the Allegheny Mountains on the road from Callaghan's. Gen. Averell endeavored to force his way through, but the First Brigade was quickly placed in position when an engagement commenced, which, for five hours, was very warm and continued at intervals until dark. That night the troops occupied the same position that they had taken in the morning. The enemy made two vigorous attacks the next morning which were handsomely repulsed, when he abandoned his position and retreated towards Warm Springs. My cavalry and artillery were ordered in pursuit. For about ten or eleven miles the road passes through a narrow and thickly wooded defile. The enemy availed himself of the advantage offered to retard pursuit by felling trees across the road.

The report of Gen. Jones shows his losses to be 20 killed, 129 wounded and 13 captured - a total of 162.

Account of the Battle of Rocky Gap by Private Samuel B. Knox, Co. K
The Leader, Pomeroy, Meigs County, Ohio
June 19, 1899

In my first letter, I wrote of one of Gen. Averell's raids which was a great success: in this I will give a brief account of the battle of Rocky Gap which defeated another daring attempt of the same officer to destroy rebel supplies and cut off communications.

Our regiment left Buckhannon, W.Va., August 21, 1863, to join the brigade at Huntersville. It required three days to make the march, and we were beset by bushwhackers almost continually. Although we lost several men by this desultory fire, we could do nothing effectual to prevent it as the enemy were experienced mountaineers and always fired from some sheltered position, where all we could see of them was a wreath of smoke curling up among the rocks or bushes.

After joining the brigade, we were still annoyed by the same wary enemy, but we contrived on the 24th to capture about 100 saddles and bridles, as

CHAPTER XIV.

well as some guns and prisoners. On the 26th, after marching about thirteen miles, we came to Rocky Gap, which is a narrow pass or defile three miles from White Sulphur Springs, W.Va. Here Capt. Von Koenig, who was in the advance, sent back word that the enemy was resisting his advance and asked for reinforcements. The gap was quite narrow, but a squad of the 2nd and 8th Virginia regiments went forward on the trot, and in a few minutes the boom of cannon was heard. The whole column then advanced as rapidly as the nature of the ground would permit, and soon the pass opened into a little valley about one mile in length and inclosed by rugged, rocky heights. There we found the enemy to be entrenched with a corn field in front. I was in a detachment from the 2nd Va., and we dismounted and went forward to the summit of a ridge to the right. A squad of the 8th Va. was ordered to ascend the hill on the left, but through some mistake they also went to the right; but the rest of the regiment remedied the mistake by seizing the hill on the left. The column of horses nearly four miles in length came up slowly, but our battery which had opened in front held its ground and even advanced after having driven the enemy back with canister. The two other regiments came up and filled up the gap; but the rebels soon gave up their position for one a half mile to the rear, where their right was posted on a rugged prominence, and their left and center protected by a temporary stockade of fence rails. One of our guns burst but the other five advanced to within about 600 yards of the enemy's position. The men were so exhausted by scaling the heights that we settled down about 100 yards from the enemy, and three hours of constant sharpshooting passed, when another effort was made by us to carry the rebel position. About one hundred men, led by Maj. McNally and Leiut. Combs, drove the enemy from the stockade, but the gallant Major was mortally wounded and fell into the hands of the enemy. About three hundred of the rebels were driven out by our cavalry and they were very roughly handled; but no united effort seemed to have been made to attain the road on extreme right as was intended.

We held the position all night and received ammunition; but as the enemy was reinforced, preparations began to be made early the next morning for a retreat. Ambulances loaded with wounded, caissons, wagons, and long columns of horses were placed in proper order for the march. Trees were partly chopped down, ready to fall across the gorge and obstruct the advance of the enemy. At about 10:30 a.m. we began to retreat in good order. As soon as we had passed the gorge, the trees went crashing down completely obstructing it; and when the enemy came up our rear guard stationed behind the fallen trees gave them a warm reception. Barricades were formed at short intervals, and at each of these the enemy was checked. We arrived at Callaghans in the evening, built fires, ate and fed our horses for the first time in thirty-six hours. After dark the fires were left burning and the march was continued to Warm

Springs. We arrived at Beverly Aug. 31st, having marched 636 miles since June 10, exclusive of about 360 miles of railroad travel and march of detachments.

Less than 1,300 of Averell's men were engaged in the battle. Gen. Jones' force numbered about 2,500.

CHAPTER XV.

DROOP MOUNTAIN.

The months of September and October were ones of intense activity, consisting of heavy picket duty, arduous scouting and severe drilling. Scouting was the regular order, and it was the exception when one or more scouting parties were not out in the mountains or valleys, watching the movements of the Confederates who were constantly hovering about. September 11th a flag of truce was sent out to ascertain the condition of our wounded at Rocky Gap. The Second Virginia went to Huttonsville on the 14th for picket duty, where they remained until the 17th, being relieved by the Fourteenth Pennsylvania Cavalry. While here Lieut. Weaver was sent with a detail of seventy-five men from the different companies, on a scout to Monterey, Crab Orchard and other points. They had several skirmishes, capturing some prisoners. On their return to camp, the horse of Sam Knox of Company K, slipped over a steep bank and crippled it so that he could not continue with the company, and was left with some Union people in the mountains, who agreed to take care of them until the return of some of the men for them. On the return to camp, Sergt. Quimby and twelve men were sent out after Knox, a distance of 43 miles. They found that the citizens had kept their word, their comrade was safe, and the horse had been cared for so that he could carry his owner to camp. When this party started for camp, on reaching Dry Fork, they learned that about 800 of the Confederates had passed at daylight in the direction of Beverly, on the road they had to travel. They at once struck down the river a few miles, then went over the hills and through the woods, arriving in camp safe, after a tramp of about two weeks. On reaching camp, they found that it was a part of this force, that had captured Lieut. Hutchinson and his party, while on picket.

On September 24, a detail for picket and patrol duty, was sent to Shaffer mountain from Company A, consisting of the following members: Lieut. J. R.

Hutchinson; Sergts. F. H. Singer, H. Smith and M. Campbell; Corps. J. Breen, C. Britch, S. Croco and Ed. Saladin, and privates A. Campbell, J. Carrigan, J. Stone, S. L. Reynolds, W. S. Taylor, J. Mclarren, J. Washington, P. Kirsch, J. Slayer, L. Henrich, W. Heine, F. H. McCleane, M. Robel, W. Ludaking, L. Metz, H. Wagner, P. Romiser, F. Dickroger, B. F. Ackelson, W. Dever, L. H. Webster, C. Werner, B. F. Kurtz. They had orders to relieve Company B and send a patrol of 20 men to the mouth of Seneca, a distance of 20 miles, each day, until the third day, when they would be relieved. After reaching the picket post, details were placed out, and nothing occurred until after 2 o'clock on the morning of the 25th. There was a heavy wind storm, and under cover of the noise and darkness, Maj. Lang, with his battalion of Confederates, captured the picket on the mountain side of the post, and Lang's force, consisting of seven officers and 132 men, completely surrounded the picket. Taylor, the guard close to camp, gave the alarm, but the darkness was so dense that the firing was all at random, until Lang's men set fire to a hay stack, when it was seen that the Union forces were surrounded. An attempt was made to escape, but it failed, and Peter Romiser was killed, and Ackelson wounded, the rest being captured, eight of whom were sent to Andersonville, the rest being imprisoned at Richmond until exchanged, being prisoners nearly six months.

Col. Latham with 152 men of the Second Virginia, went on three days' picket duty on the 26th, returning the 29th, without anything of note occurring. A Confederate scouting party, 50 strong, came within two miles of camp on the 26th, but retired in precipitate haste when their presence was learned. On the 24th one of our scouting parties that went to Greenbrier, was fired into, and lost one man wounded and two prisoners.

Intelligence was received that the brave Maj. McNally had died on Sept. 22nd, from wounds received at Rocky Gap, and on the 29th a meeting of the officers of the regiment was held, to take action on the loss of this gallant officer. Col. George R. Latham presided, and Capt. J.K. Billingsley was secretary. Capt. N. W. Truxal delivered a eulogy on the life and services of the Major, expressing in chaste and beautiful language, the estimate in which he was held by the regiment. At the close of his remarks, he offered the following resolutions, which were unanimously adopted:

Resolved; That we have learned with profound sorrow of the death of Maj. F. P. McNally, late of this regiment, and we deplore it as a calamity not only to his family and friend, but in him the country has lost a brave and intrepid officer who had won him laurels on many battle fields, gallantly supporting the glorious flag of his country, and offering his life a sacrifice on her altar.

Resolved, That we offer to his bereaved companion and aged parents our sincere condolence, hoping that the Almighty hand that "tempers the wind to the shorn lamb," may guard his helpless child and bind up the bleeding hearts.

CHAPTER XV.

Resolved, That as a testimonial of respect for the memory of our beloved brother and officer, we will wear the usual badge of mourning on our sabre belts for thirty days.

Resolved, That a copy of these resolutions be forwarded to the family of the deceased.

The month of October was a very busy one to the troops, and the service was hard and constant. On the 9th our regiment went to Huttonsville on picket duty and remained there until the 12th. On the 11th Col. Latham with 75 men, went on a scout to Elkwater, after some Confederate cavalry seen there, returning on the 16th empty handed. The picket duty was heavy and severe, and scouting parties were out nearly all the time. Thus we remained until the close of October, by which time all the preparations were completed for the successful expedition to Droop Mountain.

On the 1st of November, 1863, the order to march was again given, and the 2d, 3d and 8th Virginia Mounted Infantry, 14th Pa. Cavalry, Gibson's battalion of cavalry, and batteries B and G, First Virginia Light Artillery, Capts. Keeper and Ewing, took up the line of march, arriving at Huttonsville that evening. Lieut. Col. Alex Scott was in command of our regiment. The next day the troops crossed Cheat Mountain Summit, marching to the Greenbrier river, camping within a mile of camp Bartow. The following day we took the Huntersville road, passing through Green Bank, and camping at night at Dunmore, capturing some of the Confederate pickets, and securing plenty of hay for our horses. On the 4th we marched through Huntersville, and chased Jackson's cavalry, the Second being in the advance of the column. One squadron of the regiment was detached as the advance, under command of Lieut. A. J. Weaver, who captured two prisoners. The Third Virginia and Fourteenth Pa. Cavalry were sent to head off Jackson's cavalry, while the Second and Eighth Virginia, with one section of Ewing's battery, were ordered to march at once to Marlin's Bottoms, six miles north of Huntersville on the Greenbrier river, where Jackson's forces were supposed to be encamped. Arriving about dusk, it was found that Jackson had received intelligence of our approach, and availed himself of the privilege of leaving before our arrival, taking the road to Lewisburg, which he partially blockaded. We encamped here for the night. The hills were filled with bushwhackers, who made things lively for us. Lieut. Russell, who was on picket during the night at the camp just vacated by the enemy, destroyed a considerable quantity of small arms and accoutrements, and also burned their quarters, consisting of very comfortable log houses. The obstructions having been removed during the night, we were again in the saddle on the morning of the 5th at daylight, and followed the Lewistown pike. Cannonading was soon heard in front, which started us into a brisk trot, which was kept up until we reached Mill Point, some ten miles from where we had encamped the night previous. At this place we found the Third Virginia and Fourteenth Pennsylvania Cavalry in line of battle, with Jackson's force confronting them, whose artillery was firing at our columns. Our whole force was soon on the ground. The Second was ordered to take a position in support of Keeper's battery, when the enemy fell back and took a strong position on Droop mountain. Three men of our command were wounded in the little fight. During the night Jackson was reinforced by Genl. Echols, with his force from Lewisburg, consisting of four regiments, two battalions and a battery, thus giving the Confederates the advantage in numbers.

Shortly after sunrise on the 6th, our brigade marched to Hillsboro, where skirmishers were thrown out, and the enemy opened upon us with their batteries. Genl. Averell made his dispositions for the battle, and assumed the offensive, though the enemy had a very strong position on the mountain, and were superior in numbers. About noon Lieut. Col. Scott was ordered to dismount the Second, to fight on foot, with instructions to detach one company and post them on an elevated position, as a guard for the horses of the dismounted troops. He was then ordered to take a position between the Third and Eighth Virginia and to act in support of those two regiments. The strength of the regiment when placed in position was about 200 men, a great many being detached. On arriving at the foot of the hill where the Confederates were posted, the Second passed the Eighth Virginia, leaving them on our left, moving on for the purpose of ascertaining the position of the Third Virginia. Col. Scott was then ordered to begin his advance up the hill toward the enemy's works, which he did through briers, tree tops and obstacles of various kinds. After gaining an open piece of ground, the colonel reformed his men and moved further up the hill, where he formed in line of battle on the left of the Third Virginia. Soon battery B on the left, and the Confederate artillery, opened up, and the result was an interesting and lively artillery duel, continued for some time. This and the skirmishing were kept up until about 3 o'clock, when the infantry, under Col. Moor, was sent around by a circuitous route to turn the enemy's left and strike him in the flank and rear. The Second and Third Virginia and two companies of the Eighth Virginia, advanced in front, and the Fourteenth Pennsylvania Cavalry and Battery B and Independent Cavalry Battalion were on the left, while Battery G was on the right. Presently a few reports were heard from the direction in which the infantry had gone, followed by volleys of musketry, which were being hurled into the ranks in the rear of the unsuspecting enemy. Then came the time for the forces in front to act, when the dismounted regiments, in accordance with previous orders, came out of their hiding places and advanced to the attack in front. Battery G now opened with their guns and joined with the effective work of Keeper's battery. When our line was within ten or fifteen yards of the crest of the mountain, the enemy opened upon us, and a sheet of flame issued from the mountain top, as the Confederates poured a terrific fire of musketry

CHAPTER XV.

into the faces of our brave boys. The whole line was then pushed forward with vigor, and never flinched or wavered, but advanced with the tread of veterans and returned the fire with telling effect. The fighting was fierce and terrible, a battle to the death, the musketry fire being very rapid. We had one advantage, that as we advanced up the steep mountain, the fire of the enemy passed over our heads, and thus saved our line from being mowed down. Steadily our men advanced, driving their foe from the breastworks of fence rails, logs and stones, that they had hastily thrown up. Battery G helped materially in breaking the line of the enemy, throwing shot and shell among them when our lines were within 20 or 30 feet of their line. Indeed we were at so close quarters, that the artillery fire endangered a part of our men, though fortunately hurting none, while effective shot were being thrown into the now hard pressed ranks of the Confederates. Company B, of the Second was deployed as skirmishers, and relieved those of the Eighth Virginia on the extreme left of our line on the bluff in the woods. When the column came up on the right of the company, they filed right to join their regiment, then close to the top. As the men of the company emerged from the timber, they were saluted with shot from our own battery. C. E. Ringler got upon a high rock and tried to signal our gunners to cease, when another rattling shot saluted them. He quickly seized a tall sapling and substituted its top leaves with the front section of his white nether garment, whereupon they were relieved from this danger, but the enemy were not. After about two hours of fighting the Second and Third Virginia, with yells and cheers, loud and strong, charged into the jaws of death and fire, and carried the position by storm, driving the enemy like chaff before the wind, who retreated precipitately toward Lewisburg.

Lieut. J. B. Smith, of the Second, with some of his men, was the first to get inside the enemy's breastworks. Sergeant Keeny, of Company H, was stunned by a shot that struck a tree by him, and he claims that at least one-half hour of his life was lost by the shock. The line had advanced some distance before he regained consciousness. Lieut. A. J. Weaver, while waving his sword and urging his men forward, was struck by a musket ball, which stilled that noble heart. As he fell he said in a faint voice, "Tell Jimmie to write to Hattie." Jimmie was the bugler of the company, a lad of 15 years, now lieutenant, U.S.A., and Hattie was a lady in Baltimore, to whom the lieutenant was engaged to be married. His last words were in remembrance of her. When the breastworks were captured, Isaac Wilt, of Company K, came into the presence of a Confederate lieutenant, who refused to retreat or surrender, but with bitter oaths was urging his men back to the work, Wilt plunged his bayonet through the man, who died with oaths on his lips, cursing the men that were defending their country.

The Confederates retreated in great haste and disorder, and Gibson's cavalry battalion, which had been held in reserve, and a section of Ewing's battery, were at once sent forward in pursuit, and many of the rest of the troops, hastily mounting their horses, kept up with them, striking hard blows on the beaten and discomfited foe. Though in the hottest of the severe fighting, and punished considerably, the men of the Second were in the front in the chase, which lasted for about 12 miles. The ground was strewn with guns and accoutrements; and the upturned faces of the poor victims, formed a ghastly picture in this terrible scene of carnage. All the men behaved splendidly, and like veterans, and it is but just to say that our own regiment exhibited the qualities of true soldiers, excelled by none. Prompt, vigilant and heroic, they did their whole duty.

Lieut. Col. Scott, in his official report of the battle, had this to say: "With but few exceptions the men and officers behaved nobly. I take pleasure in making special mention of the gallantry and daring exhibited by Lieut. J. B. Smith, of Company E. He is the youngest officer in the regiment and is deserving of great credit. Adjutant J. Combs and Lieut. A. J. Pentecost, exhibited great coolness and daring, and rendered important service throughout the fight. I also mention the names of Capt. Barclay, Lieuts. J. R. Frisbie, L. P. Salterbach, A. P. Russell, Charles H. Day and Felix Hughes, as being actively engaged during the entire engagement."

The losses of our regiment in this expedition were as follows:

Killed - Charles Ritz, Company C; Andrew Bernard, Samuel Bowden, Edward Doyle and Wm. L. Hughes, Company D; Thos. J. Akers, John Murphy and Moses Moore, Company E; Lieut. A. J. Weaver, Company K.

Wounded - William Jenkins, John Kerns, Company B; Henry Emmering (died of wounds), Company C; Michael Brubach, Company D; Wm. Garroll (died of wounds), W. H. Foulke, Geo. Dent, S. L. D. Hudson, Company E; John Hope, Sergt. Thos. Williams, Company H; Lieut. C. H. Day, Company I; M. D. Kenny (died of wounds), Edward C. Maley (died of wounds), Thomas McConkey (died of wounds), John Sallyards, Company K.

On the 7th we marched to Lewisburg, where we met Gen. Duffie with four regiments of infantry and four pieces of artillery. He did not even get a shot at the enemy, but burned their camps at this place. The next day we left Lewisburg and passed through White Sulphur Springs and over the Rocky Gap battle ground, and camped on the Warm Springs road near Callaghan's. At White Sulphur Springs we released such of our men as were wounded at Rocky Gap, as were able to join us. The brave fellows were rejoiced to see us, and the meeting with their comrades was a happy and an affecting one. Gen. Duffie left us two miles from Lewisburg and went on the Union road. The Tenth Virginia and Twenty-eighth Ohio infantry and battery B left us here, and went back to Beverly with our wounded and prisoners, and cattle. We had left then only the mounted regiments, and our own battery G, the pride of the regiment. On the 9th we marched to Gatewood, about seventeen miles.

CHAPTER XV.

Lieut. Schmolze and twelve men of Company F Second Virginia, were in the advance, and they captured fifteen Confederates, with their horses and accoutrements. We were threatened by Gen. Imboden near Covington, and prepared to give him battle, but he declined it. On the 10th we marched to Green Hill on the Monterey road, and were considerably bushwhacked, one of the men of the command being killed and another wounded. The next day we marched beyond Monterey about nine miles. At Crab Bottom a part of our brigade was met by some of Thoburn's brigade, who had come out to see us. We reached Petersburg on the 13th, where we remained until the 16th, when we resumed our march. About nineteen miles from this place, we learned of the capture of a wagon train of seventy wagons, containing stores for the troops at Petersburg, by McNeill's guerillas. The Third Virginia and Gibson's battalion were sent after them, but without effect. We arrived at New Creek November 17th, and went into camp, where we remained without any special incidents, until the brigade started on the Salem raid.

Since leaving Beverly, seventeen days, we marched 296 miles, a part of the time suffering intensely from the cold, constantly subjected to the hidden attacks of bushwhackers, and having fought one of the most gallant and triumphant little battles of the war.

The following is General Averell's report of this expedition: On the 1st day of November, I left Beverly with my command consisting of the Twenty-eighth Ohio Volunteer Infantry, Col. J. A. Moor; Tenth West Virginia Volunteer Infantry, Col. T.M. Harris; Second West Virginia Mounted Infantry, Lieut. Col. A. Scott; Third West Virginia Mounted Infantry, Lieut. Col. F. W. Thompson; Eighth West Virginia Mounted Infantry, Col. J. H. Oley; Fourteenth Pennsylvania Cavalry, Col. J. N. Schoonmaker; Gibson's Battalion, and Batteries B and G, First West Virginia Light Artillery, Capts. J. V. Keeper and C. T. Ewing. The command moved on the Staunton pike to Greenbrier Bridge and thence by Camp Bartow and Green Bank to Huntersville, driving before them the enemy's pickets, and capturing or dispersing the guerrilla bands which infest that part of the country. The command reached Huntersville at noon of the 4th and it was there ascertained that Lieut. Col. Thompson, of Jackson's command was at Marlin's Bottom, with a force of about 600 men. I at once sent the Fourteenth Pennsylvania Cavalry and Third West Virginia Mounted Infantry on the direct road to Mill Point, to cut off Thompson's retreat toward Lewisburg, and the Second and Eighth West Virginia Mounted Infantry and one section of Ewing's battery to Marlin's Bottom, to attack him at that place. At 9 o'clock I received information from Col. Oley, Eighth West Virginia Mounted Infantry, commanding detachment to Marlin's Bottom that the enemy had retired toward Mill Point, blockading the road in their rear. A dispatch from Col. Schoonmaker, Fourteenth Pennsylvania Cavalry, received about midnight, informed me that Thompson had effected a junction with the remainder of Jackson's command, and that it was all in position in his front and threatening an attack. The infantry and Keeper's battery were moved about 3 a.m. to join Schoonmaker, and Oley was ordered to cut out the blockade and march to the same point as fast as possible. I reached Mill Point with the infantry and Keeper at 8 a.m. on the 5th, and found that they had just arrived, and that the enemy were retiring. This was Thursday, the 5th of November. We were thirty-four miles from Lewisburg, at which point it had been directed that my force should arrive on Saturday, at 2 p.m. It was not thought proper to press the enemy vigorously on this day, in order to keep him as far as possible from Lewisburg, and not to permit him to be re-enforced from that direction, and to gain the advantage which would follow from the arrival at Lewisburg of the force under Gen. Duffie from the Kanawha Valley. An attempt was, however, made to capture the force under Jackson by sending three mounted regiments to cut off his retreat. The rapidity of the enemy's movements made this attempt unsuccessful, and he succeeded in reaching Droop Mountain, upon the summit of which he made a stand. My advance was withdrawn from the fire of his artillery and the attack postponed until the ensuing day. On the morning of the 6th, we approached the enemy's position. The main road to Lewisburg runs over Droop Mountain, the northern slope of which is partially cultivated nearly to the summit, a distance of two and one-half miles from the foot. The highway is partially hidden in the views from the summit and base in strips of woodland. It is necessary to pass over low rolling hills and across bewildering ravines to reach the mountain in any direction. The position of the enemy was defined by a skirmishing attack of three companies of infantry. It was thought that a direct attack would be difficult. The infantry and one company of cavalry were therefore sent to the right to ascend a range of hills which ran westward from Droop Mountain, with orders to attack the enemy's left and rear. To divert the enemy's attention from this, the Fourteenth Pennsylvania and Keeper's battery made a successful demonstration upon his right. The remainder of the command prepared for action. While these movements were progressing; the arrival of re-enforcements to the enemy was announced by the music of a band, the display of battle-flags and loud cheers of the rebels on the top of the mountain. The attack of our infantry 1,175 strong was conducted skillfully and resolutely by Col. A. Moor. The guide who had been sent with him proving worthless, he directed his column nine miles, over the mountains and through the wilderness to the enemy's left, led by the flying pickets and the sound of his cannon. The intermittent reports of musketry heralded the approach of Col. Moor to his destination, and at 1:45 p.m. it was evident from the sound of the battle on the enemy's left and his disturbed appearance in front, that the time for the direct attack had arrived. The Second, Third and Eighth West Virginia dismounted, were moved in line obliquely to the right up the face of the mountain, until their right was joined

CHAPTER XV.

to Moor's left. The fire of Ewing's battery was added to that of Keeper's. At 3 p.m. the enemy were driven from the summit of the mountain upon which they had been somewhat protected by crude breastworks of logs, stones, and earth. Gibson's battalion and one section of Ewing's battery were at once ordered to pursue the routed rebels. Fragments of each regiment were already eagerly in pursuit. The horses of the Second, Third, Eighth and Fourteenth were brought up the mountain as soon as possible. The infantry pushed forward, and as soon as details had been made for succoring the wounded and burying the dead, the entire command followed the enemy until dark. It appeared from the reports of prisoners that the enemy's force had consisted of the Fourteenth Virginia Cavalry; Twenty-second Virginia Infantry, Derrick's Battalion, Edgar's Battalion, Jackson's Brigade and seven pieces of artillery; in all, about 4000 men. His loss in killed and wounded was about 250, one piece of artillery and one stand of colors. Several men of my command reported having seen and measured two other pieces of artillery abandoned by the enemy and secreted by the wayside. Time was not had, however, to look after them. I did not desire to reap more than the immediate fruits of victory that evening. It was yet twenty miles to Lewisburg, and I hoped that by letting the enemy alone during the night, he might loiter on the route and be caught the next day between my command and the force expected from the Kanawha Valley. As we went down the mountain the following morning, we could see the smoke of several camp fires along the mountains to the eastward, showing that the enemy had been somewhat dispersed. On the 7th I moved rapidly forward over an excellent road toward Lewisburg. The Fourteenth, which was in advance, reached that place at 2 p.m., and found Gen. Duffie with four regiments and one section of artillery already in possession of the town. He had reached it at 10 p.m., capturing a few stragglers and such material as the enemy had been unable to remove in his flight. I learned that a small portion of the enemy's main body had passed through Lewisburg in great disorder early on the morning of the 7th on their way to Dublin. I also learned that Gen. Lee had promised Brig. Gen. Echols ample re-enforcements at or near that point. I determined to move with my whole command to that place, and accordingly set out on the morning of the 8th. After proceeding a few miles a formidable blockade was encountered through which it was necessary to cut a passage. Gen. Duffie reported his command as unfit for further operations, as his infantry had but one day's rations and was so exhausted as to be able to march only ten miles per day. My own infantry was encumbered with the prisoners, captured property and material. I, therefore, ordered Gen. Duffie to retire to Meadow Bluff, and Col. Moor, with the Twenty-eighth Ohio Volunteer Infantry, Tenth West Virginia Volunteer Infantry and Keeper's Battery to return to Beverly, taking with him all the prisoners and such of the wounded from the battle of Droop Mountain as could be transported. Col. Moor brought from

Hillsborough fifty-five of our own and one rebel wounded. He left with those who were too badly wounded to bear transportation, Asst. Surgeon Blair, Tenth West Virginia Volunteer Infantry, and supplied them with all the rations, hospital stores and medicines which could be spared. His command reached Beverly on the 12th, bringing with it all the prisoners, property, etc., which had been captured up to the arrival of my command at Lewisburg. With the cavalry, mounted infantry and Ewing's battery of my command, I moved via White Sulphur Springs to near Callaghan's, passing through the battleground of Rocky Gap on my way. At White Sulphur I retook the wounded of my command who had been left after the battle of Rocky Gap in August last. At Callaghan's, on the morning of the 9th, I learned that Gen. Imboden, with from 900 to 1,500 men, was at Covington on his way to re-enforce Echols at Union. Not deeming his command of sufficient importance to delay my march, and knowing the impossibility of bringing him to a fight, I sent two squadrons of the Eighth West Virginia Mounted Infantry, under Maj. Slack, to drive him away from my line of march. This was accomplished after a sharp skirmish, in which Imboden was reported wounded, and one lieutenant and twenty men of his command were captured. From Callaghan's I moved by Gatewood's up the Back Creek road to Franklin; the main body of the command moved through Monterey and joined me about eight miles beyond that place. At Hightown I met Col. Thoburn, with a brigade of infantry and two pieces of artillery, whom I directed to return to Petersburg. My command reached Petersburg on the 13th where it was supplied with rations and forage. On the 17th I arrived at New Creek, bringing with me about 150 captured horses and 27 prisoners, exclusive of those which were sent from Lewisburg with Col. Moor. Several hundred cattle were captured on the march.

CHAPTER XVI.

THE SALEM RAID.

Gen. Burnside was besieged at Knoxville, Tenn., by Confederate Gen. Longstreet, and in order to raise the siege by cutting off the latter's supplies, and compel him to move his base of supplies, Gen. Averell was directed to cut the railroad, and interrupt communication between Richmond and Knoxville, at all hazards, even if his whole force was captured or destroyed. By a dispensation of Providence, Gen. Averell was enabled not only to accomplish the plans laid down, and the results desired, but as well to return to our lines with the loss of a very small number of his men, and none of his artillery.

The command left New Creek December 8, 1863, the brigade consisting of the Second, Third and Eighth West Va. Mounted Infantry, the 14th Pennsylvania Cavalry, Gibson's Cavalry Battalion, and four guns of Battery G, First West Virginia Light Artillery, all under the command of Gen. Averell. Lieut. Col. Alex. Scott was in command of the Second, and Capt. Ewing in command of the battery. The morning was bright and beautiful, and gave little promise of the terrible weather that the command would be subjected to in the long and hard campaign. We reached Petersburg on the evening of the 9th, and the next day Franklin, where we were met by the First and 14th West Va. Infantry, one section 23d Illinois Artillery and the Ringgold Cavalry. The next day we reached Monterey, where three of the Third Virginia were wounded. Here we divested ourselves of all encumbrances and prepared for the great march. Our supply train went no further, rations being issued to the men and forage for the horses, to last until we should again reach our lines. All men and officers unfit for severe duty, were sent back to New Creek, only the able bodied, well equipped and well mounted men going forward.

The Confederates were totally in the dark as to our movements, until Gen. Imboden learned of them through a young lady friend. By the time he received this information, the brigade had a fair start, and was off and away on its mission of destruction. Movements were made as if our destination was Staunton, which caused Gen. Lee to order Gen. Early from his army to Staunton, to assume command, and to meet us and our forces in the Shenandoah valley. They were completely deceived as to our real intentions. The weather became very cold on the 11th, and on the 12th rained all day, through which the command marched 21 miles. On the 13th we went 23 miles, and on the 14th 22 miles, camping near Callaghan's stand. On the 13th we overtook a body of the enemy, captured their wagons, etc., crossed the creek 13 times, which was swollen very high and was very swift, camping on its inhospitable banks. Everything in our front was brushed away from us, scouts were captured from whom we received some information, and we were aided to some extent by the loyal citizens, who gave us information about the roads, mountains, streams and bridges, and of the number of the enemy and their movements. It rained steadily and had become intensely cold, the wind blew hard from the north, and snow and sleet, and the elements, air and water, seemed to be against us. We were in sore need of food and sleep, but the march never ceased on that account. On the 14th we marched to Covington, and passed it and Sweet Sulphur Springs. The next day Red Sulphur Springs were passed, the tired troops marching all night and crossing four mountains, on whose sides and plateaus but few signs of life were to be seen.

This night the advance of the command came upon a wedding party, enjoying the festivities of the occasion, who were unaware that the hated Yankees were so near. Comrade E. F. Seaman, quartermaster sergeant of the Second Virginia, gives the following graphic account of the affair: "In our march over the mountains, between Sweet Springs and New Castle, I was in the advance guard. It was one of the darkest nights I ever saw. Almost the only light we could see was the sparks made by our horses' feet striking the rocks. When near the top of the mountain we suddenly saw a light in a window a very short distance ahead, and soon afterward heard the sound of music and the shuffling of feet in the dance. One of our scouts, who was dressed in the Confederate uniform, came galloping back and said, 'Boys, there's some fun ahead. The rebs are having a big dance in that cabin. The other scouts and myself went in and had a good time shaking the foot with those pretty girls. They are daisies, I tell you.' Waiting a few moments till all the command came up, we quietly advanced, and soon had the house completely surrounded. I was in command of the squad, and soon as we were sure of everything I went forward to the door and ordered the crowd to surrender. You never saw a company more completely thunderstruck. About twenty Johnnies, as soon as they could could collect their wits, were compelled to release their fair partners and yield themselves up to less agreeable company.

CHAPTER XVI.

'Fall in line,' was the command to the prisoners. All obeyed except one tall, finely-formed young man, who stood unmoved, with his hand resting lightly on the shoulder of a chubby maiden in white. The young thing clung closer to him with modest trustfulness, betraying no sign of fear for the sudden and rude disturbance of her joy. She was by far the calmer of the two, and was acting like a little heroine. The small left hand crept a little closer about his neck, and she said with a pleading sorrowfulness that thrilled my whole being: We have just been married, sir; and you are not going to take George away from me now, are you?

Trained by the discipline of war, I was compelled to subdue what I felt, and try to make the best of the situation. I told her as gently as I could that war was a sad thing, and that as soldiers there was nothing left for us but to do our duty, but as men we deeply sympathized with her. I assured her that her young husband, as our prisoner, should be treated with every kindness, and that, doubtless, within a few months he would be exchanged and be with her again. As the young man pressed his fair-haired bride to his bosom that new love which, in its sweetness and its purity, is the same it has always been since time began, became too strong to be longer confined. It welled up from a full heart, and, bursting its bounds, gave vent in a torrent of convulsive sobs. A silence had fallen upon us all, and I saw many of the old weather-stained men draw their sleeves quickly across their faces. Somehow I felt like it would be inhuman to speak a word. In a few moments she gained some command over herself, and, unloosing her arms, raised her tear-stained face to his. He clasped her suddenly and kissed her three times passionately. 'Good-bye, George; good-bye,' she said; 'God bless you!' Her eyes followed him to the door as we moved out. Poor thing! That was her last sight of him on the earth.

He was accidentally drowned while crossing Jackson river. In the summer of 1884, I went to the Sweet Springs, and while there got a buggy and drove over that mountain. By making inquiries I was able to find out that the bride of 20 years ago was still living, and after some search, discovered her, and had the pleasure of a short conversation with her. She never suspected, of course, that I knew her story, for 20 years had changed me as you may imagine, too much to make any recognition possible. She had remained true to her first love and refused all offers of a second marriage. Representing myself as a stranger, from common place topics I led the talk as easily as I could back to the war. She conversed very pleasantly till that subject was mentioned, when her manner became more quiet, and her gaze drifted from near objects to the long, blue horizon down the mountain, as if strained to discover something lost. I soon left, and have never seen her since."

We marched all night of the 15th, and the condition of the troops bad. Many horses were broken down, more lame, some of the men were obliged to walk, and the entering on the eventful day of the 16th of December was not as bright a prospect as we could have wished. We were about 200 miles from our base of supplies, in the very heart of the enemy's country, on the line of one of the great railways of the Confederacy, with Imboden, Jones, Fitz Lee, Echols, McCausland and Jackson searching for us, and we had, all told, not more than 1,500 men and four guns. We entered Salem, the objective point, about noon on the 16th, and immediately began the work of destruction. The column moved to the right and left, burning the mills, depot, railroad bridges, tracks and culverts for several miles each way. A general stampede was in progress among the citizens and such Confederate soldiers as were there. A passenger train was approaching the town, and one of the guns of the battery was placed in position to disable it. Comrade A. G. Osborne, corporal and gunner of the first piece, was ordered to throw the shot, and gives the following account of it: "I put in a percussion shell as soon as I heard the train coming, and had made up my mind to disable the engine, if possible, and was waiting until I could get a good view of it before firing. The smoke-stack had just come in view when Lieut. Meigs rushed up and asked me why I did not fire. I told him I was waiting for a better view so that I could put a shell into the machinery or boiler of the engine so as to disable it; but he ordered me to fire, when I could not see anything but about two feet of the top of the smoke-stack. Of course I had to obey orders, and the result was no damage to anything but the smoke-stack. Gen. Averell said after the shot that I was too quick. I told him I knew it, but that I was ordered to fire the shot by one of his staff." Before another shot could be fired the train was moving off at a rapid rate and soon was out of reach. Gen. Averell's report attached gives the amount of stores, etc., destroyed.

When the work of destruction was complete, the command prepared to retrace their steps, and about 3 p.m. of the 16th started homeward, returning through the North Mountain on the New Castle road. Not knowing the perils of the homeward march, we camped at Mason's Creek, about six miles from Salem. It rained and snowed incessantly during the night but the weary and overworked soldiers slept soundly until 5 o'clock the next morning, when the bugle called them from their slumbers to renew the march. The Fourteenth Pennsylvania Cavalry led the advance. Craig's Creek was reached about noon. The heavy rain during the night had swollen the stream to its banks, and it was full of slush, ice and driftwood. The valley was narrow, with but little ground on either side of the creek, and in many places none between the creek and the steep mountain side. The road crossed the creek seven times within a distance of ten or twelve miles. The enemy was pursuing us in large force, and there was no alternative but to ford the wild stream. The water was mid rib deep on the large horses, and the current so strong that the animals had to be kept with their breasts up the stream and worked across sideways. If the current were permitted to strike the horses sideways, which happened quite frequently, horse and rider were carried down the stream, and a number of

CHAPTER XVI.

men were drowned in this way. The artillery and ambulances were dragged through the stream with ropes by the men. The weather was so cold, part of the time below zero, that the clothing of the men was frozen stiff soon after leaving the water. The horses were covered with icicles and trembling from the cold. The whole afternoon was spent in crossing the creek, and when finally accomplished, men and horses were almost paralyzed, and suffered intensely from the cold as well as from hunger. After a few crossings had been effected it was with difficulty the horses were forced into the stream, and they were whipped and spurred to compel obedience.

Lieut. Col. Blakely, of the 14th Pennsylvania Cavalry, was ordered to cross the stream rapidly and proceed at once to New Castle, as the enemy were moving on that place. When the last fording was reached, several efforts were made to force the horses into the stream, but all efforts failed. The men found some sheaf oats and hay, and a few minutes were spent in feeding the poor brutes. Gen. Averell, without the attendance of aids or staff, came galloping up and took a survey of the ford. This one appeared more dangerous than any that had preceded it, and the general was fearful that the horses, in their weakened condition, would be unable to stem the current. He applied the spurs vigorously to his own horse, when rider and horse dashed into the stream, with many anxious hearts watching the desperate struggle of a brave man with the mad current. When he reached the opposite shore, he was cheered by the men. He acknowledged the compliment by lifting his hat and saying: "Come on boys," and then rode off hastily in the direction of New Castle.

From New Castle the 14th Pennsylvania Cavalry constituted the rear guard. Lieut. A. J. Pentecost, and a number of men composed of quartermaster and commissary sergeants, wagonmasters, etc., had charge of the wagon and ambulance train. Gen. Averell was forced into the by roads by the enemy, and their condition made it difficult to move the train, each wagon requiring a number of men to prevent its upsetting. After two days and nights of marching and skirmishing with the enemy, the advance of the ambulance corps, about 12 o'clock at night, reached the mouth of the gap leading through the mountain to Jackson river. Gen. Averell had during the day captured a Confederate courier, with dispatches, from which he learned the movements of the enemy; and in consequence of imminent danger to his command, was compelled to move rapidly to Jackson river, to prevent the enemy from burning the bridge at that point, leaving the train from 10 to 12 miles in the rear. The roadway through the mountain to Jackson river, is a deep, narrow defile, from 2 to 3 miles in length, and so narrow that it was with the greatest difficulty for anyone to pass from the rear to the front. The road bed was covered with ice, and it was impossible to prevent the horses from falling, and at times many of them would be down at once. This, with the upsetting of the wagons, greatly retarded the movements of the wagon train and rear guard. The enemy had been pressing our rear vigorously. After Averell with the main column had passed out of the gap, charged the enemy that were guarding the bridge and routed them, the Confederates under Gen. W. L. Jackson took possession of the gap and quietly awaited the approach of the train. The night was very dark and cold, and on the approach of the ambulances the horses were seized by Jackson's men and led into their camp. Three ambulances were captured in this way, and some of the men in them did not know they were prisoners until the next morning. Capt. Markbreit A.A.G., Averell's brigade, Lieut. Col. Polsley Eighth Virginia, and Lieut. McAdams, of the ambulance corps, were captured in this way.

Lieut. Pentecost, Commissary Sergeant G. H. Kirkpatrick, and Capt. W. H. Brown were riding in advance about this time, when they met a man and asked him where he was going and who he was. He replied that he was going to Jackson's camp. He held a revolver in his hand. Pentecost at once grasped his arm and took the revolver from him, at the same time informing him that he was a prisoner, which did not seem to disturb him much, and willingly accompanied his captors back to where some of the men had started a fire. Imagine the astonishment of our men on seeing a number of Confederate officers standing about the fire, in conversation with some of our own officers. The Confederates stated that we were surrounded and would be prisoners in the morning, and then retired. Lieut. Pentecost at break of day formed his detachment in line, composed of those that were with the train, and advanced toward the river some distance away. During the night the enemy had moved from our front to our rear, supposing that we would not be able to cross Jackson river, the bridge being burned, and the river swollen, and full of floating ice and drift. Col. Blakely brought up the rear with his regiment, skirmishing all the way until we reached the river. Several of the Fourteenth Pennsylvania Cavalry plunged into the river to cross, but some of them were drowned in the attempt. A citizen had been asked if the river was fordable at this place, when he stated that it was perfectly safe, which led to the drowning of our men. The citizen was at once thrown in and was drowned. A woman who lived near the burned bridge was then asked to inform us where we could find a fording place, which she at first refused to do but upon threatening to burn her house, she told us there was a ford some distance up the river. Capt. Jas. L. Kelley with a squad at once started to find it, and succeeded. In the meantime Majors Daily and Foley of the Fourteenth Pennsylvania Cavalry, kept the enemy in check in the rear, and were hard pressed. The order was then given to park the wagons and burn them, which was at once done. The enemy then sent in a flag of truce demanding a surrender, which was promptly refused, when they began to shell the hard pressed Union forces. Our men then retreated up a narrow path, along the river to the ford, two miles above. Arriving there they at once plunged into the swollen stream, and swam their horses over. Lieut. Pentecost was directed to cross the ford and take position with his men

CHAPTER XVI.

to cover the retreat and crossing of Major Daily and his battalion, which was done. The enemy having detected the withdrawal of our troops, advanced, but after a sharp contest with Pentecost, Major Daily's command succeeded in crossing safely. Had it not been for the gallant and determined resistance of Lieut. Pentecost and the genuine pluck of the men with him, Major Daily and his men would have fallen into the hands of the enemy. Our loss at the river was one officer, Lieut. Murphy troop G Fourteenth Pennsylvania Cavalry wounded, three men killed and four drowned, among the latter the unfortunate bridegroom whom we had captured on the mountain top. The ambulances with the sick and wounded, were left in the hands of the enemy. All the wagons of the brigade were destroyed by our own men.

The belated command at once started at a rapid pace for Covington, seven miles distant. The bridge at that place had also been destroyed, and again they were compelled to ford the river, which was accomplished without loss. They rode rapidly forward, expecting to join Gen. Averell and the main column at Callaghan's stand, at the junction of the Warm Springs and Rocky Gap roads, but here they found the column gone, they having given the delayed men up as lost. They rode on and caught up to the general during the night, on the top of the Allegheny mountains, where they had stopped a few hours for rest.

The command was now all together again, and Gen. Averell was taking a needed rest, and to give himself time to decide what to do next. It is said that the negroes were called to headquarters, and one, a boy perhaps twelve years old, said he knew a way across Greenbrier river by a ford far above Lewisburg. He had been there to mill with his master. Hearing this, Gen. Averell put the boy on a horse, ordered "boots and saddles" to be sounded, and then "forward." The boy led us up Oggle's Creek and down Anthony's Creek, over the Allegheny Mountains - high, rough, wild and icy. The horses were taken from the artillery and long ropes attached; men were dismounted, and drew the pieces up and down that fearful mountain path. Our advance, reached the Greenbrier River at dark the evening of December 20. We found the stream swollen and full of floating ice. It seemed impossible to cross. Gen. Averell in person directed the crossing and tested the ford. Cakes of ice from ten to fifteen feet square, and heavy enough to submerge a horse, were constantly passing. The order came to plunge and cross. This was done without loss. The command was in no mood to hesitate. Hunger, cold, exhaustion had done their utmost. But they had barely gotten under way again, when a small party of the enemy attacked them in front, but were driven in confusion by a charge of our men. Here the command turned to the right, and on the 20th entered Hillsboro, where, they went into camp. The next day they moved to Edray, where supplies were ordered, which met the almost famished men twelve miles from that place. On Christmas day 1863, the gallant, intrepid men, entered Beverly, and were now safely in our lines.

Personal adventures on this expedition were many and very thrilling, a few of which are given in the article on the scouts. The capture of the wedding party is the theme of letters from some of the boys, who evidently relish it as one of the bright spots in that dark and dreary trip. Several of the hungry boys feasted on cake to their stomach's content, and cleaned up every thing eatable that could be found about the house.

On the night of the 18th, Lieut. Russell, with Company H, was sent to the top of the mountain near the main road, to guard the signal corps, remaining all night. On the morning of the 19th they found that our command had passed, and left no orders for their relief. They soon started for the regiment, having satisfied themselves that they were left alone, and though a good many of the enemy's cavalry were between them and their regiment, they caught up with the rear guard about 9 o'clock, and the regiment about noon.

Comrade O. P. Bower, Company B, Second Virginia, with Will. Shirley, was riding in front of column, the night before Salem was reached. Shirley stopped for a few minutes' rest, Bower riding ahead, and was suddenly confronted by four Confederates, and asked where he belonged. He replied that he was one of Early's men, and parleyed with the men until four of the scouts rode up, when Bower demanded the surrender of the Confederates. A fight followed, resulting in the death of Confederate Captain Chapman, the severe wounding of one other, and the capture of Capt. Tomlinson and one man. Bower got a splendid horse in the capture. Shortly afterward they captured a wagon loaded with hospital stores, with two men and a girl. The latter was left at a house until the raid on Salem was over, when she was picked up on the retreat and came along with the regiment, going to Martinsburg. Afterward she married one of the regiment, a member of Company I, it is said, and settled near Pittsburgh. On the retreat, shortly after leaving Salem, Bower, Jos. Walton, W. A. Wiley and another member of Company D., had a lively experience with a party of Confederates, who made an attack on them. Wiley's gun was forced from his hands and an attempt made to shoot him, but Bower shot the assailant in the shoulder, at the same time calling on his imaginary force to charge the Confederates, which had the effect of driving them away, without any of our men being hurt. On the fight of the 19th Bower was captured, and had on a Confederate Major's overcoat, and a cap that once belonged to the notorious bushwhacker, Bill Harper; but in the confusion, when a Confederate charge was ordered on Averell's rear guard, Bower was foremost in the attack, but was so impetuous that he never stopped until he got in our lines, his captors firing several shots after him. He passed the ambulances just before they were captured.

S. J. Clendaniel of Company I, gives a bit of his experience of the trip, in a night's sleep he and comrades got, when the raid was about over. They slept well, but when morning came, they found themselves frozen in their blankets.

CHAPTER XVI.

The latter had been soaked by the rains, and the fearful cold weather froze them solid, but within, the men were comfortable, if such a thing were possible. A further inspection showed that Clendaniel and his comrades, eight in all, had slept on a frog pond. It was frozen of course, and they had lain on the ice, with their blankets wrapped around them, and slept soundly. But that was comfort compared to a part of that awful, horrible expedition. Hundreds of broken down constitutions attest to this day its severity.

Averell had outwitted the men who attempted his capture, and it was a bitter dose for the Confederates. The Richmond *Examiner* of December 28th had the following sarcastic article on the failure to capture Averell: The great Gen. Averell has gone, not "up the spout," but back into his den. Cast your eye upon a map, and I'll tell you how he went and how he came. He came from New Creek, a depot on the Baltimore and Ohio railroad, in the county of Hardy, along the western base of the Shenandoah mountains through Covington to Salem, burnt things generally and returned over nearly the same route. Imboden seized the gap where the Parkersburg turnpike crosses the Shenandoah, and prevented a raid on Staunton. Averell left five hundred men to hold Imboden there, and pushed onto toward Salem. That general could not pursue without uncovering Staunton - the forces threatening nearly equaling his own. Gen. Lee was informed of the situation of affairs. Here commences the reign of major generals and military science. Maj. Gen. Jubal A. Early came. Maj. Gen. Fitzhugh Lee came. Brig. Gen. Walker came. Brig. Gen. Thomas came. Their staffs came. They all took a drink. Gen.. Early took two. Brig. Gen. Wickham came. Col. Chambliss, commanding brigade, came. They smiled also.

When Averell was opposite Staunton, Fitz Lee was at Ivy depot, on the Virginia Central railroad, a day's march from that town. A fortunate occurrence, indeed. Everybody thought Averell was "treed" now. He passed through Brown's Gap and struck the valley turnpike at Mount Crawford, eight miles above Harrisonburg - a miserable mistake. One day's march lost. He then marched toward Harrisonburg - then toward Staunton. Another day gone for nothing. He finally reached Staunton, where he ought to have been on the first night. Still there was plenty of time to cut Averell off. Lee and Imboden marched day and night to Lexington, and then toward Covington. They have yet time enough to intercept.

Here was committed the fatal and foolish blunder. While Lee and Imboden were on the road to Covington, in striking distance of that place, word was sent the Yankees are marching towards Buchanan, instead of Covington. No man ought to have put credence in a statement so utterly absurd as that the enemy were going from Salem to that place. Such a statement presupposes Averell deliberately placing himself past escape, and therefore run raving mad. Such improbable rumors should never be entertained a moment, much less made the basis of important military movements. The order was obeyed. The troops turned and marched back, and at night were neither at Buchanan nor Covington.

The story is told in a few words. The Yankees passed through Covington, and, to their great amusement, escaped. The rumor about Buchanan was the tale of some frightened fool. The enemy, in terror and demoralization, fled from Salem at full speed, destroying their train and artillery. Jackson knocked some in the head; the citizens beat the brain out of others; one farmer in Allegheny killed six; some were scattered in the mountains, and are being picked up here and there; the rapid stream drowned many, but the main part have gone whence they came, wondering how they did get away. It is hardly necessary to add, the humblest private in the ranks, if he possessed sense enough to eat and drink, not only could, but would, have managed better. Old Stonewall would have marched on, caught and killed the Yankees. What Lee thought the writer don't know. They who know, say Imboden begged to go to Covington. He made it plain to the dullest mind that the Buchanan story was past belief. What's done is done.

No language can tell the suffering of our men. They were in the saddle night and day, save a few hours between midnight and day. They were beat up by their officers with their swords - the only means of arousing them - numb and sleepy. Some froze to death, others were taken from horses senseless. They forded swollen streams, and their clothes, stiff frozen, rattled as they rode. It rained in torrents, and froze as it fell. In the mountain paths the ice was cut from the roads before they ventured to ride over. One horse slipped over the precipice - the rider was leading him - he never looked over after him.

The whole matter is summed up in a couple of sentences. Averell was penned up. McCausland, Echols and Jackson at one gate, Lee and Imboden at the other. Some ass suggested he might escape by jumping down the well and coming out at Japan, i.e., go to Buchanan. Early orders them to leave a gate open and guard the well. He did not jump in. Meanwhile, the Yankees cooly came up the valley, through Edinburg, New Market, up to Harrisonburg, within twenty-five miles of Staunton - "these headquarters." This was bearding the lion in his den. Jubal took the field, at the head of Company Q and a party of substitute men, farmers and ploughboys, called "home guards." The Yankees got after him and the "major general commanding" lost his hat in the race. The last heard of him he was pursuing the enemy with part of his division - footmen and cavalry - with fine prospects of overtaking them somewhere in China, perhaps about the "great wall." The Yankees were retreating toward the "Devil Hole." Early bound for the same place. They did very little damage in the valley. Here is the moral. The marshals under Napoleon's eye were invincible - with separate commands, blunderers. A general of division, with Gen. Robert E. Lee to plan and put him in the right place, does well. Mosby would

CHAPTER XVI.

plan or execute a fight or strategic movement better than Longstreet at Suffolk and Knoxville, Jubal Early at Staunton.

The losses of the brigade on the Salem Raid were 8 killed and drowned, 8 wounded, and 122 captured; total 138. Our regiment lost 1 wounded, and 17 captured.

The following is General Averell's thrilling and complete report of this great raid, one of the most wonderful of the war: I have the honor to submit the following report of the operations of my brigade since the date of its arrival at New Creek, W. Va., November 18: Having been notified by the brigadier general commanding the department, that active service would be expected of me very soon, measures were at once taken to place the command in as good condition as possible, but owing to the meagre supply of horses, shoes, nails, coal, and forges furnished, and the shortness of the time allowed, the mounted forces of the brigade were but poorly prepared to make a long march on the 6th of December, when I received orders to move on the 8th. My orders did not contemplate the movement of any co-operative forces excepting a small force under Col. Thoburn, but after representing to the department commander the importance of such movements, and my desire that they should be made, he kindly invited me to accompany him to his headquarters at Cumberland and arrange a plan for them. I went with him to Cumberland on the evening of the 6th, and drew up a plan which was briefly, as follows, viz: Brigadier Scammon, commanding forces in the Kanawha Valley, to be at Lewisburg on Saturday, December 12; to look out northward and endeavor to intercept the enemy from that direction; to remain until 18th, taking advantage of any opportunity to strike the enemy in the direction of Union or elsewhere. Col. Moor to be at Marlin's Bottom, Friday, December 11; to feel the enemy in the direction of Lewisburg on the 12th and 13th; to remain near Frankfort until the 18th, and on his return to bring off the wounded left after the battle of Droop Mountain. Brig. Gen. Sullivan, commanding forces in the Shenandoah Valley, to be at Woodstock on Friday, December 11, to make careful demonstrations until the 18th, when he was to move toward Staunton, and threaten the same boldly on the 20th and 21st. The command of Col. Thoburn was to turn off at Monterey, and moving toward Staunton, keep the attention of the enemy fixed upon the Parkersburg pike. A copy of the above plan was given to the dep't commander and I received his promise that his orders should be given in accordance with it, with the exception of Moor's and Thoburn's commands, which were to receive orders from me. It was thought that between the two demonstrations of the Kanawha and Shenandoah forces, I might pass the enemy's lines without delay, and that the threatening of Staunton on the 20th and 21st with the operations in the direction of Union, would divert the enemy from offering any great resistance to the return of my fatigued command.

The Second West Virginia Mounted Infantry, Lieut. Col. Scott; Third West Virginia Mounted Infantry, Lieut. Col. Thompson; Eighth West Virginia Mounted Infantry, Col. Oley; Fourteenth Pennsylvania Cavalry, Lieut. Col. Blakely; Maj. Gibson's battalion of cavalry, and Ewing's battery set out from New Creek on the morning of the 18th of December, with fair weather, but with many misgivings on account of our poor condition to overcome the weary distances and confront the perils incident to such an expedition. During the march of two days to Petersburg, constant exertions were made to complete the shoeing of the horses, but lack of means and material rendered it impracticable to attain the desired object. At Petersburg, on the 10th, the command of Col. Thoburn about 700 strong joined mine, and together we proceeded southward, arriving nearly at Monterey on the 11th. The most of my train was placed in charge of Col. Thoburn and, on the morning of the 12th, my command and his started in a severe and discouraging rain storm, Thoburn toward McDowell and my command down Back Creek. The secluded road which runs along and across this now swollen stream, was pursued the ensuing day without any incident worthy of note, until our arrival at Gatewood's, where the rear guard of Jackson's forces, flying from the advance of Moor, was encountered and dispersed, and four wagons destroyed, loaded with ammunition and stores. The storm continued on the 14th, and Jackson's river was found hardly fordable. Upon arriving at Callaghan's reports reached us that Scammon had advanced and occupied Lewisburg, and that the rebel forces, commanded by Gen. Echols, had retired toward Union, under orders from Maj. Gen. Sam. Jones. We halted a few hours to rest and feed the animals, and to make a false advance in the direction of Covington. At 2 a.m. December 15, the column was in motion upon a dark and difficult road, which runs up Dunlap Creek to the pike, connecting the White with the Sweet Sulphur Springs. We reached the beautiful valley of the Sweet Sulphur about 10 a.m., and halted two hours, availing ourselves of the plentiful forage found there.

At the Sweet Springs it was learned that Echols' forces were encamped four miles from Union, to the northward, and that Gen. Scammon had retired from Lewisburg. The road to New Castle was taken at 1 p.m., and near the summit of the Sweet Springs Mountain a rebel quartermaster met us and was captured, which assured me that our advance was unknown as yet to the enemy. From the top of this mountain a sublime spectacle was presented to us. Seventy miles to the eastward the peaks of Otter reared their summits above the Blue Ridge, and all the space between was filled with a billowing ocean of hills and mountains, while behind us the great Alleghanies, coming from the north with the grandeur of innumerable tints, swept past and faded in the southern horizon. When within twelve miles of New Castle another halt was made to feed and rest, while a squadron advanced toward Fincastle, conveying to the enemy a false impression, and bringing to us some sixty horses and

CHAPTER XVI.

some prisoners. New Castle was passed during the night and efforts were made to reach Salem by daylight in the morning. A party of rebels, under Captain Chapman, reconnoitered our advance during the night, and all were captured except their leader, who, declining to surrender, was killed. The head of my column was preceded by vigilant scouts, armed with repeating rifles, mounted upon fleet horses, who permitted no one to go ahead of them.

We approached Salem unheralded, and the whistling of locomotives could be heard from that point long before it was reached by us. Four miles from Salem, a party of rebels from the town in quest of information concerning the Yankees, met us. From some of these it was learned that the division of Gen. Fitzhugh Lee, had left Charlottesville on the 14th to intercept my command, and that a train loaded with troops was momentarily expected at Salem to guard the stores at that point. I hastened with my advance, consisting of about 350 men and two 3-inch guns, through the town to the depot. The telegraph wires were first cut - the operator was not to be found, the railroad track torn up in the vicinity of the depot, one gun placed in battery and the advance dismounted and placed in readiness for the expected train of troops. An inspection and estimate of the stores contained in the depot and two large buildings adjacent were made, and upon a subsequent comparison of notes taken, found to be as follows: 2000 barrels of flour, 10,000 bushels of wheat, 100,000 bushels of shelled corn, 50,000 bushels of oats, 2,000 barrels of meat, several cords of leather, 1,000 sacks of salt, 31 boxes of clothing, 20 bales of cotton, a large amount of harness, shoes, saddles, equipments, tools, oil, tar, and various other stores and 100 wagons. A train from Lynchburg, loaded with troops, soon approached. My main body was not yet in sight, and it was necessary to stop the train; a shot was fired at it from one of the guns, which missed; a second went through the train diagonally, which caused it to retire, and a third and last shot hastened its movements. My main body arrived, and parties were sent four miles to the eastward and twelve miles to the westward to destroy the road. The depots with their contents were burned; three cars standing upon the track, the water-station, turn-table and a large pile of bridge timber and repairing material destroyed. Five bridges were burned and the track torn up and destroyed as much as possible in six hours. The "yanks" with which we had provided ourselves, proved too weak to twist the U rails, and efforts were made to bend them, by heating the centers, with but partial success. A few small store houses, containing leather and other valuable articles were destroyed in the vicinity. The telegraph wires were cut, coiled and burned for over half a mile. Private property was untouched by my command and the citizens received us with politeness.

It was intimated to some inquisitive ones that we were going back by Buchanan, but about 4 p.m. my command quitted the work of destruction and returned upon the road it came some seven miles, when it halted for the night.

The last eighty miles had been marched in about thirty hours. Little sleep had been enjoyed by my men during five days and nights; it was necessary to pause and collect our energies for the return. During the night of the 16th it rained heavily and also the ensuing day and night. My column was caught in the many windings of Craig's Creek, which was now swollen to a dangerous torrent, which uprooted trees and carried them away. Heavy caissons were swept down the stream, and great exertion and skill were required to save them. In the river and in the rain forty-eight hours, it was impracticable to keep our ammunition dry, and my command, drenched, muddy and hungry arrived at New Castle about sun-down on the 18th, in a miserable condition to make the march before us. Information that Fitzhugh Lee was at Fincastle reached me at New Castle, and that Jones was between me and Sweet Springs. At 9 p.m. while a false advance was made toward Fincastle, my column took the road to Sweet Springs. We soon encountered and drove the enemy's pickets about twelve miles, to the junction of the road with the Fincastle pike, to the Sweet Springs. The command halted and built camp fires.

The condition of my ammunition made it prudent for me to avoid a fight. It was evident from a survey of the enemy's positions, that I could not get to the Sweet Springs without a contest, and that with Lee only a few miles to my right and rear. Two ways were left, both difficult and obscure; one to the southwest leading around Jones' right, through Monroe and Greenbrier counties; the other, northeast to the Covington and Fincastle pike, which I took, as it was the most direct and dangerous, consequently the safest if I could only make the march. We left our camp fires burning and went forward in the darkest and coldest night we had yet experienced. Thirty miles through the forest and frost, brought us to Fincastle pike about noon of the 19th. It was yet fifteen miles to the bridge. The river was reported unfordable on account of the depth of the water and the obstructions formed by the ice. I had carefully calculated the possible marches of the enemy, and felt certain that we could make the march through the points they deemed most secure, but no halt could be made. When eight miles from the river a force of 300 mounted rebels opposed our advance. As soon as they were broken, they were closely pursued at a gallop to the first bridge, five miles below Covington, and thence to the bridge at Covington, both of which were saved from destruction, although faggots had been piled upon them ready to burn. The head of my column reached the first bridge about 9 p.m. and three officers and six orderlies were sent back to keep it closed up.

The approach to the river is through a gorge which opens to the stream a mile below the first bridge. There the pike from Covington passes along the right bank to Clifton Forge and Jackson's River Depot, where Jackson was supposed to be with about 1,000 men. I sent a company upon the road to Clifton Forge, with orders to dismount and move out three-fourths of a mile

CHAPTER XVI.

and hold the road until the column passed. A captured dispatch from Maj. Gen. Sam. Jones to Maj. Gen. Early, at Millborough, confirmed my opinion with regard to the position of the enemy, and gave me the information that Gen. Early's division had been added to the forces opposed to my return. The dispatch is as follows:

ON TOP OF THE SWEET SPRINGS MOUNTAIN,
Dec. 19, 1863- 7 a.m.

GENERAL: The enemy drove the pickets about twelve miles from here, near Mrs. Scott's, in the direction of New Castle, about 2 o'clock this morning. Gen. Echols has a strong position here and I think can effectually block this way to them. To avoid him, I think it probable that the enemy may attempt to escape by Covington or by Clifton Forge. Col. Jackson's troops are at Clifton Forge. I would suggest, instead of keeping any force at the Warm Springs you would place it at Morris Hill and picket at Callaghan's. I presume that you are in communication with Col. Jackson, and he may be able to give you information of the enemy's movements. I expect to ascertain the enemy's movements in the course of the morning. If he attempts to avoid Echols here and escape by Callaghan's we can reach Callaghan's before he can. Echols will hold the place here until he ascertains the enemy's movements. It is possible that they will attempt to pass Echols' right by Gap Mills, by passing one of the many gorges in these mountains to the south of this position between Echols and McCausland, who is at Newport, in Giles county. If he does that, he will pass out by the western portion of Monroe and Greenbrier; if he does so, you cannot touch him. Under all the circumstances of the case, as I see them now, I think that you should have a force at Morris Hill and a strong picket at Callaghan's. The enemy were certainly at New Castle at sun down yesterday. They cannot pass Echols here. They may escape by Clifton Forge or by Covington if you do not prevent them. Echols will give you all the aid that he can. We are closer to the enemy than you are and will be more likely to know their movements. I will endeavor to keep you informed. A portion of our small mounted force has been directed if the enemy attempts to pass from New Castle direct to Covington, or by Clifton Forge, to fall back in front of them so as to give Col. Jackson and you the earliest information.

The operator at Jackson's River will use every effort to get the above to Gen. Early and a copy to Gen. Jackson. Col. Jackson must have a copy of it.

SAM JONES, Maj. Gen.

I relied somewhat upon the demonstration which was to be made against Staunton on the next day. I also thought that Gen. Scammon might divert the force under Echols from interfering with mine. In both these trusts I was at fault. From all the information I have been able to collect, I believe the Kanawha force retired from Lewisburg on the 13th without waiting until the 18th, as prearranged, and without making an effort in the direction of Union. The detachment sent from the command of Gen. Sullivan was too feeble to make the threat upon Staunton of sufficient avail to keep Early from besetting my command upon its return. Instead of approaching Staunton on the 20th and 21st, it was retiring through New Market on the 20th. The dispositions of the rebels had been prompt and skillful; Rosser's brigade had crossed the Rappahannock at Fredericksburg on the 14th, made some demonstrations upon the Orange and Alexandria railroad near Bull Run; thence passed the Blue Ridge through Ashby's Gap; were stopped by the high water in the Shenandoah, and moved up by Front Royal to cut off the detachment from Harper's Ferry. The division of Early left Hanover Junction on the 15th; arrived at Staunton the same night; marched to Buffalo Gap the ensuing day and thence to the Warm Springs and Millborough. Fitzhugh Lee's division, leaving Charlottesville on the 14th, came into the valley, where it was deceived by Thoburn's presence and diverted by the detachment from Sullivan's command, for a day or two, when it set out for Buchanan.

At Jackson's River, though trusting in the co-operation of the Kanawha and Shenandoah forces, I acted as though they would be of no assistance to me, which was, indeed, the case. My column, nearly four miles long, was hastened across the first bridge. When all had passed but my ambulances, a few wagons and a regiment in the rear, an attack was made by Jackson's force. The company on the Clifton Forge road was driven away; three ambulances were captured and an effort was made to take the bridge, which was unsuccessful. A night attack is always appalling even to experienced troops. Unavailing efforts were made to open communication with the regiment cut off, until morning, when it appeared that the enemy was determined to maintain his position upon the high cliffs which overlooked the bridge. During the night the balance of my command had been concentrated upon Callaghan's, and an efficient defense established upon all the roads approaching that point. Finding it impossible to dislodge the enemy as long as the bridges remained, I directed them to be destroyed. The enemy at once left the cliffs and endeavored to reach the flank and rear of the regiment which remained on that side. Orders were sent to the regiment to swim the river or come to me over the mountain, around the bend; and after destroying the train, it swam the river with the loss of four men drowned. When nearly across, a formal demand from Gen. Early was received by the officers commanding the rear guard to surrender, addressed to the commanding officer of the United States forces.

CHAPTER XVI.

As my column was then in motion over the Alleghanies, no formal reply was returned to the demand.

During the night attack five officers and 119 men were lost by being captured. It was thought that had the regiment in rear been advanced steadily forward, these captures might have been mostly prevented, and we should not have been obliged to destroy our wagons and ambulances the following day. The road over the Alleghenies led us to Anthony's Creek, between the White Sulphur Springs and Huntersville. A force of the enemy was reported at Gatewood's, which is twelve miles east of Huntersville. My command was yet thirty miles from that point. If I could cross the Greenbrier and reach Marlin's Bottom before the enemy, my command would be safe. By a very obscure road the Greenbrier was reached and crossed on the 21st, opposite Hillsboro, and we encamped for the night at the northern base of Droop Mountain. My scouts thrown out kept me informed of the enemy's movements and positions.

For thirty hours after my command left Callaghan's, the enemy made great efforts to intercept my force, but they generally took wrong roads. The citizens who knew the country best regarded our capture as unavoidable. It was expected, as may be seen from the orders given Col. Moor by me, that he would remain near Droop Mountain until the 18th, but owing to orders he received from the general commanding the department, subsequent to the reception of mine, he also retired on the 4th, thus leaving 110 co-operative forces except Col. Thoburn's, in the positions I had reason to expect them to be on the 20th and 21st. Unaided, with a weary command of 2,500 men, I had marched through a difficult country in which not less than 12,000 rebels were maneuvered to effect my capture.

On the way to Edray, my rear guard experienced some trifling attacks on the 22d. The road thence to Beverly was a glacier, which was traversed with great difficulty and peril. The artillery was drawn almost entirely by dismounted men during the 23d and 24th. Couriers had been sent forward to Beverly to bring out subsistence and forage, which we succeeded, after extreme hardships, in meeting on the 24th. The officers and men undertook all that was required of them and endured all the sufferings from fatigue, hunger and cold with extraordinary fortitude, even with cheerfulness. The march of 400 miles, which was concluded at Beverly, was the most difficult I have ever seen performed. The endurance of the men and horses was taxed to the utmost, yet there was no rest for them. Believing that some retaliatory operations would be at once inaugurated by the enemy, I telegraphed to the general commanding the department that I thought it advisable to get my command into the valley as soon as possible, and set out for Webster, whence, by means of the railroad, I arrived at Martinsburg just in time to confront the enemy, who was advancing toward this place.

There is nothing of value or interest in the official report of Maj. Gen. Sam Jones, who commanded the Confederates, and it is omitted from this work.

The command left Beverly on December 27th, in a heavy rain, and on the 28th reached Webster. From there they went to Martinsburg, Va. The trip to Martinsburg was a very severe one, the cold being intense, so much so that bread froze in the box cars in which the men were transported. It will never be forgotten by those who participated in it. Upon reaching Martinsburg, our regiment went into camp without tents or covering of any kind, and suffered severely. Fuel was scarce, and there was really no condition of comfort.

General Order No. 39, War Department, dated January 26, 1864, was issued, changing the Second Virginia Infantry to the Fifth West Virginia Cavalry, by which designation it was known until mustered out of the service. The regiment remained at Martinsburg until March 19, 1864, with a vast amount of picket duty and scouting. One of the most pleasant incidents of the stay here was the visit of Gen. Milroy to the brigade on January 31, three regiments of which were formerly in his brigade. A happier meeting was seldom seen in the service. He made a speech full of the old fire, and very flattering to the boys.

At noon, March 19, 1864, the brigade left Martinsburg, went into Maryland, thence back into Virginia, and marched to Charleston, West Va., arriving there April 30, 1864.

CHAPTER XVII.

CAMPAIGNS OF 1864.

The Department of West Virginia was under the command of Gen. Franz Sigel in the spring of 1864, who was in the Shenandoah Valley in personal command of the troops there, while Gen. George Crook was in command of a large part of the forces, in the Kanawha valley. Gen. Averell's brigade, except Capt. Ewing's battery, went early in the spring to the Kanawha to operate with Gen. Crook, while the battery remained with Gen. Sigel. Gen. Grant directed the advance of these two columns, Crook to break the Virginia and Tennessee railroad at the New River bridge, while Sigel was to distract attention from Crook, by menacing the Virginia Central Railroad at Staunton.

We have first to notice the Shenandoah campaign. On May 9th Gen. Sigel's forces moved up the valley pike to Cedar Creek, thence through Strasburg to Woodstock, the cavalry advancing to Mount Jackson. Col. Moor advanced to the same place with his infantry on the 14th, and there the cavalry reported the enemy to be in force at New Market. Moor advanced still further, when the roar of the artillery announced the presence of the enemy. The Confederate force thus met was the advance of Gen. Breckenridge, who marched rapidly from Staunton to oppose him, with a force of nearly 5,000 men. Moor had four regiments of infantry, besides cavalry and artillery, of which Gen. Stahel assumed command the next morning. The Union forces were scattered along the pike and were not prepared for battle, but it was upon them. Sigel came to the front and had in line the 18th Connecticut and 123d Ohio Infantry and a small body of cavalry, under Col. Moor in the advance, to break the enemy's onset. The main line was under the personal direction of Gen. Sigel, consisting of the 34th Massachusetts, 1st Virginia, 54th Pennsylvania and a few companies of the 12th Virginia, the artillery being carefully disposed, and the cavalry was behind the center of the left flank.

291

Breckenridge moved to the attack with the veteran brigades of Echols and Wharton, a battalion of cadets and other local forces, with cavalry and artillery. Breckenridge soon drove Moor in confusion, and promptly attacked Thoburn's brigade and was checked. Imboden's cavalry with artillery charged Sigel's left flank, which, with Breckenridge in front, caused our whole force to retreat, bringing up at Cedar Creek.

Battery G had a prominent part in the expedition, being connected with some cavalry under Col. Wynkoop. On the 14th one section of the battery with the cavalry, was ordered up the valley, meeting the enemy before reaching Mount Jackson. The Confederates fell back across the river, and were vigorously shelled by the battery, continuing the retreat. Then Col. Wynkoop ordered a charge, the battery to keep on the pike, and the cavalry to be deployed right and left, after crossing the river. The bugler sounded forward, and away went the charging forces, the enemy hastily getting out of the way. The chase was continued for three miles beyond New Market, and then our forces fell back to New Market. In the meantime the rest of the army was brought up, the rest of the battery also coming up, and went into camp for the night. It was a stormy night, the rain falling in torrents, but not so hard that the battery boys forgot their cunning; for a good chicken breakfast, of the fattest and choicest poultry from the Dunkard settlement near, attested their foraging qualities. The horses were not unhitched, or their saddles taken off, being ready for a sudden attack. The next day the battle was fought, the battery being in position on the left and had to wait until our troops got past, before they could do much. As our right and centre were driven back, Col. Wynkoop was like a caged lion, as his orders prevented him from doing anything, but his time came. The bugle sounded forward, and the cavalry and battery came out on the pike. Just as they crossed it, the battery unlimbered and opened fire with canister, keeping it up for about 10 minutes, when they had to fall back, and the battle was over. Alex. McKinzie, of the battery, was killed, and Jerry Leadom had an eye shot out, and was sent to the rear. Sergt. Evans lost his hat, and when he picked it off the ground, found the top gone. It might have been the top of his head. One of their guns was disabled in this fight.

Gen. David Hunter was appointed to the command in the valley, relieving Gen. Sigel, taking charge of the army May 21. On the 26th he broke camp at Cedar Creek, and marched to New Market, where he remained until June 1, having with him Sigel's troops, reinforced until they amounted to 8,500 of all arms; including 21 guns, the infantry being commanded by Gen. Sullivan, and the cavalry by Gen. Stahel. From New Market Gen. Hunter proceeded to Harrisonburg, and June 2d found Imboden posted on the pike about seven miles ahead, whom he avoided by moving on a side road to Port Republic, a large supply train being overhauled and partly captured by the cavalry. On the morning of the 5th he advanced toward Staunton, and found that the

CHAPTER XVII.

enemy, commanded by Gen. W. E. Jones, had taken position at Piedmont, to resist the Union march. This place is on a road about seven miles southwest of Port Republic, which forks to Staunton and Waynesboro. Stahel's Cavalry soon drove in the pickets of the enemy, when the main line advanced in front of the Piedmont line, with Moor's brigade on the right and Thoburn's on the left, with Wynkoop's brigade of cavalry in rear of Moor. Then followed an artillery fire of two hours, the good work of our batteries causing the enemy to slacken their fire. Moor's brigade then attacked the Confederate left, advancing across the open and driving them through the woods to the main works; but being unable to carry the works, he fell back a short distance. The enemy then attempted to crush Hunter's right, but was effectually checked by Moor, aided by the batteries, among which were the section of Battery G, and Carlin's Battery of the same regiment, First West Va. Light Artillery. While Jones was concentrating for this attack, Thoburn moved across a ravine to gain the enemy's right flank. He gallantly charged on the woods and heights, Moor and Wynkoop co-operating, and the enemy abandoned his position, a part of his men rushing over the steep bank into the river which covered his left. Over 1,000 of the enemy, including 60 officers, were captured on the field, and among the killed was the Confederate commander. The next day others were captured, making the total number of prisoners about 1,500, to which must be added the killed and stragglers. Three guns and many small arms fell into the hands of Hunter, whose loss was about 420. Gen. Hunter then marched on to Staunton, being the first Union troops to enter the city, and here was joined by Gen. Crook's and Averell's forces from the Kanawha, fresh from the victory of Cloyd Mountain.

At the beginning of Hunter's campaign, Ewing's battery was pretty badly used up, and being short of horses, it was ordered that all of the battery but one section should be relieved. It was the only mounted battery in the command, and it was required that at least part of it should stay. The best horses and guns were picked out, and Lieut S. J. Shearer was put in command of the section. Being a part of Wynkoop's brigade, they were in the advance until they reached Staunton. On approaching Piedmont they skirmished all the time until they reached the river, where the battle was fought. It became their duty to ascertain the position of the enemy, so they unlimbered in the wheat field, and threw a shell about where they thought the enemy ought to be, and the response was one that made the valley fairly ring, killing four of Shearer's horses and wounding several. Sergeant Evans' horse was hit three times, showing the heavy fire, but fortunately none of the men were hurt. They then fell back and waited until the rest of the artillery came up, when they took another position, the other batteries forming on their right and left. The battle then opened in full earnest, and presently this section limbered up and went with Wynkoop to the right. But when they reached the river they found they could not cross it, so they returned and took a position in front of the rail breastworks, which the enemy had built, the section being on the right hand side of the road next to the river, and remained there until the battle was over. The execution that was done here was fearful. Behind these rude and frail breastworks, the enemy lay all around, many with pieces of rails driven in them in almost all shapes, and the rails on fire. Some were torn horribly, showing the worst features of the horrors of war. It was the worst sight seen during the war by many, if not all, of the troops present. After the battle was well under way, Sergeant Evans was ordered by General Hunter to take charge of and send up all the ammunition needed for the batteries. It was a new duty to the sergeant; and he had considerable difficulty with the ordnance officers, but performed his work with entire satisfaction to the authorities. That was a habit battery G had, however, and never fell short of their full duty.

The section went with the command to Staunton, and from there was sent back to Wheeling by the way of Cheat Mountain, Beverly and Webster, and were mustered out of the service, their term of enlistment having expired.

CLOYD MOUNTAIN.

On May 1, 1864, the command of Gen. Averell, consisting of three brigades, left Charleston, West Va., for an expedition southward. The Fifth West Virginia Cavalry was in the brigade commanded by Col. Oley. Nothing of interest occurred until the 4th, when our pickets were attacked and two of them captured, and our men took three prisoners. On the fifth the command marched twenty-five miles, crossing a high mountain, camping at Wyoming Court House. The next day, after a very fatiguing march of thirty miles, over rocks, roots and creeks, in single file, the troops camped for the night, and the next day went to Princeton Court House. On the 8th we left Princeton, passed the Confederate forts toward Wytheville, over mountains and through ravines, until within nine miles of Dublin station, where we met Gen. Crook's division of infantry, and camped on New River. In the morning Sergt. W. F. Graebe, of Company C, was in charge of the picket force, and in a few minutes after being placed, the enemy appeared on the road and hillside, when our men emptied their guns and struck out for camp, leaving the sergeant to meet the Confederates alone, but he was relieved by Capt. Grubb, who came in time to prevent his capture.

In the early part of the campaign, Capt. Thomas E. Day's Company E were sent out on a scouting expedition, remaining two or three days without encountering any of the enemy's forces. On the way back to camp, J. W. Stonebreaker and M. E. Moore were riding in the advance, when they discovered a Confederate soldier ahead of them, to whom they gave chase. A running fire was kept up, the chased trooper firing at his pursuers until his

CHAPTER XVII.

revolver was emptied except one barrel. This he held back for close quarters. Others of the company had joined in the chase, and the fleetest horses soon gained the front, until James A. Robinson and M. L. Lohmire galloped up to the Confederate, one on each side, and demanded his surrender. He aimed his last shot at Lohmire, who knocked the revolver upwards, and the man was a prisoner. He declared that he would never enter a Union prison, and he made good his word, escaping a few nights afterward.

Gen. Crook's forces, of which Col. Oley's brigade of cavalry, about 400 strong, formed a part, found the enemy posted in force, several thousand strong, at Cloyd Mountain, under the command of Gen's. W. E. Jones and Jenkins. They were entrenched on a wooded spur behind rail breastworks, with their guns so placed as to sweep a broad field that fronted the works, while a knee deep brook wound around the foot of the steep slope crowned by the rifle pits. "The enemy is in force and in strong position," said Crook, lowering his field glass; "he may whip us, but I guess not."

Forming under cover of the thick timber, Gen. Crook sent Col. White, with his own brigade and two regiments of Sickels' brigade, to turn the enemy's right, and the moment they were engaged moved the rest of his forces directly against the works. The advancing column was received with a hot fire as the men struggled across the open space, but after a severe fight they carried the entrenchments at all points. Crook's loss was 600, while that of the enemy was fully as heavy, if not greater. Our regiment was covering the rear and guarding the wagon train the morning of this engagement. When the main body under command of Gen. Crook struck the enemy's fortification on Cloyd Mountain, we were a mile or two in the rear. As soon as the first gun was fired, a detachment from each company amounting in all to about 100 men, was placed under command of Major Barclay and gathered forward to the scene of action. We found the rebels posted in a splendid position on the mountain, well fortified and commanding the valley about six miles from Dublin Depot, on the Virginia and Tennessee Railroad. Our infantry were just deploying through the woods to the right and left to the road. Two pieces of our artillery came forward and took up a position on a little ridge to the right of the road, and our detachment was ordered to dismount and support these guns; this we did by advancing some distance in front of the battery on lower ground, and there lay down exposed to the fire from the enemy's cannon, our own battery firing over our heads. The enemy had some large guns, twenty-four pound howitzers, and they tried hard to dismount or disable our little battery, but in vain. For one hour, while our flanking forces were getting into position, we lay there exposed to the rain of shot and shell and unable to employ the time by even firing a gun, and all we could do was to dodge the heavy shot and shell as they fell amongst us. It was as all old soldiers will admit, the most trying position in which troops could be placed. Then an hour seemed like half a day to us. At last our flankers arrived within range of the rebels lying behind the breastworks, and the troops in front ascended the hill and the fight became hot and furious. About noon our men carried the breastworks by storm, capturing the battery of twenty-four pounders and a large number of prisoners. As soon as our men reached the breastworks, we were mounted and ordered to charge the fleeing rebels; this we did with alacrity, and for awhile we kept them on the dead run capturing all who fell behind. Discovering however that we had no sabres, and were only mounted infantry; a large body of the rebels rushed into the woods alongside the road, and poured a heavy volley into us, wounding our chaplain, Rev. J.W.W. Bolton, who was charging with us, and a number of men, among others Hiram Qualk of Company I, who was shot through the breast. Of course we could not get at them on horseback, so we dismounted, and one-fourth of the detachment holding the horses, the rest rushed on foot into the woods and soon dislodged the enemy. We kept up the pursuit, driving them up hill and down valley for a mile or two, until we were overtaken by the remainder of the regiment mounted, and led by our gallant quartermaster, A. J. Pentecost, who, waving aloft a sword that he had picked up in crossing the battle field, went dashing past us. An open wood stretched across the valley in their front, and into it they rode yelling like demons. They had hardly disappeared from our sight in the woods when a terrible rattle of small arms opened up, and back they came, or some of them, and many riderless horses along with them. Close behind came 2,000 exultant rebels on a charge. It seems that 2,000 fresh troops, rushed by rail from Kentucky, had arrived at Dublin depot too late to take part in the battle on the mountain, but were thrown forward to check pursuit if possible. Our mounted men had run into them and received a withering fire, compelling an immediate change of front. We all fell back some distance until our supports came in view, when we faced about, and, with the help of the infantry drove the reinforcements whirling through Dublin depot, capturing several immense store-houses, containing several thousand stand of arms, large quantities of ammunition, bacon, tobacco, etc. Over 300 wagons, a number of caissons and quartermaster's stores of all kinds also fell into our hands. The next day, after burning all of them we could not carry away, we advanced along the railroad to the large bridge that spanned New river, where we found the rebels had made a stand, determined to save the bridge. They had some heavy artillery there, and for two hours we had a lively artillery duel, but we finally charged them and they fled before we were fairly within musket range of them, and the bridge was ours, and along with it two more siege guns. They were too heavy to transport, so we blew them up, burned the bridge and started on our return trip north.

After the battle of Cloyd Mountain, when our troops had reached Dublin depot, heavy guards were thrown out to protect the lines from the enemy, whose forces had been greatly scattered. Sergt. John Caton, of Company E, and

CHAPTER XVII.

nine of his company, were posted to the extreme right, with orders to watch for straggling Confederates. They stood guard all night, and as no relief came, in the morning the sergeant sent one of the men into camp to ascertain the reason. He soon returned with the information that the command was gone, when the sergeant and his squad double quicked to the depot. Just as they arrived there the magazine exploded, when the bursting shells created a noise and confusion that would have been amusing had it not been so dangerous. The citizens, blacks, and the guard, got out of the place as hastily as possible, and fortunately no one was hurt. Before leaving the place the troops had fired the magazine, and in their hurry, no doubt, had overlooked the guard and left it in its exposed position. Ascertaining the direction in which the troops had gone, the squad followed and overtook them four or five miles out, after traveling over the railroad track, which was made hot by the fires built along it to destroy the rails. It was a hot walk and a trying occasion for the belated men. A somewhat similar experience happened to some of the same men a little later. A band of Confederates who had charge of some wagons filled with old muskets, and had two six-pound guns, were attacked by our forces, when they hastily decamped, leaving their wagons and guns. The Union troops piled the muskets on heaps of rails and set fire to the latter, and when the old muskets got warmed up they opened a regular fusillade, bullets flying in every direction, causing the few troops near them to stampede. It was one of the biggest scares of the entire trip, and a regiment of Confederates couldn't have done as good service in routing the Yankee boys.

On the 10th we left Dublin station for New river bridge at Newbern. Our troops attacked the enemy on the heights and carried their position by a charge, capturing 100 prisoners and three siege guns, our loss being small. We marched about fourteen miles and camped on the bank of the river. Our troops burned a very large railroad bridge, destroyed culverts, etc., and the enemy burned the pike bridge, our men crossing the river on pontoons. On the 11th we crossed New river, marching twelve miles, and the next day marched about twenty miles to Salt Pond Mountain. This day the enemy tried to cut off our wagon train at Newport, but were repulsed with heavy loss. On the 13th we left this place and camped at night on the western slope of Peter's Mountain. One regiment of the enemy followed our rear guard, and we burned about forty wagons and 700 guns which we had captured. At the foot of Peter's Mountain we captured thirty-four wagons and two twenty-four pound guns from Gen. Jackson, who retreated at the mere sight of our advance guard. The next day we took the road to Lewisburg, the Fifth being in the advance of Crook's division. We passed through Salt Sulphur Springs, and drove the enemy out of the town of Union, where we camped, the Greenbrier river being too high to cross. On the 16th the division followed the road to Meadow Bluff, where we went to cross the river. All the cavalry and dismounted men under

Averell were here drawn up in line of battle, the enemy having occupied the town, who were under the command of Jackson and McCausland. The horses were kept saddled all night, and the command remained under arms all of the next day but no conflict took place.

The mountains were full of bushwhackers, who made it decidedly uncomfortable for our pickets and scouts. May 18th the command marched toward Lewisburg, our regiment as rear guard, arriving at Meadow Bluff the next day, where they went into camp. The Fifth and Seventh West Virginia Cavalry were ordered toward Gauley river, and left for there the next day. They crossed the Little and Big Sewell mountains on the Charleston road, arriving at Loup creek on the 22d where they went into camp. On the 27th, all the men except the veterans and recruits, of Companies A, B, C, D, and E, of our regiment, went to Charleston to be mustered out, their term of enlistment having expired, while Companies F, H, I, and K, with all the veterans and recruits, under Lieut. Col. Scott, went in the direction of Lewisburg, where they arrived on the 29th. Here the cavalry under Averell, and the infantry under Crook, were united. June 3d the combined forces left Lewisburg and marched in the direction of Staunton. At Warm Springs, June 5th, a number of our men in advance of the column were killed or wounded. The next day the command crossed Cow Pasture river, along a branch of the Virginia Central railroad. They passed through a very deep mountain gap, where the enemy were protected by fortifications. Gen. Crook drove them out, and the advance destroyed a very long and fine railroad bridge. On the 8th the forces reached Staunton and joined the command of Gen. David Hunter, in his expedition to Lynchburg, taking part in that memorable and unfortunate advance, and shared in the losses and hardships of the retreat.

On the trip, after the Cloyd Mountain fight, M. E. Moore, of Company E, was captured and taken to Staunton, where he had charge of thirteen of our soldiers wounded at Piedmont, and witnessed the passing of both armies through the place. Was started on the way to Andersonville, but had some boils on his arm, which he carefully bandaged, and put his arm in a sling, and was sent to City Point for exchange along with the other sick. The boys had reached perfection in foraging. Some colored folks met the line at the New River, when Will. Latta, of Company I, hailed one, asking where they had put that meat that they hid. The poor darkey denied any knowledge of contraband pork, when Latta threatened destruction to him if he did not tell, and then the colored contingent came down, and led the boys to a hiding place, where they secured seventy-two pieces of meat. Latta's chance shot produced good results. Corp. Steve Ward was then sent with a detail to look for some cattle, but came back with a quantity of the finest ham in the state. Lieut. J. B. Montgomery was sent out with a squad of his men to hunt for horses and came to a field where there was a fine assortment of just the animals he needed. He

CHAPTER XVII.

dismounted his men, who went after the horses, when the Johnnies raised a fuss about it, and Montgomery's horse holders became frightened and started for the command, compelling him and men to walk several miles before they caught up with their own horses.

During the retreat of Gen. Hunter, the battalion left of our regiment had a jolly time. On the second day out, Sergt. Steinaker of Company D, went out with a foraging party to seek something for the battalion to eat. After securing what they wanted, they started to return to the command, and after dark entered what they supposed to be their camp. Not recognizing the surroundings, D. O. Carpenter of Company I, went to a soldier and asked what regiment it was in camp, when he was told that it was the Ninth Georgia. Greatly surprised, he went to the Sergeant and told him they were in a Confederate camp, which he could not credit. They then went to another squad and made the inquiry, and were informed that it was a part of the Twelfth South Carolina. There were 15 of our boys, with a colored guide, and they started at once to get out of their bad scrape. Carpenter led the way, and they soon reached the Salem pike, when putting spurs to their horses, they galloped past the pickets, calling out to them as they passed, "Look out for us, we may be back here in a hurry." But they made no attempt of that kind, only too glad to reach our own lines, which they did in safety about midnight, saving all their forage.

The remaining companies of our old regiment, whose term of service had now expired, were sent back to Grafton by the way of McDowell and Beverly, to be mustered out. They had in charge 1,100 prisoners, captured on the expeditions to Staunton, who were turned over to the authorities. The reenlisted men, about 200 in number, were consolidated with the remnant of the Sixth West Virginia Cavalry in September 1864, all taking that name. In March 1865 they were ordered to Washington, and were engaged in provost duty until June 16, when they received orders with other troops, to proceed to Louisville, Kentucky. From there they went to Fort Leavenworth, Kansas, then across the plains to Colorado, thence to Dakotah. There they were frequently engaged with the Indians, and were highly complimented for their gallantry. Many of the men served nearly five years of service.

GOVERNOR PIERPONT'S OPINION OF THE REGIMENT.

The Historian has received the following letter from Governor Pierpont, which we place here as a fitting conclusion of the history of the regiment. No man in Western Virginia knew more about the regiment than he, and he is a capable judge of its merits as a command. After a few words of introduction, he says:

Some that came to Wheeling were mere boys. Major Oakes, the mustering officer, a very judicious man, told me that some of the boys ought to be home with their mothers, but they persevered, and those boys came out veterans. It was the first regiment I had mustered in, the three months regiments being formed before I became governor. Those that came from Pennsylvania were in citizens' light clothing, and there was a great deal of hardship and destitution until clothing was issued to them, which was some time after their muster in.

There was one pleasing feature of the troops from the two states, Ohio and Pennsylvania, that was their perfect assimilation in spirit and purpose. The Pennsylvanians seemed to feel that they were with the Virginians to defend the Virginia homes from invasion, and partook of all the enthusiasm of the Virginians in the fight. And I have always suspected that when it came to the soldiers voting on the new state constitution that they voted, but I never knew. But this is certain that whenever I heard of a fight where the Second Virginia or Fifth Cavalry, after they became mounted, was, I heard a good report of them. They were reported brave to recklessness sometimes. It was said of them that whenever they got in a close place, every man was a general, and that they were almost invincible. They certainly achieved some victories that seemed in the beginning almost hopeless. It is strange how soon men will become allied in a common cause, and the alliance seems to become a part of their nature. I frequently meet old soldiers after they have met some of those Pennsylvania comrades, and they say it is wonderful what an interest these old Pennsylvania soldiers of the Second West Virginia take in everything about West Virginia.

I am yours with great respect,
F. H. PIERPONT.

CHAPTER XVIII.

SCOUTING SERVICE.

One of the most important and effective, yet dangerous, parts of the service in Western Virginia, was that of scouting, the nature of the warfare being such that skilled men in that line of duty was an absolute necessity. The demand was speedily met, and throughout the war, there were few that equalled, and none excelled, the brave men who took their lives in their hands, and so faithfully performed their work, in the mountains in which we served. In the grand record thus made, the men from our regiment were easily at the head, and no braver, nobler, truer men ever served their country, and none ever braved death more cheerfully for the sake of right.

The nature of the service was necessarily hazardous, severe and exhausting, testing the courage of the bravest. They were required most of the time to be dressed in Confederate uniforms, thus exposed to all the risks and dangers of spies, and were expected to be ready to go at any hour, day or night, when the commander of the forces ordered. Sometimes the order came to go in pairs to visit hostile camps, learn all they could of their number and location, and run the risk of being shot as spies. Being dressed as Confederates, they would pass as good southern men, and many a letter was given them by mothers and daughters to carry to Lee's command, from which they frequently obtained very valuable information; yet in the very midst of the enemy's country they would often meet strong, faithful Union men and women, to whom the general sent them for information. They kept the scouts posted in regard to all movements of the enemy, and were valuable aids to the Union cause and true friends to the scouts. Huntersville, Franklin, Monterey and other points between the lines, were the places to which the scouts were frequently sent, and it was no uncommon thing to make long trips through the mountains, requiring the greatest care, and when near the place desired to be reached, a caution was needed that exerted to the utmost the ingenuity and care of the brave men. Under cover of night, when possible, or, at times, in broad daylight, they would slip through the picket lines of the enemy, conceal themselves on the mountain side or in the dense laurel bushes, and there watch the camp, count their tents, and note all points of information of the enemy's movements. Then they would, as quietly as they came, steal back through the picket lines, and if no accident overtook them, they generally made the trip in three or four days; but it was nothing uncommon to meet resistance and have a brisk fight with the Confederates. It was a brave and superior force, however, that could stand before them, as they were superbly armed and knew well how to use their arms.

The central figure in the scouts belonging to our own command, was C.W.D. Smitley of Company B, Second Virginia, who was the leader and chief during the entire service. One of the scouts under his command says of him, in a note to the author, that "he was a brave, cool, daring man, one in every way fitted for the position he was given; who was loved and respected by all his men and all that knew him, and a gentleman in the true sense of the word." The scouts that operated with him before Gen. Averell assumed charge of the brigade, were Sergt. A. B. Hammer and J. W. Willhide of Company B, Second Virginia, J. Paul Jones Fifty-fifth Ohio, and others, and the following civilians, names familiar to the men of our brigade and regiment: John Dove, Abe Hinkle, George Sexton, Lee Farnum and Dr. Scott Harter, brave, loyal, efficient scouts, worthy of all praise and honor for their service. These were the men who held the dangerous position of scouts, until Gen. Averell came to us, and whatever service was done in the period before that time by our scouts, the credit belongs to them.

Soon after taking command of the Fourth Separate Brigade, Gen. Averell called for a body of scouts, the following men being appointed from our regiment: C.W.D. Smitley, J. W. Willhide, Alexander Watts, Marshall Bailey, Nelinza L. Lock, Company B; Timothy Sharer, M. G. Markins, William Shirley, Company H; Robert Gaddis, Company K; nine in all. In addition to these there were Geo. W. Mooney and Jack Saylor, from the Third Virginia, and others from the Tenth Virginia Infantry, First Virginia Cavalry and Fourteenth Pennsylvania Cavalry, but whose names are not known, many of them being remembered only by their nicknames. All of them, of whatever regiment, were brave, noble, true men. Comrade Smitley says of his own regimental associates in particular, that they were "kind, considerate, obedient and reliable; and braver, truer, more loyal men never lived. I never knew one of them to flinch from duty, or give me an unkind word." He always speaks in the highest terms of all his associates, in this dangerous work.

C.W.D. Smitley was born June 6, 1838, in Cumberland, Md., moved to Bedford, Pa., when two years old, thence to Stoystown and Johnstown, Pa.,

CHAPTER XVIII.

and at the age of 21 settled with his father at Boothville, Marion county, West Va., where he was living at the breaking out of the rebellion. He and his father both voted against the ordinance of secession of their State. He attempted to raise a company for the Union service in Marion county, but the sentiment was so hostile in the locality that he was compelled to desist, and he went to Grafton and joined Capt. Latham's Company B. At the time of enlisting, Mr. Smitley was a millwright. One of his brothers, E. F. Smitley, served as one of his scouts while with Gen. Averell, and afterwards, with a younger brother, Robert P. Smitley, volunteered in Capt. Donehoo's company of the Sixth West Virginia Cavalry. They were both taken prisoners at New Creek, West Va., in the fall of 1864, and were so reduced by starvation and sickness on Belle Island, that they died immediately after getting home. Mr. Smitley made many a valuable capture during his long and eventful service of four and a-half years, but he says the best capture he ever made was a good Methodist woman at Boothville, November, 1863 - his faithful wife. In August, 1861, being on the return from a scout with A. B. Hammer, near Beverly, he was thrown from his horse, one foot remaining fast in the stirrup. The horse dragged him several rods, tramping on his left side, and broke loose from him, breaking two of his ribs. Late in October, 1861, being on a scout with A. B. Hammer, he was compelled to swim a swollen, rapid mountain stream, called Roaring Creek, to escape capture by the enemy. Not being entirely recovered from the injury to his left side, cold and exposure caused him to have typhoid fever. The company at the time was stationed at Belington, and there being no hospital near, Capt. Latham sent him in an ambulance to his father's house in Boothville. In May, 1863, while acting guide for a battalion of the Fifth West Virginia Cavalry, Maj. McNally commanding, near Franklin, he was fired on by bushwhackers, receiving a wound in his left forearm and left clavicle. On their return to camp, Mrs. Laura J. Arnold had him taken to her house and took care of him until our forces were driven out of Beverly by the enemy. On the 11th of May, 1864, Scout "Spike" Harris, First Virginia Cavalry, was shot through the heart, and Smitley was taken prisoner near Wardensville. In October, 1864, he was taken unconscious to College Hospital, Columbia, S. C., and had a long spell of fever. About December, 1864, he was removed to Asylum prison, and lacking proper clothing, shelter and food, was much exposed to the cold, causing him to have rheumatism, which has become chronic, and for twenty-six years has been a sufferer from it. He finally escaped and joined Sherman just as he was entering Columbia, S.C. He is now living at Burlington, Ohio, in the enjoyment of the respect and confidence of all that know him, surrounded by his family of ten children, seven boys and three girls.

John W. Willhide was born December 16, 1839, in Frederick county, Md. His grandfather came from Germany in the year 1778. His father, William Willhide, was born in eastern Maryland, and was married to Harriet Darcy.

The union was blessed with seven children, six boys and one girl. He moved to Western Virginia in the year 1856, where he resided until his death. He was a carpenter by trade. John W. still remained in Maryland, where he learned the wagon making trade, and in the year 1859 he went to Webster, Western Va., where he started a wagon shop. He had but fairly got started, when the excitement over secession aroused the people. Then the call for troops followed, and Mr. Willhide was among the first to cast his lot with the friends of the Union, joining Company B. He served out his term of three years faithfully, most of the time being in the secret service, and while in this service was wounded in the left hip, the full circumstances of which are given in one of the expeditions, in this article. At the close of his service he returned to Webster and started a wagon shop, which he has followed ever since. In the year 1870 he married Caroline Adams, their union being blessed with three children, two boys and one girl. He has been elected Justice of the Peace in his town for the last twelve years. He is a member of the M. E. Church, having been connected with that society for 24 years. A brave soldier and a true citizen.

Robert Gaddis is of Irish birth and parentage, having come to this country with his parents before he was nine years of age. His early life was passed like that of other country lads, and nothing eventful occurred in his life until just before the secession movement began to take form. He left home before Christmas, 1860, and found his way to Parkersburg, W.Va., where he was when companies began to form to suppress the rebellion. He was naturally of a bold, reckless disposition, and found congenial work in the excitement of the time, becoming a member of Company K, of which he was appointed a corporal. He was a brave soldier, a true son of his native country, and as true, noble, and loyal one of his adopted country. He now lives at Newbern, Ind., an honored citizen.

Marshall Bailey was born in Taylor county, Va., March 10, 1843, his father being engaged in farming. In the summer he worked on the farm and attended school during the winter. He read history a great deal and became so interested in the early struggles of his country, and so imbued with the military spirit, that he acquired a strong desire to be a soldier. The opportunity came with the breaking out of the rebellion, and he became a member of Company B, at the early age of 18. He served faithfully during his term of three years, was one of the most active of the scouts, and received his discharge in the summer of 1864, retiring with credit and a most honorable record. He attended school during 1865 and 1866, and engaged in teaching, following that calling until he was married, March 30, 1868. He then returned to the farm, and has since been engaged in that occupation. He has two sons and one daughter. In 1878 he removed to a farm in Harrison county, where he is an honored citizen, attending to all the duties of civil life as faithfully as he did those of military life.

CHAPTER XVIII.

Moses Golden Markins, of Company H, was born in Brown county, Ohio, and before enlisting was a farmer. His tragic death is related in one of the scouting expeditions. He was a noble hearted man, fearless and tried, and his death was a great grief to his comrades. He left a wife and four children.

Timothy Sharer, of Company H, was a brave, loyal, intelligent scout, who never failed in the trying hour of duty. He was killed in a hand to hand encounter with Mosby's men, the odds ten to one against him, near Bunker Hill, in the summer of 1864, as related by Lee Farnum, the celebrated scout, who was an eye witness of the affair.

Nelinza L. Lock, Company B, a true soldier, loyal to the heart, was daring and faithful scout, one that could be trusted in any emergency. While in swift pursuit of a Confederate cavalryman on the Droop Mountain expedition, when almost in reach of the man, his horse fell among some rocks, causing a dangerous wound in his head, from which he died at his father's home in Webster, W. Va., January 5, 1865, aged 24 years and 7 months. He was an upright young man, liked and respected by all. He is interred in the National Cemetery at Grafton, W. Va.

William Shirley, a boy of 19 when he enlisted, entered the service at Ironton, O., with Company H. He was detailed as one of Smitley's scouts, and served with his country as a true soldier, meeting the demands of duty whenever the call came.

Alex. Watts, a brave Western Virginian, enlisted in Company B, and was a true, good man and brave soldier.

It is not possible in a work like this, giving the history of an entire regiment, to give in full, or in detail, sufficient to show the great service of these scouts. It would require a volume of itself, and a very large one, to do that; but in order to give some fair idea of the perils, hardships and dangers encountered by our scouts, a few of their adventures are given in the succeeding pages.

After the battle at McDowell, in May, 1862, between Gen. Milroy's Brigade and Stonewall Jackson's force, and we had joined Gen. Fremont at Franklin, Smitley was sent out to watch Jackson's movements. Fremont's "Jessie Scouts" believed that the enemy were menacing our front with a view of again attacking us. Smitley left alone and went as far back as McDowell, and then went to within nine miles of Staunton where he learned that Jackson had gone down the Shenandoah Valley. He joined some Confederate scouts, passed himself off as a Western Virginia refugee, went down the valley to Willow Springs, where he left the scouts and returned up the valley, retraced his steps to Monterey, then to Franklin, reporting his observations to Gen. Fremont, by which time Jackson had attacked Gen. Banks. It was while returning from this scout that Smitley had one of his most lively adventures. When he arrived at Monterey, early in the morning, and very much, worn out, he called on Mrs. James Whitelaw, a true friend of the Union, for something to eat, and to rest for an hour. He was told that the Confederate cavalry were expected every moment. After eating a hearty meal, her negro boy, by the name of Henry Madison, was set to watch for the coming of the enemy, while Smitley took a needed rest. He had barely closed his eyes when the boy came running up stairs shouting, "Massa, de rebs is comin." Looking out of the window toward the court house he could see the Staunton pike, one-fourth mile from town, and sure enough there came a company of cavalry. A boy ran out of town and met them, and their yell and the speed of their horses, convinced him that he was reported. Picking up his revolver and leaving his breech-loader in the room, he ran out through the garden and stable and crawled along a little hog path, under some thick, small laurel, within a few rods of the stable, and before he had scarcely time to get under this rather insecure cover, the cavalry were all around him. Every moment Smitley thought their horses would tramp on him, but he hugged the ground closer than he ever did before in his life. The thick laurel proved a safe refuge, and in a few hours the search ceased. In the afternoon he heard a negro boy singing near him. It proved to be Mrs. Whitelaw's boy, who had watched him hide, and he came close to where the scout lay, and told him as he passed, to lie still until midnight, and passed on without stopping. About 11 o'clock that night, Mrs. Whitelaw and the negro boy came to him, and brought him something to eat, and the rifle which he had left in the room. They walked a few hundred yards further from town, and sitting down on a log, Mrs. Whitelaw told him that the cavalry had gone towards Franklin, leaving a small squad as picket, on the Beverly pike near town. It was a bright starlight night, but no moon. In a few minutes Smitley noticed a boy pass near them into a ravine, running up towards the mountain. Smitley got behind him and followed as swiftly as he could, coming within a few steps of the boy before he heard him, and as he turned, Smitley's revolver was full in his face, and he was compelled to throw up his hands and march to the scout. He had seen the boy frequently before, whose name was Fleming, and about 14 years old. He knew Smitley's occupation, and the latter charged him with reporting him to the cavalry, which he did not deny. Mrs. Whitelaw fearing the boy would be killed, begged that his life be spared, though she knew it might cost her life for harboring a spy. She freely staked her life on the boy's word of honor that he would not betray her, and he never did. After guiding Smitley safely around the pickets, he was released on his honor, and the scout reached his camp in safety.

About the 10th of June, Smitley was sent out to observe the movement of the enemy, taking with him John Dove. In flanking the enemy, and while going through a little cove in the mountain, in the direction of and about twenty miles from Brock's Gap, they stopped for dinner; but before they had the pleasure of dining, they came near tasting of rations not nearly so palatable. A notorious bushwhacker by the name of Wilson, with a number of his men,

CHAPTER XVIII.

burst unceremoniously into the house. Wilson advanced to within a yard of where Smitley sat, placed his double barreled shot gun against his breast, both barrels cocked, and with the most terrible oaths, informed Smitley that he was a Yankee spy, and that he intended to blow his heart out. The fellow's eyes glared like a tiger's, and his countenance was that of an arch demon, while he shrieked in his anger and hate. Smitley looked him calmly but firmly in the eye, with a cynical smile on his face, till the fellow's eyes dropped, when in a fearless, firm tone he spouted, "Coward, base villainous coward"; and then pointing to his insignia of rank, denoting that he was a Confederate officer, assured the cowed wretch in a calm manner, that they were nothing but what they represented themselves to be. The man was somewhat chagrined, as Smitley threatened him with punishment for his threats. They all then sat down together and partook of a very good dinner, after which the valiant bushwhacker showed the scouts a near way to Brock's Gap, accompanying them several miles.

After escaping from Wilson, Smitley and Dove went by way of Franklin, thence to Circleville, and from there about six miles further up the river, where Dove's brother lived, who was a miller. When they entered the house they found one of Capt. Elsie's "Dixie Boys," who seemed much frightened, and in a few minutes left and went to some of his comrades at the mill, a short distance from the house. Dove and his brother not having seen each other for several years, entered into conversation, during which they were brought to a realizing sense of their danger, by a noise outside, and upon examination saw that they were surrounded. Smitley called to the "Johnnies" that they need not be afraid of them, as they were only two, and invited them in, assuring them they wouldn't be hurt. This bit of levity put them in a good humor, and they accepted the invitation. Smitley undertook to convince the visitors that they were Jackson's scouts, but they were suspicious, when Smitley asked them if they were not Capt. Elsie's "Dixie Boys." They said they were, when the scout asked them to take him to the captain, and he would convince them that he was all right. To Smitley's disgust and disappointment, they took him at his word, and immediately started to camp. The two scouts were both mounted, and were permitted to retain their arms, though closely guarded on both sides. Toward dusk they neared Capt. Elsie's camp, Smitley all the while studying how to avoid meeting the captain. On the way they had to cross a creek, and the guards were required to go over a foot log, while the scouts rode through the stream on horseback. When the guards were all on the log, and were in poor situation to handle themselves, Smitley and Dove put spurs to their horses and made a dash down the stream. As quickly as possible the guards turned their guns upon the scouts and fired, one of the bullets striking Dove, who fell from his horse. He had sat upright on his horse and made a good mark, while Smitley leaned to the side of his horse away from the guards, and thus escaped, but his horse was struck, though not disabled, and on he went at a rapid rate down the stream. The guards followed, firing as they went, but doing no damage. As he neared Capt. Elsie's camp, on a narrow piece of road between the creek and the mountain, he leaped from his horse, dropping one of his revolvers, and clambered up the hillside. Soon the guards had his horse and revolver, and were planning for his capture, but by this time it was quite dark, and he kept on to the summit of the mountain, and there spent the night, keeping out of range of the enemy. At daylight he observed that he was but a few miles from where he had his exciting experience with the "Dixie Boys." He then started for Petersburg, and probably about 9 o'clock in the morning came to an open place in the woods on the ridge, and thinking there might be a path across there, he stopped and listened. Hearing nothing he started to walk rapidly across the open space, and was about half way when a noise attracted his attention, and looking down toward the river, saw at first a woman on horseback ascending by a mountain path, and close behind her followed six of the "Dixie Boys," some of them the very ones from whom he had escaped. It was raining quite hard by this time, and they trudged along with their guns shouldered, hunter fashion, their slouch hats dripping with wet. At the sight of the woman he stopped suddenly and stood like a statue, eyeing the little procession, holding his revolver, intending to fire as soon as discovered. The path which they were following made a circuitous course around where Smitley was standing, and was not more than 50 or 60 feet from him. He was caught wholly unawares, and was amazed, and as well frightened, but eyed the men closely, expecting every moment that some one of them would look in his direction and discover him. But from the depressing influence of the rain, and the long toilsome night racing after Smitley, they all passed by without noticing him, though he was a prominent object standing in the open space. He hurried out of the open space and into the woods, and proceeded as well as he could on his way to Petersburg. When in the neighborhood of the Harman settlement, he met a deserter from the Confederate army, by the name of Martin Bennett, who persuaded him to stop at his mother's house, and said he would accompany Smitley to Petersburg. They reached the house at dusk, and had been there but a few minutes when a little child rushed into the house saying, "The rebs are riding down the road." They ran out from the back of the house and hid in a field of grain, and lay there until the visitors left. They searched the house but gave it up after a while and left. When they were gone, the fugitives returned to the house, ate their supper and started on their journey. They followed the river, avoiding the road as much as possible, and stopped at the Carr settlement all night. The next morning they safely reached Petersburg, where the scout reported to the general by telegraph.

After reporting from Petersburg, and while awaiting orders from the general, Col. S. W. Downey, commanding the post, tendered Smitley his

CHAPTER XVIII.

valuable private horse, an iron grey of great speed and powers of endurance, and requested him to scour the country between Petersburg, Brock's Gap and Moorefield, and ascertain the movements of the enemy. He left Petersburg in company with Q. M. Sergt. J. Paul Jones, Fifty-fifth Ohio, and rode in the direction of Brock's Gap, falling in with some of the enemy's cavalry, learning their intention to surround and capture our telegraph station and commissary stores, at the ford of the river below Moorefield, which was guarded by a part of two companies of Col. Downey's regiment, the Third Maryland Infantry. Smitley and Jones excused themselves to get something to eat, promising to join the cavalry at Moorefield. As soon as they were out of sight, they rode rapidly to the ford, intending to report to Col. Downey by telegraph. The operator told them that communication was cut off with both Petersburg and New Creek. Smitley then went to the lieutenant commanding the post, apprised him of his danger, and advised him to move into the woods, and when the Confederates had the empty camp surrounded, give them a dose of the kind of medicine they gave us - bushwhacking. He replied with an oath that he knew his own business, and the scouts returned to the telegraph office, a tent on the river bank, where they got a substantial supper. Hitching the horses convenient for speedy use, Smitley went to sleep, resting until near morning, when hearing a commotion in camp, he sprang to his feet. A messenger from the lieutenant commanding met him, saying that a flag of truce had come in with the information that they were surrounded by Col. Harness' cavalry, demanding immediate surrender, and wanting to know what the scout thought about it. Smitley mounted his horse, told the messenger to tell the lieutenant he knew his own business, and, with Jones, rode part round the enemy's lines, near enough for them to see the grey clothes and mistake the scouts for their own men. Finding a weak place in their ranks on the road to Mr. Van Meter's, Smitley and Jones made a dash for liberty, and had passed several rods beyond their lines, before they took in the situation. A few of them pursued, but soon gave it up, after firing several shots, which the scouts escaped by lying flat on their saddles. The horses being saddled all night, the girths were quite loose, and Jones' saddle turned and was lost while the horses were at full speed. He was compelled to ride fifteen miles bare-back, a great hardship to him, as he was a large, fleshy man. Smitley and Jones were the only ones that escaped. Smitley left Jones at New Creek, turned Col. Downey's horse over to the quartermaster, and started for Front Royal, arriving early on the third morning after leaving New Creek, and reported to Gen. R. C. Schenck.

Miss Belle Boyd, who later acquired considerable notoriety as a southern spy, was at Front Royal on parole. Being suspected of violating her parole, one of Gen. Schenck's aids requested Smitley to see if he could entrap her. He went to one of the prominent southern citizens of the village under an assumed name, and representing himself to be a paroled Confederate officer, secured boarding. The host was exceedingly hospitable and communicative, informing him that Miss Boyd was in town. Smitley affected surprise and eulogized her valuable services to the southern cause. He soon learned that Miss Boyd was the sensation of the village, that the intensely loyal Confederates idolized her, and that she had a large following of Federal officers, who were ready to do her homage. Smitley's advent to the inside circles of the village, and his expressed admiration of Miss Boyd's exploits as a spy, were carried to her by his host's daughter, and the same afternoon he received an invitation through the daughter, to take tea with the fair scout, at one of the southern residences. He went, was introduced, and found her to be a lady of culture, a brilliant conversationalist, expert with the piano and rather pretty. In the course of the evening, a number of young ladies called, accompanied by Federal officers, and Miss Boyd appeared to be the centre of attraction. Toward the officers Smitley assumed a lofty, patronizing air, but with the ladies was exceedingly bashful and diffident. When the doxology of the occasion, "The Bonny Blue Flag," was being sung and played by Miss Boyd, he stepped forward and sang the bass, with all the feeling and power of his strong voice, though his heart burned within him to sing "Down with the Traitors and up with the Stars." This effort settled his social status with the Confederates, and thereafter he was one of the "charmed circle." He stayed in the village several days as Lion No. 2, and secured Miss Boyd's confidence to such an extent, that she informed him boastingly of the manner in which she was violating her parole, and urged him not to consider a parole binding to the much hated Yankees. About the third evening of his stay, at an evening party, a Federal officer in the secret of Smitley's identity, to whom Miss Boyd turned a cold shoulder, became so incensed at her marked attention to the scout, that he tauntingly told her that Smitley was a Yankee scout. She scornfully resented the accusation against his loyalty, but a night's reflection on the situation brought her early in the morning to Smitley, greatly agitated and shedding tears like a child. Her informant was the staff officer who requested Smitley to entrap her.

While Pope's army was in camp near Culpepper Court House, Va., the Shenandoah valley now being left open to the Confederate army from Staunton to Winchester, C.W.D. Smitley and John W. Willhide were sent out as scouts, to watch any movements of the enemy in the valley. They were furnished with paroles as though Confederate soldiers, and permitted to go home to await exchange. At a little town about 18 miles southeast of Winchester, there were stationed some four or five companies in command of a colonel, where they received some valuable information. They found no trouble here, but got into serious difficulty near Strasburg, where the scouts were recognized as being with the Union army when it passed through there but a short time before. The alarm was given, and a chase began for Winchester, where Union troops were stationed. Willhide's horse was failing fast from the long chase, but he

CHAPTER XVIII.

saved himself by changing horses with a little negro boy, who was going to the mill. Quite a number of shots were exchanged during the chase. They finally succeeded in getting within our lines. They remained in the valley several days, and receiving news of the battle of Cedar Mountain, and the subsequent falling back of our army from the Rapidan, they started for Staunton, thence by way of the Staunton and Fairmont pike for Beverly. On the way they were expecting to come on the rebel pickets, and at one place, (it was dark, just before daylight), they stopped to rest at the roadside. Willhide sat on a dark object which proved to be a rotten log, in which was a lively yellow jacket's nest. In a moment Willhide was attacked by the ferocious insects, and being stung severely, he jumped and yelled. That moment there was a blaze of muskets in that direction, for indeed they were right on the rebel pickets, but in the darkness the scouts were able to escape. Otherwise they found no difficulty until they reached Crab Bottom, where they found about a regiment of Confederates in camp, and lay there within 500 yards of the camp from before daylight until 2 p.m. After securing all the information they could, they left the pike and took to the mountains for a distance of about 20 miles. After leaving the pike they met several Confederate foraging parties who supposed the scouts were in the same business. Striking the pike again at Greenbrier river, near Camp Baldwin, a measure of safety was felt, but they had not gone far up Cheat Mountain until they found that there were some Confederate soldiers in their front, and not far ahead of them. There being no other way to get across the mountains, they decided to take their chances and go ahead. Passing up the mountain a short distance, there were indications that others had joined the soldiers, and that the force was fully 100 men. Some distance ahead of this, the scouts discovered the men, who were cooking their suppers in the road where there was a short bend, having their guns stacked. Riding slowly until near the party, a stir was made, among them to get their guns, and the scouts made a dash right through the party. Many of the Confederates had to get out of the way hurriedly to avoid being run over, and the others failed to get their guns until the scouts passed them, but in a moment, almost, the bullets began to fly thick and fast, and kept pouring into the retreating scouts until they got out of range, one striking Willhide, passing through his hip, and another hitting his horse in the neck, but the horse was not hurt much, and could still travel. The continuous fast riding and the loss of blood made Willhide very weak, but they did not dare stop, and rapidly rode to the summit of the mountain. Here Smitley dismounted and dipped up water in his hat for Willhide to drink, as he could not dismount. They then went to the White house at Cheat Mountain pass, and Smitley left Willhide here and went ahead to make some arrangements to get his comrade to Beverly. At the pass they met three men who had been north for some purpose, and were then going home, who took Willhide in the house and cared for him until the next day about 12 o'clock. It was here learned that the Confederates were Capt. Marshall's company, which was raised in the Beverly valley. During this time, Smitley was trying to get to Beverly, and had great difficulty with the pickets, who at first refused to let him through the line or take him to Beverly; and orders were given that if they were fired on that night, to kill him. Smitley knowing that the Confederates were on the road coming that way, was very uneasy, as he knew that they might be fired on at any time. The night passed without an attack, and the next morning he was taken to Beverly, where he was known by Col. Harris, who was in command. That officer sent some cavalry out after Willhide, who brought him in, it being twenty-four hours from the time he was shot, until his wounds were dressed. He was taken to Mrs. Jonathan Arnold's residence, and this noble Union and Christian woman nursed and cared for him like a mother. To her Willhide, as well as the others of his regiment, owes a debt of gratitude that can never be paid.

About the time of Gen. Milroy's last trip to Beverly, Smitley and George Sexton were sent to Crab Bottom to learn the truth about a report that the Confederate government was herding a large lot of cattle there. On returning they met, near Franklin, Capt. C. T. Ewing, of the Second Virginia, with his company, equipped as mounted infantry, accompanied by the brave and efficient scout, Abe Hinkle, on their way to destroy the saltpetre works of the enemy, two miles south of Franklin. The captain asked the two to join him for a short time, which they did. Smitley had learned that there was a small squad of Confederates loitering about Gen. Boggs', in Franklin, all of whom knew Smitley. He told the captain of the facts, and asked him for some men whom he would lead by a short and unfrequented road in the rear of Gen. Boggs' house and capture the squad. The captain did not think it prudent to divide his men so Smitley and Sexton concluded to go alone. Capt. Ewing was to come in on the north side of the town, on the main road, as rapidly as he could, while the two scouts were to secure a position in a deep gulch on the west side of town, immediately in the rear of Boggs' residence, on the route by which they supposed the Confederates would try to escape. They rode swiftly in order to get in position before Capt. Ewing would enter the town. When within a hundred yards of the gulch, being on higher ground than the town, they saw Ewing within a few hundred yards of town, horses at full speed, and women, children and negroes running in every direction over town. The scouts dashed into the gulch, about 150 yards in the rear of Boggs' where a small outbuilding and large barn concealed from their view the enemy, until almost in the midst of them. Both discovered them almost at the same instant, their horses at full gallop, Smitley being under cover of the buildings, while Sexton, in the excitement of the occasion, rode right among them, when he tried to convince them that he was one of their scouts. They were too sharp for that, having recognized Smitley at first glance, and would have fired instantly

CHAPTER XVIII.

but for the commotion in town and this dash in the rear. Smitley, though he felt personally safe until Ewing should come, knew that unless something was done instantly they would kill Sexton. He dismounted, and, leading his horse, walked right into the group, addressed Boggs, son of the general, and informed him that they were surrounded, and that there would be less danger in surrendering to two men than to a regiment. With a terrible oath he sprang toward Smitley and, placing his revolver against his temple, demanded to know which way our forces were coming. While trembling with affected fear, Smitley stuttered and stammered, but could not speak, but pointed in the direction they had come. They started, with the scouts as prisoners, to reach the timber, but before they reached the river they were met and surrounded by Capt. Ewing's men and all were captured. The return to our lines was afterward effected in safety.

In October, 1863, Gen. Averell wanted a scouting party to go to Monterey valley, to ascertain about what force the enemy had there, and if they were making preparations to move. Chief Smitley detailed John W. Willhide, Robert Gaddis, Moses G. Markins and John Sallyards for the work. There was a Union force under Capt. Powell, of about 100 men, on picket 12 miles from Beverly, at the base of Cheat Mountain, and the general gave the scouts an order on Capt. Powell, to escort them over the mountains. On the opposite side of Cheat Mountain stood the remains of an old house, commonly known as the "Gumhouse," a dangerous place for the lonely scout, and a few miles beyond it, at Green Bank, was a Confederate camp, and they always aimed to waylay any scouting parties that came along, and close their service for all time, hence the escort. All went well until the escort turned homeward. Marshall and Waumsley's guerillas observed them pass into the little Greenbrier Valley, and prepared an ambush for their return. Between the Gum House and Cheat river, near what the old Second knew as the Deadening, they felled trees across the road; and the escort, led by the intreped Markins, in dusk of evening, just as they made a short turn in the road, a very difficult place to flank, were immediately in front of the blockade, when they discovered it, and instantaneously with the discovery came a volley from the bushwhackers. Markins in the advance, was most exposed, and, as he afterward related, fell the first volley. The escort, not wholly unprepared, fired at the flash of the enemy's guns, and literally hewed their way through the enemy and around the blockade, almost at the identical spot where Willhide, on a former occasion, had received the terrible wound in his hip. Strange to relate, they all returned to camp but the brave scout. The day following, the General ordered a company of cavalry to go to the place of ambush and search for the scout. It being dark on their arrival, they did not find him, though it seemed passing strange, as he lay in the middle of the road, just where he fell from his horse, until return of scouts over fifty hours later. Markins says the enemy came to him the next day and he begged them for God's sake to raise him up and give him water, which they refused with an oath. The other scouts went forward unaware of the terrible fate that had befallen their brave comrade, and reached the home of a Union man in the early part of the night, where they put up for the night. About 3 o'clock in the morning they were wakened for breakfast, the good woman of the house having prepared an excellent one. They had just sat down to eat when they heard some one shouting, "get out, get out," at the top of his voice, which arrested all further proceedings. The family had intended to go to Monterey that morning, had risen early for that purpose, and had sent their boy out to what they called a hacking, to get the horses. The boy saw some Confederates approaching the house, and gave the alarm. The scouts jumped to their feet at once, rushed out of the house, and lay down in some brush, where they concealed themselves the best they could. In a few minutes the house was surrounded by the enemy, demanding the surrender of the scouts, the latter being so close that they could hear every word that was said. The woman of the house denied that any scouts were in the house, and when asked why the boy had given such an alarm, replied that they were going to mill that day and had to get up early, and the boy was calling them out. They threatened to burn the house if she did not tell, but she stoutly denied having seen any scouts. They then hunted everywhere for them, and even tore up the floor, which was made of puncheons. After a fruitless search they very reluctantly left. The scouts remained in hiding all day, and during the time noted many items of information of value. The Confederates then returned to their camp rather crest fallen. About 11 o'clock that night, the scouts started on their return tramp, having received considerable information of value from their friends. They slept part of the night, resuming their journey the next day. Toward evening they came near a house, in front of which two horses, saddled and bridled were standing. They naturally concluded that the riders must be inside, and the chances for a tempting prize were good. Willhide suggested that they undertake the capture of both men and horses, which was agreed to. They slipped up to the side of the house, the typical log structure of the mountains, cautiously went to the door, which was shut, drew their revolvers ready for use, and then pulled the latch string, and there sat two southern cavalrymen, talking to two girls. The scouts made themselves known, disarmed the soldiers, and taking them with them hurried away, as they wanted to reach Greenbrier river by dark, which they did, and again started to climb Cheat mountain. To pass the old "Gum House" was now their greatest danger, and Gaddis proposed to take the advance while the other two followed with the prisoners and horses. The night was dark, and the prospects none the brightest. Gaddis was to fire his revolver if he came on any great danger. He passed the old house in safety, when coming to a bend in the road, he saw some dark objects in front of him. While examining closely to ascertain what the objects

CHAPTER XVIII.

were, he heard his name called, which was repeated, and upon inquiring who called, the answer came, "Oh Bob, I am shot." Gaddis then recognized him as the brave, faithful, Markins, who had received his death wound as stated. His piteous cry for help rang in Gaddis' ears for months afterward. The scouts went on to camp, turned over their prisoners, and an ambulance was sent for Markins, who died soon afterward.

On the return from Salem, while in camp the first night out, about 3 or 4 o'clock in the morning, Smitley detailed Gaddis, Sharer and George Mooney, to ride to New Castle about eight miles ahead, to see a doctor there, who was a Union man, and get from him information in regard to the movements of the enemy. They reached their destination about daybreak, rode up to the doctor's house and made known to him their business. He told them to get out of that as quickly as possible, and pointing across the town said there is a major and twenty-five men. As he spoke some of the gray coats appeared, and the scouts moved away, with the Confederates following. Soon it was a chase for capture or freedom, some of the horsemen coming out of the different streets, and dashing rapidly after the retreating scouts, called upon them to surrender, but that was something not to be thought of. Firing began, and it was now only a question of endurance of men and horses, as a fight between equal numbers was out of the question. The scouts dashed down the river, being unable to cross it, until they came to a very narrow road, which terminated in a bluff that ran out into the river. They were hemmed in by a mountain on one side and the Confederates on the other, and there was no escape, and they prepared to sell their lives as dear as possible. They knew it was death to be captured, and they preferred to die fighting rather than die as prisoners. They dismounted, drew their Henry rifles, and as the enemy came in range let them have the best they could from their trusty guns. This checked them for a few minutes, and then the firing became general, but even that must come to an end, as the scouts were outnumbered eight or ten to one, and were almost out of ammunition. Soon a loud shouting and cheering was heard from the opposite side of the river, and there came a body of Averell's brave boys, just in the nick of time, and at once opened fire on the now frightened Confederates. The firing had attracted their attention and they surmised what was wrong and came hastily to the aid of the hard pressed scouts. Now the chase took another form, and the Confederates were driven back to the town, the scouts charging them with vigor, driving them through the alleys and across lots, and succeeded in capturing all of the party, with the help of their relief, except the major and a few of his men. The general and his command soon came up, and went into camp.

Desiring information of the condition of affairs ahead of him, Gen. Averell here sent out Gaddis, Sharer and Mooney, to ascertain all they could. The order was to go to the top of a mountain, some three miles distant, and see if any of the enemy were in sight. All went well until they got near the top of the mountain, when they met a body of twenty-five or thirty Confederates, who were distant about 150 yards. Although dressed in Confederate uniforms, it availed the scouts nothing, as their enemy opened fire on them at once. The scouts wheeled their horses and started to run, but it was evident they were in close quarters. Gaddis rode a horse that he had captured, an animal of worth, that had carried him through many a hard scrape, and he told his associates to ride on as fast as they could, and as their pursuers came around a bend in the mountain, he would give them a few shots and check them. Looking up the mountain, he saw several Confederates riding at the top of their horses' speed, aiming to get ahead of him on the road. The one in the lead was a large, red faced man, with long red whiskers parted in the middle, and was a wild, daring, fearless looking fellow, mounted on a large black horse. Just as Gaddis passed the road this man came down and fired at him, and Gaddis at him, but neither checked his horse for a moment. Now it was a race down the mountain road, and no race course ever afforded so exciting a chase. Gaddis' pursuer was not more than ten steps behind him, and he in turn was followed by his men, all in hot pursuit, and shooting every chance they got. The Confederate called on Gaddis to halt, who replied with a shot, and in turn the Confederate bullets whistled all around him. They soon emptied their revolvers, and Gaddis' only safety now lay in the swiftness and endurance of his horse; but it was worn with the terrible work of the campaign and soon the Confederate began to gain on him, and drawing his saber, prepared to use it on the brave scout. He is close by the side of Gaddis, has raised his saber for the fatal blow, when Confederate and Union scout, together, rush into the midst of a body of Union soldiers. Gaddis called out hastily to his comrades to shoot the man, and willing hands send leaden messengers after him as he dashed up the road, but none seemed to hit him, and he escaped. After the general had sent out the scouts, he sent a picket post of ten men, who were the means of saving the lives of the hard pressed scouts.

When Gen. Averell's command reached Huntersville, on the return from the Salem raid, it became necessary to send out some of the scouts to mislead Imboden's forces, who were trying to cut our brigade off on the retreat to Beverly. Rob't Gaddis, Will Shirley and Geo. Mooney were selected for the dangerous work. Their instructions were to start up the valley, ride all night, and scatter the news far and wide that they were Echols' men sent to Imboden to tell him that Averell was coming up the valley, and to be prepared to intercept him, while Echols would press Averell closely. Having done this, the scouts were to take the nearest route to Beverly. The three brave men started on their mission after dark, rode all night and the next day until noon without any serious trouble. Occasionally they met citizens to whom they told their story. About noon they ran into a Confederate lieutenant and sixty men, who hailed the scouts and asked them to what command they belonged, while the

CHAPTER XVIII.

scouts also questioned them. The three men said they belonged to Echols' command, and told the same old story. The lieutenant said that they were there on the lookout for Averell, as they did not know exactly which road to expect him, and when told that he was coming up the valley, they were jubilant, and made the scouts take dinner with them. They fed their horses, put a shoe on Shirley's horse and were pleasant and kind. Gaddis and comrades accepted the situation and made the best of it, and when ready to start, the lieutenant sent a man with them to lead them to Imboden's camp. The guide took them past the road that led to Beverly, but when he departed they hastily rode back to the right road, put spurs to their horses and dashed toward Beverly. They were now in a section in which they had frequently scouted and knew the road well. They had gone but a short distance when they met a boy on horseback who was going to the mill. One of the scouts said he knew the boy and expressed a fear that he would be recognized, but they pulled their hats over their faces and rode past very fast, went on some distance and came to a house. They dismounted, fed their horses and went into the house, where there were a man and woman. Mooney was uneasy and restless, and the man acted as if suspicious, but the wife prepared them a meal. Mooney objected to staying and kept going to the door frequently, on the lookout. The woman had just got the meal ready, and the scouts were in the act of sitting down, when Mooney appeared with a look on his face that they well understood, when they rushed to their horses, mounted and were away on the run. Looking back they saw coming the lieutenant and his men, who had entertained them at dinner. Now came the race for life. They were about 23 miles from Greenbrier river, the day was cold, there was a deep snow on the ground, and the problem was to reach that river which, once crossed, they had a fair chance of escaping. The company fired at the scouts, when about 300 yards apart, but the bullets fell short of their aim. The fugitives made good use of their horses, but Shirley's horse soon showed signs of lameness where he had been shod, and before many miles had been gone, he had to abandon him. Coming to a spur of the Alleghenies, they went straight up the mountain side, jumped off their horses, and with gads forced the poor beasts up the mountain. Reaching the top, they could see away down in the valley, but the mountain side here was too steep for the horses to descend. Gaddis being fleet of foot, told Shirley to mount his horse, while he went afoot. The horsemen had to go a considerable distance before they reached the valley, and by the time they arrived there, Gaddis was in waiting, and mounted behind Shirley. They were now fully a mile in advance of their pursuers. A few miles further on they came to a house, and a horse hitched outside. Here the roads forked, one in the direction of camp Allegheny, now deserted, and the other to camp Bartow. They rode up to the house and shouted, when the door opened and a Confederate officer stepped out, followed by about a dozen men wearing Union overcoats.

The officer was dressed in his own uniform, and the scouts were put on their guard, and prevented from getting into serious trouble. Saluting the officer, Gaddis asked him which of the roads led to camp Bartow. The officer hesitated, when the question was repeated, an answer was given, and Gaddis said, "We are in a hurry, as Averell is coming up the valley, and we are warning all our men to get away and save themselves; the whole valley is full of them." They again put spurs to their horses, giving the officer no time to ask further questions, and rode rapidly until they came to a bend in the road, where there was another house, and five more Confederates ran out and started up the mountain side. The scouts shouted at them to get away, as Averell's men were coming, and they seemed very willing to obey. On they went until they met an old woman. They asked her if there were any more of their men out that way, to which she replied yes, at the next house down the road, where her son was. They told her about Averell coming, when she pleaded with them to hurry forward and tell her son, which they promised to do. They then asked if there were no more troops, and she said no, that all the rest were in the houses they passed. This was a grateful relief, as they had begun to think that Confederates grew on the bushes in that neck of the woods. Hurrying on, they came to the house, when the old woman's son looked out, and he was told the same old story. The scouts had made good time, and were nearing Greenbrier river, and if their horses could only hold out to Cheat Mountain, then they could cross the mountain on foot, and consider themselves safe. Soon they reached the river, which was swollen, and was a raging torrent; but it was not half so wild and dangerous as the foes behind them, so they plunged into the cold, dashing stream and were soon safe on the other side. They had no fear of the enemy crossing after them, and when about 300 yards away, they saw their pursuers coming, who galloped down to the stream, but concluded not to attempt to swim it. They fired at the scouts, when the latter waved their hats and cheered their discomfited foes, but saved their ammunition for the future, not returning the fire. They rode over Cheat Mountain to Huttonsville, where they met Union troops from Beverly, and the next day Averell's belated and worn troopers, rode into the place, safe again within our own lines.

In the winter of 1864, while Averell's command was in camp at Martinsburg, Mosby's cavalry caused considerable trouble, picking up every straggling soldier they could find and capturing our horses. The general received information that they were encamped at Winchester, but to be sure of it, he sent out six of his scouts, to ascertain the truth. It was a bitter cold evening when they went out, and they got as far as Bunker Hill, where they stopped with a family with whom they were acquainted. It was now snowing, and they concluded to wait until it ceased. After while Gaddis and Sharer concluded to go ahead, and when within four miles of Winchester, stopped at the house of an Irishman, who pretended to be a Union man. He built a fire, put the horses in the stable

CHAPTER XVIII.

and fed them, and said Mosby's men were in Winchester the previous day. About five o'clock in the morning the two scouts started for Winchester, rode up over breastworks that were on their side of the town, and saw enough to convince them that there were Confederates there in plenty. They returned to Bunker Hill, the other scouts having left with the loss of their horses. Upon the return of the party to camp, there was a good deal of chaffing about it, but the General was in no pleasant humor over it. Gaddis, Sharer and Mooney determined to get even with Mosby's bold rangers, so on the next Sunday night the three started for Bunker Hill, intending to stop at the house where there was a young lady, the house being watched by the Confederates, to capture any of the Union horses that might be hitched at the place. The scouts reached there, about 9 o'clock at night, tied their horses to the portico in front of the house, made the family go up stairs, while they watched below. They kept a good look-out, and about three o'clock in the morning they saw three horsemen ride up to a white church, which stood off to the left a short distance, going behind the building, where two of the men dismounted, while the third held the horses. The scouts had had the house entirely darkened, so they could not be seen. In the room where they were watching, was a front door and one window. Their plan was for Mooney to stand at the window, Sharer was to hold the knob of the door in his hand and keep it slightly ajar, while Mooney was to keep his hand on Sharer's shoulder. Out of this room on the north side of the house stood another small porch, and in the dark corner of it Gaddis was to crouch close, as the Confederates had to pass within ten feet of where he was. It was bitter cold and starlight, and Gaddis had taken off his boots so as to be able to give a lively chase, and his position was a rather uncomfortable one. Mooney was to watch through the window, and as they came up to cut the horses loose, he was to give Sharer a push, who was to throw open the door and fire, and then Gaddis was to jump out and shoot also. The plan worked well. The two men approached on tip toe, each having a knife in one hand and a revolver in the other, passing close by where Gaddis stood. Just as they got to the horses ready to cut them loose, Mooney shoved Sharer, who threw open the door and fired at the men, and Gaddis jumped out also and fired. They fired in turn, when the whole five engaged in the lively fusilade for a few minutes, but no one was hit, though Sharer had a very close call. The horses broke loose and ran away, and the Confederates took to their heels to get away. One was a lieutenant, who was followed by Mooney and Sharer, and the other an orderly sergeant, who was pursued by Gaddis. The lieutenant was soon killed and the horse holder escaped, but Gaddis had a serious time with his man. Both were very rapid runners, the advantage being with Gaddis, and as they ran a running fire was kept up, Gaddis firing all his loads but one. The race was kept up for about 300 yards, when Gaddis overtook his man, grabbed him, and a scuffle followed. The sergeant turned and fired at Gaddis, the ball grazing his temple, but not severe enough to draw blood, but he was stunned and fell to his knees, still holding to his man. The sergeant put the muzzle of his revolver under Gaddis' right eye, pulled the trigger, but the cap snapped, and no explosion followed. This aroused Gaddis, whose vigor returned, and the scuffle was resumed. The sergeant drew his knife but before he could use it Gaddis' revolver went off, and the man begged Gaddis not to shoot again, as he would surrender. Just then Mooney came running up, and thinking it was a struggle for life, he fired into the man, and he fell dead to the ground. The fight over, they now turned their attention to their horses, but they were nowhere to be found, until they returned to the house, where they stopped, when the young lady, Miss Amy White, rode up with the three horses, which she had gone after and secured. The scouts found $25 in greenbacks on the dead men, which they presented to Miss White for her daring and heroism. The parents of the sergeant requested his body, which was given them.

When Gen. Sigel assumed command of the forces in the Shenandoah valley, in the spring of 1864, Smitley's scouts were ordered to report to his headquarters for duty. They did so, when Smitley as chief, and Willhide, Bailey, Lock, and E. F. Smitley were retained, the rest going with General Averell to the Kanawha valley. To these General Sigel added others, among whom were two brothers from the First West Virginia Cavalry, named Harris, familiarly known as "Spike" and "Lasses." The scouts were placed under the direction of Gen. Julius Stahel. On May 10, 1864, they were ordered to report to Gen. Sigel's headquarters in Winchester. The general told Smitley he had sent 500 cavalry to Moorefield, and it being long past the time they should be heard from, and having sent several other scouts for information without any of them returning, the general felt considerable anxiety about them and inquired of him if he had a scout suitable for the emergency. All members of the old Second Virginia would understand the situation. Sending 500 cavalry over there at that time, with green scouts, meant their capture or a bad defeat; to send green scouts to see about them, meant for McNeil or Mosby to pick them up as soon as outside our lines. Smitley's scouts, that were suitable, being overworked, he offered his services. The general demurred at first, then asked how many men he wanted with him, and how soon he could make the trip. Smitley told him if the cavalry were not captured he could go to them and return in about thirty hours; if captured, he could get reliable information and return in twelve hours, and would go alone. But the general decided he must have a lieutenant and twenty-five cavalry with him. Scout "Spike" Harris had a few hours previously, complained to Smitley of fancied partiality to the old Second scouts in his details, and requested to go along the next time and he would prove he was true blue. So Smitley hunted the poor fellow up, taking him to what proved his grave. About 11 p.m., May 10th, Smitley and Harris, a lieutenant and twenty-five cavalry left Winchester, the lieutenant with written

CHAPTER XVIII.

dispatches and Smitley with oral, in case the written ones failed to go through. They were nearly all night getting outside our lines, and a little after daylight they passed through Wardensville. Soon after, coming to a stream of water, along the shore of which their road led, a short bend disclosed to them about fifteen or twenty rebel cavalry approaching, not more than 150 yards off. Harris was riding close by Smitley's side. Smitley turned, and anticipating his question, Harris said, with a suppressed oath, "we will go through them quicker than croton oil." Smitley led and sent Harris to keep the rear closed up. The enemy in sight proved a very small obstruction, as they, no doubt, felt secure in their backing. Close to their rear was a regiment of cavalry, into the midst of which the scouts plunged, horses at full speed. To say the rebels were thunder struck would be very weak language, as they literally rode some of them down, and the little squad they first met was simply whirled by them into the midst of their friends. The reader can imagine the confusion. Harris proved to be a prodigy of strength, valor and ingenuity in eluding the grasp of the enemy. In the shock, friend and foe were mixed indiscriminately. Harris, whose suit of blue was covered with one of grey, coming in contact with rebels in blue, cursed them for Yankees, and in tones of thunder, would call on them to surrender, at the same time knocking them right and left; this did not turn back or stop the fight, but they cleared their way in any manner they could, and, singular to relate, escaped in the confusion without a scratch, although pursuit was immediately instituted by the enemy. Smitley and Harris were the only ones to escape capture and they were now inside the enemy's lines; and if the reader will picture to himself a ring hunt for game, he will have the best description that could be given of their condition. Having made up their minds to return to camp with such information as they had been able to glean during the day, they halted at a farm house for supper and horse feed, so much needed. They fed their horses on the ground close to the door. Entering the room they found a bright fire in the old-fashioned fire place and sat down to wait a few moments for supper. Having carried a brace of heavy revolvers about his waist twenty-four hours, Smitley loosed his bolt and placed them on the floor by his chair. In a moment he was asleep. Harris must have remained awake, as it appeared but a moment till he, in a loud voice, called out, "the rebels are coming." Smitley was startled, and, half awake, thought Harris was hurrying him to supper, when the report of a revolver brought him to a realization of his surroundings. There was a door and window on each side of the room, and three rebels had entered the room. Harris had escaped through a door on the opposite side. As Smitley was rising from his chair, a rebel picking up his revolver off the floor, he was grazed on one temple by a bullet fired by Harris through the window. Harris made things lively until his revolvers were emptied, and then ran from the house, when he was shot through the heart and instantly killed, while Smitley was a prisoner.

CHAPTER XIX.

PRISON LIFE.

The following sketch of prison life is furnished by Jacob G. Matlick of Company B, and it so well covers the horrors and incidents of life in two of the most noted of the southern prisons, that it is used in the history of the regiment, as representing the experiences of the many comrades of our regiment, who languished in prison, some of whom gave up their lives in this horrible manner. No pen is equal to the task of portraying the suffering, the depths of despair and the horror experienced in these infamous dens, and it will not be attempted here, but a plain recital of what actually occurred will be given.

"While returning off the Salem raid in December, 1863, a detail of four men was made from Company B for provost guard, composed of Joseph M. West, Edward B. Creel, William. E. Stafford and Jacob G. Matlick, and it fell to our lot to guard the prisoners. The slow progress made by the prisoners on foot, made quite a gap between the advance and the provost guard, and the ambulances and wagon train also in the rear. The Confederates observing this weak point, and taking advantage of the darkness charged past our stragglers and ambulances, and the provost guard were fully apprised of their danger only when confronted with drawn sabers and revolvers. The four of Company B were in the rear of the line of prisoners, and were captured, though most of the others in front escaped with the prisoners in their charge. Just how many of our men were captured that night is not certainly known, but of the whole command not many beyond one hundred. The Confederates took us about a half a mile further down the river to an old shed, where we were kept until the morning of the 20th, and were then taken to a building near by and some raw beef and flour issued for our use. On the 22d we started in the direction of Staunton, arriving there the evening of the 24th, tired, hungry and foot sore.

They marched us up southwest of the depot, on a high bleak knob, facing the northwest, and the wind was blowing very hard and cold from that direction. At this point there were several stables that their cavalry had quartered their horses in the previous winter, and we thought we would get to sleep in them that night out of the cold, wind, but that was denied us. They let us lie on the bare, frozen ground, without fire, where we suffered most intensely. We endured the cold the best we could, and early on the morning of the 25th, we were put aboard the cars and sent to Richmond, the coaches being good ones. We arrived in Richmond about 8 p.m., and were put in Scott's old tobacco building. The week following they sent in the noted 'Majah Tunnah', to search us, who took from us everything he could find of value except our clothes. We were stripped naked and our clothes thoroughly overhauled. It was in that building that we had our introduction to the 'N'Yaarkers' or raiders, who infested every prison, and were almost as great a terror to the poor prisoners as their inhuman keepers. We were kept here until January 1, 1864, when we were taken to Belle Isle, and turned loose in that miserable pen, which consisted of about four acres, with an embankment thrown up around it, and a ditch on the inside which served as a dead line. We were counted off in hundreds and so numbered to draw rations. The island consisted of about ten acres opposite the upper end of Richmond. The prison was in command of one Lieut. Bossieux, a rather young man, a southerner by birth. He was assisted by two Sergeants Hight and Marks, who were very cruel, as also was the lieutenant, when angered. Outside the prison pen was a bakehouse, made of boards, the tents for the accommodation of the officers and guards, and a hospital also of tent cloth. Running from the pen was a lane enclosed by high boards, running to the water's edge. At night it was closed by a gate at the pen, and thrown open in the morning. About one half of the ten thousand prisoners there at that time had tents, and the remainder slept and lived out of doors. That memorable New Year's Night is remembered by many thousands to this day, on account of the extreme cold, and many succumbed to the grim monster that night. I was lucky enough to get in a tent by finding two comrades, James Calihan and Kidd Simpson, who were left to care for our wounded at Rocky Gap the 27th of August, and had a tent, but Stafford saved himself only by running all night up and down the street in the center of the camp. Next day we all got together and crowded into the tent, making nine in one little A tent. We had but little cover, lay on the ground, putting our feet under each other's arms to keep them from freezing. No language is adequate to convey the least conception of the awful misery and suffering endured on that island that fall and winter. We were on the island two months and eight days, and many who went on there when we did starved to death long before we left, and many were the insane caused by hunger and exposure. Men, more ghastly than death itself, were stalking around the camp, not knowing where they were

CHAPTER XIX.

wandering, with feet frozen hard. Yet we are told that we did all this for the money we got; but in the face of all the suffering we endured, with death on every hand, we were offered plenty, and freedom, if we would but renounce the old flag and join the Confederate army. We told them we would rot first, as many did, and as many more, perhaps, might as well have done, the way they have since suffered. I appeased somewhat the pangs of hunger by finding an old friend on the island, whom I knew as a former school teacher and class leader, and by the aid of the guard at the gate I got an interview with him. He visited me occasionally and brought me what he could that I needed most, and gave me some Confederate money, which helped me through the prison. If any of the boys would commit any misdemeanor, Lieut. Bossieux would not give us any rations for that day, adding misery to want, for we received only a piece of corn bread about two inches square, each day, or a pint of field pea broth, and it covered with bugs, or about two spoonsful of rice for a day's rations, and no meat, except once or twice during our stay there. So strong became the craving for animal food, that the white bull terrier belonging to Lieut. Bossieux, round and fat, was one day decoyed into a tent, a blanket was thrown over him and his throat cut, within a rod of where his master stood and then skinned and cooked into a savory meal of many hungry men. When the lieutenant learned the fate of his four footed friend, he raged and stormed with anger, and stopped our rations for a day, and meted such punishment as he could. One of the saddest scenes we saw on the island, was five poor fellows, reduced to skeletons, who burrowed under the hard crust of the sand on the southside, beside the ditch, where they could lie in the sun in day time, and at night could be out of the wind, as they had no covering. One cold morning they were found dead, and were carried out and laid to rest. We had no wood issued to us that would do any good toward warming us, the issue being about three sticks to a hundred men, and that was split up fine to do our little cooking in our quart cups, that we might chance to have to do. The sanitary commission sent a man through with some clothing, that was issued to us some time in January. I got a blanket, that did the nine much good; also a copy of the New Testament, which the boys eagerly read, and which I have yet in my possession, a priceless treasure to myself and family. We were so starved that when we tried to go to sleep at night, we dreamed of seeing great quantities of good things to eat, but when we were about to partake of them, we would awaken to find that it was merely a dream, and our hunger was intensified. Thus we suffered and endured, until the last week in February when they began to take out about five hundred prisoners at a time, and they told us they had agreed to exchange, so there was a rush to get out first, but our nine waited until the third call. On March 8th, about 10 a.m., we left the island, crossed into Richmond, and were taken to the Pemberton tobacco warehouse, where we were kept until about 4 a.m. of the 10th, when we were taken to the southside of the city and put into a lot of box cars as close as we could stand, having no room to sit or lie down. We went through Petersburg, reaching that evening a station called Gaston, in the edge of North Carolina, where we were taken out and camped in a piece of woods, and, it being fairly warm, we enjoyed a clean place to sleep. They gave us some hard tack, about enough for one meal, and it was here that I bought some meat, the first we had eaten for over two months. On the morning of the 11th we were again put into stock cars and started for the unknown to us, passing through Raleigh, thence to Charlotte, where they side-tracked us and locked us in the cars and kept us over one night. The next morning we continued our journey, passing through Columbia, S.C., to Augusta, where we were changed into box cars, and given an ear of corn to eat, and where some of the sick were sent to the hospital, one of whom had the small pox. We continued our advance until, on the night of March 15th, we reached a small station called Andersonville, Sumter County, Ga., sixty miles south of Macon, and were there taken out and marched about three-fourths of a mile southeast, and counted off into hundreds, and driven, as so many brutes, into what was known to the Confederates as Camp Sumter, and to us the hated Andersonville. We were so stiff and tired that we could scarcely walk, but when the gates of that prison closed upon us, we soon stretched ourselves on the bare ground and slept soundly. But when the fog had cleared away in the morning, we began to realize our terrible condition.

ANDERSONVILLE PRISON.

This place was one of the stations on a rudely constructed, rickety railroad, that runs from Macon to Albany, the head of navigation on the Flint river, which is 106 miles from Macon and 250 from the Gulf of Mexico. Andersonville was about sixty miles from Macon and about 300 miles from the Gulf. The camp was simply a hole cut in the wilderness. It was as remote a point from our armies then, as the Confederacy could give. The place was an immense pen about one thousand feet long by eight hundred wide, and contained about sixteen acres. The walls were formed by pine logs twenty-five feet long, two to three feet in diameter, hewn square, which were set in the ground five feet, leaving the walls twenty feet high. The logs were placed so close together as to leave no crack to see the outside world. The pen was divided in the center by a creek about three feet wide and ten inches deep, running west to east, on each side of which was a bog of slimy ooze about one hundred and fifty feet wide, in which one would sink to the waist. From this swamp the sandhills sloped north and south to the stockade. There were two entrances to the stockade, one on each side of the creek, midway between it and the ends, called the 'north gate' and the 'south gate.' These were constructed double, by building smaller stockades around them on the outside, with another set

CHAPTER XIX.

of gates. At regular intervals of about fifty feet along the top of the stockades, little perches were built on the outside, in which were the sentries, who overlooked the whole inside of the prison. When we first went there the prison was commanded by one Col. Piersons, who would nearly every day ride in and talk to us, and the guards were reasonably good, much unlike the cruel wretches that guarded us from Richmond to Augusta, who would rather run a bayonet through a Yank than eat. We received about a pint of meal per day and about two ounces of bacon. At that time there was plenty of wood in the camp, cut from the tops of the timber and hewn from the logs, which we used to make fires to cook by. With the large area of the prison and plenty of wood, we were having a fairly good time for prisoners, but the water was bad, as the stream from which we obtained it was at best but a swamp and the drainage of swamps, with all the Confederate camps on it above, and afterwards our cook house was located on it immediately above the prison.

But our good time was fast disappearing, for about March 25th Col. Piersons, with his command, was ordered to the front, and for guards they robbed both the cradle and the grave, and worse than all, they sent that frenzied old Swiss, Capt. Henry Wirz, to command us. He was a small brained, small souled, incompetent fellow, and as cowardly and cruel as he was small in all the elements of manhood. He had the respect of no one, and had the intense hatred of every prisoner. By the 10th of April our wood was exhausted and it began to get very warm in the day time, and in consequence of the heavy fogs at night, it would get very cold, so as to chill even those who were well dressed and had blankets. The diarrhea and scurvy began to be much worse, exhausting the men very fast, causing a score or more of deaths per day, out of the 12,000 prisoners then in the pen. To make our condition still worse, the raiders were robbing indiscriminately, and taking money, rations, blankets, clothing, or anything they wanted. They managed to get plenty to eat and have good clothing and blankets, so that they were strong, and being armed with clubs, could do about as they pleased, with but little resistance on the part of their victims, who were so much worn down that they were unable to cope with the scoundrels. On the 3d of July a lot of new prisoners came in, when the raiders cried out, 'fresh fish,' and attacked them. The prisoners were mostly West Virginians, and gave them a hard fight, but as usual the cut throats ran to each other's rescue and came out ahead. Complaints were made to the quartermaster about the outrages, and while he was coming in the South gate on the afternoon of the 3d, with a load of rations, a man was carried out whose head had been beaten into a jelly by the raiders. Taking in the situation, being aware of the conduct of the raiders in the past, he ordered the wagon out and said we should not have another ration, until we got the raiders out, saying he would furnish a guard to protect our men, if they would catch the scoundrels and hand them over to the guard at the gate, who would take care of them until we should rid the camp and dispose of them. Our men soon formed vigilance committees all over the camp, and armed with clubs, and protected by the guards, they soon ran down and took out all the raiders, over 100, and by dark the work was done. The morning of the 4th we drew our rations, but the best of all was that we were rid of the raiders, who were then tried by regular court martial, organized by Key, the head of the movement against the raiders, in which both sides were represented before a competent court by attorneys, and witnesses heard. Six were regularly and duly proven guilty of murder in the first degree, and were sentenced to be hanged. About thirty were found guilty of maltreatment to fellow prisoners, and were sentenced to wear a ball and chain furnished by the Confederates, while the remainder were turned loose in the camp, under the watch of the vigilance committees, which were so thoroughly organized that they kept all in peace and quiet.

The following account of the execution of the raiders, is from Comrade J. L. Ransom's diary, as written at the time, a part of which is here used: 'The morning of the 11th, lumber was brought into the prison by the guards, and near the south gate a gallows was erected for the purpose of executing the six raiders condemned to death. At about 10 o'clock they were brought in under guard by Capt. Wirz, and delivered over to the police force. Capt. Wirz then said they had been tried by our own men, and for us to do as we chose with them, and that he washed his hands of the whole matter. Their names were as follows: John Sarsfield, 144th New York; William Collins alias 'Mosby', Company D, 88th Pennsylvania; Charles Curtis, Battery A, 5th Rhode Island Artillery; Pat. Delaney, Company E, 83d Pennsylvania; A. Muir, United States Navy; and Terrence Sullivan, 72d New York. After Wirz had made his little speech, he withdrew his guards, leaving the condemned at the mercy of the enraged prisoners, who had all been more or less wronged by these men. Their hands were tied behind them, and one by one they mounted the scaffold. Curtis, who was last, a big stout fellow, managed to get his hands loose, and broke away on a run through the crowd and down toward the swamps. He reached the swamp and plunged in, trying to get over on the other side, presumably among his friends. It being very warm, he over exerted himself, and when about the middle of the swamp, he gave out and could go no further. The police started after him and waded in and helped him out. He was then led back to the scaffold and helped to mount it. All were given a chance to talk. Muir, a good looking fellow in marine dress, said he came into prison four months before, perfectly honest; and as innocent of crime as any fellow in it. Starvation, with evil companions, had made him what he was. He spoke of his mother and sisters in New York, that he cared nothing for himself, but the news that would be carried home to his friends, made him want to curse God that he had ever been born. Delaney said he would rather be hanged than live there as the most of them had to live on the allowance of rations.

CHAPTER XIX.

If permitted to steal he could get enough to eat, but as that was stopped, he would rather hang. He bade all good bye. He said his name was not Delaney, and that no one really knew who he was, therefore his friends would never know his fate, his Andersonville history dying with him. Curtis, with an oath, said he didn't care, only hurry up and not be talking about it all day, making too much fuss over a small matter. William Collins, alias "Mosby," said he was innocent of murder, and ought not to be hanged. He had stolen blankets and rations to preserve his own life, and begged the crowd not to see him hanged, as he had a wife and child at home, and for their sake to let him live. Sarsfield, made quite a speech. He had studied law at the outbreak of the rebellion, had enlisted and served three years in the army, had been wounded in battle and furloughed home. After the wound had healed, he returned, was promoted to first sergeant, and also commissioned as lieutenant, but never mustered in, being taken prisoner. He began his downward course by stealing parts of rations, gradually becoming hardened as he became familiar with the crimes perpetrated, and here he was. The others did not care to say anything. While the condemned were talking, they were interrupted by all kinds of questions and charges from the crowd, such as 'don't lay it on too thick, you villain,' 'get ready to jump off,' 'cut it short,' 'you was the cause of so and so's death,' 'less talk and more hanging,' etc. About 11 o'clock they were blindfolded, hands and feet tied, and told to get ready, when the nooses were adjusted and the plank knocked from under. 'Mosby's' rope broke and he fell to the ground with blood spurting from his ears, mouth and nose. As they were lifting him back to the scaffold he revived, and begged for his life, but it was no use, and he was soon dangling with the rest, and he died very hard. It had been a good lesson. There were still bad ones in camp, but we had the strong arm of the law to keep them in check.

During the hanging scene, the stockade was covered with rebels, who were fearful a break would be made if the raiders should try to rescue their friends. Many citizens, too, were congregated on the outside in favorable positions for seeing. Artillery was pointed at us from all directions, ready for action in short order. Wirz stood on a high platform, in plain view of the execution. After hanging for half an hour or so, the six bodies were taken down and carried outside. The raiders had many friends who crowded around and denounced the whole affair, and but for the police there would have been a big riot. Many both for and against the execution, were knocked down. Negroes came in to take down the scaffold, and the prisoners took hold to help, and the result was they carried away the whole thing, ropes, and all, for kindling, and relics to be carried north as mementoes of the horrible affair. The person who manipulated the drop, was taken out on parole of honor, as his life was in danger. The prisoners now settled down to peace and quiet, talking exchange and hunting 'greybacks', which every man who had any pretense to cleanliness at all had to do. Morning and evening we would strip ourselves and give our clothing a thorough search for the little creepers, that we might not be literally leached to death as many were. Each day we thought it could get no worse, but each recurring day brought with it additional horrors and new scenes of trouble, with hotter weather, and the camp in worse condition. Although the camp was enlarged with about six acres, the men lay thick all over the ground, in all conditions imaginable, some beyond the conception of the human mind in their horror. Some were naked and bronzed by pine smoke and exposure, and thousands lay upon the ground with but little clothing, the most ghastly and horrible looking objects, enough, it would seem, to bring pity to the heart of a demon, dying at the rate of about 100 per day. The bodies of the dead, all besmeared with filth and vermin, were carried out of the south gate by fellow prisoners, between the hours of 8 in the morning and four in the evening, and there laid in rows, each body labeled with name, company and regiment, if known, where they lay until next day, when they were loaded in a wagon like wood in a rack, and hauled to the cemetery about forty rods northwest of camp, where they were buried in a shallow ditch, one hundred in a ditch. The keeping of the sanitary condition of the camp was entrusted to the prisoners, the police force among them enforcing good order and seeing that the camp was kept in as good condition as circumstances would permit. The commander of the forces provided clubs and a few shovels and gave the police an extra ration of bread. During the first twenty-one days of June it rained hard every day, washing the camp clean. Through July and August we had frequent showers. One afternoon, early in August, there came one of those violent rains and flooded the camp six to eight inches deep, and flowed through the camp with such force as to break the stockade on the east. As soon as the guards noticed the break they fired two guns as a signal to get out, and a strong force was soon on the spot to prevent an escape if one was attempted. The storm did a good thing for the camp in washing out the filth, leaving it much more wholesome. The 12th of August there happened what we termed a 'Providential dispensation.' The water in the little creek was so indescribably bad, that no one could use it except in case of extreme necessity, and the prisoners on the southside had dug a few wells the best they could, which furnished nearly enough for that side, but they could not get water so easy on the north side, as the ground was higher and the water deeper. A nice, flowing spring broke out on the northside, between the dead line and the stockade, about half way between the north gate and the stream, and came trickling down under the dead line. The prisoners soon had a receptacle fixed to receive the water, and police stationed so that all could be supplied. Whatever the cause of it, it was a providence to the suffering thousands that were blessed by it. W. E. Stafford became very sick, and it was soon discovered that he was breaking out, and knowing that he had been exposed to the smallpox, he was

CHAPTER XIX.

examined by a physician, and it was pronounced smallpox. He was at once removed to the smallpox hospital and soon recovered, but remained out of prison while there. He came into the enclosure occasionally and ministered to his suffering comrades. About the first of July the cords of my legs began to contract so I could not walk, and my legs were drawn to near an angle of 45 degrees from the knees. In addition to this I took chronic diarrhea in a very bad form, and my gums became swollen and my teeth all loose. I was in a most deplorable condition, and on looking around me each morning and seeing the great numbers of dead and dying, I could not help being impressed with the terrible realities of death, for thus I sat for nearly two months, 'without one beam of hope or spark of glimmering day.' During that long and horrible time, I noticed many who would be walking about, and in a few days would be silent in the cold sleep of death. My observations led me to note that every one of intemperate or dissipated habits, soon fell an easy prey to the dread destroyer, but those who had lived temperate in all things stood the hard trial much better. Also, that those of strong will power were able to endure more, and stood better chance of recovery. Comrade E. B. Creel, though suffering horribly, was not affected to the extent of his other comrades, but kept on his feet. Lindsey Sexton, of Company K, was of very great help to me in my unfortunate and helpless condition.

As time passed on our situation grew worse, as the thousands were crowded into the prison. The greatest number in the prison at anyone time was 33,114, making about 1700 to the square acre. The whole number received during its occupation was 45,613, whole number of deaths 12,912. After Sherman took Atlanta the Confederates began to get scared, and the last of August began preparations to transfer us to other prisons, and the last of September there were left 8,218 that could not walk, none being permitted to go except those who could walk to the depot. During September of one-third of these died, during October one out of every two died, and in November one in every three died.

Such was the mortality, and from no other cause than bad treatment, for they could have located the prison on a river where we could have had plenty of good water and thus kept clean, and we know from the word of people of the neighborhood, that they could have given us plenty to eat, and especially vegetables of any kind that would have saved our suffering from scurvy and diarrhea, which was the prime cause of over 8,000 deaths. They could have fed us on sweet potatoes, of which the country had an abundance when matured. But no, that would not suit that old tyrant, General Winder, the fiendish old tory, who was told when he located the prison, by people living there, that it was a very unhealthy place, to which he answered that that was what he wanted, where the 'd--n Yankees would die as fast as they could catch them.' During August I became so bad and exhausted that I could not help myself, only as I lifted myself about with my hands on the ground, while in a sitting posture. Under the excitement of prospective exchange, or from some other cause, I began to get better, and by the 8th of September I could stand and walk a little.

No one can conceive the surprise of the prisoners when on the morning of September 6th, the seven first detachments nearest the south gate, were ordered to be ready to march at any time, and all that could not walk should stay behind, and in the afternoon they were called out to be sent to our lines for exchange. The men of the Fifth West Virginia Cavalry were in the fifteenth detachment, and there, as on Belle Isle, it would come our turn to go out in the third lot, following the numbers consecutively. As the second call was made on the night of the 7th, on the morning of the 8th we were expectantly looking for orders to march at any moment, and were buoyed up by the hope of getting home, or at least getting out of the hole of death in this camp. Every man that could possibly walk at all, was by the aid of a comrade practicing, that he might pass muster, which was to walk to the depot, three-fourths of a mile. About noon that day, September 8th, the call was made, ordering our detachment out. I could barely make out to walk a little, but by the aid of comrades Creel and Sexton, I succeeded in supporting myself until we were passing Wirz's quarters, when in order to pass, each one had to walk alone, and by a great effort, unsupported, I succeeded in satisfying the miserable tyrant. The gentle touch of the elbows of my comrades, gave me the required strength. Arrived at the depot we rested about two hours, when we were put into box cars, after receiving each a piece of corn bread weighing about six ounces, and we were on our way to Macon. We reached Macon that evening, and were side tracked on the east side of the Ocmulgee river, where we remained until the morning of the 9th, crowded together as so many hogs, and suffered intensely, when we started for Savannah, where they said we would be exchanged, reaching that city about sunset. It was a very rough ride over the jolting rails. I was seized with a severe attack of diarrhea, which completely exhausted me, so that I could not help myself at all. The train ran into the city on to a beautiful street, lined on both sides with live oaks, where the prisoners were ordered out. Neither myself nor Creel could walk by that time, so both tumbled out in the sand and lay there. Those that could walk were at once marched away to a stockade west of the old brick jail, and we that could not walk, lay there in the street until about 9 o'clock, when some loyal ladies came along with a bucket of coffee and some soft bread. Ministering angels were they, but a lieutenant came along at the same time, with wagons and a guard to take us away, and he drove the ladies away, but not until we had received a cup of coffee, the first delicacy for nine months. We were loaded into the wagons, which were drawn by mules, driven by colored teamsters, and started up street. To our happy surprise a lot of good eatables were thrown into the wagon, at a place

CHAPTER XIX.

where we stopped. It was noticeable that the teams frequently stalled, once or twice in each square, and at every stop, colored cooks from the basements of wealthy residences, would come with waiters in hand, and pour into the wagons a lot of food. It was after dark, but their forms were easily discernible, proving to the sick and weary prisoners, that the loyal blacks were still their true friends.

By the time we got to the old jail enough had been given us for a fair supper, the first in many weary months. That was all we received from the time we left Andersonville on the 8th until the 12th. We were hauled to a nice green on the west side of the city, known as the old United States parade ground, near the United States marine hospital, and there they laid us on the bare ground, which was called a hospital, without any attention whatever, except a strong guard to keep us from running away, when none of us could walk. On Sunday, the 11th, the ladies of the city came out by the hundreds, and with well filled baskets, who would have given us all the delicacies of the season, but that infamous wretch, the most inhuman of his kind, Lieut. Davis, would not let them come near us, but they persisted until late in the evening, when he put them all under guard, and kept them there until long after dark. On that day they set up a lot of A tents on the ground, and we then lay in them, a paradise compared to Andersonville, as we had a clean place to lie and pure air to breathe, though we got very little to eat. If that cruel scoundrel, Davis, had permitted it, the loyal ladies of the city, of whom there were scores, would have kept us in plenty to eat, but that would have been human, and the inhuman wretch forbade it.

The first guards we had at Savannah were a lot of marines dressed in the old regulation uniform, and were a nice lot of fellows. But the cradle and the grave were again robbed, and new guards were put on. The young men were the most cruel, while the old men were reasonably good, many of whom, it is believed, were loyal at heart. We remained in these tents about four weeks, and were then transferred to a board stockade beside the marine hospital where some of our officers had been confined. There were A tents in there and boards to lie upon. That was the Savannah hospital. They put about three hundred of us in there, but we fared no better. The men died very fast of the various ailments, even of mosquito bites, the blood was so poisoned with gangrene. If we became able to walk, we were sent away to Blackshear, Fla., or to Millen. We soon caught on in our mess, and when the Confederates would come in and order out any that could walk, we would lie down in our tents and could not walk, for we feared we could not find a better place. Exhausting diarrheas and other sickness, incident to our condition, still prostrated us and I was so low that I believed death near, but a change for the better came, and I partially recovered. One Sunday in October, a Confederate colonel and his wife came into the prison and talked with us very kindly and sympathetically, and inquired very minutely about our condition and treatment. Seeming to realize our condition, he told us that on the next Thursday he would send into us sugar, coffee, rice, soft bread, vegetables and meat, but the boys had been lied to so much, that they would not believe him. Late on Thursday, when nearly all of the most sanguine began to despair of the fulfillment of the promise, the gates were thrown open and the promised luxuries were at hand. Only those who had starved for ten long months, in the most abject conditions of life, could appreciate such a blessing as this was to us, and for the next four weeks we reveled in the good things of life. But we began to suffer from cold, as we wore the same clothing as that in which captured, and it was very thin, incapable of protecting us from the cold, damp north winds that had begun to blow down the Savannah river, and some days it was very severe, for we got barely enough wood to do our cooking.

About that time we learned that our government had arranged for the exchange of ten thousand sick and wounded, after first exchanging the marines. Accordingly, about the 15th of November, a well-dressed, hearty-looking set of Confederates, made their appearance in the sentry perches around the top of the stockade, who said they were the men sent there by the Federal government to be exchanged for the ten thousand sick and wounded; that there were but few sick in the northern prisons, and that they had been up north fattening up, and that their government would now exchange, and that they would all go into the ranks able for effective duty, while we never would be able to do service. On the evening of the 17th of November they began to parole us, there being at that time one hundred and eighteen of us in that prison hospital, and we had so improved that we could walk fairly well. Some time after midnight they got through paroling us, and we went to our quarters but could not sleep, we were so happy over the prospect of release. On the morning of the 18th we were taken out and down to the wharf and put on a transport, when we started down the river. A few of us had not given much credence to the report of exchange, on account of many former deceptions practiced on us, but when about noon we came near to Fort Pulaski, and caught sight of 'Old Glory,' the loved stars and stripes, floating over the Federal steamer New York, our feelings were such that no imagination could conceive. Eyes were flooded with tears and our hearts seemed ready to burst with the joy that filled them; and when we stepped beneath that dear old flag, for which we had dared to offer ourselves a living sacrifice, we could not cheer, but we sank down into quiet weeping, thankful for escape from our living tombs. We were provided with good food and taken down to our steamers, the Baltic and the Atlantic, and were put on board the Atlantic, where we were well cared for and provided with everything needed for our comfort. We remained anchored there until Tuesday, the 22d, when the steamers had received their cargo of living freight and then sailed for Annapolis, Md., arriving there on the 25th. Those able were

CHAPTER XIX.

sent to Camp Parole, while the others were sent to the hospital, thence to their regiments, or to their homes for discharge.

The author of this work desires to add to this account, as an instance of the sad results of the horrors of prison life, the subsequent history of comrade Matlick, who went into the war vigorous and healthy. He arrived home near Tunnelton, Preston county, West Virginia, December 18, 1864, just one year from the time he was captured, and was discharged from the service Jan. 12, 1865. In February, he went to Clark county, Mo., and bought a farm and applied himself to that calling. He returned to Preston county, West Virginia, in November, 1866, and was married to Miss Maggie A. Falkenstein, returning to his farm in Missouri in February following. Owing to the exposures and hardships endured while on the marches, raids, in camp, and in his long imprisonment, he could not rally sufficiently to stand the labor of farming, and broke down completely in 1869, and could hardly exist, to say nothing of work, in the next five years. In 1872, this man, who had suffered untold horrors, a dozen deaths, was granted the sum of $8 per month as a pension, from date of discharge. Recovering partially in 1873, he engaged in merchandising in Scotland county, Mo., in 1874, and remained at it until 1884, by which time his constitution had become so racked and weakened from the effects of his army life, that he broke completely down, and became subject to violent spasms, so much so that he became a charge to his family. In September, 1886, he removed with his family, wife and four children, to Kirksville, Mo., where the latter could have the advantage of good schools. His pension was raised from time to time, until at last fair justice was done in 1887, by increasing it to $50 per month. In all these years of married life, a noble wife has ministered to his every want, and now when the cursed seeds of Andersonville cruelty have developed into the full growth of physical ruin, she is a tower of strength to him, and as loyal as in those stormy days of the early sixties, when in her West Virginia home, she cheered him as he went to protect the flag, and received him as one from the dead, on his return from the blasting breath of prison life. Reader of this, when you hear thoughtless people minify the work and sufferings of the volunteer of 1861-65, reflect a moment, then ask yourself if you would care to accept the life of suffering for the pitiful pay received, or rather if it was not a service of the loftiest patriotism and sublimest courage.

CHAPTER XX.

ESCAPE FROM PRISON.

At the close of the advance of Gen. David Hunter on Lynchburg, Va., in June 1864, a detail was made of a few men whose term of service was about to expire, who were directed to take the advance of the troops placed in command of the wagon train, which was ordered to be sent back to the Kanawha valley, in advance of the main column. In this detail were Martin V. Sweet, First New York Cavalry; Joseph H. Anderson, First New Jersey Cavalry; Horace Penniman, First Maryland Infantry; and Frank S. Reader, Fifth West Virginia Cavalry, who were captured, and afterward associated in an escape to the Union lines. This detail was the advance of the troops that guarded the train, and as well did a great deal of scouting on their own account, securing a number of fine horses, a large quantity of forage, and cleared the immediate section of the marauding bands that hovered in the rear of Hunter's army. When near the head of the Kanawha valley, the advance had considerable fighting with small bands of the enemy, and we held our own against all comers, and pressed steadily forward, until we came to the river near Lewisburg. Here, while about a mile in advance of the main column, the latter was attacked by a force of the enemy, our little party was cut off from the command, and for two days was hunted and driven by sleepless foes. We endeavored to regain our lines, but were unable to do so, being forced to follow a road into a little town by the name of Liberty. When we attempted to pass out of this place, we found three of its four roads guarded by Confederate horsemen, who quietly took our measure, ready for fight or chase. A road was left open, however, leading to the White Sulphur (Greenbrier) Springs, which we followed. As we passed beyond the town, in fording a small stream, a body of cavalry came dashing upon us, and demanded our surrender. Finding that we were outnumbered, and that we must either surrender or escape by a dash

337

into the mountains, we chose the latter, and put spurs to our horses, when they plunged through the waters, and carried us into the depths of the mountains, followed by a storm of bullets. We could not stand and fight, as none of the party had arms fit for use, on account of the want of cartridges, the entire party not having a half dozen all told. In a severe little fight the day before, all our stock was used up, and being cut off we could not replenish. It was a day full of adventures, as we, by feints and threatenings, tried to keep our pursuers at bay. Toward evening we eluded them and spent the night in the great mountains. In the morning we abandoned our horses, and under the leadership of Reader, the little band undertook to make its way to Beverly, by a route he had before passed over. Toward noon, as we were quietly walking along, faint from hunger, we were surprised by a company of cavalry charging squarely upon us, and we were prisoners of war, our capture occurring June 20, 1864.

Our first experience as prisoners was a long tiresome march, hurrying at times through the narrow valleys, and again secreting ourselves amid the hills, until we reached Covington, where we were committed to jail, being lodged together in a small cell. A few days here, and our little squad was put in line of march for Lexington. The burning of the Military Institute there by General Hunter's command, had provoked the wrath of the citizens, and they threatened vengeance on any of the soldiers of Hunter's army who might fall into their hands. We knew this and were somewhat apprehensive over it. Upon our arrival in the town, we were placed in the upper room of a store-house, where we had a full view of the street and surroundings. Toward evening a large and noisy crowd of citizens assembled in front of the building, and a demand went up from the crowd for the Yankees. We inquired as to their purposes, when one of the excited number cried out that they wanted to hang us for burning their houses. We were then notified that it was necessary to search us, and we were deprived of everything we had except the scanty clothes we wore. This ceremony over, our attention was again called to the cry from the street. It became quite stormy, and we had become serious over the matter. Staring death in the face in this manner was new to us. Each of us had many times braved the storm of battle; but it was the first time that we had had the prospect of getting a rope seriously around our necks. Seeing that there was real danger of violence from the citizens, the commander of the post ordered out a strong guard, and by it we were conducted to the jail, and there securely locked in a strong cell. Our new quarters were not a success in the way of comfort. It was a small cell and it was crowded full. We remained in here about twenty-four hours, unable to rest or sleep, when the order came to get in readiness for a march. Our destination was first the city of Lynchburg, thence Andersonville. Upon leaving Lexington, the guards were instructed to watch us closely, and if any prisoner attempted to escape, to shoot him. The march was a hard one in the fearful heat of the sun, without food, until we reached

CHAPTER XX.

the bank of the Virginia and Ohio canal in the evening, when a little flour was given us, out of which we made a few "flapjacks." The next day we were put aboard a canal boat, and thus carried to Lynchburg.

Upon our arrival in that city on the evening of the 1st of July, we were conducted from the canal to our first regular prison house. This consisted of an old tobacco warehouse, filthy in the extreme, and totally unfit for the habitation of human beings. The amount of room was inadequate to the number of persons incarcerated, and the consequence was that sick, wounded and healthy prisoners were stowed away together, regardless of their condition. The first thing that attracted our attention upon entering the lower room of the building, was a sight revolting and horrible. A number of sick persons lay together, crowded into a corner, where the poor fellows were suffering terribly. There was no friendly hand to relieve them, and no help of any kind, except the miserable comfort afforded by their fellow prisoners. Many of them lay in their own filth, dirty, ragged, haggard, the very pictures of despair. Our entrance but added to their misery. They were already crowded too much, and now, that place had to be made for us, they were crowded still more, until the appealing looks from their poor, weak eyes drove their well comrades to suffer anything rather than add to their discomfort. There was but little rest or sleep, and the suffering was severe on the part of the most robust.

We remained here until the 3d of the month, when most of the well prisoners were removed to another building, a tobacco warehouse, located in the heart of the city, which was a great improvement over the first quarters. There were about 700 prisoners all told, confined in this building, and so far as circumstances would admit, were a jolly set of fellows. One of our first acts, was for a few choice spirits to get together and plan an escape for the evening of July 4th. Our desire was to pass the guards and strike for the Blue Ridge Mountains, and follow that range until we should reach the Union lines. When we attempted to pass the guards we found a double line around the prison and we were ordered back, with the threat of close confinement if we were again found out at night. Six attempts were made to get away from this prison, but we were always foiled in some way. It was at this time that our party of four determined that we would never permit ourselves to be taken to the prison pens of Georgia, but would try to escape every time we saw a possible chance. By this we stood and never faltered. We passed nineteen days in Lynchburg prisons, and had little complaint to make, except that which came from most Confederate prisons, the want of food. The supply we received here was totally unfit for food and insufficient for our wants, and there were but few that were not affected by it. Violent diarrheas, utter prostration and emaciation, and a weakness that was a pitiable sight, were some of the fruits that attested to our treatment. There was but little cruelty beyond that of depriving us of what we needed to support life. Lynchburg was but a fraction in the subtotal of suffering in prison life, and not unlike that of the other prisons in the south.

On the morning of July 19th, we were ordered to get ready for a trip to Georgia. In due time we were marched out and counted off, when 230 persons were taken from our prison and 270 from another, making in all 500 poor creatures bound for what we regarded as a living tomb. At the station we were given each about three-fourths of a pound of wheat bread, as our rations for the day. Soon we were aboard the cars, and after a very tiresome ride, reached Burkesville Junction about 6 o'clock p.m. Here we were taken from the cars and marched to a camping place a few rods distant, there to remain until the arrival of a train from Richmond, which was to take us to Andersonville. The train came up presently, but it was some minutes before we got into it, and we had ample time to examine the cars, and see if they offered any hope for a way of escape. They were baggage cars, with a large door on each side, at each of which two guards were stationed. Our little party of four held a council of war, and briefly discussed the best means of getting out of the cars while on the way. We agreed upon a desperate venture, full of peril, and if unsuccessful, was almost certain death to us. It was, that each of the four should sit near one of the guards and, at a given signal, be ready to leap from the cars with him, and then trust to our skill and strength in overcoming him and making our escape. We had already agreed on a point at which we should leap from the train. It was about 20 miles south of Burkesville Junction, on the Danville road, from which we could reach our lines at Petersburg, Va., by traveling about 120 miles in a direct line, northeast direction. We had a small map from which we had traced our course, and from which all our plans had been made.

Penniman and Reader were selected to ascertain the best way to accomplish our purpose. While doing this, Sweet and Anderson entered one of the cars and found some boards loose on the left side of the car at the rear end. In the confusion and noise then existing, they forced these boards off and made a hole large enough for a man to crawl or jump, through, without much difficulty. Having done this they concluded that this afforded a better and safer means of escape than the guard capturing scheme. In the meantime the other two were arranging for the other plan, and had agreed upon where they should sit and how they were to operate, when their attention was attracted by their names being called in a whisper by their comrades. Immediately they joined each other, when the hole in the car was shown them, the new plan explained and agreed upon, and we gathered around the opening, which the evening shadows obscured from the guards inside and outside.

In front of us were the four guards, sitting with their guns in their hands, and in the dim light permitted in the car, narrowly watching every movement on the part of the prisoners. On the top of each car were four other guards, watching for any that might try to escape, and in the rear car was a company

CHAPTER XX.

of others to relieve those then on duty. The guards were quite communicative at times, freely talking to us about the country and other subjects that were valuable to us in the escape. They told us the names of the stations as we passed along, and about 9 o'clock we stopped at a station beyond which we intended to make our leap. While leaving here quietly and slowly the guards become quiet and stillness reigned in the car. Outside, however, the clatter of the wheels and the patter of the rain, which was now steadily falling, drowned all the noise we could make. The train was running about ten miles per hour and we were nearing the point fixed for our leap. One of the boys peered into the darkness, when he was startled by the gleam of a bayonet. Hanging down over the side of the car, was the gun of one of the guards, who was seated on top, with the bayonet fixed, and the reflection of the dull light from the inside of the car, on its bright surface, gave us a view of it far from being comfortable. The chances now were, that in getting from the car, we would disturb this guard, who could alarm the rest on the top of the train, and have it stopped in time to follow us. We decided to go ahead and run the risk. Once out of the train and in the woods, we would have a fair chance for escape, which was all that we asked.

We were now about half way between two stations, and the guards were doubled up against the closed doors resting and listening when any undue noise occurred. One of them was facing us but a few feet distant, and had been keeping a sharp eye on us, but was now more intent on getting a good rest. His gun was leaning forward almost within reach of us, and we could at the same time with one hand almost reach a gun on the outside of the car, and with the other almost touch one on the inside of the car. We were hedged about with guns, and when the critical moment came, we looked into each other's faces inquiringly, trying to read the determination of each in this testing hour. There was no weakness on the part of either, but the word was passed, "do or die." Sweet was selected to take the lead and first leave the car. At the proper moment the word was passed to him from his comrades, to jump, and he leaped from the car into the pitchy darkness and rain. Hastily following went Anderson, plunging into the bushes, and next Reader, who fell into the mud, under the edge of the train, the wheels almost grazing his head, while last of all went Penniman, alighting close to the end of a stone abutment. Our escape seemed to be unobserved, as there was no alarm of any kind given, and the train went on its way, leaving the four alone in the edge of the woods. As soon as the train had passed, we rushed together, and clasped hands, congratulating each other on our success thus far. We found that we had alighted from the car within the distance of about one hundred yards from where the first and last of the squad had reached the ground.

An inventory of our stock of goods, showed us possessed of one jack knife, one clay pipe, one comb, two pounds of smoking tobacco, scraped from the floor of the Lynchburg prison, and we ought to have had one block of matches, which cost us one cent per match, but it was lost in getting out of the car. We began to discuss the best way to proceed, when we were surprised by a light at a house a few yards from us, followed by the voice of some one, evidently looking for us, as he had doubtless heard our voices. We hastily stepped under the cover of the trees, where we would not be seen, and watched the place until all became quiet again, and we were safe from danger in this direction. We had learned from the guards and our little map, that Petersburg, the point aimed at by us, was in a northeast direction from where we had left the train, but how to get started in the right direction, was a problem we could not solve. Not a star was visible, nor could anything else be seen but the faces of the anxious fugitives, as they stood in earnest consultation. But to stay in this place was to invite recapture, and we decided to go in some direction and trust to our usual good fortune for a favorable result. Sweet was unanimously selected leader of this forlorn hope, as he was admirably fitted for such a duty, and he accepted the post of honor. A rough guess was made as to which direction north was, and then we struck off through the woods at a rapid gait, but were soon checked by the thick undergrowth of bushes and briers, into which we plunged, sometimes sprawling at full length as we became entangled in the vines and briers. An hour's experience of this sort of traveling was enough to wear us out, and our progress was very slow. Disheartened, tired and hungry, we sat down on a log, in the midst of a dense forest, not knowing whither we were going. The rain drops were falling from the boughs of the trees, the wind occasionally moaned through their branches, and behind us we could hear the rumbling of the cars we had left about two hours before, a combination of sounds that did not produce harmony to our minds. Presently the clouds parted, and a mellow light diffused itself through the trees, and peeping forth from behind the great clouds, the stars blinked at us, and kept at it so persistently, that our spirits rose. We found an open space in the woods, and when the clouds had passed further away, the dipper met our gladdened eyes, and the pointers bade us see the North star, shedding its sweet light upon us. The countenance of a friend could not have imparted more cheerfulness than did that polar star, which seemed to say to us - " Follow me and you are safe."

With renewed courage we went forward, and after we had walked as we supposed about an hour, emerged from the woods and reached a plantation. The first thing done there was to hunt something to eat, but as there were no blacks in sight, we deemed it unsafe to venture near the house, and entered a patch of potatoes instead. Here we found a small quantity of peas in the pod, of which we ate, finishing our repast on the potatoes we dug fresh from the ground. It was high living, as we had not enjoyed such a fresh, wholesome meal for weeks. We had not been long here when we heard voices at the house and some one calling a dog. As we hurried outside the enclosure,

CHAPTER XX.

some one gave the dog the word of command, and he came at us on a full run. We ran as quietly as we could, passing around the lower end of the garden and up a ravine, hiding behind some bushes when the dog stopped. Nothing further occurring, we passed quietly on and came to an orchard which we entered. Here we found an abundance of small, green apples, to which we helped ourselves, eating them with great relish, and filling our pockets for the next day. We pursued our journey, and soon were warned by the approach of dawn that great care must be exercised and a place of hiding found for the day. This place we soon found, located among some thick underbrush in the edge of a heavy wood, where we were secure from observation, but could see what was going on in the outside world. We had marched nearly all night, and were only about eight miles from where we started. We could yet hear trains passing on the road we had so unceremoniously left. We must have made a large circuit, as we certainly walked seven hours. This was fixed on our memory as one of the most terrible nights of our entire experience in life, but it was only the beginning of a series of such, now remembered as horrible nightmares. The quiet of our hiding place soon lulled us to sleep, and we slept soundly until broad daylight. We awoke with the sun brightening everything about us and very much refreshed. We had now before us a day of peril and anxiety, to avoid discovery by persons passing. We were greatly alarmed in the forenoon; when two men entered the woods and began chopping timber. They remained within a few rods of us all day and chopped away, unconscious of the prize within their reach. They ate their dinner in the woods, and how aggravating it was to us. Already suffering acutely from hunger, it increased our misery to see these men enjoying their dinner.

Toward dark we ventured out from our hiding place, and walked through a part of the woods to see what prospect there was for a forward movement. It being too early to leave the woods with safety, we lay down under some bushes until after dark, then started for a house near at hand, but seeing no blacks about, we avoided the house and came out on the Petersburg pike, which we followed for some distance. Fearing that we might meet some one on the road, we turned off into the woods and kept under cover of the grand old oaks. The walking was similar to that of the night before. The vines and underbrush were so thick that it was almost impossible for us to keep on our feet, and every now and then we found ourselves plunging headlong into a bunch of briers or clump of bushes, coming out of the scrape pretty well demoralized. We had the advantage of a bright clear night, which enabled us to pick our way when the wood was not too dense, and the walk was thus rendered the less tiresome. Having the North star clearly in sight, we experienced no difficulty in keeping the right course. We had no adventures of any kind during the night, and had an uninterrupted walk of fully six hours, making good time and headway.

When it was almost daylight we camped in a clump of thick bushes where we remained all day, sleeping most of the time, and did not see a person outside of our party. We were hungry enough to eat almost anything, and our thirst was so intense as almost to madden us. We forgot it only when we fell asleep. Instead of camps, battle fields, prisons, short fare and ill treatment, we dreamed of our dear old homes, the happy scenes and sports of boyhood, and the well filled tables of the land of plenty. How we entered the enjoyment of this sweet vision of peace, and reveled in the love and blessings afforded us there, banishing sorrow, healing wounds, relieving hunger, and comforting us in our misery. But when the hour of awaking came, how different the surroundings. The intensity of suffering cannot be forgotten, nor can it be described. Toward evening we ventured from our hiding place, and in a short time took our first meal on the tramp. We saw a house a short distance from us, which we went as close to as we dared, and watched the opportunity to hail a friendly black. In a few minutes we heard one of them coming, singing one of their quaint and weird plantation songs. We never heard the measured singing or chanting of one of these songs of plantation life, without seeming to recognize in it the sadness and misery of a life of slavery, and a sense of pity was felt by each for the unfortunate slaves. Yet with the degradation of the life, and, we would suppose, the blunting of their sympathy, and all feeling for others who might suffer, they entered into our feelings and expressed a sympathy for us, that was full of human kindness. More than this, they helped us whenever they dared to do so, and not once in all our weary efforts to escape, or in our entire army life, did they ever betray us.

When the black came within hailing distance, we called him to us. We stated to him our situation, and found him to be quite intelligent, and ready to do us a service. We informed him we were Union prisoners trying to escape, and asked his assistance in giving us something to eat and putting us on the best road to our lines. He cheerfully agreed to aid us and left to see his wife about it. In a short time they both returned, each bearing a plate of corn bread and fried bacon, and some vessels filled with milk. Ah, what a feast was that! A better supper, we thought, we had never sat down to and it was eaten with a relish. Nearly three days of fasting and now we were feasting. Faithful friends were they. We talked freely with them about our future plans, and they gave us some advice that was valuable to us afterward, giving explicit directions how we should proceed on our way, and with many words of cheer, heartily shook hands with us and bade us good by.

We pushed on and as closely as possible followed their directions. We soon came to Nottaway river, and had a great deal of trouble crossing it. We had evidently taken a wrong road, which brought us to a broken-down bridge. By hard work we got across the stream and rested on its pretty banks. Before leaving the little river, we took a good drink, not knowing when we should get

CHAPTER XX.

another, as water was scarce in that section, except in these running streams. We made but little progress, as we were constantly bewildered, not knowing whether or not we were on the right road, passing over many miles of road and woods, but to very little purpose. We became tired towards morning, and lay down in the midst of a clump of dwarf oak to await daylight, and the assistance of a friendly black. We soon fell asleep, and awoke on the morning of the 22d, feeling refreshed, and encouraged by the fact that we had escaped recapture for sixty hours, and began to feel confident that we would be successful in getting home to our friends. We spent a part of the day in what we called "skirmishing," consisting in cleaning our clothes and persons of the vermin with which we had become covered in prison. These dirty pests, together with the little black gnats and mosquitoes that filled the woods, rendered our situation extremely disagreeable. In order to hide ourselves from the eyes of any who might pass through the woods, we had to confine ourselves to a compass of perhaps twenty feet, from daylight until dark, and be annoyed by the vermin and insects. It was a miserable day. We would occasionally be able to get a few minutes' sleep, but it was generally troubled by dreams of the scenes through which we had passed, and we would awake tired and unrefreshed.

We struck out about nine o'clock in the evening and made our way to the edge of the woods we were in, when Sweet started in the direction of some houses to see what chance there was for something to eat. He first encountered a warlike hog, which grunted and snorted at him until he was compelled to hide among the trees, for fear the noise would betray his presence. He again went toward the houses and attracted the attention of a negro boy, who took to his heels very much frightened. By considerable persuasion he was quieted, and we got him to come to us. We asked him about affairs at the houses, but the little fellow was suspicious, and would say nothing until he went and saw his mother, telling her of the presence of strangers, when she came to us inquiring what we wished. We told her who we were and what we wanted, but she was afraid at first to trust us. The slaves had become notorious as aids and guides to escaping Unionists, and the Confederates were in the habit of dressing themselves in the garb of Union soldiers, when they would pretend to be escaping prisoners, in order to find out who among the slaves helped such persons. She was afraid we were of that kind of spies, and was loth to help us, but we soon convinced her that we were Union prisoners fleeing from prison. We then asked her for food when she invited us into her house. We sat down in her rude cabin, where she baked us some excellent corn bread, in the red hot wood coals, and fried us the last bacon she had in the house. It was a dish fit for a prince, and there never was a set of belated fellows so fortunate as we were. With this food and plenty of sweet milk, hunger was soon satisfied, and we were ready for a night's tramp. We bade her good bye, started on our journey, accompanied by one of her boys, whom she sent to guide us a few miles. We crossed the Nottoway river and followed the Dinwiddie road, pushing on to a large gate, where our guide left us.

We had been cautioned by our black friends, that if we met Confederate soldiers, or citizens, on the road, in small numbers, to say nothing to them but pass right on. They said there were a great many desertions from the Confederate army, and that the deserters would not disturb us if we let them alone, but that if interrupted, they would likely give us trouble. It was a fortunate bit of advice, and we had occasion to profit by it this night. We met two armed persons, dressed like Confederate soldiers, so far as we could tell who paid not the slightest attention to us, but walked gravely on as if they were alone in the world. We set them down at once as deserters, but what they took us for we never learned. From this on we had a difficult time to keep on the right road after all the good instruction given us. We walked once about two miles out of our way, bringing up near a plantation house, and had to retrace our steps and take a new start. We then followed the highway some distance, and got on the wrong road, which almost led us to recapture. We turned aside into an orchard to get some apples, where we filled our pockets for next day's eating, and decided to go into camp. But upon looking about us we were surprised to see about twenty fine horses grazing in the orchard, and, as the surroundings looked suspicious, we decided to go into the depths of a heavy pine forest on the right of the road. We camped under a thick clump of the great jagged trees, a lonely place, surrounded on all sides by huge pines, which we found secure enough for our purpose.

When daylight appeared, Penniman made a reconnoissance through the woods, to ascertain our whereabouts. He returned in about an hour, with the information that he had been conversing with a slave, who told him we were within a mile of a Confederate camp, which was directly behind the orchard that we thought of stopping in, near a place called Blacks and Whites. The horses we had seen belonged to the officers in the camp. This was startling intelligence to us, and we did not need the caution of our black friend to keep very quiet. Occasionally we could hear sounds coming from the camp, the calls of a bugle telling us plainly enough that we had no friends in that quarter. We put in the time until evening eating the green apples we had picked, and in low conversation, with occasional naps of sleep, which were necessarily shortened by the persistent attacks of the gnats and mosquitoes.

When his day's work was finished, and night came, the black joined us and guided us to a plantation about two miles distant. Upon nearing the house, he bade us lie down close to a large spring of water and await his return, when he would bring us our supper. It was a delightful place, where we quenched our thirst and rested beneath some stately trees. We remained here perhaps an hour, when another black approached, and announced himself as our guide for the next few miles. He had us secrete ourselves in some bushes near by,

CHAPTER XX.

where we waited until he went and got our supper. In a short time he and his wife made their appearance, with an excellent repast both in quality and quantity. Supper over, and we were ready to resume our journey. The good old woman, black and ignorant as she was, did us all the service she could, and as we parted, wrung our hands and bade us a hearty God speed.

Her husband took the lead and told us to follow him closely. He went on a swinging, rapid walk, through the woods and bushes, over stumps and logs, leading us into several falls and plunges into the bushes, but all the while making a bee line for the point he wished to reach. Finally he stopped at a cross roads, leaving the camp at Blacks and Whites in our rear. Here he left us, directing us to some cabins to the left, where we would get another guide. He had proved himself a true friend, and we parted from him with regret. Upon reaching the cabins of the slaves to which directed, we knocked at the door of one of them, and were admitted with a cordial welcome. One sprightly young fellow volunteered to guide us to a point some nine miles distant, thus establishing him to return in time to get some sleep. Several of the blacks were awakened, who gathered about us, all shaking hands as we extended ours to them, gratified to meet some of the Union soldiers. They were full of sympathy for us, and offered anything they had that would add to our comfort. Our guide led us a lively race for about eight miles, following a path through the woods. He was constantly on the alert, and was apprehensive of the presence near us of some of the enemy, and it required all our skill and urging to keep him with us.

We had gone perhaps about eight miles, when we had an adventure that threatened to be serious, but proved to be laughable. A foraging train of the Confederates was in camp on the side of the road a short distance ahead of us, but of course we knew nothing of it until we reached it. When nearly to it we were halted by two armed men, evidently on guard duty, who saw only the black and Anderson, who were in advance, the rest of us several yards behind them. When they saw the rest of our squad coming up in single file and in good order, they broke into the woods on a full run, not waiting long enough even to fire an alarm. We heard one of them in a few minutes call to the other, and we went silently on our way. It was an astonishing occurrence to us. They must have thought that a whole company was advancing, and that the best thing for them to do was to get out of the way. It was a sight to see our poor guide. He was badly demoralized and scared, but we quieted him down, though we were nearly as badly frightened as he was. We stepped aside into the woods and continued our walk, cautiously looking in every direction. In a few minutes we were right in the midst of a train of foraging wagons, and had no time to recover ourselves or retrace our steps. Several teams were standing together, and in most of the wagons the teamsters were stretched out asleep, but, standing at the end of one of the wagons, was one fellow that wasn't asleep. He was wide awake, and was trying to get something out of the wagon. He being occupied gave us our chance, and we quietly stepped behind some trees and awaited the fellow's good pleasure. He went to the other end of the train presently, and we moved off out of sight. We supposed that the fellows who took to the woods belonged to this train, and were either on guard duty or just coming into camp. We heard no more of them, but suppose they stopped somewhere long enough to tell of what a mighty host of Yankees had driven them into the woods.

We struck off to the right of the train, and advanced about a mile, when we stopped for consultation. Our guide begged to be relieved from further duty, and as we did not want to subject the poor fellow to further danger, we dismissed him. As a reward for his services, Reader gave him his vest, the one remaining relic of civilized life in the party, which he carried off in triumph. We went to a safe distance from the train and settled down for the next day, the 25th. It was an uneventful one, nothing occurring that gave us any concern. We found that we had camped in the midst of a berry patch, where there was any quantity of huckleberries and some blackberries. Of these we ate freely and heartily. Toward evening the rain began to pour down in a steady stream, drenching us thoroughly, and we were finally driven from our shelter, passing through the woods, bringing up at a tobacco drying house in the clearing. Here we were sheltered from the rain, but were in full view of some houses that were about half a mile distant, across some fields. We saw some of the folks in the houses, but none came near us, so we were not disturbed. After dark we went into the open place to look for something to eat. It was Reader's turn to go to a house and he advanced for that purpose, when he suddenly came close to a woman, who evidently lived in one of the houses. Not being anxious to form her acquaintance, he asked some questions of her and retired to the woods. As no further notice was taken of him, it is probable the woman did not suspect who he was.

We left this neighborhood, and passing through another wood, we came to a large plantation, upon which there was a fine residence and other evidences of thrift. Anderson went toward the house to hunt something to eat, and attracted the attention of a black and brought him to us. We questioned him all about our location, our proximity to Dinwiddie Court House, and the nearest road to it, and then asked him to get us something to eat. He very intelligently gave us all the information we needed, but on the all absorbing question of eatables, he was compelled to deny us. He said that there were four Confederate officers at the house who were to be waited upon, and it would be impossible for him to get us anything without discovery. He offered to do all in his power for us, and took us into a stable, where there were four fine horses, owned by the officers, saddled and bridled ready for use, which we might take, and he would not inform on us. It was a great temptation, but

CHAPTER XX.

we could not consider it for a moment, as by doing this, we would have to pass through Dinwiddie Court House, the only available road being through there, where a regiment of Confederate cavalry was stationed. These facts we learned from the black, who advised us to try it on foot a while longer, and gave us clear directions for avoiding the troops at Dinwiddie, and making our way to Petersburg. He put us on the way to the road, and left us then to our own resources. We got on the road at the scene of the previous night's adventures, but the wagon train had left, not leaving a sign that it had ever been there, except the torn down fences, the rains having obliterated all marks of the wagons and horses. The rain was pouring down, the roads became so slippery that we could scarcely walk, and it was so dark that we could not see where we were going, or see each other, and we kept together by the sound of our voices. We went a mile, perhaps, through this intense darkness, when finding it almost impossible to go further, we took shelter under a tree, huddling close together, and waiting patiently for the cessation of the rain. The air was cool and our suffering became very severe. The rain drops fell from the branches and leaves, chilling us through, every drop seeming to penetrate the flesh, and soon we were shaking with the chills that seized upon us. We became almost unable to move, and were benumbed and sore, and when we attempted to walk, found it a painful effort. But we couldn't stay there, as we struck off through the woods, and presently found that we were lost in the great woods. We retraced our steps as best we could, and by groping and feeling our way back, arrived at the road, which we then closely followed.

The rain having partially ceased after walking some distance, we were soon able to reach open ground, and had not gone far when we saw lights to our left proceeding from houses. To these we made our way and found them to be some negro cabins, at the door of one of which we knocked, and entreated the inmates to permit us to enter and warm ourselves. They opened the door, and told us to be seated near the fire, when they heaped on wood, and soon had a blazing fire, in front of which we sat and warmed our chilled bodies. There was not a morsel to eat in the house, so they could not accommodate us in this way. A black from another plantation was visiting at this place, and told us that if we would go with him, he would give us something to eat, and a good fire to warm and rest by. We accepted his invitation and started with him. He took us about three miles through the woods, bringing up in front of a long row of cabins. He led us into a workshop, closed the door, and told us to keep very quiet while he made preparations for us in his cabin. In a few minutes after leaving us he returned and took us with him, giving us a place before a blazing fire. He then went to work and cooked us an excellent meal of corn bread and bacon. By the time we had finished, day was breaking, and he told us we would be safer now in the woods, and went with us to find a secure hiding place.

We passed through an orchard, picking up some of the apples, and found a safe place not far from the cabins. He told us that he would return to us in the evening, and guide us a few miles that night, and then we were left to ourselves. The day was clear and bright, and the sun soon warmed us and dried our clothing. While nothing occurred of a startling nature, the day was one of much anxiety to us. Confederate cavalry in squads passed us frequently, and as we lay within a few rods of the road, we had a good view of them. Several times we were very much frightened by the near approach of the horsemen, some of whom seemed as if they must know we were hidden there, by the manner in which they rode towards us, in some cases being within a few feet of us. But the bushes hid us from them. A wagon train also passed, and there was enough going on, in connection with the vigorous attacks of mosquitos and gnats, to keep us awake and vigilant.

As soon as it was dark enough, our friend came to us with a good supper, and he then said he was ready to guide us a short distance and led us a few miles, leaving us at a plank road which led to Dinwiddie, giving us directions for the night.

We had not gone far when a turn in the road found us in the midst of another wagon train. We could see that the wagons were loaded with provisions, but we were too much alarmed by the unexpected turn affairs had taken, to think of foraging on our own account. Every person about the train was asleep, and we were not observed. We retraced our steps, and made a circuit through the woods around the train, until we had safely passed all danger. We pushed forward rapidly, and by the time this little adventure had been forgotten, we encountered another wagon camp, in which all the teamsters were not asleep. The train was a large one, heavily loaded with hay and produce. Before we realized our position, we were among the wagons, and, worse than all, in the presence of one of the teamsters, who was busy working about a team. He barely spoke to us, and being intent on his own business, paid no further attention to us. We hurried along until we were at a safe distance. This thing of running into these wagon trains had become monotonous, and we determined to keep in the woods, though we would thus make slower time. We observed this caution for a while, but presently ventured out on the road again.

We had not gone far when we were startled by the sound of horses approaching us. We stepped back into the woods out of sight and watched the approach of the new danger. A squad of cavalry cantered along the road, passing us almost near enough to strike us with their sabres. We barely had time enough to get out of their way. Fortunately they did not see us, or our adventures as escaping prisoners would have come to an end. They went on their way, and left us in some embarrassment as to what course next to take. From the description given us by our black friend, we felt satisfied we were close to Dinwiddie, and that the utmost caution must be observed. Turning

CHAPTER XX.

down over the hill to our left, we came to Stony Creek, which passes near the town, and lay down on its banks for a short time. We had not lain there long, when we were aroused by a terrific noise, coming apparently from across the stream. We were on our feet in an instant, and though the clatter was kept up for some time, we could not discover what it was. It was sufficient to impel us to move forward, and we walked along the creek a short distance until we heard voices. We got under cover and soon ascertained that we were near the bridge that crossed the creek on the road that we had been traveling, and that it was guarded. At the time we heard the voices a relief was being put on, as near as we could understand, and when this was done, no sound was heard but the murmur of the waters in the creek. Our intention was to cross the bridge, as we did not expect to find it guarded, but we could not do that, so we went into a piece of woods, near at hand, and put up for the day.

We were more exposed during this day than any place we had yet stopped. A few small bushes were all that kept us from the view of passersby. Persons were constantly passing on the road a few rods distant, but none discovered us. Near us on the creek was a mill that kept up a great deal of noise, which was in our favor, drowning whatever noise we made. The day was thus passed, with but very little sleep, and not a morsel to eat. About dark we left our little camp and went to the creek, finding a crossing place near the mill. Once over the creek, we climbed a little bluff and went into the woods, stopping near some houses. Sweet and Penniman went to the houses and secured a black, who came to us, and with whom we had a long talk. We were concerned about getting past Dinwiddie, the most dangerous place on the route until we should get near our lines. He agreed to guide us around the town, and leave us where we could proceed safely without the services of a guide. We followed after him, and felt perfectly safe as long as he kept before us. He was very cautious and careful and would not pass any exposed place without first carefully examining it, and satisfying himself that the way was clear. We passed the guards with but little trouble, and went around the town, keeping to the right, and avoiding the troops that were encamped in the place. Our guide left us at the edge of a wood, after explaining to us what direction we should take. We went into the woods and became lost, traveling for some time in a circle, and finally emerging from the woods at the place we entered. This was decidedly provoking, but we enjoyed a hearty laugh over it, and started in again. This time we came out all right. We then followed the edge of the woods for some distance, when we entered a pine forest, where the trees were so close together, that we could scarcely crowd through a part of it. We were walking along busily engaged in laying plans for future operations, when a shrill cry broke upon the stillness of the night, and caused the hair to rise on our heads. It sounded like the cry of a child in distress, but we understood fully what it was, though we had never heard it before. Any of the readers of this who have had occasion to be much in a Virginia forest, remote from thick settlements, will not need to be told that it was the cry or scream of what is usually known as the wild cat or lynx. It followed us a short distance for an hour or more, emitting its piercing cries, and was a cause of terror to us, though no attempt was made to attack us. The next night we were followed by it or another one, until almost daylight, and then this annoyace ceased.

Late in the night, as we were pushing rapidly forward, Sweet suddenly disappeared in our front. We couldn't imagine what had become of him, when one of us called out: "Hello, Sweet; where are you?" "All right," was the response, "come on." Anderson was next, and after sliding a few feet on an inclined rock, went over the edge of it, the others of the party following fast and hard, all alighting in the mud, and barely missing a large number of rocks that were to our left. It gave us an opportunity for a hearty laugh, and we concluded to hunt a camp, as the night seemed to be full of mishaps and scares. We walked up a small hill, coming to an open space, where there were a few houses. To these we went and tried to get something to eat, but it was a failure. Daylight was near at hand and it behooved us to hunt a hiding place. This we found without any trouble, and lay down hungry and tired.

We experienced nothing unusual in this day's solitude, except that we were very hungry, and had nothing with which to satisfy it. The air was hot and close, and with the attacks of the gnats and mosquitos, sleep was out of the question. Toward dark we moved eastward to the edge of the woods, hoping to find something that would alleviate the suffering we were undergoing from hunger. We saw some cabins at a distance, to which it was agreed we would send one of the party to seek for food. It was Reader's turn to forage, and he went within a short distance of the cabins, when seeing some one coming from that direction, he stopped and took refuge behind a tree. He supposed it to be a black, but was very much astonished to see instead a man with a blanket thrown across his shoulder and a haversack strapped to his side, and apparently fully equipped. There was not enough light to tell certainly whether he was armed, but he had all the appearance of an armed soldier ready for the march. He noticed Reader, and having passed him a few feet, stopped and said:. "Who are you?" There Reader stood, not knowing what to do or say. Capture seemed inevitable, and he thought, with sinking of heart, of his three comrades safely hidden in the woods behind him. It was the worst scrape of the whole trip, and it looked as if all his hardships and suffering to keep away from Andersonville, were to go for naught. Two ways were open before him, submit to recapture, or run and risk being shot. He chose the latter. All this occurred in a few moments, and before the new-comer had time to say or do anything further, Reader deliberately turned from him and walked away, until he had got some distance from him, when he turned off into the woods on a run to where he had left his comrades. Singularly enough, no attempt was

CHAPTER XX.

made to follow him, but he was permitted to depart in peace. It was the most puzzling event that had occurred to us. We could not come to any satisfactory reason for the fellow's conduct, except that he was a deserter from the Confederate army, and was himself anxious to avoid discovery. A large force was but a short distance from us, and it is possible that he was deserting from them. We at once changed our quarters, going to a thick part of the woods, where we remained for awhile. Hearing nothing further that was suspicious, Reader was sent to try what he could do at the same cabins, this time following a safer course. When he reached the cabins he saw a negro woman sitting in a door, with her back to him.

Desiring not to alarm anyone, as the plantation house was but a few rods distant, he stepped up to the woman, laid his hand on her shoulder and spoke to her. To his surprise and consternation, she jumped to her feet and ran across the room, screaming at the top of her voice. Her cries could be heard at all the houses in the immediate neighborhood, and the alarm would certainly bring some one to the place. He hurried at once to the rear of the cabin and hid against the side of an outside chimney. The mud between the logs of the building having fallen out in many places, he could see all that was going on in the house. The inmates were badly frightened and greatly excited, and scarcely knew what they were doing. The woman calmed down sufficiently to order a boy to take a big dog and go out and see what had scared her. They went on their errand, but fortunately were not zealous enough in their search to hunt very closely for the fugitive. Presently one of the men of the family, a burly black, came into the house, and learning the state of affairs, went on the search of Reader, whom he found in a few minutes. The latter gave an account of the scare he had been the innocent cause of, which amused the old darky greatly. Reader told him what he was after, that we were escaping Union prisoners and desired food. He promised to bring it to us in a few minutes, and showed a place where he would meet the party. Reader then returned to his comrades and related to them his second adventure. The black came to us in a short time with some fried apples, swimming in grease, a dose that would have sickened an ordinary stomach. This was the best that he could do, as he said they had not a pound of meal for their family. It was a grievous disappointment to us, but there was no remedying it now. He gave us directions how to reach the road that led to the Weldon railroad, and cautioned us as to the presence of Confederate soldiers almost everywhere. We pursued our journey, and got along very well for a while, when the rain began to pour down in torrents, and we became again lost in another of those Virginia forests. The rain ceased in a short time, but we were deep in the woods, not having the remotest idea of what course we should take, not being able to see the stars, or anything else that would indicate the points of the compass. We at last reached a fence, beyond which we saw a house, which we approached and found to be empty.

Being apparently some distance from any other house, we concluded to put up in it for the day. It was a new house, the best place we found on our trip in which to rest, and being free from the little pests that annoyed us in the woods, we were able to rest and sleep.

At dusk we went to the edge of the woods near a house, in which lived a family of poor whites. We rested within a few rods of this house until it was quite dark, when Anderson went to it, called the man of the house to one side, and learned from him all about the location of the Confederate forces in that vicinity. Anderson led the man to believe that he was a Confederate, and thus received from him a good deal of valuable information. We learned that in order to get to our destination, we had to pass three camps of cavalry, one stationed at Ream's station, one at Stony Creek, and the other camp between the two places, the extreme right wing of Lee's army, and from that time on, we were not at any time half a mile from armed men. Almost from the hour we jumped from the train we were really so situated, but not in so great a degree as now, when we were never out of sound of the call of the bugles. A moment's exposure in daylight and we were as sure of recapture as that we lived. Having received this valuable information, Anderson returned to us, and we pursued our tramp on the Boydton plank road. We had not gone far when we got into difficulty with the enemy's pickets and barely escaped capture. We avoided them by striking off into the woods and keeping as quiet as possible.

Of all our experiences in the woods this was the worst. It was a swamp of the most treacherous kind, in which we sank as we stepped along, making the walking exceedingly tiresome and slow. We walked along in this as we supposed about two miles, when we were brought to a stand still, by a little stream that impeded our progress. We followed its course for some distance, when we stopped at some logs, which we hoped would afford a crossing place. Penniman got off by himself, hunting an open place in the woods, where he could see the stars, so as to shape our course, and called to the rest of the party to come to him. The words had scarcely left his lips, when the stillness of the air was broken by - "Who goes there?" coming from the opposite side of the little stream. We found ourselves face to face, almost, with the Confederate pickets, and the question was how to escape from them. We at once hurried back further into the woods from the stream, thoroughly arousing the pickets, the click of whose guns sounded ominous. We sat down at the foot of a large tree, and became as quiet as we could, awaiting developments from the other side. We lay thus for perhaps an hour, during which time the guards were relieved, and our case was evidently overlooked. There was no further attempt made to find us, and they doubtless thought we were wandering negroes.

As soon as the relief took their place we were ready to proceed. Just then the artillery opened up north of us, at Petersburg, indicating the direction we were to go. We were not long in getting out of that place. We picked our

CHAPTER XX.

way carefully and cautiously, until we had got out of reach of the guards, and soon were out of the woods, on the road on which the pickets were stationed. We kept our eyes and ears open for them, and were fortunate to avoid them at this time. Taking our course from the North star, we struck directly east, aiming to get across the Weldon railroad before morning. We soon reached Stony Creek, when, looking behind us, we saw a light, which we supposed came from a house. It was at once proposed to return to the house, and see if we couldn't get something to eat. We had about concluded to do so, when the call from a bugle was sounded, and we saw at once that the light came from a camp of soldiers. We were but a short distance from one of the camps we so greatly feared. We did not stay long here, but waded the creek and hurried into the woods. When we had gone a short distance, we could see plainly the camp fires and the troops in motion, and soon were in the midst of camps and guards, and it required all our ingenuity and care to avoid them. The forces were nearly all in motion, and though we were often almost in their grasp, we succeeded in dodging them. It was not a pleasant thing to stumble within a few yards of a squad of armed men, standing in some cases around a camp fire, but this became so common to us in our experience that night, that we almost expected it.

Soon we heard a train coming up the railroad, and we went into a more open space to watch it, when we saw to our left a camp fire, probably not over fifty yards distant, behind a little knoll, and a number of soldiers stretched about the fire. We crawled on our hands and knees near to an empty log house a few rods in front of us, to ascertain our whereabouts. What a sight met our view! All around us were the enemy in camp, the guards stationed everywhere, and we were in their hands once again, if they but closed in on our hiding place. They seemed to be getting ready in some of the camps to go on a march. At a distance we saw the lights of one camp of cavalry, where the bugles were sounding and the troops in motion, but we did not care to investigate the surroundings, and cudgeled our brains how to get out of the bad scrape we were in. Before us was the Weldon railroad, which we had to cross to reach our lines, and we tremblingly moved toward it. Now crawling along, again on our hands and knees, and again for a few yards on our feet, we moved to the important place. When we had gone a short distance we heard a train coming, and we lay down in the corn into which we had now found our way, which was sufficiently high to screen us from view. We were but a few yards from the track, and as the train came thundering along, we were close enough to see the soldiers on it. The train was going in the direction of Petersburg, and was full inside and on the top, with armed soldiers. When the train got past we drew a long breath, relieved that this danger was over. We then went close to the railroad track and took a view of the surroundings. The road was strongly guarded, but a few minutes' absence of the guards would enable us to cross the track in safety. Watching our opportunity, when none of them seemed to have an eye on where we were, we passed hastily over the road and hurried into the woods beyond. The critical point was behind us, and we sat down in the forest and rejoiced in our safety.

This day, the 29th, was an exciting one. Our high spirits of the night before were considerably dampened. It was the most dangerous day that we had experienced, and it seemed scarcely possible that we could get out of it as well as we did. We lay all day within less than one mile of one of the camps of cavalry. Their bugle calls could be heard distinctly, and hundreds of the men were in sight all the time. A party of them came within less than twenty feet of us, and could have nearly stirred us out with their guns, but fortunately did not learn of our whereabouts. We put in an uneasy day and could get no more sleep, and even our hunger was forgotten in the great danger that beset us. We struck out through the woods when darkness fell upon us, and when we reached a clearing, we saw a house a short distance off, to which Penniman went for something to eat. When he reached it he found the place surrounded by guards, and would have been captured had it not been for a black, who pulled him back to a secure place, as the guard approached. Inside the house several officers were enjoying the hospitalities, and there was no chance to get anything to eat. He returned to us in a few minutes and related his adventure with unstinted praise for his rescuer.

We crossed through another wood stopping near a house. Here Sweet made up his mind to have a drink of water and something to eat, at the risk of his life. He went to the house and entered it, and as he entered at one door a Confederate soldier went out of another one, and started to the woods on a run. Sweet got a drink, but did not deem it prudent to stay long enough to get anything to eat. The Confederate pickets were too near for comfort, and we got out of that place just as soon as our weary limbs could carry us. We got on to the Prince George Court House road, and found an old tobacco case, with an engraving of General Meade on it. This satisfied us that the Yankees had been there. A little further along, on a high point of land, we saw a body of horsemen, but of which army we could not tell. We debated the question for some minutes whether we should make ourselves known to them, but finally concluded not to do so, satisfied to endure still greater fatigue rather than run the risk of recapture. We then left the road, crossed down through a field to our left, and came out on the Petersburg pike, which we followed, and soon came to a house, where we waked up the inmates, requesting them to tell us how far it was to our pickets. We represented ourselves as Confederates, and of course they thought we meant the pickets of that army, and they told us that it was two and one-half miles, at the crossing of Mill creek by the pike we were on. We received from them all the information we wished, as to the number of the Confederate forces near, the distance we were from them, and our best and

CHAPTER XX.

shortest course to all the principal points. We bade them good night, thanking them for their information, and went into the orchard, where we filled our pockets with green apples for use in camp next day. We then went into the woods near to the picket lines and camped, hidden securely among the bushes, almost within gunshot of our lines.

We had a good sleep, but were awakened early by one of the most tremendous noises we had ever heard. As we learned afterwards, it was caused by blowing up the fort in front of Petersburg. Soon a terrific cannonading was begun, and we became deeply interested in it. There we lay and listened, eating the green apples we had secured, and spent some time in trying to clean ourselves of the vermin, and in resisting the attacks of the gnats and mosquitos. We had eaten no food for several days, and our hunger was intense. We had a quantity of salt which we used on our green apples, thus avoiding any ill effects from such food, but there was no sustenance in it. We had become very weak, and our nerves were almost shattered by the intense strain to which we had been subjected for some weeks, so much so that the firing of the guns about us kept us in constant dread. But strange to say, in all this suffering and weakness, we did not lose our hope and cheerfulness of spirit, nor did we ever for a single moment think of giving up our struggle for freedom. While listening to the cannonading at Petersburg, we were startled by the report of a field piece not far in our front, then another and still others, until we made ready to vacate our hiding place, feeling sure that mischief was in store for us. Presently we could hear the rapid firing of carbines, all the time moving to where we were secreted, and we hurried from the place. We went to the edge of the woods, and followed it, keeping to the right and under cover of the trees. The wood was circling to our left, and we had not followed it far when we could see that the firing was now near the spot we had left. We walked thus perhaps two or three miles, the firing on our left, until we came to a point where we could see the contending forces, perhaps a mile distant in a direct line, and had a full view of the scene of action. A fight was in progress and it was a brisk one, but we could not make out then which of the lines was our own army, but we could see that one of the armies had been driven into the wood where we were hidden in the morning, and from which we were driven. We learned after our arrival in our lines that the forces occupying our hiding place were Confederate cavalry, which had been forced there by a force of Union cavalry. The former were those that we had seen in motion during our secret night marches, and the bugle calls found an explanation.

As we could go no further without discovery, we lay down in a piece of woods to our right, and watched the progress of the battle as best we could. While thus engaged, a company of cavalry galloped past us in the direction of the Confederate forces. We were within a hundred yards of the road, but as the troops were covered with dust, we could not distinguish their uniforms, to tell to which army they belonged. One of us went into the field to see if we could make them out, but was not able to do so. In the hope that they would return, Penniman went down to the road and hid in some bushes, where he could have a full view of them and not be seen himself. It was an anxious waiting for us. If they were Union cavalry we were saved, but if they were of the enemy, then our chances of escape were very few. Soon we heard the clatter of the horses' feet on the return. Near and nearer they came, and all eyes were strained to get a view of them. Oh what intensity of emotion was crowded into that minute of waiting! Penniman, at his outlook, was eagerly scanning the road, and his eyes never left the troopers from the moment they came in sight until they filed past him. He waited patiently to see something about them that would show to what army they belonged.

The company came up to where he lay and went rapidly by him, when out of the grime and dust, the blue of some of the uniforms showed itself, and the truth flashed on him that they were Union soldiers. Jumping to his feet he waved his hat and called out at the top of his voice: "Come on, boys; thank God we're safe." Instantly scores of carbines were raised and covered us, when we called to the troops, "Don't fire; we are Union soldiers," and every carbine fell and we rushed to them, safe beneath the authority of the stars and stripes.

INDEX

Note: individual soldier names can also be found in the company rosters in Chapter III.

1st Indiana Infantry 193
1st Iowa Cavalry 20
1st Maryland Infantry 337
1st New Jersey Cavalry 208, 337
1st New York Cavalry 337
1st Pennsylvania Cavalry 209
1st Separate Brigade 151
1st West Virginia Cavalry 146, 186, 187, 201, 213, 236, 302, 303, 320
1st West Virginia Infantry 11, 37, 273, 291
1st West Virginia Light Artillery xii, 21, 180, 244, 265, 269, 273, 293
1st West Virginia Veteran Infantry 16
2nd West Virginia Cavalry 131
2nd West Virginia Infantry xi, xii, 9, 15, 17, 20, 26, 31, 32, 33, 34, 36, 49, 60, 67, 68, 76, 137, 140, 142, 144, 145, 146, 148, 149, 150, 158, 167, 168, 173, 174, 177, 179, 180, 181, 184, 194, 196, 197, 199, 201, 202, 203, 204, 205, 210, 211, 213, 217, 224, 225, 226, 232, 233, 234, 236, 237, 238, 244, 245, 246, 247, 249, 251, 255, 256, 257, 263, 264, 265, 266, 267, 268, 269, 270, 273, 274, 280, 284, 290, 300, 302, 312, 313, 320
3rd Arkansas 175
3rd Maryland Infantry 309
3rd Ohio 174, 179
3rd Pennsylvania Cavalry 243
3rd West Virginia Cavalry 208
3rd West Virginia Infantry 15, 149, 187, 204, 205, 213, 217, 225, 226, 238, 244, 245, 250, 252, 255, 256, 257, 265, 266, 267, 269, 270, 273, 284, 302
4th New York Cavalry 208, 209

4th Separate Brigade 16, 148, 150, 151, 241, 243, 254, 302
5th Ohio 15
5th Pennsylvania Artillery 105
5th Rhode Island Artillery 328
5th U.S. Artillery Battery B 99, 100, 102
5th West Virginia Cavalry xi, xii, xiii, 15, 68, 91, 153, 154, 155, 241, 290, 294, 297, 298, 300, 303, 332, 337
5th West Virginia Infantry 15, 16, 186, 205, 213, 224, 225, 226
6th Ohio 167, 173, 174, 178, 179
6th Ohio Infantry 17
6th West Virginia Cavalry 15, 51, 53, 62, 71, 80, 90, 92, 100, 110, 116, 125, 132, 244, 299, 303
6th West Virginia Infantry 83
7th Ohio 201
7th West Virginia Cavalry 16, 298
8th West Virginia Infantry 16, 149, 206, 236, 237, 244, 245, 250, 252, 255, 256, 257, 261, 265, 266, 267, 269, 270, 272, 273, 278, 284
9th Georgia 299
9th Indiana 181, 189, 194
9th West Virginia Infantry 16, 186
10th West Virginia Infantry 136, 148, 238, 249, 255, 256, 258, 268, 269, 271, 272, 302
12th Battery Ohio Light Artillery 213
12th Ohio 185, 186
12th Pennsylvania Cavalry 195
12th Pennsylvania Regiment 107
12th West Virginia Infantry 291
13th Indiana 177, 181
14th Indiana 173
14th Ohio 124
14th Pennsylvania Cavalry 149, 150, 152, 161, 244, 245, 249, 250, 251,

359

254, 255, 257, 263, 265, 266, 269, 270, 271, 273, 276, 277, 278, 279, 284, 302
14th Virginia Cavalry 271
14th West Virginia Infantry 20, 273
15th Ohio 97
17th West Virginia Infantry 21, 61, 86
18th Connecticut 161, 291
20th Ohio 97
22nd Virginia Infantry 271
23rd Illinois Artillery 273
25th Ohio 181, 184, 201, 204, 205, 213
25th Virginia 48
28th Ohio Infantry 268, 269, 271
31st Virginia 48
32nd Ohio 181, 201, 204
34th Massachusetts 291
54th Pennsylvania 291
55th Ohio 302, 309
60th Ohio 16
62nd Ohio 85
72nd New York 328
73rd Ohio 203
75th Ohio 201, 204
82nd Ohio 204, 213, 224, 225, 226, 227
83rd Pennsylvania 328
88th Pennsylvania 328
100th Pennsylvania Regiment xii, 124
123rd Ohio Infantry 291
144th New York 328
147th Regiment of Virginia Militia 25

A

Accomac, VA 10
Ackelson, Benjamin F. 264
Adams, Caroline 304
Adams, Robert M. 79, 225
Ailes, Ann 103
Akers, Thomas J. 268
Alexandria, VA 10, 11, 33, 60, 143, 226
Allegheny, Camp 93, 192, 200, 317
Allegheny College 7, 163
Allegheny County, PA 29, 36, 43, 75, 77, 97, 103, 104, 107
Allegheny County, VA 256, 282

Allegheny Heights 191
Allegheny Mountain 27, 38, 39, 41, 43, 72, 74, 96, 98, 104, 123, 131, 183, 191, 192, 194, 199
Allegheny Mountains 11, 107, 144, 181, 200, 260, 279
Allegheny, PA 43, 45, 46, 78, 136, 137, 139
Anderson 88
Anderson, Joseph H. 337, 340, 341, 347, 348, 352, 354
Anderson, Samuel Read 175, 176
Andersonville, Georgia 39, 40, 41, 65, 69, 73, 74, 75, 81, 82, 83, 91, 94, 95, 99, 111, 112, 117, 118, 264, 298, 326, 329, 333, 335, 338, 340, 352
Andrews, Virginia H. 138
Anisansel, Henry 186
Anthony's Creek 257, 259, 279, 289
Antietam 44, 229
Appomattox 46, 131
Arbogast, Charles 250, 251
Arbogast, George 250
Arlington Heights 67, 230
Armentrout 50
Armitage, Mary Jane 193
Armstrong County, PA 47
Armstrong, Helen M. 43
Armstrong, Rudolph 253
Army of the Potomac 85, 148, 216, 229, 241, 243, 246
Army of Virginia 140, 142, 213, 229
Arnold, Laura J. 303
Arnold, Mrs. 161
Arnold, Mrs. Jonathan 87, 171, 312
Ashby's Cavalry 16, 207
Ashby's Gap 288
Ashby, Turner 16, 208, 209
Athey, Armida 32
Averell, General William Woods xi, xii, 16, 27, 29, 46, 88, 91, 123, 137, 148, 149, 150, 152, 153, 154, 155, 161, 241, 242, 244, 245, 246, 251, 252, 253, 254, 259, 260, 262, 266, 269, 273, 276, 277, 279, 280, 281,

INDEX

282, 283, 291, 293, 294, 298, 302, 303, 313, 315, 316, 318, 320

B

Back Creek 259, 272, 284
Bailey, Marshall 302, 304, 320
Bailey, Mary F. 59
Baker 169
Baker, Asbury C. 51, 58
Baker, Bishop Osmon C. 158
Bakerstown, PA 77
Bald Knob 143
Baldwin, Camp 181, 199, 311
Baltimore, MD 6, 44, 68, 121, 163, 195, 267
Baltimore & Ohio Railroad 30, 37, 51, 59, 60, 86, 101, 115, 136, 186, 281
Banks, Nathaniel Prentiss 212, 213, 215, 219, 305
Banks, Surgeon W.A. 162
Barbour County, WV 21, 22, 55, 56
Barclay, Douglas D. 29, 30, 70, 76, 146, 162, 268, 295
Barclay, Jane Ferguson 29
Barnhart, Henry 235
Bartlett, Josiah 241
Bartow, Camp 265, 269, 317
Bates, William Brimage 196
Battery G xii, 180, 229, 230, 244, 250, 252, 266, 267, 268, 273, 292, 293, 294
Baum's Battery 179
Bayard, George Dashiell 208
Beauregard, Pierre Gustave Toutant 23
Becca Creek 174, 175, 177, 178, 181
Belington, WV 23, 49, 50, 53, 56, 60, 87, 189, 231, 235, 303
Belle Island 65, 303, 324, 332
Bellevernon 170
Belleville, VA 158
Belmont County, OH 17, 79, 85
Belmont Guards 76, 95, 96
Benham, Henry W. 59, 185, 186
Bennett, Martin 308
Benwood, WV 110

Bernard, Andrew 268
Berry, Jonathan 211
Bethany, WV 97
Beveridge, Jacob 200
Beverly, WV 13, 17, 37, 39, 44, 49, 61, 62, 64, 67, 68, 71, 72, 73, 79, 82, 83, 87, 93, 95, 98, 100, 101, 102, 105, 110, 111, 115, 117, 120, 125, 128, 137, 144, 146, 147, 150, 158, 159, 160, 161, 167, 168, 169, 171, 173, 178, 180, 181, 189, 231, 235, 236, 237, 238, 239, 244, 245, 253, 256, 259, 262, 263, 268, 269, 271, 280, 289, 290, 294, 299, 303, 306, 311, 312, 313, 316, 318, 338
Bibey, William 50
Big Springs 183
Billingsley, James K. 121, 264
Billingsley, W.H. 252, 253
Bird, John 257
Black, Col. S.W. 141
Black, James 44
Black, Joseph 145
Blacks and Whites 346, 347
Black, Sergeant 183
Blair, Assistant Surgeon Jonathan R. 272
Blakely, William 152, 277, 278, 284
Blenker, Louis 209
Blenker's Division 203, 212
Blue, Capt. Richard W. 133
Bluemont Cemetery 59
Boggs, William Robinson 312
Bohlen, Henry 209
Bohlen's Brigade 16, 220
Bolton, Rev. J.W.W. 18, 157, 158, 160, 161, 162, 163, 164, 213, 296
Boothe, Paton G. 50
Booth, Jane 56
Boreland, Col. 243
Boreman, Arthur I. 6, 61
Bosley, William K. 17, 168, 169
Bossieux, Lt. 324, 325
Bowden, Samuel 268
Bower, Basil F. 79, 84, 87
Bower, Oliver P. 50, 59, 280

Bowman, Richard 145
Bowser, William 183
Boyd, Belle 309
Boyles, Samuel J. 61
Bracken's Cavalry 181, 184
Braxton County, WV 186
Breckenridge, John C. 8, 291, 292
Breck's Battery 105
Breen, John 264
Bridgeport, OH 17
Britch, Charles 264
Broad Run 218, 222
Brock's Gap 194, 306, 307, 309
Brohard, Humphrey F. 59
Brooks, Bonaparte 145
Brown, Adam 251
Brown, Bailey 48, 49
Brown, Capt. W.H. 152, 278
Brown County, OH 305
Brown County, WI 44
Brown, George W. 131
Brown, John 67, 124
Brown's Gap 281
Brownsville, PA 122
Brown, W.H. 30
Brown, William G. 4
Brubach, Michael 268
Buchanan, VA 281, 282, 286, 288
Buckhannon, WV 16, 98, 107, 144, 147, 149, 161, 169, 231, 235, 236, 237, 239, 245, 247, 249, 260
Buckley, Eunice C. 164
Buell, Capt. Frank 220, 229
Buell's Battery 229, 230
Buffalo Gap 288
Bull Pasture 120, 202
Bull Pasture Mountain 203
Bull Run 20, 229, 230, 288
Bull Run, First Battle of 23, 33, 37, 243
Bull Run, Second Battle of 15, 18, 27, 31, 32, 38, 39, 40, 41, 54, 55, 60, 63, 64, 65, 66, 67, 73, 74, 75, 80, 81, 82, 83, 85, 87, 88, 92, 93, 95, 101, 111, 112, 113, 114, 116, 118, 122, 126, 127, 128, 137, 142, 144, 162, 185, 194, 222, 223

Bunker Hill 88, 111, 113, 305, 318
Burdett, J.S. 4
Burkesville Junction 340
Burns, Henry 107
Burnside, Ambrose E. 273
Burskell, Henry 225
Bushfield, Joseph M. 67
Butcher, George S. 225

C

Calihan, James 324
Callaghan's, VA 256, 258, 260, 268, 272, 274, 279, 284, 287, 288, 289
Callahan, James 253
Campbell, Alexander 264
Campbell, Archibald W. 11
Campbell, Col. 204
Campbell, Michael 264
Camp Chase 239
Camp Parole, MD 335
Cantwell, Col. 226
Capon Springs, WV 249
Carlin's Battery 293
Carlisle Barracks, PA 242
Carlisle, Camp 17, 49, 62, 67, 70, 79, 97, 110, 115
Carlisle, John S. 2, 4, 5, 17
Carney, William W. 150, 253
Carnifex Ferry, WV 185
Carpenter, David O. 299
Carpenter, Thomas W. 50
Carrigan, James 264
Carroll, Col. 210
Carr settlement 308
Cassidy, Peter 225
Castillow, David A. 145
Castillow (of Company E) 88
Cather, Fabricius A. 23, 48, 57
Caton, John H. 296
Cedar Creek, VA 46, 291, 292
Cedar Mountain, VA 15, 31, 45, 60, 137, 141, 160, 215, 311
Cedar Run, Camp 142
Centreville, VA 31, 229
Ceredo, WV 15

INDEX

Chain Bridge, VA 111, 144
Chambers, A.J. 78
Chambliss, Col. 281
Chantilly, VA 31
Chapman, Captain 280, 285
Charleston, SC 45, 89, 121
Charleston, WV 16, 155, 162, 290, 294, 298
Charlottesville, VA 285, 288
Chase, Ira 225
Cheat Mountain 14, 51, 64, 74, 93, 105, 136, 140, 159, 167, 173, 174, 175, 176, 178, 181, 184, 189, 190, 192, 194, 199, 200, 245, 265, 294, 311, 313, 314, 318
CHEAT MOUNTAIN 145
Cheat River 13, 38, 39, 40, 41, 45, 49, 50, 52, 54, 108, 111, 167, 174, 175, 177, 232, 313
Chester County, PA 43
Chester, Joseph W. 149
Circleville, WV 307
City Point, VA 132, 298
Clark County, MO 335
Clark, Noah 104
Clark, Sarah 104
Clarksburg, WV 2, 15, 48, 58, 62, 70, 79, 98, 101, 136, 147, 151, 153, 154, 158, 163, 164, 231, 235
Clary, Col. R.E. 142
Clay County, WV 186
Clear Spring, MD 246
Clemmer, J.C. 162
Clendaniel, Silas J. 170, 183, 252, 281
Cleveland, Grover 31
Clifton Forge, VA 287, 288
Clover Lick, WV 200
Cloyd's Mountain, VA 15, 19, 65, 69, 91, 122, 123, 137, 155, 162, 293, 294, 295, 296, 298
Cluseret, Gustave P. 16, 194, 206, 209
Collier, Cornelius 145
Collins, William 328, 329
Colmer, Jacob 70, 77, 150, 162
Combs, John 110, 114, 145, 149, 155, 258, 261, 268

Comley, Captain 145
Conger, Captain 208
Connellsville, PA 107
Connellsville Railroad Shops 45
Cool, Watt 239
Cooper, William P. 48
Corken, Mary E. 45
Corrick's Ford, WV 13, 23, 49, 59, 97, 167, 194
Cotton Mountain 137
Couch, Darius Nash 195
Covington, VA 256, 269, 272, 274, 279, 281, 282, 284, 286, 287, 338
Cow Pasture River 298
Cox, Jacob W. 225
Cox, William I. 145
Crab Bottom, VA 201, 269, 311, 312
Crab Orchard, VA 263
Craft, Sarah 105
Craig's Creek 276, 286
Craig, William 110
Creel, Edward B. 323, 331, 332
Cristy, Antony 144
Critchlow, David xii, 124
Croco, Samuel K. 264
Croghan, George 186
Crook, George 16, 29, 91, 155, 164, 186, 291, 293, 294, 295, 298
Cross Keys, VA 16, 27, 28, 31, 32, 39, 40, 54, 57, 60, 67, 75, 96, 101, 112, 116, 121, 126, 127, 128, 137, 160, 205, 209, 210, 211, 223
Crow, John N. 252
Culpepper Court House, VA 215, 310
Culpepper, VA 215, 219
Cumberland County, PA 43, 106
Cumberland, MD 32, 60, 254, 283, 302
Cummins, Dr. R.H. 32
Curtin, Andrew Gregg 36, 97
Curtis, Charles 328
Custer, George Armstrong 131
Cutlip, William 88

D

Darling, Mame F. 123

363

Darling, Merrian xii
Davis, Asbury S. 253
Davis, August 225
Davis, Jefferson 21, 217
Davis, Lt. 333
Davis, Sgt. 230
Day, Charles H. 85, 268
Day, Lt. 184
Day, Thomas E. 84, 146, 294
DeBeck, Capt. 220
Dehaven, Jehu 183
Deitrick, Chris 225
Delaney, Pat. 328
Dennison, John H. 51
Dent, George 268
Derrick's Battalion 271
Dever, Henry 145
Dever, William 145, 264
Devore, A.A. 115
Dickroger, Frederick 264
Dieckmann's Battery 221, 229, 230
Dillon, George F. 253
Dinwiddie Court House, VA 346, 348, 349, 350, 351
Dixie Boys 307, 308
Donaldson, Gen. 175
Donehoo, Capt. 303
Doph, Fred 51
Dougherty, Caroline A. 78
Dove, John 302, 306, 307
Downey, Col. S.W. 308, 309
Doyle, Edward 268
Droop Mountain, WV 27, 29, 30, 40, 46, 52, 54, 57, 61, 64, 65, 72, 73, 81, 82, 86, 91, 104, 108, 111, 112, 114, 126, 128, 130, 137, 150, 152, 241, 263, 265, 266, 270, 271, 283, 289, 305
Dry Fork 50, 52, 54, 55, 263
Dublin Depot, VA 155, 162, 271, 294, 295, 296, 297
Duffie, Alfred N. 268, 270, 271
Dumont, Col. 12
Dunlap Creek 284
Dunmore, WV 265
Dunn, Alexander 225
Dunning, Col. 15
DuPont, Capt. 105
Dushane, Captain 141
Duvall, Isaac H. 16
Dwyer, Theophilus 252, 253

E

Early, Jubal A. 209, 274, 280, 281, 282, 287, 288, 289
East Pike Run Township, PA 105, 121
Echols, John 266, 271, 276, 282, 284, 287, 288, 292, 316
Ecker, David 70, 76, 184
Edgar's Battalion 271
Edinburg, VA 207, 282
Edray, WV 279, 289
Eichbaum, Thomas S. 135, 155
Elk River 238
Elkwater, WV 30, 41, 63, 64, 83, 113, 159, 167, 170, 173, 174, 175, 178, 179, 180, 181, 182, 184, 190, 194, 202, 265
Ellenboro, WV 79, 163
Ellsworth, Col. 37, 49
Elsie, Capt. 307, 308
Elzey, Gen. 209
Emmerig, H. 145
Emory, Col. W.H. 243
Ethan Allen, Fort 143
Evans, Henry A. 97, 107, 108, 229, 230, 250, 251, 292, 293, 294
Evans, Rufus E. 108
Ewell, Richard S. 141, 206
Ewell, Robert S. 211, 222
Ewing, Chatham T. 97, 102, 103, 149, 200, 202, 204, 205, 229, 233, 234, 236, 245, 250, 251, 255, 256, 265, 267, 269, 271, 272, 273, 284, 291, 293, 312

F

Fairfax County, VA 20
Fairfax, VA 10
Fairmont, WV 5, 7, 9, 22, 26, 59, 163, 164, 190

INDEX

Falkenstein, Maggie A. 335
Fanzell, Matthew 145
Farnum, Lee 302, 305
Fellowsville, WV 51
Ferguson, Abijah 36
Ferris, Frank 146, 234, 235
Fetterman, WV 22, 23, 48, 49, 146
Fife, John 251
Fincastle, VA 285, 286
Finsley, Amelia 69
Finsley, Justice 69
Fisher's Hill, VA 46
Fitzsimmons (of Company D) 144
Five Forks, VA 46
Flemington, WV 52, 58, 59
Fleming (young boy) 306
Flesher, Henry C. 28, 110, 141, 142, 145
Floyd, John B. 173, 178, 184, 186
Foley, Shadrack 278
Ford, Dr. Sample 18, 32
Forrest, Nathan Bedford 196
Foulke, William H. 268
Fowler, Mary 43
Frankfort, WV 283
Franklin County, PA 26, 157
Franklin, WV 53, 113, 140, 160, 194, 203, 204, 206, 234, 249, 255, 272, 273, 301, 303, 305, 306, 307, 312
Fredericksburg, VA 288
Freeman's Ford, VA 31, 32, 216, 219
Fremont, John C. 15, 16, 28, 29, 33, 42, 44, 57, 140, 199, 202, 204, 205, 206, 209, 210, 211, 212, 213, 305
French, John C. 79, 86, 87, 238, 253
French, Mary Porter 86
Frew, William 102
Frisbee, John R. 218, 230
Front Royal, VA 288, 309

G

Gaddis, Robert 302, 304, 313, 314, 315, 316, 317, 318, 319, 320
Gainesville, VA 137, 218, 222, 223, 226
Gap Mills, WV 287
Gardner, James 225

Gardner, James A. 225
Garnett, Robert S. 12, 13, 23, 49, 59, 60, 194
Garroll, William 268
Gaston, NC 326
Gatewood's, VA 258, 259, 268, 272, 284, 289
Gauley Bridge, WV 136, 162
Gauley Mountain, WV 186
Gauley River 185, 186, 298
Gazzam, Captain 70
Gettysburg, PA 195, 246
Getze, Henry 62
Gibson, Billy 250
Gibson, Jr., Thomas 70, 75, 77, 89, 184
Gibson's Battalion 244, 245, 254, 255, 257, 265, 267, 269, 271, 273, 284
Glenn, George 48
Glover's Gap, WV 37
Goff, Nathan 145
Gordon, Elizabeth 43
Gordonsville, VA 89
Graball (of Company I) 183
Graebe, William F. 62, 66, 69, 235, 253, 294
Grafton Guards 48
Grafton House 23
Grafton Sentinel 21
Grafton, WV 2, 5, 12, 17, 21, 22, 23, 31, 33, 37, 43, 48, 49, 51, 55, 56, 58, 59, 61, 70, 97, 98, 101, 104, 111, 115, 120, 136, 149, 194, 239, 244, 299, 303, 305
Graham, William 27
Graham, William H. 42, 46, 253
Granger, Gordon 242
Grant, Ulysses S. 24, 46, 58, 291
Great Run 220
Green Bank, WV 181, 192, 200, 265, 269, 313
Greenbrier 264, 289
Greenbrier Bridge, WV xi, 258, 269
Greenbrier Camp 181
Greenbrier, Camp 200
Greenbrier County, WV 286, 287, 337
Greenbrier River 63, 91, 122, 265, 279,

365

289, 297, 311, 314, 317, 318
Greenbrier Valley, WV 313
Green Hill 269
Grover, Gen. Cuvier 227
Grove, Robert 70
Grover's Brigade 227
Groveton, VA 218, 222, 223
Grubb, Andrew 125, 130, 294
Gum House 313, 314
Guyandotte, WV 187

H

Hagans, Harrison H. 146, 236
Halleck, Henry W. 195, 246
Hall, Elijah 225
Hall, Moses S. 238
Halpin, Jack 169
Hammer, Amos B. 56, 57, 302, 303
Hampshire County, WV 186
Hancock's Veteran Corps 42
Hanover Junction, VA 288
Hansbrough, George W. 22, 23, 48
Harman settlement 308
Harness, Col. 15, 309
Harper, Bill 50, 56, 205, 280
Harper's Ferry, WV 37, 195, 288
Harper's Mills 254
Harris, \ 303, 320
Harrisonburg, VA 16, 28, 206, 208, 209, 281, 282, 292
Harrison County, WV 7, 57, 60, 157, 304
Harrison Guards 48
Harrison, Henry N. 154
Harris, Thomas Maley 136, 238, 245, 258, 269, 312
Harrisville, WV 158, 163
Harter, Dr. Scott 302
Hart, George 251
Hartranft, John Frederick 105, 137
Hayes, Albert C. 36, 41, 42, 44
Hayes, Rutherford B. 25
Hay Market, VA 222
Hays, Alexander 136
Hays, Charles McClure 30

Hazlett, Dr. R.W. 18, 31, 32, 160, 170, 171, 217, 233
Hebron, WV 157, 158
Hedgesville, WV 162
Heine, William 264
Heintzelman, Samuel P. 230
Hemmenway 241
Henrich, L. 264
Hewes, David T. 15
Hightown, VA 259, 272
Hight, Sgt. 324
Hill, Daniel Harvey 216
Hillsboro, WV 266, 272, 279, 289
Hill, Wallace 229
Hinkle, Abe 302, 312
Hixenbaugh, Charley S. 170, 252
Hollister, Simpson 79, 84
Hooker, Joseph 195
Hope, John 268
Howe, Daniel 202
Howe, Lemuel B. 253
Howe, Samuel J. 183
Howe, William 202
Hubbard, Chester D. 4
Hudson, S.L.D. 268
Huggins, Jacob G. 97, 105
Hugh, Col. 51
Hughes, Felix 268
Hughes, William L. 268
Hunter, David xi, 16, 29, 58, 122, 123, 292, 293, 294, 298, 299, 337, 338
Hunter, John A. 42, 92, 96
Huntersville, WV 39, 61, 96, 130, 159, 173, 179, 180, 184, 194, 200, 245, 249, 252, 255, 256, 258, 259, 260, 265, 269, 289, 301, 316
Hurst, Kate 107
Hutchinson, James R. 45, 263, 264
Huttonsville, WV 146, 173, 176, 177, 181, 184, 236, 245, 253, 263, 265, 318
Hyman's Battery 201, 205

I

Imboden, John D. 147, 232, 237, 254,

INDEX

255, 269, 272, 273, 276, 281, 282, 292, 316, 317
Independent Brigade 31, 140, 142, 213, 214
Independent Cavalry Company of Cincinnati 245
Indians 91, 106, 107, 132, 133, 242, 299
Ivy Depot, VA 281

J

Jackson Court House, WV 28
Jackson, Henry G. 18, 79, 84, 85, 87
Jackson, H.R. 175
Jackson Independent Blues 107
Jackson, John 124, 125
Jackson River 133, 137, 152, 256, 275, 277, 278, 284, 287, 288
Jackson River Depot, VA 287
Jackson's Brigade 271
Jackson, Stonewall 13, 16, 57, 141, 142, 171, 204, 206, 209, 210, 211, 215, 222, 305
Jackson, W.H. 242
Jackson, William Lowther \ 181, 245, 249, 256, 258, 265, 269, 270, 276, 278, 282, 284, 287, 288, 297, 298
Jackson, William S. 259
James, Hamilton B. 79, 85
Janes, Bishop E.S. 163
Jenkins, Albert Gallatin 185, 186, 295
Jenkins, William 268
Jennings, David A. 130
Jessie Scouts 305
Johnson, Andrew 24
Johnson, Capt. 202, 219
Johnson, D.F. 145
Johnson, Gen. E. 181, 182, 184, 204
Johnson's Battery 57, 69, 204, 205
Johnston, Eleanor 76
Johnston's Battery 84, 88
Jones, Col. 181
Jones, Gen. Samuel 26, 61, 147, 237, 250, 255, 259, 260, 262, 276, 284, 286, 287, 288, 290
Jones, Gen. W.E. 293, 295

Jones, George 237
Jones, J. Paul 302, 309
Jones, Mr. 107
Jones, S.G. 145

K

Kanawha River 162, 231
Kanawha Valley, WV 5, 15, 16, 85, 136, 155, 162, 185, 270, 271, 283, 291, 293, 320, 337
Kane's Rifles 209
Kearney, Philip 230
Keeny, Michael B. 267
Keeper, John V. 265, 269, 270
Keeper's Battery 249, 255, 266, 270, 271
Kelley, Benjamin Franklin 11, 12, 37, 186, 194, 246
Kelly, J.B. 211
Kelly's Ford, VA 31, 32, 55, 126, 137, 216, 217, 229
Kenny, Marquis D. 268
Kent, Samuel 183
Kerns, John 268
Kevill, Michael 225
Kiger, John P. 124, 125, 129, 130
Kimball, Nathan 173, 177
Kincaid, Albert 230
King's Division 219
Kingwood, WV 4, 51
Kirkpatrick, George H. 135, 147, 152, 278
Kirsch, Philip 264
Klein, Jacob 62, 69
Knight, Daniel W.S. 48
Knight, D.S.K. 23
Knox, Samuel B. 260, 263
Knoxville, TN 273, 283
Kramer, George 225
Kreps, Major 218, 222
Kurtz, Benjamin F. 145, 264

L

Laing, Sarah Robinson 108
Lamb, Daniel 3, 7
Lancaster County, PA 131

Lancaster, Hugh \ 183
Lander, Frederick W. 12
Lane, Brigadier Gen. Joe 193
Langfitt, Martha J. 91
Lang, Major 45
Lang, Theodore F. 264
Larimer, General William 136
Latham, George R. 20, 21, 22, 23, 24, 25, 48, 49, 50, 51, 56, 57, 60, 88, 143, 144, 146, 147, 149, 155, 158, 200, 203, 205, 234, 236, 247, 264, 265, 303
Latham, James W. 158
Latham, John 20
Latta, William L. 298
Laurel Fork, WV 72, 73, 167
Laurel Hill, WV 12, 13, 17, 49, 50, 60, 97
Lawton, Alexander Robert 222
Leading Creek 147, 232, 235
Leadom, Jerry 292
Lee, Fitzhugh 242, 276, 281, 282, 285, 286, 288
Lee, Robert E. 46, 58, 123, 131, 173, 175, 178, 186, 195, 216, 229, 246, 271, 274, 281, 283, 301, 354
Leese, John N. 145
Lee's Springs, VA 25
Lessig, Samuel 251
Letcher, Gov. John 1, 48, 176
Lewisburg, WV 152, 175, 179, 250, 256, 258, 265, 266, 267, 268, 269, 270, 271, 272, 279, 283, 284, 288, 297, 298, 337
Lexington, VA 281, 338
Liberty, WV 163
Little Meadows 183
Lock, Nelinza L. 302, 305, 320
Lohmire, M.L. 295
Long, Major 203
Longstreet, James 142, 222, 273, 283
Loomis, D.W. 144
Loring, William W. 175, 176, 242
Lost River, WV 254
Loup Creek, WV 298
Love, Eli Nathan 32

Lowe, Col. 186
Lowery, Fielding 141
Ludaking, William 264
Luther Day Post, No. 395, G.A.R. 87
Lynchburg, VA 16, 69, 89, 122, 173, 285, 298, 337, 338, 339, 342
Lyons, Samuel 232

M

Macon, GA 27, 45, 89, 326, 332
Madison, Henry 306
Mail, W.H. 211
Maley, Edward C. 268
Mallonee, Helen V. 58
Manassas, VA 23, 142, 218, 222, 225, 243
Mannington, WV 49
Mansfield, Gen. 44
Marcy, Emma P. 138
Marcy, General R.D. 138
Marietta, OH 124, 131
Markbreit, Leopold 151, 278
Markins, Moses Golden 122, 302, 305, 313, 315
Marks, Sgt. 324
Marlin's Bottom, WV 258, 265, 269, 283, 289
Marshall, Capt. 312, 313
Marshall, Lawrence 251
Martin, Calvin B. 253
Martin, G. 145
Martin, John F. 51
Martinsburg, WV 44, 61, 88, 91, 153, 154, 161, 246, 280, 290, 318
Martin, Theodore 225
Mason's Creek, VA 276
Matlick, Jacob G. 51, 323, 335
Maury, D.H. 242
May, Charles A. 242
May, James 70
McAdams, Lt. 278
McAleer, James 253
McCausland, John 276, 282, 287, 298
McCleane, F.H. 264
McClellan, George Brinton 12, 13, 23,

INDEX

29, 37, 42, 44, 67, 71, 138
McClellanville, SC 90
McCloy, George E. 170
McClure, William F. 251
McConkey, Thomas 268
McConnelsburg, PA 195
McCook's German Brigade 185
McCoy Post No. 1, G.A.R. 131
McCoy, Robert 149
McCoy, Robert A. 145
McCoy, William 145
McCrea, John A. 144
McDonald, Lt. 181
McDowell, Irvin 142, 212, 213, 215, 219, 223
McDowell, VA 15, 31, 57, 60, 136, 160, 201, 202, 203, 223, 284, 299, 305
McGarvey, H. 145
McGilvery, John 245
McGully, William 217
McKeesport, PA 29, 32
McKennan Infantry 115, 122
McKennan, William 115
McKinzie, Alex. 292
Mclarren, J. 264
McLean, Mr. 46
McLean's Brigade 220, 223
McMasters, Gilbert 102
McMillan, James B. 225
McNally, Francis Patrick 28, 110, 147, 150, 184, 251, 253, 258, 261, 264, 303
McNamara, Mary 29
McNeil, John Hanson 320
McNeill's guerillas 269
McPorter, George 3
Meade, George G. 44, 195, 246, 356
Meadow Bluff, WV 162, 186, 271, 297, 298
Meigs County, OH 260
Meigs, John R. 150, 276
Meigs, Montgomery C. 150
Mendel, George 68
Metcalf, James 251
Metz, Louis 264
Mexican Rangers 66

Middletown, VA 212
Millborough, VA 256, 287, 288
Mill Creek 356
Miller, Conrad 70
Miller, George W. 33, 253
Mill Point, WV 265, 269, 270
Millspaugh, Dr. Theodore 33
Milroy, Gen. Samuel 192
Milroy, Martha 192
Milroy, Robert Huston 15, 28, 29, 30, 31, 57, 76, 141, 142, 143, 144, 145, 160, 181, 182, 192, 193, 194, 195, 196, 199, 202, 203, 204, 205, 209, 210, 213, 214, 216, 217, 219, 223, 224, 225, 229, 230, 232, 233, 234, 290, 312
Milroy's Brigade 15, 16, 57, 85, 141, 209, 215, 222, 224, 230, 305
Mingo Flats, WV 179
Moats, Andrew 79
Monongahela, PA 141
Monongahela River 5, 115
Monroe County, OH 17, 68, 79, 84
Monroe County, WV 286, 287
Monroe, Rev. Thomas H. 162
Monroe Rifle Volunteers 26
Monterey, VA 13, 31, 54, 60, 104, 160, 184, 200, 201, 202, 249, 255, 263, 269, 272, 273, 283, 284, 301, 305, 313, 314
Montgomery Academy, NY 33
Montgomery, AL 2
Montgomery, James B. 122, 123, 146, 298
Moody, Col. 181
Moody, Dwight L. xii
Mooney, George W. 302, 315, 316, 317, 319, 320
Moor, Augustus 233, 270, 271, 283, 289, 291, 292, 293
Moore, Caroline 32
Moorefield, WV 15, 206, 243, 249, 254, 259, 309, 320
Moorehead, Gen. 125
Moore, Marion 145
Moore, M.E. 91, 294, 298

Moore, Moses 268
Moor's Brigade 16
Moran, Lt. Col. Robert 18, 25, 26, 205
Morgantown, WV 7, 132, 163, 190
Morris, Bishop Thomas A. 158
Morris Hill, VA 287
Morris, Thomas A. 12, 13, 23, 49
Morton, Col. 97
Morton, George 104
Morton, Howard 104, 105, 229, 250, 252
Morton, Randall 104
Mosby, John Singleton 105, 283, 305, 318, 320
Mosby's Rangers 89
Moss, John W. 3, 20, 124, 158, 160, 174, 177, 205
Moundsville, WV 62, 67
Mountain Department 15, 16, 160, 199, 204
Mount Crawford, VA 281
Mount Jackson, VA 96, 207, 208, 211, 212, 291, 292
Muir, A. 328
Mulligan, James A. 61
Murphy, John 268
Murphy, Lt. 279
Murraysville, WV 158
Murry, John 225
Myer, Henry 253
Mysenberg, F.A. 140

N

Nashville, TN 26, 195, 196
Newbern, IN 304
Newbern, VA 297
New Castle, PA xi, 106, 109
New Castle, VA 274, 276, 277, 284, 286, 287, 315
New Creek, WV 15, 16, 26, 64, 81, 82, 98, 132, 152, 161, 186, 194, 269, 272, 273, 281, 283, 284, 303, 309
Newman, Juliet A. 20
New Market, MD 85
New Market, VA xii, 101, 105, 108, 123, 208, 225, 282, 288, 291, 292
Newport, VA 287, 297
New River 186, 294, 297, 298
New River Bridge, VA 291, 296, 297
Northampton, VA 10
Northern Brigade 145, 233
North Fork of the South Branch of the Potomac River 255
North, Lt. G.H. 150
North Mountain 254, 276
Northwest, Camp 255
Northwestern Virginia Railroad 12
Northwestern Virginia Turnpike 48
Norton, U.S. Marshal 97
Nottoway River 346
Nuzum, T.C. 51

O

Oakes, John 253
Oakes, Major 22, 37, 97, 115, 299
Oakland, MD 97, 98, 163, 164
Oaks, John 183
Oggle's Creek 279
Ohio River 42, 78, 79, 102, 131, 167, 191, 194
Oley, John Hunt 255, 257, 269, 270, 284, 294, 295
Orange and Alexandria Railroad 288
Orange Court House, VA 89
Osborne, A.G. 107, 276
Osborne, S.J. 106, 201, 251
Otto, William 42, 170
Owens, John D. 18, 27, 97, 168, 182, 184, 205

P

Parkersburg, WV 3, 4, 6, 15, 18, 20, 86, 94, 124, 129, 130, 131, 158, 162, 163, 231, 304
Patrick, Gen. 219
Patterson's Creek 155
Patton, George S. 259, 260
Peaks of Otter, VA 284
Pegram, John 12, 13, 31, 167
Pemberton Prison 132, 325

INDEX

Penniman, Horace 337, 340, 341, 346, 351, 354, 356, 358
Pennsylvania Railroad 27, 96
Pentecost, Alex. J. 135, 136, 137, 138, 139, 140, 142, 144, 145, 147, 148, 149, 150, 151, 152, 153, 154, 155, 268, 277, 278, 279, 296
Petersburg, VA 46, 131, 326, 340, 342, 343, 349, 354, 355, 356, 357
Petersburg, WV 20, 194, 206, 249, 254, 255, 269, 272, 273, 284, 308, 309
Peter's Mountain 297
Peterstown, WV 186
Philippi, WV 5, 6, 12, 22, 23, 37, 49, 55, 60, 132, 189, 194, 235
Phillips (bugler) 245
Piedmont, VA 91, 108, 123, 293, 298
Pierce, Col. 195
Pierpont, Francis H. 2, 3, 4, 5, 6, 7, 8, 9, 11, 97, 136, 299, 300
Piersons, Col. 327
Piggott's Mill, WV 185
Pike Run, PA xi, 122
Pike Run Squad 103
Pittsburgh, PA xi, 26, 27, 29, 30, 33, 36, 41, 42, 43, 44, 45, 46, 47, 68, 70, 75, 76, 77, 78, 92, 95, 96, 97, 102, 103, 104, 105, 106, 107, 108, 123, 136, 137, 138, 141, 144, 208, 231, 280
Pittsburgh Zouaves 102
Plankey, Edward 62, 66, 67, 68, 69, 178
Plummer Guards 27, 30, 97, 103, 104, 105, 106, 108
Plummer, Joseph 97
Point Pleasant, WV 144, 231
Pollock, Capt. R. 150
Polsley, Daniel H. 4
Polsley, John J. 256, 278
Pomeroy, Chaplain 161
Pomeroy, OH 260
Pope, John 15, 16, 28, 29, 42, 44, 68, 69, 140, 160, 212, 213, 214, 215, 218, 219, 223, 224, 310
Porter, Andrew 242
Porterfield, George A. 12, 22, 23, 48

Porter, Fitz John 143, 223
Porter, R. 86
Port Republic, VA 209, 210, 292
Potomac River 11, 32, 111, 246
Princeton Court House, WV 294
Prince William County, VA 20, 86
Pulaski, Fort 334

Q

Qualk, Hiram 252, 296
Quest, James 225
Quimby, George A. 130, 131, 182, 192, 263

R

Ramsey, Col. 13
Ransom, J.L. 328
Rapidan River 215, 311
Rappahannock River 25, 60, 216, 288
Rappahannock Station, VA 216, 219
Ray, Samuel 253
Reader, Ellen Smith 123
Reader, Frances 123
Reader, Frank Smith xi, xii, 123, 337, 338, 340, 341, 348, 352, 353
Ream's Station, VA 354
Red Sulphur Springs, WV 274
Reed, Calon 145
Reed, Jefferson 145
Reeves, Mary C. 122
Reger, Naomi 56
Reinbeau, Mrs. E.P. 30
Reneker, Mary Bell 105
Reno, Jesse Lee 223
Reynolds, Joseph Jones 173, 174, 175, 178, 179, 194, 223
Reynolds, Samuel L. 264
Richardson, Thomas B. 145, 237
Richmond Examiner 281
Richmond, VA 1, 2, 4, 6, 7, 11, 20, 21, 41, 45, 46, 51, 65, 66, 69, 91, 99, 100, 124, 132, 141, 186, 210, 215, 264, 273, 324, 325, 327, 340
Rich Mountain, WV 12, 17, 31, 49, 62, 71, 79, 136, 169

Riley, Joseph 79
Rimmel, John 145
Ringgold Cavalry 273
Ringler, Cyrus E. 50, 59, 61, 267
Ripley, Stephen 229
Ritchie County, WV 17, 79, 84, 87
Ritchie Court House, WV 84, 86
Ritchie, Jacob 225
Ritchie Squad 88
Ritz, Charles 268
Roaring Creek, WV 180, 303
Robel, Michael 264
Roberts, Benjamin S. 147, 234, 235, 236
Roberts, Charles M. 149
Roberts, Christian 37
Robertson River 215
Robinson, James A. 295
Robinson, John A. 48
Robinson, Richard 232
Rocky Gap, WV (see also White Sulphur Springs, WV) 18, 19, 29, 30, 34, 38, 46, 53, 55, 63, 66, 69, 74, 75, 80, 81, 82, 83, 84, 87, 92, 94, 95, 98, 99, 100, 101, 102, 104, 108, 114, 117, 118, 128, 137, 149, 162, 249, 250, 259, 260, 261, 263, 264, 268, 272, 279, 324
Rolf, August 67
Romiser, Peter 264
Romney, WV 186
Rook, A. Boyd 97, 229
Rosecrans, William S. 12, 13, 29, 71, 169, 185, 186, 199
Rosser's Brigade 288
Rosser, Thomas L. 132
Rowand, Weston 186
Rowe, Frederick 251
Rowlesburg, WV 51
Rucker, Col. D.H. 144
Rumsey, Will 152, 153, 154, 155, 255
Rush, Morgan 253
Russell, Andrew P. 114, 265, 268, 280
Russell's Place, OH 114
Rust, Col. 175, 176
Rutherford, J.N. 148

S

Safford, Dr. C.D. 162
Saladin, Edward 264
Salem Raid 27, 29, 30, 53, 54, 55, 61, 65, 73, 74, 75, 77, 82, 99, 100, 101, 104, 108, 112, 117, 122, 123, 127, 128, 129, 139, 150, 152, 153, 241, 269, 273, 283, 316, 323
Salem, VA 105, 276, 280, 281, 282, 285, 299, 315
Sallyards, John 268, 313
Salterbach, Louis P. 67, 68, 268
Salt Pond Mountain, VA 297
Salt Sulphur Springs, WV 297
Sankey, David xi
Sankey, Ira D. xi, xii
Sarsfield, John 328, 329
Savannah, GA 117, 332, 333
Savannah River 334
Saylor, Jack 302
Scammon, Eliakim P. 258, 283, 284, 288
Schaub, Fred 253
Schenck, Robert C. 57, 142, 195, 203, 209, 222, 223, 225, 226, 227, 309
Schmitz, Charles 225
Schmolze, William 269
Schoonmaker, James M. 150, 154, 258, 269
Schott, Henry 145
Schurz, Carl 222, 226
Scott, Alexander 26, 27, 42, 76, 92, 96, 137, 143, 145, 146, 232, 265, 266, 268, 269, 273, 284, 298
Scott, General 242
Seaman, Elias F. 135, 138, 139, 153, 274
Seneca, WV 81, 82, 205, 264
Sewell Mountains 162, 298
Sexton, George 302, 312
Sexton, Lindsey 331, 332
Shaffer Mountain 167, 168, 233, 263
Sharer, Timothy 302, 305, 315, 318, 319
Shearer, Samuel J. 106, 229, 250, 293
Sheets, John 145
Shenandoah Mountain 201
Shenandoah Mountains 203, 281

INDEX

Shenandoah River 208, 288
Shenandoah Valley 16, 33, 46, 150, 206, 243, 274, 283, 291, 305, 310, 320
Sheridan, Philip 46, 58, 131, 150
Sherman, William Tecumseh 69, 90, 303, 331
Shields, James 28, 210
Shields, Sadie K. 47
Shirley, William 280, 302, 305, 316, 317
Shuman's Cavalry 203
Sickel's Brigade 295
Sickman, Alfred 43, 97, 103, 182
Siegfried, Rev. Simeon 21
Sigel, Franz xi, xii, 16, 44, 57, 123, 140, 141, 213, 214, 215, 219, 223, 224, 229, 291, 292, 320
Simon, Jacob 252
Simpson, Kidd S. 253, 324
Singer, Frank H. 47, 264
Sistersville, WV 62, 163
Sivert, Charles W. 217
Slack, Hedgeman 272
Slaughter Mountain 67
Slayer, Jacob 264
Smith, Capt. 178
Smith, Capt. Frank 236, 245
Smith, David L. 36, 43
Smith, Eleanor G. 26
Smith, Fort 243
Smith, Hugh 237, 253, 264
Smith, James B. 88, 89, 90, 91, 267, 268
Smith, John 152
Smith, Lewis E. 115, 120
Smith, Thomas 225
Smith, Thomas B. 95
Smitley, C.W.D. 89, 302, 303, 305, 306, 307, 308, 309, 310, 311, 312, 313, 315, 320, 321
Smitley, Robert P. 303
Smythe, Douglass G. 92, 96, 167
Snyder, Harmon 245
Sold, Carrie 139
South Fork 254, 255
Sperryville, VA 213, 214, 215
Sponholtz, A. 146
Stafford, William E. 51, 323, 324, 330

Stahel, Julius 105, 207, 209, 227, 291, 292, 320
Starke, William E. 222
Staunton-Parkersburg Turnpike 167, 175, 177, 181, 200, 204, 269, 281, 283, 306
Staunton, VA 91, 122, 123, 132, 173, 199, 256, 259, 260, 274, 281, 282, 283, 288, 291, 292, 293, 294, 298, 299, 305, 310, 311, 323
Steadman, Fort 137
Steinaker, William 299
Stephens, E.W., G.A.R. Post, Wheeling 69
Stephens, W.A. 136
Stevens, Webster A. 18, 135
Stewart, William R. 131
St. Marys, WV 79
Stonebreaker, J.W. 294
Stone, John 264
Stony Creek, VA 207, 351, 354, 355
Strasburg, VA 160, 194, 206, 207, 211, 212, 291, 310
Stratton, Charles 140
Strickel, Fritz 225
Stuart, James Ewell Brown \ 141
Sturgis, Samuel Davis 213
Sudley Ford, VA 222
Suffolk, VA 283
Sullivan, Jeremiah C. 177, 283, 288, 292
Sullivan, Owen 70
Sullivan, Terrence 328
Sulphur Springs, VA 216, 217, 219, 220, 221
Summersville, WV 185, 186
Sumter, Camp. *See* Andersonville; *See* Andersonville
Sumter, Fort 34, 36, 42, 46, 48, 96, 115, 136, 158, 243
Sutton, WV 186
Swamp Dragons 249
Sweet, Martin V. 337, 340, 341, 342, 345, 351, 352, 356
Sweet Springs Mountain 284, 287
Sweet Springs, VA 256, 274, 275, 284, 286

Sweet Sulphur Springs, VA 274, 284

T

Taggart, John N. 251
Taliaferro, Wiliam B. 204
Tarr, Campbell 4
Taylor County, WV 17, 21, 22, 48, 56, 59, 79, 304
Taylor, William S. 264
Thaw, William 102
Thayer, Caroline A. 21
Thayer, Dr. A.H. 133
Thoburn, Joseph 272, 283, 284, 288, 289, 293
Thoburn's Brigade 269, 292
Thomas, Brig. Gen. 281
Thomas, George Henry 195
Thomas, John R. 33
Thompson, Francis W. 22, 154, 269, 284
Thompson, Lt. Col. 269
Thompson, Rev. J.R. 196
Thompson, William P. 48
Thompson, W.P. 22, 23
Thornton, WV 12
Tomlinson, Capt. 280
Townsend, E.D. 153, 244
Trowbridge, C. Fred 148, 254
Truxal, Norval W. 115, 121, 264
Turk, Lorenz 253
Tygart Valley River 48
Tyler, Capt. 97
Tyler, C.H. 242
Tyler County, WV 87, 88, 157

U

Union Church, VA 209
Union, WV 65, 162, 268, 272, 283, 284, 288, 297

V

Valley River Falls 49
Van Meter, Mr. 309
Vanwinkle, P.G. 9
Vierheller, Christian 62, 68

Virginia and Tennessee Railroad 153, 291, 295
Virginia Central Railroad 281, 291, 298
Virginia Military Institute 338
Von Koenig, Baron 254, 256, 257, 261

W

Wagner, Henry 264
Walcott, Major 98
Walker, Brig. Gen. 281
Walker, Capt. C. 66
Walker, Thomas J. 202
Walters, Martin 237
Walton, Joseph 280
Wardensville, WV 194, 254, 303, 321
Ward, Stephen H. 298
Warm Springs, VA 250, 255, 256, 258, 259, 260, 262, 268, 279, 287, 288, 298
Warren, Fitz Henry 20
Warrenton Springs, VA 216, 221
Warrenton, VA 31, 142, 218, 222, 229
Washington County, IN 192
Washington County, OH 131
Washington County, PA xi, xii, 17, 32, 86, 87, 103, 105, 109, 115, 121, 123, 137
Washington, D.C. 5, 11, 16, 21, 32, 37, 46, 68, 90, 129, 144, 153, 160, 162, 213, 214, 229, 231, 242, 243, 244, 299
Washington, George 157
Washington, John 264
Washington, PA 31, 104, 115
Washington Rifle Guards 37, 46
Washington Rifles 43, 136
Waterloo Bridge, VA 31, 76, 80, 94, 127, 137, 217, 221, 230
Watts, Alexander 302, 305
Waumsley's guerillas 313
Waynesboro, VA 293
Weaver 184
Weaver, Arthur J. 50, 130, 132, 192, 263, 265, 267, 268
Webb, Aden 253

INDEX

Webster County, WV 238
Webster, George 184, 201, 213
Webster, L.H. 264
Webster, WV 12, 23, 49, 97, 110, 115, 153, 167, 245, 289, 290, 294, 304, 305
Weible, William 237
Weldon Railroad 353, 355
Werner, Charles 264
Wesley, John 2
Western Virginia Bushwhackers 203
Western Virginian 21
West, Joseph M. 323
West Liberty, WV 58, 97
West, Oliver R. 36, 42, 43, 184
Weston, WV 28, 148, 158, 186, 235, 237
West Union, WV 116, 118, 147, 237, 238
Wetzel County, WV 17
Wharton, Gabriel C. 292
Wheeler, Ella 103
Wheeler, Joseph 196
Wheeling Intelligencer 11
Wheeling, WV xi, 2, 3, 5, 6, 7, 11, 17, 20, 22, 23, 26, 27, 28, 29, 31, 32, 37, 42, 49, 56, 57, 62, 63, 66, 67, 68, 69, 70, 77, 79, 85, 88, 91, 95, 97, 107, 110, 115, 125, 130, 136, 138, 154, 155, 158, 163, 231, 294, 299
White, Amy 320
White, Carr B. 295
Whitelaw, Mrs. James 305, 306
White Sulphur Springs, WV (see also Rocky Gap, WV) 29, 31, 55, 102, 137, 250, 253, 256, 260, 261, 268, 272, 284, 289
Wickham, Williams Carter 281
Wigner, R.H. 79, 238
Wiley, John B. 225
Wiley, William A. 280
Willey, Waitman T. 4
Willhide, John W. 302, 303, 310, 311, 312, 313, 314, 320
Williams, Gen. 196
Williamson, D.F. 30, 31, 182
Williamsport, PA 246

Williams, Thomas 268
Williamstown, WV 158
Williamsville, VA 202
Willow Springs, VA 305
Wilson (bushwhacker) 306
Wilson, Daniel 48, 56, 57
Wilson, James 145
Wilson, James Lewis 132, 133
Wilson's Cavalry 21
Wilt, Isaac 145, 267
Winchester, VA 46, 81, 83, 88, 126, 129, 194, 195, 196, 232, 246, 254, 310, 318, 319, 320
Winder, John Henry 331
Wirz, Henry 327, 328, 329, 332
Wise, Henry A. 60, 173, 178, 184, 185, 186
Woods, Elizabeth 109
Woods, John 145
Woodstock, VA 207, 283, 291
Woodville, WV xi, 123, 126, 140, 141, 160, 214
Woodward, R.M. 51
Wright, Joseph 50, 60
Wynkoop, John N. 292, 293
Wyoming Court House, WV 294
Wytheville, VA 294

Y

Yingst, David R. 250
Yonking, Jackson 145
Young, Captain 30
Youngstown, OH 108

Z

Zantzinger, Camilla 133
Zeigler, Caroline 106
Zeigler, John L. 186, 226
Zeigler, Phillip 251

www.ingramcontent.com/pod-product-compliance
Lightning Source LLC
Chambersburg PA
CBHW071648160426
43195CB00012B/1391